Causes Of Crime

Biological Theories in the United States 1800-1915

By
Arthur E. Fink

A Perpetua Book

A. S. Barnes & Company, Inc.

New York

To

K. B. F.

PREFACE

AMERICAN students of criminology have been familiar with the background of European research into the biological factors of crime causation. Long before De Quiros' summary in 1911, European works had been known in this country, but no systematic presentation of American thought in this field had been made. One has but to review the literature of science of the last century to appreciate this void. American authors of textbooks in criminology have paid homage to the earlier works of Europeans, but they have consistently failed to indicate their awareness of the necessary groundwork which had been laid here by American physicians, prison administrators, and other students of human behavior. Much the same may be said of the encyclopedia writers, including those within the social science fields. This failure to mention American contributions in the textbooks and encyclopedias (as well as in the more general works) may be due to a variety of reasons. Either there was no work done in America, or it was of such an inconsequential nature as not to justify or require historical consideration; or else it had been neglected by scholars. Careful study of the intellectual history of the period from 1800 to 1915 reveals an astonishing variety and quantity of work on the causal factors in human behavior. Similarly, the quality was often of such a character as at times to merit world-wide attention. The conclusion is inevitable that the historical record of the early labors is bare because social historians have failed to probe into and interpret the nature and extent of these accomplishments. This study undertakes to meet this need.

Attention to matters of crime causation in America began, tritely enough, with the first colonizations, and a history of such thought would extend over three centuries. Much of it is contained in the theological concepts of man's original depravity and sin, and while conceivably it could be dealt with in terms of hereditary endowment, it might also be included as social his-

tory. However, since it was decided to include the non-environmental factors only, a starting point both logical and practical
was the beginning of that period when scientific concepts were
displacing the metaphysical and theological in the description
of the world of natural phenomena. This brought into the foreground the work of the early American physicians who had already gone beyond the limits of the physical body of man and
had seen him as a human being operating in relation to other
human beings. When those relations with his fellow men were
abnormal, that is, when they deviated too far from a standard
set within the prevailing culture, then quite naturally that behavior was regarded as criminal if accompanied by a certain legally defined state of mind. As such it came within the purview
not only of the physician but of the State as well. No man perceived this fact more clearly or was more aware of its relation
to man's physical state than was Benjamin Rush, certainly one
of the most eminent of early American physicians.

Our study begins with Benjamin Rush (whose early work
even antedated phrenology) and continues almost unbroken
through the long line of those American physicians who saw beyond the limits of hospital or consulting room into the larger
area of human relationships. The material used is gathered very
largely from their writings, but not to the neglect of the important contributions from the non-medical field. In some instances the work of the physicians is definitely original. This is
particularly true in those cases where their experience brought
them into intimate and first-hand contact with the criminal, either
in private practice or in institutional work. In other instances
they were certainly influenced by contemporary thought abroad,
of necessity by the earlier alienists, and later by the students of
criminal anthropology.

The period covered is from the time of Benjamin Rush to
William Healy; from the last decade of the eighteenth to the
second decade of the twentieth century. Prior to Healy, despite the
individual approach, the offender had been classified as a type—a
criminal anthropological type, a mental type, etc. Healy's con-

tribution was his establishment of the case study of the individual offender and his concept of the essentially dynamic character of the human personality. This method and this concept stand out so boldly in contrast to the studies of the preceding hundred years that they may be said to signalize a new approach to the study of the individual offender in the United States. In the present pages the material is presented from the biological, anthropological, and psychological points of view. A perspective is thus afforded of the researches of William Healy and of those who followed him in substantiation of the claim that his monumental volume of 1915 marks the transition from the old to the modern era in this country. This treatise covers the period before 1915.

A word remains to be said about cause and causation. This treatise indulges in no discourse on scientific cause; for such the reader is referred to contemporary works on methodology, of which there is no lack. The use of cause and causation is governed by the usage of the period under consideration. It will be seen that much of what passed for cause in the nineteenth century would be termed correlation today. Nevertheless, on the basis of these correlations the students of that day drew many valid conclusions, as well as some others that would not and did not stand up under the scrutiny of a later methodology. It is no derogation to point out these errors, but it is sheer intellectual arrogance to appraise them by other than the knowledge and practice of that day. The methodology of today, which we feel is so much superior, will have to stand up to the same test tomorrow.

I wish to acknowledge my immense obligation to the library of the College of Physicians of Philadelphia for the privilege of examining the rich literature on its shelves. May I personalize this by expressing my deepest appreciation to Dr. Edward B. Krumbhaar, chairman of the Library Committee, who made the valuable resources of the library available. To the late Dr. Henry H. Donaldson of the Wistar Institute of Anatomy and Biology, to Dr. Charles W. Burr, Emeritus Professor of Mental Diseases at the University of Pennsylvania Medical School, and to Dr.

Edgar A. Doll, Director of Research, Vineland Training School, I owe thanks for helpful suggestions on certain of the chapters which they read.

To Professor Thorsten Sellin, of the Department of Sociology of the University of Pennsylvania, who suggested this study, I am grateful for his kindly yet incisive counsel and for his continuing encouragement. To Malcolm G. Preston, of the Psychology Department, and to Ray H. Abrams of the Sociology Department of the University of Pennsylvania, I owe a debt greater than friendship seems able to repay for their careful examination and valuable criticism of the manuscript.

ARTHUR E. FINK

Philadelphia

CONTENTS

I

PHRENOLOGY

STUDENTS of the historical development of criminology, and particularly of criminal anthropology, are accustomed to trace its origins back to physiognomy and phrenology, and in some instances to still earlier sources. Lavater is usually associated with physiognomy, Gall with phrenology. That Gall is here discussed is no depreciation of Lavater, but rather a recognition that at the time when European thought reached America phrenology was largely in the ascendant. The consequence was that physiognomical doctrines never enjoyed a comparable vogue in America.[1]

Historically, physiognomy was antecedent to phrenology. By the ending of the eighteenth and the turn of the nineteenth century physiognomy—the belief that character could be read by observation and measurement of the face—had enjoyed its period of greatness and was already in decline. It was giving way before the anatomical researches being conducted by Franz Joseph Gall, a physician whom Nordenskiöld, the historian of biology, described as "without doubt one of the most brilliant anatomists of his age."[2] Gall (1758-1828), as a student, had noted that some of his fellows with pronounced characteristics had certain head conformations. His early awakened interest in these rough correlations was carried through his years as a private physician and as physician to an insane asylum. These experiences, together with his observations upon the so-called lower classes (i.e., those largely found in penal and charitable institutions), suggested to him the essentials of his system. First known as the author of

[1] It will be noted later that occasional physiognomical references were made by American students, but they were so unrelated that they can hardly be said to form the unified doctrine which was the case in Europe. Furthermore, when these references did appear they evidenced the influence of the newly developing schools of criminal anthropology of the last quarter of the nineteenth century rather than the physiognomical doctrines of Lavater of a hundred years before.

[2] Erik Nordenskiöld, *The History of Biology*, New York, 1915, p. 310.

two chapters of a work published in Vienna in 1791 entitled *Philosoph-medinische Untersuchungen ueber Natur und Kunst im kranken und gesunden Zustande des Menschen*, Gall continued his researches on the brain, and by the year 1809 had begun the publication of four volumes on the anatomy and physiology of the nervous system. In the first two of these he had the collaboration of John Gaspar Spurzheim (1776-1832), who, from 1800 to 1804, had attended Gall's lectures, and who from 1804 to 1813 had been first his pupil and later his associate. By 1813 these two had agreed to separate, and the remaining volumes as completed by Gall first appeared in 1819 in Paris. The complete title stamps it as the first great work on phrenology: *Anatomie et physiologie du système nerveux en général, et du cerveau en particulier, avec observations sur la possibilité de reconnaître plusiers dispositions intellectuelles et morales de l'homme et des animaux par la configuration de leur têtes*. Gall's last great work of six volumes, entitled *Sur les fonctions du cerveau et sur celles de chacune de ses parties*, appeared in 1825, three years before his death.

Much of Gall's early examination of heads was done among persons found in jails and lunatic asylums, and it is understandable that he believed he saw some connection between the characteristic head forms and the type of behavior which brought these individuals to such institutions. Supplementing this by studies of heads and head casts of non-institutionalized individuals, he found his material shaping into a coherent whole which seemed to him to justify a new scientific theory. This came to be known as phrenology, although the term as such did not originate with Gall.[3]

Three main propositions supported phrenology. First, the exterior conformation of the skull corresponded to its interior and to the conformation of the brain. Second, the mind could be ana-

[3] The term "phrenology" is said to have been used first in 1815 by Thomas Ignatius Forster (1789-1860), an English naturalist and astronomer. As early as 1806 he had begun to study the psychology of Gall, later making the acquaintance of Spurzheim, with whom he studied the anatomy and physiology of the brain. See Thomas Ignatius Forster: "Sketch of the New Anatomy and Physiology of the Brain and Nervous System of Drs. Gall and Spurzheim, Considered as Comprehending a Complete Phrenology," *Pamphleteer*, V (February 1815) 219-244.

lyzed into faculties or functions. Third, these faculties were related to the shape of the skull. Corollaries to these propositions
held that, in general, the brain was the organ of the mind, and
that certain areas of the brain contained organs to which corresponded an equal number of psychological characters, or powers.[4]
Gall originally identified twenty-six of these psychological characters (subsequently increased to thirty-five by Spurzheim) which
he divided into the affective powers on the one hand and the
intellectual powers on the other. Within the affective powers was
a further division into the propensities and the sentiments, while
the intellectual powers were separated into the perceptive faculties and the reflective faculties.

Pertinent to an understanding of the criminal nature were the
so-called lower propensities, particularly amativeness, philoprogenitiveness, combativeness, secretiveness, and acquisitiveness.
These served to account for crime, unless (and the phrenologists
made this very important qualification) they were altered in their
expression, or were made subservient to some of the more dominant faculties or higher sentiments, or were ruled by the intellectual powers.[5]

[4] The modern expression "psychological characters" is used here as being less con-
fusing than the word "faculties" which the phrenologists used loosely in several meanings.

[5] The line of descent in phrenology is: Gall, Spurzheim, George Combe. Gall, German born, practised medicine in Vienna. His researches in anatomy—particularly of the
brain—predicated upon a physiognomical base led him to the enunciation of theories
unpalatable to the Austrian government. Leaving Vienna he traveled over much of
Europe, finally settling in Paris in 1807. Here the Institute of France, which included
Cuvier and Pinel, in 1808 rejected the memoir which he and Spurzheim had jointly
prepared for membership. The anatomical studies which he pursued up to the time of
his death in 1828 furnish the very substantial basis for his fame as an anatomist.

Spurzheim (1776-1832), like Gall, was German born, and studied medicine in
Vienna. It was here that he became associated with Gall. Together they left Vienna,
eventually going to Paris to continue their studies. It was Spurzheim, rather than
Gall, who carried their doctrines abroad to Great Britain and America. For it was
he who came to America, as his biographer Nahum Capen put it, at the pressing invitation of "various scientfic bodies in Boston, and other cities," and it was here that
he died, in 1832. See Nahum Capen, *Reminiscences of Dr. Spurzheim and George
Combe*, New York, Boston, 1881, p. 5.

Gall is regarded as the originator of the system of phrenology, while Spurzheim is
known as its first popularizer and propagandist. Essentially his system differed only
in amplifying terms from that of Gall. In addition to his collaboration for a time
with Gall, Spurzheim prepared, independently, works on phrenology. Of especial interest to American students was his American edition (revised from the London edi-

PHRENOLOGY IN AMERICA

Our first step in tracing the influence of phrenological doctrines on American theories of criminal behavior shall be to consider at some length the work of Charles Caldwell. For it was Caldwell who first introduced phrenology into this country in 1821-1822, after having attended Spurzheim's lectures in Paris in the summer of 1821. For the next twenty years Caldwell was the stormy petrel of the medical, theological, and philosophical controversy over the merits of phrenology. During this period its status as a science was attacked especially by physicians, its fatalism was decried by theologians, and its assumptions and conclusions denied by philosophers. Throughout it all Caldwell was phrenology's staunchest proponent—its vindicator. His *Elements of Phrenology*, published in 1824, was a reprint, at the request of his students, of his lectures to them in the medical department of Transylvania University, in Kentucky. It will bear study in our attempt to understand the phrenological explanation of crime.[6]

---

tion) in 1832 of *A View of the Elementary Principles of Education, Founded on the Study of the Nature of Man*. Included in his discussion of education and morality was a consideration of the correction and reform of malefactors, which was centered around certain penological principles founded on phrenology. Among other things he noted the irresponsibility of idiots and madmen, and observed that there is a moral "idiotism" as well as an intellectual idiotism. "Some individuals may possess intellect and strong animal feelings but very weak moral sentiments which seldom, if ever enter into activity, so that such persons constantly follow their animal propensities." See John Gaspar Spurzheim, *A View of the Elementary Principles of Education, Founded on the Study of the Nature of Man*, 1st American Edition from 3rd London, Boston, 1832.

So too the work of the Scotsman George Combe (1788-1858) was merely a restatement and occasional elaboration of Spurzheim's writings. By his own admission their only difference concerned the function of the organ which to Spurzheim was inhabitiveness and which Combe called concentrativeness. Trained in the law and in moral philosophy, Combe at first denounced phrenology, only later to be its most fervent and zealous advocate. Like Spurzheim he traveled to America.

[6] Charles Caldwell was born in North Carolina in 1772. He studied medicine under Rush, Shippen, Wistar, and Physick, and had hoped to succeed to Rush's chair at the University of Pennsylvania. Failing this he resigned his professorship of Geology and the Philosophy of Natural History at the University of Pennsylvania to become the organizer of the medical department of Transylvania University in Lexington, Kentucky, and Professor of the Institutes of Medicine and Clinical Practice. In his capacity as Dean and Professor he journeyed to Europe in 1821 to purchase books for a medical library and to secure the requisite material for instruction. It was during this summer that he attended the lectures of Spurzheim in Paris. Later he left Transylvania University to found another medical school at Louisville, Kentucky. From 1795 when,

Beginning with the fundamental proposition that the brain was the organ of the mind, an organ that was compound and not simple, Caldwell proceeded in the manner of Gall and Spurzheim to mention three regions or compartments—the one being the seat of the active propensities, another, of the moral sentiments, and the third of the intellectual faculties.[7] These propensities, sentiments, and intellectual faculties each had a specific cerebral organ which produced a cranial protuberance. The pressure of these protuberances rendered their size and location a matter of observation. Thirty-four psychological characters were listed (Spurzheim listed thirty-five, Gall twenty-six) of which three—philoprogenitiveness, destructiveness and covetiveness—were related specifically to criminal behavior. Concerning philoprogenitiveness it was noted that of twenty-nine females who had been guilty of infanticide the development of this organ was defective in twenty-seven. Of destructiveness it was said that when not properly balanced and regulated by superior faculties it led to murder; while of covetiveness ("acquisitiveness" in other writers) Caldwell remarked that unless restrained and properly directed by the higher faculties it led to great selfishness and even to theft. His description of the passion for acquiring things without regard to their value to the taker or to the consequences of the taking anticipated much of the later controversy on irresistible impulse, kleptomania, and moral insanity. After declaring that phrenology taught that man derived his propensities from nature, Caldwell declared that the propensities were much more powerful in some than in others, and hence were more difficult to control. Individual differences were noticed even among the members of the same family, where it might be presumed that children would enjoy the same degree of health and education.

In this hierarchy of propensities, sentiments, and intellectual

---

at the age of twenty-three years, he translated from the Latin Blumenbach's *Elements of Physiology*, to the date of his death in 1853 he was a voluminous writer. Admittedly gifted, his career was marked by violent controversies in which he was often to be found as attacker as well as defender. Phrenology was but one of the many causes he vehemently championed. See *Dictionary of American Biography*, III, p. 406.

[7] Charles Caldwell, *Elements of Phrenology*, Lexington, Kentucky, 1824.

faculties the higher controls the lower. The sentiments control the propensities, while with the aid of the will the intellectual faculties enlighten, direct, and govern the whole. It is not predictable whether the intellectual faculties will operate for good or evil; it is more certain that the sentiments will incline to virtue, while the propensities become vicious only by excess. Suppose, Caldwell said, that an individual had the organ of covetiveness strongly developed but uncontrolled by other faculties. The result would be dishonesty and theft. But opposing and seeking to control this organ were the organs of conscientiousness and benevolence, together with the intellectual organs. At this point the counteracting organs of piety, the love of approbation, and self-esteem are called into play while the will throws its support on the side of virtue and subdues completely the propensity to vice. Or take the organ of destructiveness which, if uncontrolled, would lead to murder; it was opposed and overcome by conscientiousness, benevolence, love of approbation, self-esteem, piety, the intellectual faculties, and the will. Thus, while any single propensity or sentiment if uninfluenced by any of the others may lead to vice and crime, yet the functions of the organs were so united in due proportion that harmony and perfection are achieved.[8]

A strong propensity to commit a crime, Caldwell held, by no means implied a necessity to commit it. Defending himself from the charges of fatalism, he insisted that man was a free agent, and that in all cases where actual insanity did not exist, the higher faculties could govern the lower, provided they were properly called into action. If they were not thus called the fault was not in Nature, but in the individual who misused her gifts.

When we take into view the effect which education may be made to produce in weakening propensities, and in strengthening the moral sentiments and the intellectual faculties, we are forced to acknowledge that, in the constitution of man, nature, according to the principles of

[8] Caldwell, in common with other phrenologists, neglected to specify why virtue is so consistently triumphant. Is it because of the system of checks and balances which was necessary to show that phrenology was more favorable to liberty than any other system of mental philosophy?

Phrenology, has done everything necessary and practicable, to constitute moral freedom and to give virtue an ascendancy over vice. If man, then, misemploys and abuses the dispensations of heaven, the fault is his own, and he must abide the consequence. Hence the future accountability of moral agents is perfectly compatible with the doctrines of Phrenology. That science, therefore, has no tendency to the legitimation of crime.[9]

No other American phrenologist was as prolific or wrote with such vehemence as did Caldwell in the twenty-year period following his introduction of phrenology into this country. Never accepted by the medical profession, phrenology had passed out of the stage of scientific controversy by 1841, the date of Caldwell's last article of defense. Yet during the two previous decades (1820-1840) much of his medical writing was explicitly phrenological. For example, in his remarks on mental derangement he spoke of intemperance which may pervert the moral, the animal, or the intellectual organs.[10] Admitting that his thoughts were tinctured by phrenology, he dwelt on the possibility of murder by one whose organ of combativeness was in a state of excessive excitement, and remarked that if the organs of destructiveness, acquisitiveness, and secretiveness were affected very likely there would be produced an irresistible propensity to theft. After stating that man is not born with organs which are by nature essentially of evil tendency, he specifically added that there are no organs necessarily of theft and murder, but that theft and murder result from the neglect and abuse of the organs of combativeness, destructiveness, and secretiveness.[11] Later Caldwell emphasized this in the following style: the crimes that disturb society are murder, theft, assault and battery, fraud, treason, and rape, these being the product of five unrestrained animal propensities which are known as destructiveness, combativeness, acquisitiveness, se-

[9] Caldwell, op. cit., pp, 79-80.

[10] Charles Caldwell, "Thoughts on the Pathology, Prevention and Treatment of Intemperance, as a Form of Mental Derangement," Transylvania Journal of Medicine and Associate Sciences, V (July-August-September 1832) 309-350.

[11] Charles Caldwell, "Phrenology Vindicated, in Remarks on Article III, of the July Number, 1833, of the North American Review, Headed 'Phrenology,'" Annals of Phrenology, I (October 1833) 1-102.

cretiveness, and amativeness. When these are held in subordina-
tion by the higher faculties these crimes do not exist. Restrain
destructiveness, he insisted, and there will be no arson or murder; restrain combativeness and there will be no assaults; restrain
acquisitiveness and there will be neither theft nor robbery; restrain secretiveness and there will be no fraud or treason; and
finally, restrain amativeness and there will be no violation of
female chastity. While each of these organs may function alone,
there stand opposed to them at least six other organs and their
faculties. Two or three of them are nearly or even quite as
powerful—benevolence which whispers kindness and mercy,
veneration which interposes the prohibitions of religion, conscientiousness which proclaims the injustice of the deed. In addition there is love of approbation which warns of the loss of reputation, and causality which admonishes of the ruinous effects of
such lawless violence. And again Caldwell wrote:

If man, therefore, continues vicious and unhappy, the fault and
misfortune are attributable to himself; not to anything in the cast of
his destiny which he cannot control. Whatever he does, he does freely,
though in strict subservience to the influence of motives. I shall only
add, that flagrant immorality, profligacy, and crime, are as essentially
the product of functional excess, or structural derangement of the
brain, or of both united, brought on by abuses which might have been
avoided, as pneumonia is of similar affections of the lungs, hepatitis of
the liver, or dyspepsia of the stomach.[12]

Once more, in an article vindicating phrenology, Caldwell emphasized that man had no organ of crime, but that he had several organs that might lead to crime if they were abused or mis-
applied, or unless they were prevented from acting to excess.[13]
He reaffirmed the rôle of the countervailing organs to the lower
propensities and added to the list the organs of self-esteem,
firmness, and comparison. Continuing, he declared that there
was a confederacy of moral and reflecting organs and faculties

[12] Charles Caldwell, "Thoughts on the Most Effective Condition of the Brain as
the Organ of the Mind, and on the Modes of Attaining It," *American Phrenological
Journal and Miscellany*, I (August 1839) 409.
[13] Charles Caldwell, "Phrenology Vindicated Against the Charges of Fatalism,"
American Phrenological Journal and Miscellany, II (December 1839) 98-110.

that could be arrayed against a single animal organ in order to withhold it from crime. They, the countervailing organs, could effect their purpose as certainly and as easily as seven or eight men could prevent a single man within their reach from perpetrating murder. How could these animal organs be reduced in power when they threaten criminal action? In the same way that any organ of the body could be reduced in tone and weakened in action—by protecting them from unnecessary exercise and excitement. Just as other organs were strengthened by exercise and enfeebled by inaction, so too with these animal organs. Furthermore, the union of faculties leaning toward virtue was more powerful than any single animal propensity which could lead to vice. And finally, the animal propensities act not in unison but separately, each seeking its own gratification.[14]

The address of John Bell, in March 1822, before the Central Phrenological Society of Philadelphia a month after its organization, followed closely the introduction of phrenology by Caldwell.[15] Bell, a physician, and later medical editor of considerable standing in Philadelphia (which was then the medical center of the western hemisphere), recognized that man was possessed

[14] In view of the dominating part which Caldwell played in the early history of phrenology in the United States it is significant that his autobiography carried only a line or so of reference to phrenology. His own bibliography contained seventeen items on phrenology extending from his first book on phrenology in 1824 to his latest work in 1841. Caldwell was writing his autobiography up to the time of his death in 1853, but already phrenology had been rejected. It seems a fair inference that he was unwilling to dwell upon that phase of his life, and that the editor of his autobiography and several biographers have concurred with him on that score.

[15] The Central Phrenological Society of Philadelphia was organized in February 1822 with Philip Syng Physick, professor of Anatomy at the University of Pennsylvania, President; Dr. Benjamin H. Coates, Recording Secretary; and Dr. John Bell, Corresponding Secretary. Bell, but twenty-six years old, was undoubtedly influenced by George Combe, the Scotch follower of Spurzheim, for Bell was the American editor of Combe's *Essays on Phrenology,* published in Philadelphia in 1822. This volume contained Bell's address on phrenology already referred to, while in the same year Nathaniel Chapman, professor of Theory and Practice of Medicine at the University of Pennsylvania, published it in the *Philadelphia Journal of the Medical and Physical Sciences,* of which he was the editor.

Coates, a year younger than Bell and already a physician of promise in Philadelphia, delivered a lecture before the Society in 1823, on comparative phrenology. See Benjamin H. Coates, "Comments on Some of the Illustrations Derived by Phrenology from Comparative Anatomy," *Philadelphia Journal of the Medical and Physical Sciences,* VII (1823) 58-80.

of strong animal feelings and propensities which could and did impel him to the commission of crimes, but he denied that man was necessarily or irresistibly led away by these lower propensities, pointing out that higher and nobler faculties may predominate in his behavior.[16] More than a decade later Bell was still an ardent supporter and defender of phrenology, and at the same time editor of the *Eclectic Journal of Medicine*, lecturer on the Institutes of Medicine and Medical Jurisprudence, Member of the College of Physicians of Philadelphia, and of the American Philosophical Society.

Following Caldwell and Bell a number of other writers issued works on phrenology, stressing particularly the propensities of destructiveness and acquisitiveness as likely to conduce to crime. Amos Dean in 1834 followed substantially the system of Gall and Spurzheim[17] as did also Silas Jones, who in 1836 insisted that the propensity of destructiveness was manifested in its grosser forms of breaking, stabbing, poisoning, drowning, and murdering when it was not dominated by the balancing and directing influences of the higher sentiments.[18] Haskins' work was more in the nature of a history, giving valuable background on the work of Gall, Spurzheim, Combe, and Caldwell,[19] while that of J. Stanley Grimes in the same year was based upon Gall and Spurzheim, but amplified by the author.[20] In 1837 appeared *Phrenology Proved, Illustrated, and Applied*, by the Fowlers— O. S. and L. N.—which by 1840 had appeared in its ninth edition.[21] Aside from Boardman's book in 1847[22] there was hardly another work published on the subject without the imprimatur of one or the other of the Fowlers, or of Fowler and Wells, successors. By this time phrenology had definitely passed out of

[16] John Bell, "On Phrenology, or the Study of the Intellectual and Moral Nature of Man," *The Philadelphia Journal of the Medical and Physical Sciences*, IV (1822) 72-113.

[17] Amos Dean, *Lectures on Phrenology*, Albany, 1834.

[18] Silas Jones, *Practical Phrenology*, Boston, 1836.

[19] R. W. Haskins, *History and Progress of Phrenology*, Buffalo, N.Y., 1839.

[20] J. Stanley Grimes, *A New System of Phrenology*, Buffalo, N.Y. 1839.

[21] O. S. and L. N. Fowler, *Phrenology Proved, Illustrated, and Applied*, Philadelphia, and New York, 1837.

[22] A. Boardman, *A Defence of Phrenology*, New York, 1847.

the realm of scientific discussion save for an occasional rare instance of which note shall be made here.[23]

That phrenology was not without its respectable adherents was indicated, among other instances, by the enunciations of Benjamin Silliman, editor of the *American Journal of Science and Arts,* professor of chemistry in Yale College, and a member of numerous scientific bodies. Following the lectures of George Combe in 1840, resolutions of appreciation were offered by Governor Edwards (in a meeting presided over by Chief Justice Daggett, of the State of Connecticut) and seconded by Professor Silliman.[24] If further evidence on this score be necessary, the record of the reception of Combe on his trip to America in 1838-1840 stands open to inspection.[25] In Philadelphia, for instance, the committee appointed to carry resolutions to Combe following his lectures consisted of: Nicholas Biddle, who was a trustee of the University of Pennsylvania, a member of the American Philosophical Society, and President of the Board of Trustees of Girard College; Joseph Hartshorne, a member of the American Philosophical Society; Benjamin Richards, a trustee of the University of Pennsylvania as well as one of the managers of the Eastern State Penitentiary and a former Mayor of Philadelphia; William Gibson, professor of surgery at the University of Pennsylvania, and a member of the American Philosophical Society; Thomas Harris, president of the Philadelphia Medical Society and a member of the American Philosophical Society; and Alexander Dallas Bache, President of Girard College, formerly professor of chemistry at the University of Pennsylvania, and member of the American Philosophical Society. In other cities such as Boston, New York, Albany, Buffalo, New Haven, the experience was not unlike this. (This recalls the earlier visit of Spurzheim in 1832, when he attended the Yale commencement

[23] For a sprightly review of the Fowlers see the article by Carl Carmer entitled "That Was New York, the Fowlers, Practical Phrenologists," in the *New Yorker* for February 13, 1937, pp. 22-27.

[24] "Phrenology," *American Journal of Science and Arts.* XXXIX, October, 1840, pp. 65-88; see also Benjamin Silliman, "Plea in Behalf of Phrenology," *American Phrenological Journal and Miscellany,* III (December 1840) 130-141.

[25] George Combe, *Notes on the United States of America During a Phrenological Visit in 1838-9-40.* 2 volumes, Philadelphia, 1841.

exercises, and was invited by President Quincy of Harvard to that school's commencement as well as to the meeting of the Phi Beta Kappa Society. It was at that same time that Spurzheim commenced his lectures at the Boston Athenaeum and at Harvard.)

Amariah Brigham, superintendent of the New York State Lunatic Asylum at Utica, and founder of the *American Journal of Insanity*, was a stout believer in phrenology, maintaining it in the *Journal* from its founding in 1844 until his death in 1848. In the second volume he wrote of criminals as being unfortunate victims of a physical organization which was defective and in which the influence of the higher faculties was small while that of the propensities was great. Those whose animal propensities governed them constituted nine-tenths of our criminals.[26] Brigham's assistant at Utica, H. A. Buttolph, who was later superintendent of the New Jersey Lunatic Asylum at Trenton and, following that, of a State Asylum for the Insane at Morristown, New Jersey, continued Brigham's interest in phrenology even after 1849. Indeed, in October 1849, the month following Brigham's death, Buttolph presented in the pages of the *American Journal of Insanity* an article on the relation between phrenology and insanity, in which he recognized that disease could affect the organs of the feelings, exciting, depressing, or perverting them so that the end result was some sad and unlooked-for catastrophe.[27] Of the phrenological approach to the problem of moral insanity he wrote:

The bare mention of the fundamental principles of the science, that the mind is composed of a plurality of faculties, depending upon the brain for their manifestations, that through disease of this organ, the social, moral, and animal, no less than the intellectual powers, are subject to derangement and impaired responsibility, is sufficient to solve the whole mystery attached to "moral insanity."[28]

Almost forty years later (although phrenology by that time

[26] Amariah Brigham, " 'Journal of Prison Discipline,' and Lunatic Asylums," *American Journal of Insanity*. II (October 1845) 175-183.

[27] H. A. Buttolph, "Relation Between Phrenology and Insanity," *American Journal of Insanity*, VI (October 1849) 127-136.

[28] *Ibid.*, pp. 131-132.

had passed into the "practical" stage of boardwalk divination) Buttolph still insisted on the utility of phrenology, particularly in connection with mental derangement, for he wrote then:

It proves that one or more of these organs may be injured or diseased, and their functions impeded or altered, without necessarily affecting the remainder and thus explains how a man may be insane on one feeling or faculty, and sound on all the rest; and, consequently, how, when a different organ is diseased, the faculty or feeling that is deranged may be different and yet the disease itself remain exactly of the same nature. . . . Phrenology shows that in like manner, morbid excitement of the cerebral organs of combativeness and destructiveness may produce raving violence and fury. . . .[29]

PHRENOLOGICAL STUDIES OF AMERICAN PRISONERS

Professional phrenologists from time to time reported on the examination of prisoners' skulls. Among the first of these reports was that upon the examination of the skull of Le Blanc, who had committed a murder in Morristown, New Jersey. The phrenologist making the examination after execution declared, without knowing the criminal, that he was a thief who would murder for money. Le Blanc's skull was described as having a large posterior lobe, while the middle lobe in which were situated the organs of destructiveness, secretiveness, and acquisitiveness was very large.[30] In the next issue of the *American Phrenological Journal and Miscellany* the skull of Tardy, the pirate, was described as having the organs of combativeness, destructiveness, acquisitiveness, secretiveness, self-esteem, and firmness very well developed, while those of veneration and conscientiousness were small.[31] The same organs were found to be very large in the skull of Miller, a murderer.[32] In another instance it was observed that the organ of ideality was invariably small in crimin-

[29] H. A. Buttolph, "On the Physiology of the Brain and Its Relations in Health and Disease to the Faculties of the Mind," *American Journal of Insanity*, XLII (January 1886) 303.

[30] "Character of Le Blanc," *American Phrenological Journal and Miscellany*, I (December 1838) 89-96.

[31] "Phrenological Developments and Character of Tardy the Pirate—with Cuts," *American Phrenological Journal and Miscellany*, I (January 1839) 104-113.

[32] "Phrenological Developments and Character of William Miller," *American Phrenological Journal and Miscellany*, I (May 1839) 272-286.

als. When the wax facsimile of Fieschi (who had attempted to assassinate the King of France) was studied, it was declared that Fieschi had the organ of destructiveness well developed while his social feelings and moral sentiments were defective.[33] Of two skulls presented to L. N. Fowler he identified one as being that of a man possessed of very weak moral powers, with strong animal feelings and propensities of which the strongest were combativeness, destructiveness, alimentiveness, and firmness, which if perverted would make him quarrelsome, cruel, desperate, and stubborn. With this man, who turned out to be Robert Morris, who had been hanged for murder, destructiveness and firmness had a controlling influence making him cruel, desperate, and possessed of a murderous disposition.[34]

Another phrenologist, Dr. K. E. Burhans, examined fifteen prisoners in the St. Louis jail, described each head and what it betokened, predicted the character of the crime, and was thereupon informed of the charge against the prisoner. The description and the prediction corresponded remarkably! For instance, the account of the examination of prisoner #2 reads as follows:

The organs of Combativeness and Destructiveness predominate in this head; there is some want of Conscientiousness. Under the influence of spiritous liquors he is capable of great wilfulness and cruelty to his friends, and even to his children. Free from artificial excitement, his conduct would not be very violent. *Charge:* an assault, with intent to kill his daughter—it is said under the influence of spiritous liquors.

Of another prisoner it was reported:

He is combative and destructive, more so than anyone whose head has been yet examined. He is capable of great bravery and daring. He is bold and vigorous in his enterprises; taciturn and gloomy, with little hope; considerable Acquisitiveness and Secretiveness. His organization would make him dangerous to others and to himself, in despondency. *Crime:* theft and assault, with intent to rob.

Concerning a third, it was noted:

[33] "Phrenological Developments of Fieschi; Who Attempted to Murder the King of France," *American Phrenological Journal and Miscellany*, I (August 1839) 438-440.
[34] "Examination of a Skull," *American Phrenological Journal and Miscellany*, II (June 1840) 427-428.

His brain is small and his capacity is limited. He is without any degree of conscience. His organization would make him deceitful, cunning, and cruel; and he would be more disposed to steal than to commit any other crime. Charged with theft.[35]

Peter Robinson, a murderer whose skull was examined, had destructiveness, self-esteem, secretiveness, and acquisitiveness very well developed, while he was deficient in benevolence and cautiousness.[36] So too with James Eager, of whom it was observed that his drinking habits and his immense amativeness were the cause of the murder. It was noticed that his organs of combativeness and destructiveness were both large.[37]

One of the few prison administrators who was influenced by phrenological doctrines and especially by the writings of George Combe (Combe had made phrenological analyses of prisoners' heads in American prisons in 1838) was the matron of Mount Pleasant State Prison in New York State, E. W. Farnham. It was she who edited the American edition of Sampson's *Rationale of Crime*, a book based avowedly on phrenology. In addition to endorsing its beliefs Miss Farnham elaborated with extensive footnotes and appendices on the application of phrenological principles to the study and treatment of the criminal.[38]

As was to be expected, the phrenological propensities were used occasionally by writers of prison reports to explain criminal behavior. The reports of the Eastern State Penitentiary in Philadelphia from 1856 to 1865 recorded the predominant passions as causes of crime in the following categories: combativeness, amativeness, destructiveness, acquisitiveness. The 1856 report, for instance, listed the crimes of four hundred and sixteen pris-

[35] "Phrenological Examination of Prisoners," *American Phrenological Journal and Miscellany*, III (November 1840) 83-85.

[36] "Phrenological Developments and Character of Peter Robinson, Who Was Executed April 16th, at New Brunswick, N.J., for the Murder of A. Suydam, Esq.," *American Phrenological Journal and Miscellany*, III (July 1841) 452-459.

[37] "Phrenological Developments and Character of James Eager, Executed for the Murder of Philip Williams, May 9, 1845," *American Phrenological Journal and Miscellany*, VII (August 1845) 263-268.

[38] M. B. Sampson, *Rationale of Crime, and Its Appropriate Treatment; Being a Treatise on Criminal Jurisprudence Considered in Relation to Cerebral Organization*, American Edition, from the Second London Edition, edited with Notes and Illustrations by E. W. Farnham, New York and Philadelphia, 1846.

oners as being due in fourteen, or 3.8 per cent, of the cases to
combativeness, in thirty-four, or 8.17 per cent, of the cases to
amativeness, in seventy-two, or 17.3 per cent, of the cases to destructiveness, in 295, or 70.9 per cent, of the cases to acquisitiveness, while in one case jealousy was the cause.[39]

Stolz, while not a prison official, wrote from the phrenological
point of view in his work on the cause and cure of crime. Believing in the inheritance of acquired characteristics he emphasized the fact that one possessing pronouncedly the organ of
combativeness who did not control it would pass it down to the
next generation. Similarly Stolz believed that he who exercised the opposing principle to combativeness or any of the other
lower propensities would hand to his descendants lessened propensities.[40] Reeve, too, who wrote on the prison question, indicated his belief in phrenology by citing an example of a phrenologist who after examining a stranger informed him that his brain
combinations showed him to be instinctively a thief. True enough
the man said he was a thief, without the power to fight off an
irresistible impulse.[41] Gorton, though writing on moral insanity,
also confirmed this belief in the potency of the propensities of
acquisitiveness, secretiveness, destructiveness, and combativeness
as instigating to criminal behavior unless checked by the higher
sentiments of self-respect and moral feeling.[42]

A century after Gall's work on cerebral localization the American physician Lydston declared that clinical evidence supported
it, deploring the fact that Gall's ideas had been monopolized almost entirely by charlatans, quacks, and literary pirates.[43] Indeed
Lydston held that the trend of modern criminology was in the

[39] *Twenty-Seventh Annual Report of the Inspectors, Warden, Physician, and Moral
Instructor of the Eastern Penitentiary of Pennsylvania*, 1856, p. 42.

[40] John Stolz, *The Cause and Cure of Crime*, Philadelphia, 1880.

[41] Charles H. Reeve, *The Prison Question*, Chicago, 1890.

[42] D. A. Gorton, "Moral Insanity," *American Medical Monthly*, XVI (June 1898)
81-92.

[43] George Frank Lydston (1858-1923) received his medical training at the Bellevue
Hospital Medical College, New York, and was later resident surgeon at the State
Immigrant Hospital, Ward's Island, New York. He subsequently engaged in medical
practice in Chicago. For many years he held a lectureship, and after 1891 a professorship on genito-urinary and venereal diseases at the Chicago College of Physicians
and Surgeons. At one time he held a chair of criminal anthropology at the Kent College

direction of the theories of cerebral localization as laid down by Gall.

If there be aught of truth in Gall's theory of localization, it is not beyond the bounds of possibility that certain moral faculties are presided over by special cell areas, and that injury or disease of these centres may be productive of vicious or criminal impulses. That the posterior and middle lobes of the brain in general preside over the moral faculties of the mind, the anterior lobes being the intellectual inhibitory centres, is fairly well established. It follows, then, that disease of what may be termed the moral centres, and disease of the inhibitory centres may alike produce moral perturbations. The relation between coarse brain disease and insane criminality is so well established that neither theoretic nor clinical evidence is wanting to support it.[44]

SUMMARY AND CONCLUSION

Introduced into America by Caldwell, propounded, defended, and vindicated by him (did he not say that phrenology was as likely to be doomed to extinction as that the sun should retrograde in its path?), endorsed by many, chiefly non-medical laymen, phrenology resisted for a time the repeated onslaughts of the medical and theological professions, but finally succumbed. Ultimately it fell into the hands of the pseudo-scientific and eventually of the quack. For some it answered the riddle of human behavior until such time as the developments of psychology denied it the eminence it once so defiantly struggled for.

Some understanding of the inadequacy of phrenology as an interpretation of human behavior can be gained by noting for a moment its beginnings and subsequent development. As a student Gall observed that those of his fellows with unusual memory ability had projecting eyes, from which he later concluded that an undue prominance of any part of the head indicated a corresponding development of the brain beneath. Likewise an underdevelopment of the brain was responsible for an under-

---

of Law in Chicago. He was the author of over one hundred books, papers, and pamphlets on medical topics. See *Dictionary of American Biography*, XI, 513.

[44] G. Frank Lydston, *The Diseases of Society*, J. B. Lippincott Co., Philadelphia, 1904, pp. 155-156.

sized development of any of the head parts. Gall also learned by clinical observations that injuries to certain parts of the brain caused loss of eyesight or paralysis, etc., which caused him to deduce the theory of brain localization. Thus for criminals the overdevelopment of certain parts of the brain resulted in certain identifying cranial protrusions, which indicated a dominance of the lower propensities. Similarly the lack of protuberances of other parts of the head was due to an underdevelopment of the subjacent brain, indicating the impotence of the higher sentiments and the intellectual powers. Gall, Spurzheim, and some of the later "practising" phrenologists may have found these anatomical peculiarities in certain individuals, but in no instance was any evidence presented to prove this was true only of the criminal population. Furthermore the mere fact that a man was a criminal, i.e., incarcerated in a penal institution, was taken to mean that his skull bore these identifying features. In other words there was no control group established for comparison purposes.

A corollary to this was the failure of the phrenologists themselves to perform the necessary research to establish a scientific basis for their body of knowledge. Especially was this true with Caldwell, in America, who defended phrenology from attacks on all sides by the simple expedient of flawless logic based upon certain a priori assumptions rather than upon any research which he had actually made. Phrenology sought to reject the Calvinian dogma of man's innate sinfulness only to set up in its place another dogma just as unsurely grounded and partaking of the same "unprovability."

That phrenology made so little real contribution to the study of crime causation was due essentially to the failure to recognize the fact, now well known, that no single portion of the brain can determine that complexity which we call human behavior. Just as we have come to know intelligence as a multi-factored phenomenon, so too we have come to regard behavior as a resultant of many forces within the brain and body of the individual. Psychology of the last hundred years has not confirmed the phrenological analysis of the mind into a number of faculties or functions, and with this central principle unsubstantiated, the behavior theory which rests upon it has long since been repudiated. And certainly no psychology of today will support the position that an excess of a function is correlated with an excess of brain development and consequent protrusion.

Rejected by the physiologists, who denied the connection between the exterior of the skull and the brain, as well as by the philosophers, who refused to accept the analysis of mind into faculties with spatially distinct organs, nevertheless phrenology is historically significant in the rôle it played in the development of a scientific psychology. As Boring put it, "It is almost correct to say that a scientific psychology was born of phrenology, out of wedlock with science."[45] Likewise rejected by the students of human behavior, it should be recognized that while the practical application of phrenological doctrine may have been of slight value, yet phrenology gave impetus to a new orientation of causation—individual study rather than philosophic reflection upon the nature of crime.[46]

[45] Edwin G. Boring, *A History of Experimental Psychology*, New York, 1929, p. 55.
[46] See also, Joseph Jastrow, *Wish and Wisdom*, New York, 1935, pp. 285-303; George Malcolm Stratton in Joseph Jastrow, *The Story of Human Error*, New York, 1936, pp. 326-328.

II

INSANITY

DESPITE the extensive popular interest in phrenology in America and the work of a few notable physicians on its behalf, it never received a wide acceptance in scientific circles. An even earlier and more continuing study of human behavior lay in the relation between insanity and crime.

Historically, the two—insanity and crime—were at times indistinguishable; the criminal was the madman (often possessed of a demon), the madman was the criminal. Later, as the madman was identified and segregated the criminal remained. When the criteria for establishing insanity were clear there was little difficulty in separating the insane from the criminal. Yet as these gross criteria were more and more refined, controversy replaced agreement as to who was insane and who was criminal.

The difference of opinion was more than dialectical, for upon it depended the practical issue of treatment or punishment. Courts of law recognized the lack of responsibility of the insane man for his acts and accordingly confined him to an asylum or retreat where hospital services were available. The criminal, on the other hand, was held accountable for his deeds and was committed to prison. The one institution embodied the philosophy of treatment, the other of punishment.[1]

The distinction between the acts of an insane man and a criminal was early made, in 1838, by Isaac Ray upon the basis of motive or intent.[2]

---

[1] The term "insanity" is used in the setting of the period under discussion. The current expression—"mental disease"—does not convey the full flavor of the period as does "insanity."

[2] Isaac Ray (1807-1881), a native of Massachusetts, received his medical training at Harvard Medical School after having served in the offices of several well-known Boston physicians. After a period of private practice in Portland, Maine, he became medical superintendent of the State Hospital for the Insane at Augusta, and later, in 1845, the superintendent of the newly organized Butler Hospital at Providence,

Crime is not necessarily the result of madness, not even when perpetrated under the excitement of fierce and violent passions; in the true sense of the word, it is never so, but is always actuated by motives; insufficient it may be, but still rational motives, having reference to definite and real objects.[3]

In contrast to this is the situation where mental derangement is present:

The causes, which urge the insane to deeds of violence, are generally illusory—the hallucinations of a diseased brain—or they may act from no motive at all, solely in obedience to a blind impulse, with no end to obtain, nor wish to gratify. Madness too is more or less independent of the exciting causes, that have given rise to it, and exists long after those causes have been removed, and after the paramount wish or object has been obtained. In short, madness is the result of a certain pathological condition of the brain, while the criminal effects of violent passions merely indicate unusual strength of those passions, or a deficient education of those higher and nobler faculties, that furnish the necessary restraint upon their power.[4]

In his discussion of intellectual mania (monomania), general and partial; moral mania, general and partial; dementia; febrile delirium; and suicide, Ray consistently distinguished between the act which was both criminal and criminal by intent, and the act which was criminal in execution but not in intent. The one was crime, the other the anti-social act of the insane man. The one called for full responsibility and punishment under the criminal law, the other for the dispensation of the law according to existing knowledge of the nature of the mind of the actor.

Rhode Island. In 1867 he retired, owing to poor health, and spent the rest of his busy life in Philadelphia, principally writing and consulting on professional matters. Ray was one of the founders of the Association of Medical Superintendents of American Institutions for the Insane (later the Medico-Psychological Association), at one time its president, and a frequent contributer to its *Journal*. He was also a member of the Philadelphia College of Physicians, and a founder of the Social Science Association. In 1838 he published *The Medical Jurisprudence of Insanity*, which was recognized as the outstanding book in the field for over a generation and which eventually went through six editions. During his lifetime he published over one hundred articles and books, including *Mental Hygiene* in 1863, and *Contributions to Mental Pathology* in 1873. See *Dictionary of American Biography*, XV, 404.

[3] Isaac Ray, *A Treatise on the Medical Jurisprudence of Insanity*, Boston, 1838, p. 52.

[4] *Ibid.*, p. 53.

Other colleagues confirmed Ray as they reported their observations in the *American Journal of Insanity* (the journal of the Association of Medical Superintendents of American Institutions for the Insane). Nine years after the publication of Ray's book, Amariah Brigham[5] noted that marked changes in behavior were often due to diseases of the brain or at times to accidental injuries to the brain. Persons so affected who previously were lawabiding suddenly lost all powers of self-control and literally seemed driven to the commission of the most heinous deeds.[6] A decade later (1857), Edward Jarvis, a frequent contributor to the *Journal*, a member of the association, and a practitioner who took insane patients into his home, maintained that it was the mental disorder which preceded the criminal acts, depriving the person of the power of discriminating between right and wrong and impelling him to commit the anti-social offense.[7]

Nor was the legal profession at this time without its working distinction between crime and insanity as contained in its definition of legal responsibility, a definition enunciated in 1843 in the McNaghten case. In this case (in which the jury returned a verdict of insanity in the trial of McNaghten for the killing of Mr. Drummond, secretary to Sir Robert Peel) the House of Lords put certain questions to the judges. The answers of the judges became rules which confined legal, and occasionally medical, opinion on the subject of insanity and crime for many years. It was held that when the doer of an illegal act could not distinguish between right and wrong he was an insane man and his act was not a crime for which he was legally responsible. Simi-

[5] Amariah Brigham (1798-1849) had practised general medicine prior to his appointment to the superintendency of the Retreat for the Insane at Hartford, Connecticut, in 1840. Two years later he became superintendent of the newly organized New York State Lunatic Asylum at Utica which he helped to open in 1843. In 1844 he undertook the publication and editorship of the *American Journal of Insanity*, the first journal of its kind in the English language. He was the author of two books, entitled *Influence of Mental Cultivation on Health*, and *Influence of Religion on the Health and Physical Welfare of Mankind*, as well as a later work, *An Inquiry Concerning the Diseases and Function of the Brain, the Spinal Cord and the Nerves*.

[6] Amariah Brigham, "Crime and Insanity," *American Journal of Insanity*, IV (July 1847) 67-72.

[7] Edward Jarvis, "Criminal Insane, Insane Transgressors and Insane Convicts," *American Journal of Insanity*, XIII (January 1857) 195-231.

larly, if the doer of an illegal act was under an insane delusion as to circumstances, which, if true, would relieve him of responsibility, or if his reasoning powers were so depraved as to make the commission of his act the natural consequence of his delusion, then he was an insane man, and his act was not a crime. All other illegal acts are crimes and all other doers are held to be criminals, and hence were legally responsible. American courts followed these rulings which were early presented by the celebrated lawyer and writer, Francis Wharton, in 1855. Wharton's treatise was a model for close reasoning, scholarly grasp, and succinct presentation, being the first of many treatises on medical jurisprudence written by American lawyers. Indeed Wharton's book may be regarded as being as able a work for the legal profession as Ray's, seventeen years earlier, was for the medical.[8]

As is to be expected, much of the question of crime and insanity revolved around homicide and the responsibility of the perpetrator of the act, a subject discussed by John P. Gray, superintendent of the New York State Lunatic Asylum, in 1857.[9] Where these acts were the product of a diseased brain in which actual physical changes had taken place, Gray declared the acts to be those of an insane man. His three categories were: crimes occasioned by delusion; crimes in which the offender, though suffering from cerebro-mental disease, had committed the offense under the influence of some motive not of a delusive character; crimes where with general symptoms of cerebro-mental disease neither delusion nor motive were discernible.[10] By far the larger number of his fifty-two cases of homicides or homicidal attempts fell within the first class. Further analysis showed fourteen of

[8] Francis Wharton, *A Monograph on Mental Unsoundness*, Philadelphia, 1855.

[9] Following his medical training at the University of Pennsylvania, John P. Gray was resident physician at Blockley Hospital (later Philadelphia General Hospital), and at twenty-eight the superintendent of the New York State Lunatic Asylum. For many years he was editor of the *American Journal of Insanity*, a position in which he succeeded Amariah Brigham, his predecessor at Utica. On many occasions he was a medical witness in the courtroom, never failing to characterize moral insanity, dipsomania, and kleptomania as psychiatric myths. At one time he was professor of psychological medicine at Bellevue Medical College and at the Albany Medical' College. See *Dictionary of American Biography*, VII, 521.

[10] John P. Gray, "Homicide in Insanity," *American Journal of Insanity*, XIV (October 1857) 119-145.

these fifty-two cases to be acute mania; three sub-acute mania; two paroxysmal mania; four chronic mania; twenty-four dementia; four melancholia; and one mania *a potu*. Though he called the offenses under consideration crimes, Gray recognized them to be the product of mental disease.

That in insanity there is developed a disposition to the extreme violence of murder, and that this disposition is, at times, irresistible, no one familiar with the insane will for a moment pretend to doubt; and from such observation as cases have thus far afforded we cannot but adopt the opinion that the morbid tendency to homicide is but one of the many violent impulses of the insane state—one among the many manifestations of perverted instinct exhibited *in* the disease; and that the homicidal act, in irresponsible persons, generally, if not always, has for its origin and development such motives or disturbance of feelings as usually influence the insane to other carefully planned or sudden acts of violence; and that a full and reliable history of cases of sudden or more or less persistent homicidal propensity will reveal the fact, that, *in all instances,* anterior to any such impulse, there existed for a time *physical disease,* or at least perceptible disturbance of the physical health and a change in the mental condition; or, in other words, a *state of insanity.*[11]

Eighteen years afterwards Superintendent Gray offered a series of cases (fifty-eight in one article, and sixty-seven in the second) of attempted homicides which he classified as: those in which the homicidal attempt was made during a paroxysm of insanity; those in which the homicidal attempt was made by manifestly insane persons, from motives and conditions which might influence a sane mind as anger, revenge, etc.; those in which the insanity was said to have developed after the homicidal attempt; and cases of epilepsy.[12] His classification of the forms of insanity followed his earlier study, with the exception that here he included paresis as one of the forms. Throughout, Gray insisted that the insane person acts from motives which, were the premises correct, might influence a sane mind; nowhere, however, will he permit himself to accept the theory of impulsive acts or impulsive insanity.

[11] John P. Gray, *op. cit.,* pp. 142-143.
[12] John P. Gray, "Responsibility of the Insane—Homicide in Insanity," *American Journal of Insanity,* XXXII (July, October 1875) 1-57, 153-183.

While most of the members of the legal and medical professions differentiated the disposition of the offender who committed an illegal act by providing for confinement of the offender not guilty by reason of insanity, Dr. William A. Hammond believed that even if it were the act of an insane man such a person ought to be punished—delusions did not justify homicide.[13] In 1873 in his work on insanity and its relations to crime he stated: "Again, some of the insane are such monsters of depravity that they should be slain, upon the same principle that we slay wild and ferocious beasts."[14] Later Hammond reaffirmed this position, speaking this time of "love of killing," irresistible impulse, suggestion, imitation (possibly reflecting an influence of the French sociologist Tarde), "reasoning mania."[15]

Like the asylum superintendent, who in most instances was a physician, the prison physician saw the offender and the insane as patients within his institution. While the superintendent and the physician may have regarded their charges differently because of the nature of their respective positions, they agreed substantially that many forms of insanity were contributing factors in the commission of crimes, even when perpetrated by those capable of entertaining criminal intent. "Indeed," wrote Comegys Paul, physician to the Eastern State Penitentiary of Pennsylvania, "certain phases of crime, as the homicidal tendency, suicidal impulse and moral idiotcy cannot be separated clearly from so many phases of insanity, and it is with this class that the

[13] Such an extraordinary opinion was pronounced by a physician of unusual abilities and attainments. Graduated from medical school at twenty years of age, Hammond became at thirty-two the holder of a chair of anatomy and physiology at Maryland University. Within two years he was Surgeon-General of the United States Army, 1862-1864. Later he established himself as an alienist in New York City, becoming at first lecturer and then professor of diseases of the mind and nervous system. He wrote extensively on nervous diseases, insanity, and insanity in its medico-legal relations. In addition he was the editor of the *Quarterly Journal of Psychological Medicine and Medical Jurisprudence*, 1867-1872, of the *New York Medical Journal*, 1867-1869, of the *Journal of Nervous and Mental Disease*, 1867-1883. See *Dictionary of American Biography*, VIII, 210.

[14] William A. Hammond, *Insanity In Its Relations to Crime*, New York, 1873, p. 54.

[15] William A. Hammond, "Madness and Murder," *North American Review*, CXLVII (December 1888) 626-637.

medical officer of a large prison soon comes to be familiar."[16]
Paul went on to add that in cases where the parents had been
or were periodically insane, the children usually had a propensity to thieving and to other crimes. He recognized certain criminals as having such a disposition to commit crimes that no sooner
did they finish one term of imprisonment than they began another. This was equivalent, according to Paul, to an incurable
form of insanity. In this connection he remarked that the prisoner described by Charles Dickens in his *American Notes* for
whom so much sympathy was created both here and abroad, was
imprisoned at the Eastern State Penitentiary seven times and in
other prisons five times. Paul very seriously questioned the
mental condition of this prisoner who, he declared, had always
enjoyed good health and had every capacity to make an honest
living. Of syphilis, he wrote that the degeneration of nerve element induced by it was always followed by a corresponding derangement of thought, failure of intelligence, and the development of a criminal propensity. Such was the action of the gummatous tumors situated in the brain, as well as of the thickening
of the cerebral arteries.

The prison physician's tables purporting to show the relation
between insanity and crime as factors in hereditary transmission
were being confirmed constantly by the physician practising outside prison walls. John Stolz so declared, adding too that crime
was a manifestation of a depraved condition of the mental as well
as of the physical organism.[17]

Moral perversities of character may be hereditary, or exist from
birth, when the whole life of the individual is morally unhealthy; or
they may be due to various causes, the effects of which are seen in a
profound change in the conduct. Examples of the former kind are
numerous, where inertness or obtuseness of the moral nature, and a
controlling activity of the lower propensities, have been witnessed from
childhood, and over which threats, rewards, and punishments were
without influence. In some cases, persons in whom mental derangement has never appeared become the subject of a gradual change of

[16] *Forty-Ninth Annual Report of the Inspectors of the State Penitentiary for the
Eastern District of Pennsylvania for the Year 1878.* Physician's Report, p. 107.

[17] John Stolz, *The Cause and Cure of Crime*, Philadelphia, 1880.

feeling and conduct. As the cloud gathers, there is increasing suspicion and moroseness, and, without perhaps knowing the reason, the patient's friends regard him as an altered man. At last the storm bursts, and some outrageous act is committed. If it is not a breach of law, he is declared insane, and sent to an asylum; if the law has been violated, he is probably declared a criminal, and sent to prison or execution.[18]

Stolz spoke of a "debilitated stock," "a low organization or defective endowment," "a nervous system incapable of the higher controlling functions," while Edward C. Mann's description was of a mind laboring under the tyranny of a bad organization."[19] Mann, medical superintendent of an inebriate asylum, president of the New York Academy of Medicine, and author of a work on nervous diseases, observed that sometimes when there had been no previous symptom of a disease, the commission of a crime marked the period when the insane tendency had passed into actual insanity. Too often this was the sign used by the law court to signify the change from an insane man to a criminal. According to Mann two groups of people inhabited the borderland between crime and insanity. One group evidenced some insanity but more of crime, the other some of crime but more of insanity. Mann also wrote of the trance state, by which he meant loss of memory and consciousness for a time during which criminal impulses might dominate the mind and impel the commission of any or all kinds of crime. Given a latent tendency to disease from congenital or acquired vices, Mann continued, from cerebral conformation or nutrition, still no psychologist or alienist could predict with any certainty whether the fully formed, fully developed attack would fall on the purely mental and intellectual side—and hence insanity—or upon the moral side—and hence crime. "A great criminal or a raving maniac may be the result of the evolution of the morbid psychic force."[20]

Edward C. Spitzka, professor of nervous and mental disease

[18] *Ibid.*, p. 215.
[19] Edward C. Mann, *A Manual of Psychological Medicine and Allied Nervous Diseases*, Philadelphia, 1883.
[20] *Ibid.*, pp. 624-625.

and of medical jurisprudence in the New York Post-Graduate Medical College, in his work on insanity published in 1883 (generally accepted as the first systematic treatise on insanity since Rush), maintained that crime could be committed when persons were afflicted with various forms of insanity such as melancholia, mania, transitory frenzy, primary mental deterioration, senile dementia, paresis, and monomania.[21] Rather than adopt homicidal mania as a separate classification of mental disease, he insisted upon speaking of the lunatic with insane homicidal impulses, and he made the same distinction with regard to pyromania and kleptomania. These morbid impulses (the expression "morbid impulses" is quite characteristic of this period) he regarded as symptoms which might occur in any variety of mental disease. They are not disease entities in themselves, Spitzka insisted. By the same token moral insanity should be denied as a separate disease. Without using the term "crime" specifically, Spitzka wrote:

The patients suffering from the ordinary psychoses are dangerous to society in the following ways: 1st. They may commit homicide, either under the influence of hallucinatory terror of imaginary pursuers, insane hatred of rivals in their affection, or of alleged seducers of their partners in life, an insane desire for notoriety because of disappointments in insane aspirations, or under supposed inspiration from on high. 2nd. They may commit arson or incendiarism either from similar motives as those just enumerated, in the thoughtlessness and carelessness of dementia, as the result of morbid projects—for example, when a paretic dement burns down his house to build a palace in its place—or in obedience to the pyromaniac morbid impulse. 3rd. They may make delusional charges, or false charges from malicious motives, against others, and procure the punishment of innocent persons. 4th. They may make indecent assaults, either on account of satyriasis, or sexual perversion, and scandalous exposures of their persons from sexual motives, or in the abstraction of dementia. 5th. They may destroy valuable property under the influence of delusions or insane antipathy. 6th. They may propagate their disorder.[22]

---

[21] Edward C. Spitzka, *Insanity, Its Classification, Diagnosis and Treatment*, New York, 1883.
[22] *Ibid.*, p. 398.

It cannot be emphasized too often here that the greater part of the question of the rôle of insanity in criminal behavior is bound up with the concept of legal responsibility, and that physicians, asylum superintendents, lawyers, and judges were obliged to accept this as a central consideration. Joseph Draper, the superintendent of the Vermont Asylum for the Insane, saw three classes of persons involved in criminal conduct each constituting a departure from the normal. There were those who lacked a moral sense, those who had definite disease of the brain, and those who have had such a pathological condition but in whom it has subsided, leaving what Draper called "mental cicatrices," which permanently impaired normal functioning. He was willing to admit cases upon whom no legal responsibility could be placed, and others still enjoying partial responsibility for their conduct. However, he felt the doctrine of insane irresponsibility had carried too far, instancing the case of Guiteau, the assassin of President Garfield, and declaring that if the defense had gained its point of "not guilty by reason of insanity," the precedent would have invited many similar murderous acts.[23]

Benjamin Rush and Isaac Ray had each used the term "monomania" as descriptive of a certain form of mental disease, and had been followed by most, if not all, writers since then. In time "monomania" developed into such a cover-all and catch-all term that Edward Spitzka, in 1883, declared that probably no word in the nomenclature of mental science had been used so confusedly, and had led to so much misunderstanding. It was not, however, until the decade in which Spitzka wrote that, under the influence of the Germans, Kraepelin and Krafft-Ebing, "monomania" began to be replaced by "paranoia." Thus it was, in 1888, that the superintendent of the Boston Lunatic Asylum, Theodore W. Fisher, wrote of paranoia in relation to the defense of homicide. In one case, the defendant, a victm of paranoia, was committed by the court to an asylum, while in another case the defendant offering the same defense was convicted.[24]

[23] Joseph Draper, "The Responsibility of the Insane Outside of Asylums," *American Journal of Insanity*, XL (October 1883) 113-126.

[24] Theodore W. Fisher, "Paranoia in Relation to Hallucination of Hearing, With Two Cases of Medico-Legal Interest," *American Journal of Insanity*, XLV (July 1888) 18-31.

Within the next decade alienists had generally accepted paranoia as a distinct entity and had recognized its rôle in abnormal behavior. Julius B. Ransom, physician to Clinton State Prison (New York), divided insane criminals into five classes, of which the paranoiac was the first.[25] Henry E. Allison, superintendent of the New York State Asylum for Insane Criminals, identified crimes committed by paranoiacs, as well as by paretics and those suffering from dementia praecox.[26] Eugene S. Talbot, a physician and dentist, who had been asked by Havelock Ellis to write a volume on degeneracy for the "Contemporary Science Series," also treated of the relation of paranoia to crime.[27] Of this same class of offenders Carlos F. MacDonald, a professor of mental diseases and medical jurisprudence as well as ex-president of the New York State Commission in Lunacy, wrote in 1899, a year after Talbot's book, as follows:

It is in a widely different and much more frequently represented form of disease among the so-called criminal insane—insane persons charged with crime—that the application of the legal test of responsibility has proven so unsatisfactory, namely, the "dangerous insane," a large proportion of whom are paranoiacs, or, in other words, victims of systematized delusional insanity which older writers were wont to call "monomania," "reasoning mania," or partial insanity. . . . Many of the victims of this form of insanity, contrary to popular belief, but as every experienced alienist knows, possess a perfectly clear knowledge of right and wrong in the abstract and also comprehend, abstractly, the nature and legal consequences of acts similar to those which they have committed. Paranoiacs also are frequently actuated by most powerful motives in the commission of crime, motives similar in character to those which frequently govern sane persons, namely revenge, vindication of personal honor, self-defence of life or property, etc., but if we seek for the foundation of these motives we shall find that, unlike the motives of the sane individual, they are not founded on reality, but are the offspring of a diseased or disordered intellect, a psychopathic state, which has deranged the psychical apparatus, so to

[25] Julius B. Ransom, "The Physician and the Criminal," *Journal of the American Medical Association*, XXVII (October 10, 1896) 788-796.

[26] Henry E. Allison, "What Constitutes an Insane Criminal, and What Status Does He Occupy?" *Albany Medical Annals*, XVIII (December 1897) 569-582.

[27] Eugene S. Talbot, *Degeneracy; Its Causes, Signs and Results*, New York, 1898.

speak, and left it awry, even though the logical apparatus remains intact.[28]

Chauncey Adams spoke of an insane person as being analogous to the paranoiac but without delusions. Such a person reasoned with ease, but labored under false premises and beliefs, and seemed unmindful of his acts or of their consequences once he had been seized by an overwhelming and imperative desire.[29] W. Duncan McKim and G. Frank Lydston each recognized the paranoiac as one of the most dangerous types of insane and as very likely to commit murder when under the dominance of a fixed delusion.[30]

Isaac Ray, as early as 1838, had distinguished between the criminal and the insane, but it was fully half a century later before this distinction had been elaborated into the categories of the criminal insane and the insane criminal. Insanity was the core of the disorder in the criminal insane, while criminality was the essential element in the case of the insane criminal. In a half-dozen articles extending from 1892 to 1893 Henry E. Allison, who had been a member of a commission to erect the Matteawan State Hospital for the Criminal Insane, and later its first medical superintendent, stressed this distinction. According to him the criminal insane were not naturally criminals, but, on the contrary, when in health were useful and law-abiding members of the community. It was, however, by reason of insanity and while "laboring under stress of disease and such duress of mind as to render them irresponsible" that they committed flagrant and violent acts in serious violation of the law. In one of his earliest articles Allison described these persons, the criminal insane, as believing their false ideas which are the product of their diseased minds, hearing voices, seeing visions, feeling themselves plotted against, persecuted, their very lives threatened until they can restrain themselves no longer and finally

[28] Carlos F. MacDonald, "The Legal Versus the Scientific Test of Insanity in Criminal Cases," *American Journal of Insanity*, LVI (July 1899) 28-29.

[29] Chauncey Adams, "Insanity in Its Relation to Crime," *Medical Times*, XXVIII (November 1900) 321-324; XXIX (January 1901) 5-8.

[30] W. Duncan McKim, *Heredity and Human Progress*, New York, 1901; G. Frank Lydston, *op. cit.*

yield to an overpowering impulse. They reason as do other people, but upon false premises, and their acts are the product of their distorted sense impressions, and their interpretations of them. To them their hallucinations, their delusions, their inner promptings have an actual existence, and it is upon the basis of this assumed reality that they justify their acts.[31] In subsequent articles Allison reinforced his theme, noting that these persons usually knew the difference between right and wrong, but that they seemed powerless to do other than they have done. He also observed that the criminal insane differed from the insane criminal in that the latter were habitual offenders whose acts were not the result of mental disease nor prompted by the delusions of a deranged mind.[32]

In some instances there were others than physicians who remarked upon the close similarity of insanity and crime. Such was Frederick Howard Wines, a leader in the field of social welfare, who, in extemporaneous words to the inmates of Elmira Reformatory in 1886, said:[33]

1. The basis of insanity is physical, its manifestations are physical, mental, and moral. The same is true in large measure of criminal propensities.

[31] Henry E. Allison, "On Motives Which Govern the Criminal Acts of the Insane," *American Journal of Insanity*, XLIX (October 1892) 198.

[32] Henry E. Allison, "Insanity Among Criminals," *American Journal of Insanity*, LI (July 1894) 54-63; "Some Relations of Crime to Insanity and States of Mental Enfeeblement," *Journal of the American Medical Association*, XXVII (September 19, 1896) 646-650; "What Constitutes an Insane Criminal, and What Status Does He Occupy?" *Albany Medical Annals*, XVIII (December 1897) 569-582; "Insanity and Homicide," *American Journal of Insanity*, LV (April 1899) 627-638; "Hospital Provision for the Insane Criminal," *American Journal of Insanity*, LX (July 1903) 111-121.

[33] Frederick Howard Wines was the son of Enoch C. Wines, famous as teacher, author, prison reformer, and philanthropist. Trained for the ministry, he occupied a pulpit in Springfield, Illinois, for several years. In 1869 he was appointed the first secretary of the newly organized State Board of Public Charities of Illinois, and continued in that office for thirty years, with the exception of a four-year interval occasioned by a political upheaval in the state. He was one of the prime movers in the organization of the National Conference of Charities and Correction, was a delegate to the Second International Penitentiary Congress in 1878, and from 1887-1890 was secretary of the National Prison Association. In 1895 he published his famous book on *Punishment and Reformation*, which enunciated the advanced principles of his day in the field of penology. He was Special Agent for the 10th Census of defective, delinquent, and dependent classes, and Assistant Director of the 12th Census. See *Dictionary of American Biography*, XX, 386.

2. Insanity and crime are both hereditary—to what extent is not definitely known. The predisposition to both is often congenital.

3. The approach of insanity and the growth of criminal character are alike gradual, in many instances, and unsuspected by the victim of either.

4. The change from innocence to depravity corresponds with the alteration in personal character observable in the insane.

5. The lunatic and the criminal both form theories, to account for the perversion of which they are more or less conscious, which are very far removed from the truth.

6. The manifestations of insanity assume one of two opposite forms —undue exaltation or undue depression; in either form they present the appearance of a pronounced self-consciousness, amounting to egotism, and often accompanied by hallucinations or delusions. In this particular the resemblances between insanity and crime are striking.

7. As insanity tends to make progress and to end in dementia, so does the habitual criminal sink into moral imbecility—the complete loss of moral perception, depravation of moral tastes and inclinations, and paralysis of volition.[34]

The person acting from an irresistible impulse has been placed in various categories; he has been described as a monomaniac, as morally insane, as a paranoiac, etc., and in 1896 he was placed in one more category. In sub-division three of his five sub-divisions of the insane criminal, Julius B. Ransom, the prison physician already referred to, placed the phrenasthenic or psychopathic criminal, this person of irresistible impulse, feebleness of will, with morbid tendencies to murder. Members of this class, he held, committed crimes apparently without motive and purely from impulse, or from the satisfaction of the criminal act itself. In contrast to this Ransom noted the reasoning phrenasthenic whom he deemed almost synonymous with the morally insane. His fifth class "consists of a large body of persons tainted by a common and clinic form of mental alienation all of whom are apt to become criminal," a description he borrowed from Ferri, the Italian criminologist.[35] Another classification by, Arthur

[34] Frederick Howard Wines, *Punishment and Reformation*, Thomas Y. Crowell Co., New York, 1895, p. 215.

[35] *Ibid.*, p. 792.

Sweeney distinguished between the type of criminal who committed crime under the influence of passionate impulse and another whom he called the instinctive criminal, the latter presenting well-marked signs of physical and psychical abnormality.[36] Alonzo B. Richardson, superintendent of the State Hospital in Columbus, Ohio, found a close relation between criminality and mental disorder and defect, for he observed that there were those who had a natural tendency toward criminal conduct and in whom there was no power within the individual himself to prevent or protect him from the execution of these tendencies. In others the criminal act was the outgrowth of a delusive idea, as in the case of the woman who murdered her children because she believed that a life of disgrace and infamy awaited them otherwise. Or again, there was a class of which it was true that the criminal conduct was in marked contrast with the former life of the individual to such an extent that it could be said that the criminal act was the result of disease. Finally, Richardson spoke of another group whom he called moral imbeciles, those individuals without physical defects, not enfeebled intellectually, who apparently had no identifiable mental disease yet who manifested an utter incapacity to judge of the moral quality of their acts. Of these more shall be said in the discussion of moral insanity and feeble-mindedness in succeeding chapters.[37]

By the turn of the twentieth century, asylum superintendents were noting in their reports the rôle of dementia praecox in the production of criminal behavior. For example, Butler Metzger, assistant physician of the Massachusetts Asylum for Insane Criminals, analyzed four hundred cases in 1901, and found a high proportion of cases of dementia praecox.[38] Other physicians made note of the defense of dementia praecox in trials for murder, as Charles W. Hitchcock did in 1906.[39]

[36] Arthur Sweeney, "Crime and Insanity," *Northwestern Lancet*, XVII (May 15, 1897) 203-211.

[37] Alonzo B. Richardson, "The Relation of Criminality to Mental Defect," *Cleveland Medical Gazette*, XIII (December 1897) 87-88.

[38] Butler Metzger, "The Insane Criminal," *American Journal of Insanity*, LVIII (October 1901) 309-314.

[39] Charles W. Hitchcock, "A Case of Dementia Praecox of Medico-Legal Interest," *American Journal of Insanity*, LXII (April 1906) 615-626.

Few writers approached the study of crime with more appreciation of European works coupled with a broad experience as practitioner and teacher than did G. Frank Lydston.[40] Without attempting to write a book on criminology, he did manage to bring out of his reading and experience a work which, for its time, ranked beyond anything else that had been produced in the border field between medicine and sociology. As a physician he had been able to see that there were more than physiological, psychological, and anthropological factors involved in criminal behavior. He also had an understanding of the social factors. He recognized, for instance, that a neurosis may, in many cases, be an underlying cause of crime, that *mania furiosa* was a frequent cause of assault and murder, that melancholia was frequently associated with suicidal impulses. He did, however, question whether kleptomania was a separate disease entity, claiming that it should be used only in the case of stealing by those unequivocally insane. Head injuries, he declared, might be a contributing element in abnormal behavior, as might also conditions of cerebro-toxemia which irritated the temporal and occipital lobes, and inhibited the functions of the frontal lobes.[41] Hugo Münsterberg, a psychologist at Harvard, agreed with Lydston and others that mental disease was a contributing factor in illegal acts, but insisted that offenses committed under such circumstances should rightly be considered acts of the insane and not crimes.[42] So, too, I. L. Nascher distinguished a category of criminal acts due to mental incapacity to distinguish between right and wrong, declaring them to be insane acts which should not be included under the head of criminality. In 1914 he wrote:

The pyromaniac, the kleptomaniac, the aged individual who assaults a child during an attack of sexual fury which occasionally occurs in senile climacteric, the religious maniac who kills to make a sacrifice to God, are criminals in respect to their acts, but not in relation to their mental capacity. The pyromaniac and the kleptomaniac are impelled by an uncontrollable morbid impulse which they know is

[40] See biographical note on Lydston in the chapter on *Phrenology*, pp. 16-17.
[41] G. Frank Lydston, *op. cit.*
[42] Hugo Münsterberg, *On the Witness Stand*, New York, 1908.

wrong. The religious maniac and the senile dement who commits rape do not know that they do wrong.[43]

Others, said C. H. Anderson, know the nature and quality of their acts, but the desire is so irresistible that it seems to be performed under the dominance of an automatism outside their will.[44]

Perhaps no other physician of the period with which this treatise ends wrote more on the relation of insanity and crime than did Paul E. Bowers, physician in charge, of the Indiana State Prison. Based upon his experiences with prisoners, he went so far as to state that he must almost accept the theory of Lombroso that criminality was a psychosis in itself.[45] In his study of one hundred recidivists he found 12 per cent insane, 38 per cent constitutionally inferior, 17 per cent psychopaths. "At least fifty-six of them bore the burden of some neuropathic taint which bequeathed to them an instability of the nervous system and a sensitized physical economy for the action of degenerative influences."[46] As for the various forms of mental disease and their relation to crime, no single writer brought them all together in one volume as did Bowers in 1915 in his *Clinical Studies in the Relationship of Insanity to Crime*. In his opening section of this work he remarked that there was probably no type of crime that had not been committed by insane persons, and in many cases the only distinction between these acts and those of the normal person had been the motives which prompted them, respectively. On the one side were the impulsive acts of the insane in response to overpowering obsessions and imperative ideas, on the other were the acts of cunning and skill which at times baffled detection, yet both were the acts of the insane and in each instance reflected hidden pathological sources.

The most dangerous of insane patients, Bowers continued, was

[43] I. L. Nascher, "Psychanalysis of Criminality," *American Practitioner*, XLVIII (May 1914) 233-238.

[44] C. H. Anderson, "Are Criminals Insane Individuals?" *Illinois Medical Journal*, XXV (April 1914) 227-229.

[45] Paul E. Bowers, "Prison Psychosis. A Pseudonym?" *American Journal of Insanity*, LXX (July 1913) 161-173.

[46] Paul E. Bowers, "The Recidivist," *Journal of the American Institute of Criminal Law and Criminology*, V (September 1914) 407.

the paranoiac who harbored within the recesses of his diseased mentality systematized delusions of persecution. Homicide, homicidal attempts, assault and battery, blackmail, perjury, impersonation of officers, and sexual crimes were the most frequent and characteristic offenses of the paranoiac. For the paranoiac who had built up his world of ideas around one central theme —say persecution—his system was entirely logical, and would be logical even to the so-called normal, were his original premises granted. While harboring his delusions of persecution he was a potential homicide. In contrast were the crimes of those suffering from dementia praecox. These "were characterized by more or less defect of reason and judgment, a marked emotional poverty, a more or less complete state of indifference, a condition of puerility and often a thoughtless, senseless, and impulsive brutality."[47] In the hebephrenic type were to be found the crimes of petit larceny, trespass, vagabondage, drunkenness, the breaking of box cars, sexual crimes, and public prostitution in the female. Their crimes were marked by impulsiveness, a lack of premeditation, thoughtlessness, with little effort to escape the consequences of the criminal acts. In the catatonic form the victim made vicious assaults, committed murders, and destroyed property by incendiarism. In the paranoid form (of dementia praecox) there were delusions of persecution leading to assault, homicide, theft, blackmail, and perjury.

While the crimes of paranoiacs and the victims of dementia praecox constituted a large proportion of the criminal offenses committed by the insane, those due to general paralysis, or paresis, were comparatively rare. Bowers reported only five patients of the latter among a total admission of 205 to the Indiana Hospital for Insane Criminals. Paretics seemed to have little awareness of the nature and quality of their acts, and were readily identified by the profound change which took place in their mode of life. Their crimes were those of immorality, alcoholic debauch, indecent behavior, thievery, dishonest speculation, forgery, but rarely homicide and suicide. Crimes deriving from

[47] Paul E. Bowers, *Clinical Studies in the Relationship of Insanity to Crime*, Michigan City, Indiana, 1915, p. 35.

manic-depressive insanity were also infrequent. Bowers discerned a cyclical characteristic in certain criminals which strongly resembled the alternations of this type of insanity. In the manic stage the acts were usually destructive but seldom criminal, while in the depressive phase suicide was the most common act, though occasionally the obsessions provoked murderous assaults. Concerning hysterical insanity, Bowers spoke of "the exaggerated impressionability to external stimuli, the abnormal tendency to stimulation, the excessive emotionalism, the volitional impairment," which rendered the victim highly susceptible to criminal behavior. The delusions of persecution might lead to homicidal assaults; the basic eroticism might lead to sexual crimes; hysteric derangement, especially in females, might lead to blackmail and false accusations. In the male hysteric it may take the form of attempted murder or suicide. Suicides, homicides, and infanticides might follow from puerperal insanity. Sexual crimes and frequently homicides accompanied senile dementia, and much the same might be said for arterio-sclerotic dementia, with the exception that in the latter sexual crimes and homicides might be more frequent because of the paranoid nature of the affliction. Head injuries might also be productive of criminal acts; Bowers called these "traumatic psychoses," and "traumatic psychopathic states."

For some time before 1915 the term "psychopathic personality" had been used to describe persons who did not seem to fit into other categories, who were neither identifiably insane nor yet sane. The expression "constitutional psychopathic inferior" was often used correlatively, and it was this person whom Bowers described as follows:

He is unable to stand the strain imposed upon him by the ordinary conventions of society; without assistance he cannot occupy the place that he should in the social order. Indecision, inability, vacillation and dependency are his chief characteristics.

The C.P.I. (as he came to be known) lived on the borderline between insanity and crime, now on the one side, now on the other. In this class was to be found the pathological liar. Standing with the psychopathic personality and the constitutional inferior was a third class—the sexual pervert. It was the latter who was given to rape, incest, sodomy, and necrophilia, any of which in turn might lead to other crimes including murder.

The final classification that Bowers took up was what he called "constitutional immorality." This class included persons who could not refrain from crime because their "degenerative organizations" predisposed and impelled them to immoral and illegal acts. The moral sense, being the last to be acquired by the human being, is not possessed by these persons. They were without a moral sense, for since it is the first to be lost (if once acquired), then these persons either lost it, or it had been destroyed. "Constitutional immorality" was Bowers' own term for what others had called just as loosely "moral imbecility" or "moral insanity."

INSANITY AND COURT TRIALS

In an earlier section of this chapter mention was made of the McNaghten case and its bearing upon American trials where the defense of not guilty by reason of insanity was set up. American psychiatrists have not always seen eye to eye with the courts in instances where insanity was present or purported to be present. Traditionally the legal criteria of insanity had been "the nature and quality" and the "right and wrong" test laid down in the McNaghten case,[48] or in some jurisdictions the "irresistible impulse" test.[49] Yet in many instances asylum superintendents, practising alienists, or others who have served as medical witnesses in a criminal trial have protested the failure of the judge to charge the jury properly, or have deplored the verdict of guilty when the evidence patently demonstrated the mentally diseased state of the defendant.

[48] In this case the judges made answer to the House of Lords in part as follows: ". . . to establish a defence on the ground of insanity, it must be clearly proved that, at the time of committing the act, the party accused was labouring under such a defect of reason, from disease of the mind, as not to know the nature and quality of the act he was doing, or if he did know it that he did not know he was doing what was wrong." James FitzJames Stephen, *A History of the Criminal Law in England*, London, 1883, volume 2, p. 158.

[49] In the Ohio case of *State* v. *Thompson* in 1834, Judge Wright instructed the jury that if the defendant at the time could discriminate between right and wrong, and was conscious of the wrongfulness of the act, and had the power to forbear or to do the act, he was responsible.

In some cases alienists testified to a condition which they termed "monomania" (Samuel B. Woodward in 1845, Charles H. Nichols in 1850, Charles K. Mills in 1884); in others they described a state known as "pyromania" (Amariah Brigham in 1849); and in still others a disorder called "mania transitoria" (Edward Jarvis in 1869). Indeed the whole gamut of mental disease defenses was run in numerous trials during the last half of the nineteenth century. The most famous trial was that of Charles J. Guiteau for the murder of President Garfield in 1881, in which Guiteau's plea of insanity was unsuccessful.

The significant point to note for our purposes here is that mental disease was recognized as a real factor in the causation of crime. This was obviously so in the cases where acquittal was granted upon such a defense plea, but was also true even in cases of conviction, for in many cases juries and the informed public were aware of the part played by mental abnormality but were unwilling to permit the offender to escape punishment. For example, in the Guiteau case the defendant was obviously a victim of paranoia, yet public opinion and even most alienists would permit no jury to exculpate the man who had killed the President of the United States.[50] In other cases mental disease was recognized as present, but not to such a degree as to exculpate the offender. As to just what degree of mental abnormality must exist to render the person legally irresponsible is a question as confused today as it was in eighteenth-century England or nineteenth-century America. Neither the defense of delusion made by Lord Erskine in behalf of Hadfield in 1800, nor the McNaghten principles of 1843, nor the doctrine of irresistible impulse of 1834 have settled the issue conclusively. Occasionally in America a scientific approach was made in those

---

[50] "Review of the Trial of Charles J. Guiteau," *American Journal of Insanity*, XXXVIII (January 1882) 303-448. Eminent alienists who testified to the insanity of Guiteau included the following: James G. Kiernan, Charles H. Nichols, Charles F. Folsom, Theodore W. Fisher, William W. Godding, James H. McBride, Walter Channing, Edward C. Spitzka. Witnesses called by the prosecution included the following physicians who testified to Guiteau's sanity: Fordyce Barker, Noble Young, Francis Loring, Allen McLane Hamilton, Samuel Worcester, Theodore Dimon, Selden H. Talcott, Henry P. Stearns, Jamin Strong, Abram M. Shew, Orpheus Everts, A. E. MacDonald, Randolph Barksdale, John H. Callender, Walter Kempster, John P. Gray.

cases in which a commission examined the offender before trial, and determined upon the basis of this whether he should be committed to a hospital for the criminal insane or be made to stand trial without the defense of insanity. One of the earliest of these commission examinations was that made in 1875 and noted in the *American Journal of Insanity;* another followed in 1888, and a third in 1890.[51]

EPILEPSY

Nowhere in America was there developed any theory of criminal behavior based upon epilepsy such as was encountered in the work of Cesare Lombroso. Epilepsy, of course, was known to American alienists, and while they recognized the likelihood of the epileptic committing an illegal act during his seizure, yet epilepsy as such was not conceived as the fundamental cause of criminal acts. "Veritable monomaniacs and not unfrequently dangerous," was part of Amariah Brigham's description of them in a contribution in which he admitted they were prone to commit crimes during certain periods of their disorder; at other times, and for years perhaps, they were entirely rational.[52] Francis Wharton, in his treatise on the legal aspects of mental unsoundness, remarked that in addition to the lack of criminal intent during the height of the attack there was seldom the evil intent, recognized by law as necessary to constitute a crime, present in the period preceding or following the attack.[53] Despite the justifiable defense of epilepsy at law, there were still juries who convicted upon the defense of epilepsy even when a clearcut case of epilepsy was evident to medical witnesses. This situation was deplored by Isaac Ray when a committee of which he

[51] "Case of Perrine D. Matteson, Indicted for Murder in the First Degree," *American Journal of Insanity,* XXXI (January 1875) 336-344; W. W. Godding, "A Judicial Advance—The Daley Case," *American Journal of Insanity,* XLV (October 1888) 191-206; J. B. Andrews, "A Medico-Legal Case—the People vs. William Manley," *American Journal of Insanity,* XLVII (October 1890) 152-165. In another case, after examination by a commission the defense was disallowed and the defendant was subsequently convicted and executed—Judson B. Andrews, "The Case of Peter Louis Otto. A Medico-Legal Study," *American Journal of Insanity,* XLV (October 1888) 207-219.

[52] Amariah Brigham, "Crime and Insanity," *American Journal of Insanity,* IV (July 1847) 67.

[53] Francis Wharton, *op. cit.* 116-119.

was a member held a defendant to be a victim of epilepsy who, despite that fact, was convicted by a jury and later executed.[54] Meredith Clymer, a specialist in nervous and mental diseases, admitted that criminal acts might arise from epilepsy,[55] as did W. J. Conklin, physician to the Dayton, Ohio, Hospital for the Insane, who wrote that the mental condition of epileptics might manifest itself prominently in three directions: 1st. In temporary outbursts of delirium or uncontrollable fury. 2nd. In a perversion of the moral qualities. 3rd. In an attack of regular maniacal excitement, lasting from a few hours to several weeks. Conklin added that the form of disease known as mania transitoria was usually a manifestation of epilepsy.[56] This latter opinion was shared by M. G. Echeverria, a special student and prolific writer on epilepsy, and physician-in-chief to the New York Hospital for Epileptics and Paralytics.[57] In his book Echeverria cited cases of epileptic insanity with homicidal impulse, as well as instances of homicidal furor and suicide associated with epilepsy.[58] John Ordronaux, professor of medical jurisprudence at Columbia University and New York State Commissioner in Lunacy, reported two cases of epileptic homicide, in both of which a commission inquired into the mental condition of the defendants, and in one instance the death sentence was commuted to life imprisonment when the commission reported a case of epilepsy and arrested development.[59]

"Moral epilepsy" was the term introduced by Edward C. Mann to describe a state growing out of disorder of the central nervous system which resulted in temporary criminal impulses

---

[54] Isaac Ray, "Epilepsy and Homicide," *American Journal of Insanity*, XXIV (October 1867) 187-206.

[55] Meredith Clymer, "On the Mental State of Epileptics and Its Medico-Legal Relations," *Medical Record*, V (November 1, 1870) 363-366, 409-413.

[56] W. J. Conklin, "The Relations of Epilepsy to Insanity and Jurisprudence," *Transactions of the Ohio Medical Society*, 1871, pp. 251-295.

[57] M. G. Echeverria, "On Epileptic Insanity," *American Journal of Insanity*, XXX (July 1873) 1-51; also "Criminal Responsibility of Epileptics, as Illustrated in the Case of David Montgomery," *American Journal of Insanity*, XXIX (January 1873) 341-425.

[58] M. G. Echeverria, *On Epilepsy*, New York, 1870.

[59] John Ordronaux, "Case of Isabella Jensch—Epileptic Homicide," *American Journal of Insanity*, XXXI (April 1875) 430-442; also "Case of Jacob Standerman," *American Journal of Insanity*, XXXII (April 1876) 451-474.

returning with a certain regularity. Concerning victims of this disease he wrote:

Such criminals are temporarily seized with the deepest remorse and are fortified with the best resolutions. They behave for a time in the most exemplary manner, until they relapse again, which relapse is unanimously attributed by them to an irresistible impulse.[60]

At another place Mann describes the affliction as

... a morbid affection of the mind centres which destroys the healthy coördination of ideas and occasions a spasmodic or convulsive mental action. The will cannot always restrain, however much it may strive to do so, a morbid idea which has reached a convulsive activity, although there may be all the while a clear consciousness of its morbid nature.[61]

In addition to the convulsive type of epilepsy Mann described a form in which no convulsions and no complete loss of consciousness are encountered. During such an attack the victim might still commit acts of a homicidal or suicidal nature in answer to instantaneous impulses. Patients in certain forms of epilepsy might entertain delusions of fear and persecution and might commit criminal acts as a result of such delusions. James G. Kiernan, professor of mental diseases at Milwaukee Medical College, and lecturer on forensic psychiatry at the Kent College of Law, Chicago, noted the great likelihood of criminal acts during the period when the patient loses consciousness of his act.[62] Likewise, Edward C. Spitzka and William A. Hammond mentioned this tendency of the epileptic to commit violent acts during his attack or preceding or following it.[63] In a case where the defense of epilepsy was put forth only to be disregarded by the jury, P. M. Wise, medical superintendent of the Willard Asylum for the Insane, thought the conviction unjust because he believed that epileptics might appear to have criminal tendencies and even commit criminal acts with all the appearance of legal normality,

[60] Edward C. Mann, *op. cit.*, p. 120.

[61] *Ibid.*, p. 128.

[62] James G. Kiernan, "Medico-Legal Relations of Epilepsy," *Alienist and Neurologist*, V (January 1884) 12-32.

[63] Edward C. Spitzka, *op. cit.*, p. 37. William A. Hammond, *A Treatise on Insanity in Its Medical Relations*, Appleton, New York, 1883, pp. 630-639.

and yet they might be actually insane at the time.[64] In fact, said A. E. Osborne, superintendent of the California State Home for the Feeble-Minded, the first intimation of the criminal tendency might be the evidence of the commission of the crime itself.[65] J. B. Ransom, in his classification of the insane criminal (already referred to), described his psychic epileptic as being apt to perpetrate outrageous murders during the epileptic seizure, the acts being of such a nature as to be entirely inconsistent with the previous character of the person.[66] W. J. Furness and B. R. Kennon, assistant physicians of the Manhattan State Hospital, attested to this lack of reason or motive, remarking upon the perversion of the moral qualities, and also upon the amnesia during the seizure and period of the criminal acts. They cited cases of other epileptics who did not suffer this blankness of mind and could give a full account of themselves before, during, and after the attack, but declared their inability to restrain an irresistible desire to commit the criminal act.[67] Of the acts of epileptics H. E. Allison wrote:

Epileptics often commit crime while under the influence of frenzy or while in epileptic states, and retain no memory of the act whatsoever. Many of them are tractable during the interval, but troublesome and dangerous periodically. Many most shocking crimes have been committed by epileptics. Most of their deeds are of a sudden and impulsive character. As a rule, they are at the time unconscious of the nature and quality of their act, nor do they know that it is wrong. In fact they are oblivious of the whole affair, and after the effects of the convulsion have passed away retain no knowledge of the occurrence. Criminal acts may also be committed, not in frenzy, but by epileptics who have reached a state bordering on dementia as the result of their disease.[68]

The close relationship between crime and epilepsy was evidenced,

[64] P. M. Wise, "The Barker Case. The Legal Responsibility of Epileptics," *American Journal of Insanity*, XLV (January 1889) 360-373.

[65] A. E. Osborne, "Responsibility of Epileptics," *Medico-Legal Journal*, XI (1894) 210-220.

[66] J. B. Ransom, *op. cit.*, p. 792.

[67] W. J. Furness and B. R. Kennon, "The Legal Responsibility in Epilepsy," *State Hospitals Bulletin*, II (1897) 66-77.

[68] H. E. Allison, "What Constitutes an Insane Criminal, and What Status Does He Occupy?" *Albany Medical Annals*, XVIII (December 1897) 576.

said Albrecht Heym, professor of nervous and mental diseases in the Chicago Clinical School, in the high proportion of the epileptics found in the criminal population in contrast with that of the general population. In the choleric and impulsive form epilepsy might incite brutal assaults, in the epileptic stupor where hallucinations were present homicide was very likely, and even in dream-like states crimes were committed.[69]

Despite the remarks made by Lombroso in the introduction to August Drähms' book on the criminal, Drähms could not subscribe to the view that there was an anthropological resemblance between epileptics and criminals, nor to Lombroso's theory of the epileptoid nature of the criminal. That this condition might be characteristic of older countries where the "race-stock" has degenerated Drähms might concede, but he was unwilling to accept it for any part of the New World.[70] On the other hand, W. Duncan McKim asserted that epilepsy was a fruitful source of crime, citing instances of the automatism of many epileptic criminal acts in which the actor might have no notion of what he had done.[71] The blank state of mind of the epileptic was recognized by William P. Spratling, who was in charge of the Craig Colony for Epileptics in New York State. The epileptic was incapable of distinguishing right from wrong when under the control of a seizure, his inhibitions were impaired or destroyed, and he was no more responsible for his acts than a railroad engine is for the damage it does when it is running without a driver.[72] The statement quoted earlier from P. M. Wise to the effect that the epileptic might seem normal while committing a crime during a condition of psychic epilepsy was corroborated by T. H. Evans, who cited two cases in support of his view.[73] Epilepsy, to G. Frank Lydston, was related to

---

[69] Albrecht Heym, "Epilepsy in Its Forensic Aspect," *Chicago Clinic*, XII (September 1899) 344-346.

[70] August Drähms, *The Criminal*, New York, 1900, pp. 118-119.

[71] W. Duncan McKim, *op. cit.*, pp. 140-144.

[72] William P. Spratling, "Epilepsy in Its Relation to Crime," *Journal of Nervous and Mental Disease*, XXIX (August 1902) 481-496; also "The Legal and Social Standing of the Epileptic," *Medical News*, LXXXIII (July 18, 1903) 112-114.

[73] T. H. Evans, "The Epileptic Criminal: With Report of Two cases," *Medical Record*, LXVII (February 25, 1905) 295-296.

toxemia, being due to some "autogenetic" irritant poison acting upon the nerve centers. It was frequent among criminals, by which Lydston did not mean that it would always cause criminality, but rather than the same nervous degeneracy might underlie both epilepsy and criminality. It did lead to crime, however, because it lowered the moral standard. The *furor epilepticus* was characterized by maniacal outbursts, not infrequently of a homicidal nature.[74] S. P. Goodhart and Harriet C. B. Alexander each commented upon the relation between epilepsy and crime, the former noting: ". . . with true paranoia it is the one undisputed form of psychic aberration which is conceded as an honest defense in criminal cases where its presence can be demonstrated";[75] while the latter maintained that epileptics constituted fifteen per cent of the prison population, the epileptic criminal really combining both the insane criminal and the criminal insane. The epileptic, she held, was capable of committing any kind of crime during the epileptic mental state.[76] According to Paul E. Bowers, epilepsy was responsible for more pathological offenses than any other form of positive mental disease.[77] The mercurial nature of the epileptic was provoked by the merest trifles, Bowers continued, into criminal outbursts of violence; his delusions of persecution often produced homicidal assaults; his automatic acts in psychic epilepsy or the post-epileptic stage accounted for many acts of a criminal nature of which the epileptic was entirely unaware.

CONCLUSION

In America, it must be repeated, there was no equivalent for Lombroso's epileptoid criminal base. Nor were there any theories, save an occasional one, that epilepsy was more responsible for crime than was any other form of mental disease. The prevailing thought, if the record is read correctly, was that

[74] G. Frank Lydston, *op. cit.*, pp. 213-214.

[75] S. P. Goodhart, "Forensic Import of Psychic Epilepsy," *Medical Times*, XXXVII (May 1909) 143.

[76] Harriet C. B. Alexander, "Legal Aspects of Epilepsy," *Alienist and Neurologist*, XXVII (May 1906) 170-188; also "The Degenerate and Crime," *Woman's Medical Journal*, XXV (1915) 265.

[77] Paul E. Bowers, *op. cit.*, p. 24.

epilepsy was but one of the many causal factors of criminal behavior, not necessarily more important nor less important than others. There was substantial agreement upon its manifestations, and upon the nature of its rôle in the criminal act—the violent seizure, the periods preceding and following, the distinction between this and what was known as "psychic epilepsy," wherein the derangement was entirely mental and not involved with muscular response. There was, too, substantial agreement upon the nature of the legal responsibility of the epileptic.

The nineteenth century and the first decade of the twentieth formed a period which saw the chains struck from the insane and their elevation from beasts to the stature of men. There was still restraint needed, and much of the controversy in the shift from custody to care revolved around the kind and extent of restraint. During this century or so there were alternations of opinion upon the curability of the insane; in the first quarter their case seemed hopeless, during the middle half insanity was deemed the most curable of diseases, but by the end of the century the soberer view of psychiatrists was that in the light of their past experience and their present knowledge one could hardly predict any high rate of recovery from mental disease. Psychiatrists were armed with considerably more knowledge, but they had to come through the long period of preoccupation with classification before they could comprehend the dynamic nature of the human material they were dealing with.

During all this time lay, legal, and medical opinion were agreed that there was a definite relation between insanity and crime. The agreement ended there, however, for immediately as the question of legal responsibility arose there was considerable difference as to the extent to which mental abnormality excused the offender from the consequences of his act. In this respect we stand today perhaps no farther ahead, if ahead at all, than Isaac Ray of exactly one hundred years ago.

III

MORAL INSANITY

IN THE previous chapter on insanity and crime there were scattered references to a disorder called moral insanity. No one was quite clear as to just what constituted moral insanity. Most physicians had been able to distinguish insanity from sanity, insanity from criminality, but when the concept of moral insanity recurred in the literature there was considerable difference of opinion as to whether such a condition existed, of what it consisted and how it might be identified. The effort to deal with this concept—to explore its reality or unreality—shall be traced in this chapter.

The term "moral insanity" was first used by the English ethnologist, physician, and writer, James C. Prichard (1786-1848), in his treatise on insanity published in 1835. He distinguished the principal varieties of insanity as moral insanity, monomania, mania, and incoherence or dementia. All of these were modifications of intellectual insanity, being disorders of the intellectual faculties, except moral insanity, of which Prichard wrote:

. . . madness consisting in a morbid perversion of the natural feelings, affections, inclinations, temper, habits, moral dispositions, and natural impulses, without any remarkable disorder or defect of the intellect or knowing and reasoning faculties, and particularly without any insane illusion or hallucination.[1]

Thus early came the attempted distinction between the intellectual, cognitive, knowing aspects of man's mental life, and the feeling, conative, emotional part. A disorder of the latter was called moral insanity, of the former, intellectual insanity. For the remainder of the nineteenth century, psychiatrists were to dispute this dichotomy.

[1] James Cowles Prichard, *A Treatise on Insanity*, London, 1835.

48

Prichard's contribution (if an expression that caused endless controversy can be called a contribution) was the term, but the condition had been described years before. At the beginning of the century the French alienist and asylum physician at Bicêtre and Salpêtrière, Philippe Pinel, had described this as *manie sans delire*, while Benjamin Rush, called America's first psychiatrist, had written to Dr. Joseph Priestley in 1795 of this diseased state of the will in which the understanding was unimpaired.[2] Later, in his lectures on the study of medical jurisprudence at the University of Pennsylvania in 1810, he spoke as follows: "By moral derangement I mean that state of the mind in which the passions act involuntarily through the instrumentality of the will, without any disease in the understanding."[3] Rush associated an irresistible impulse with this moral derangement and instanced two cases of murder and homicide in substantiation. Another case concerned a young lady who told Dr. Rush that she was happily blessed with husband and children, yet she had such paroxysms—with perfect control of her reasoning powers—that she longed for an axe so that she might split their heads and lay them all dead at her feet. Regarding the state of mind of persons who took life under the influence of this morbid state of the will Rush continued:

1. It is committed without provocation or malice, either of a sudden, or of a chronic nature.

[2] Few men in the early development of medicine in America have been more fruitful than Benjamin Rush, 1745-1813. Born in Philadelphia County, he was apprenticed for six years to one of Philadelphia's most prominent physicians, following which he completed his medical training at Edinburgh University. At twenty-four years of age he was elected professor of chemistry in the college of Philadelphia, and when, in 1791, this institution merged with the University of the State of Pennsylvania to become the University of Pennsylvania, Rush was appointed professor of the institutes of medicine and clinical medicine. During the Revolutionary War he was appointed surgeon-general of the Middle Department. He was active during the yellow fever epidemics which ravaged Philadelphia in 1793 and 1797, although his therapeutics of the lancet and calomel were severely attacked by many of his contemporaries. For many years he served on the staff of the Pennsylvania Hospital, formulating many of their policies of care and treatment of the insane. Rush in addition to being a stimulating teacher was an active practitioner, an original researcher, and a tireless writer. His book on *Diseases of the Mind* was a pioneer work in America.

[3] Benjamin Rush, *Sixteen Introductory Lectures to Courses of Lectures Upon the Institutes and Practice of Medicine*, Philadelphia, 1811, p. 380.

2. It is usually committed upon near relations, and friends; and often by persons of the most exemplary moral and religious characters.

3. It is sometimes committed upon a child or an idiot, in order to provoke death by the law; supposing it to be a less crime to kill innocent persons for this purpose, than persons who might suffer from dying in an unprepared state; and preferring that mode of getting rid of life, to perishing by suicide.

4. It has been committed by parents upon their children, under the pressure of extreme poverty, in order to prevent their suffering from the same evil.

5. It is sometimes committed by persons under the influence of delusive opinions in religion.

6. Circumstances of greater and more deliberate cruelty attend it, than common murders.

7. It is never accompanied by robbery.

8. It is sometimes followed by suicide, or by attempts to maim their own bodies; and

9. It is never, or rarely, succeeded by an attempt to escape; but, on the contrary, the persons who perpetrate it, generally confess what they have done; and sometimes not only surrender themselves up to justice, but demand its utmost vigor.[4]

Nor did Rush find this moral derangement confined solely to acts of killing, for he cited instances of theft in which persons of comfortable or affluent circumstances took goods of little value without making any effort to derive any profit from them or even to conceal them. It was significant that Rush remarked upon this propensity to steal as early as 1786, in an address before the American Philosophical Society entitled "An Inquiry Into the Influence of Physical Causes Upon the Moral Faculty," which he used years later in his *Medical Inquiries and Observations*.

Do we ever observe partial insanity, or false perception on one subject, while the judgment is sound and correct, upon all others? We perceive, in some instances, a similar defect in the moral faculty. There are persons who are moral in the highest degree, as to certain duties, who nevertheless live under the influence of some one vice. I knew an instance of a woman, who was exemplary in her obedience to every command of the moral law, except one. She could not refrain

[4] Benjamin Rush, *op. cit.*, pp. 386-387.

from stealing. What made this vice the more remarkable was, that she was in easy circumstances, and not addicted to extravagance in anything. Such was her propensity to this vice, that when she could lay her hands upon nothing more valuable, she would often, at the table of a friend, fill her pockets secretly with bread. As a proof that her judgment was not affected by this defect in her moral faculty, she would both confess and lament her crime, when detected in it.[5]

Rush's contributions closed with his remarks in his *Diseases of the Mind,* the first work in America on insanity.

In the course of my life, I have been consulted in three cases of the total perversion of the moral faculties. One of them was in a young man, the second in a young woman, both of Virginia, and the third was in the daughter of a citizen of Philadelphia. The last was addicted to every kind of mischief. Her wickedness had no intervals while she was awake, except when she was kept busy in some steady and difficult employment. In all these cases of innate, preternatural moral depravity, there is probably an original defective organization in those parts of the body, which are occupied by the moral faculties of the mind.[6]

For fully three-quarters of the nineteenth century the bulk of our knowledge of the mental diseases was a product of the experience of American physicians in private or state asylums, together with contributions from European sources, the chief of which was English. The earliest record of moral insanity named as such in America was in the report of Dr. Samuel B. Woodward, superintendent of the Massachusetts State Lunatic Hospital, for the year 1836. Accepting the categories of Prichard (whose book had appeared the year before), Woodward declared at least one-fourth of the patients in the hospital were victims of moral insanity, being characterized neither by delusions nor by hallucinations but by a highly excited state of the feelings, by uncontrollable passions, by a derangement of the moral powers, and having perverted habits of life. In commenting upon

[5] Benjamin Rush, *Medical Inquiries and Observations,* Philadelphia, 1805, second edition, II, 15.
[6] Benjamin Rush, *Medical Inquiries and Observations upon the Diseases of the Mind,* Philadelphia, 1812, pp. 359-360.

a female patient who twice attempted to strangle an attendant, Woodward pointed out that the patient owned no hostility towards the attendants, but she vowed that a feeling possessed her that she must kill them. She admitted that she had no motive, nor delusion, but that she felt she had to act in obedience to a power that she could not and dared not resist.[7] Woodward cited several homicides (which Isaac Ray used in his book two years later) as well as lesser offenses in his institution, and concluded that they furnished him with conclusive evidence of the existence of moral insanity.

Reference has been made to Rush's lectures on medical jurisprudence in 1810. It remained, however, for Isaac Ray, in 1838, to present the first systematic treatise on the medical jurisprudence of insanity. This treatise, which grew out of his interest in insanity coupled with his extensive acquaintance with the European literature, was destined to stand alone for almost fifty years, being described by Frederick P. Henry, the historian of the Philadelphia medical profession, as a work which has "not only never been rivaled nor approached in his own country, but has scarcely been surpassed in any other." In his *Medical Jurisprudence of Insanity* Ray presented the doctrine of moral insanity, elaborating it as no other American has ever done, before or since. He remained, throughout his long and useful life, its ablest defender.

Ray's treatment of the subject of moral insanity began with his classification of insanity into two sections: the first comprising those cases of defective development of the faculties—idiocy and imbecility; the second those cases of "lesion" of the faculties subsequent to their development—mania and dementia. Under idiocy and also imbecility he subsumed those cases which resulted from congenital defect or which resulted from an obstacle to the development of the faculties supervening in infancy. Under mania he subsumed the twofold division of intellectual mania and affective mania, each of which had further divisions of general and partial mania. Under dementia he classified cases

[7] Samuel B. Woodward, *Reports and Other Documents Relating to the State Lunatic Hospital*, Boston, 1837, Appendix, p. 173.

"consecutive to mania, or injuries to the brain," and cases of "senile dementia, peculiar to old age." Moral insanity came under affective mania, and could be either general or partial. In beginning his discussion of moral mania Ray accepted Prichard's definition of moral insanity, remarking that it was the same disorder that Pinel designated as *manie sans delire*. General moral mania involved the entire moral nature, and Ray quoted cases from Pinel, Prichard, and Hoffbauer illustrating actions entirely devoid of moral awareness or sensitivity in which there was absolute perversion of the moral faculties without evidence of intellectual impairment. Of partial moral mania he wrote:

In this form of insanity, the derangement is confined to one or a few of the affective faculties, the rest of the moral and intellectual constitution preserving its ordinary integrity. An exaltation of the vital forces in any part of the cerebral organism, must necessarily be followed by increased activity and energy in the manifestations of the faculty connected with it, and which may even be carried to such a pitch as to be beyond the control of any other power, like the working of a blind, instinctive impulse. Accordingly, we see the faculty thus affected, prompting the individual to action by a kind of instinctive irresistibility, and while he retains the most perfect consciousness of the impropriety and even enormity of his conduct, he deliberately and perseveringly pursues it. With no extraordinary temptations to sin, but on the contrary, with every inducement to refrain from it, and apparently in the full possession of his reason, he commits a crime whose motives are equally inexplicable to himself and to others.[8]

Of the irresistible propensity to steal, Ray observed, first, that it was often to be found in people who showed abnormal conformations of the head (an early note on criminal anthropology, based on a case borrowed from Gall and Spurzheim) which were accompanied by an imbecile condition of the understanding; second, it was not unfrequently noted in cases of mania (again Gall is cited); third, it had been known to follow diseases or injuries of the brain, and therefore must be dependent on morbid action; fourth, it was sometimes followed by general

[8] Isaac Ray, *A Treatise on the Medical Jurisprudence of Insanity*, Boston, 1838, pp. 186-187.

mania; fifth, it was sometimes produced by certain physiological changes in the animal economy (Gall was cited as to the stealing proclivities of pregnant women).

The last and most important form of moral mania that will be noticed consists in a morbid activity of the *propensity to destroy;* where the individual without provocation or any other rational motive, apparently in the full possession of his reason, and oftentimes, in spite of his most strenuous efforts to resist, imbrues his hands in the blood of others; oftener than otherwise, of the partner of his bosom, of the children of his affections, of those, in short, who are most dear and cherished around him. The facts here alluded to are of painful frequency, and the gross misunderstanding of their true nature almost universally prevalent, excepting among a few in the higher walks of the professions, leads to equally painful results. In the absence of any pathological explanation of this horrid phenomenon, the mind seeks in vain, among secondary causes, for a rational mode of accounting for it, and is content to resort to that time honored solution, of all mysteries of human delinquency, the instigation of the devil.[9]

This is the disorder that was various called monomanie-homicide, monomanie-meurtrière, melancholie-homicide, homicidal mania, homicidal insanity, instinctive monomanie. It has been admitted by Pinel, Gall, Spurzheim, Esquirol, Georget, Marc, Andral, Orfila, Broussais, Burrows, Connolly, Combe, Prichard, Hoffbauer, Platner, Ethmuller, Henke, Otto, and Rush. In its simplest form it was the (apparently) unmotivated desire to destroy life, prompted solely by an irresistible impulse without any appreciable disorder of mind or body. In yet another class of cases that Ray cited the exciting cause was of a moral nature, operating upon some peculiar physical predisposition, and sometimes followed by more or less physical disturbance.

Instead of being urged on by a blind, imperious impulse to kill, the subjects of this form of the affection, after suffering for a certain period much gloom of mind and depression of spirits, feel as if bound by a sense of necessity to destroy life; and proceed to the fulfilment of their destiny with the utmost calmness and deliberation.[10]

[9] Ray, *op. cit.*, pp. 197-198.
[10] *Ibid.*, p. 213.

Of yet a third and final type of this murderous propensity Ray wrote:

. . . though it is not properly homicidal mania, there exists some hallucination, and the individual acts from motives—absurd and unfounded it is true—but still, motives to him. In consequence of the universal prevalence, in some shape or other of religious fanaticism, and of the excitement of the religious sentiments thereby produced, a perversion of these sentiments is one of the most common exciting causes of the murderous propensity in this class of cases. When thus excited its fury knows no restraints, and whole families are slaughtered in a single paroxysm.[11]

Ray concluded his discussion of partial moral mania by noting that the various forms of homicidal insanity possessed one feature in common—the irresistible, motiveless impulse to destroy life. This irresistible impulse was characterized by certain elements, which are similar, incidentally, to those described by Rush. First, the criminal act evidenced symptoms of the incubation of insanity; second, the impulse was excited by some trivial or imaginary circumstance; third, the victims were either closely related to the homicidal maniac or were entirely unknown to him; fourth, there was an utter absence of remorse or grief; fifth, the deed being accomplished confession was made voluntarily; sixth, in some instances the criminal act was the only sign of insanity, in others it was preceded or followed by open insanity; seventh, some pleaded insanity, or entire ignorance, while others denied that they labored under any such condition.

As an alienist, as an expert witness, and as an author on medical jurisprudence Ray was not unmindful of the distortions to which such a doctrine as moral insanity might be subjected by the wily and the vicious in their attempt to escape the legal consequences of their criminal acts. He took occasion to distinguish homicidal insanity from criminal homicide. The former was committed without motive, the latter never without motive. The former had only the homicidal act in view, the latter often accompanied the crime of murder with some other crime. The homicidal maniac showed neither grief nor remorse; the crimin-

[11] *Ibid.*, pp. 226-227.

al either denied or confessed his guilt. The homicidal maniac (or monomaniac, because driven with only one idea) seldom planned his act and after perpetration voluntarily surrendered himself; the criminal's plans were carefully set and escape was a part thereof. The homicidal maniac acted alone; the criminal generally with accomplices.

MORAL INSANITY SUPPORTED AND DEFENDED

In the decade following the pronouncements of Prichard and Ray there had been little disagreement over the condition each had described as moral insanity. In 1844 the Association of Medical Superintendents of American Institutions for the Insane began the publication of the *American Journal of Insanity*. In its pages the members carried on their discussions of disease entities along with problems of institutional management, etc. Amariah Brigham, the first editor, was disposed to accept the doctrine of moral insanity, and up to the time of his death in 1849 he insured its favorable presentation in the *Journal*. By 1861 the opposition had grown so powerful that Ray was called upon to meet the objections. He maintained his original definition of moral insanity, and while he took cognizance of the objections to the term "moral" he nevertheless doubted whether "emotional" or "affective" would signify the same thing or that they would be any more acceptable than the term "moral." He repeated that it was the derangement of the moral powers that constituted the essence of the disorder.

It seems hardly necessary to prove to one who has taken the first lesson in psychology, whether normal or abnormal, that the affective and intellectual powers work together, each in its proper sphere, in determining the thoughts, feelings and movements of the individual, and that the absence of one or other would produce an imperfect and disjointed result. It is but a plain corollary of this position, that a morbid condition of one or the other, must produce a similar effect. In many of the cases where the person is impelled by an irresistible impulse to commit some criminal act, it is stated that the feeling was contemplated with horror, and successfully resisted, until at last, having steadily increased its strength, it bore down all opposition.[12]

Two years later, in the same journal, Ray again replied to objections, this time specifically in answer to an article by Dr. Andrew MacFarland, superintendent of the Illinois State Hospital for the Insane.[13] He defended the term "moral insanity," arguing that whether the term moral or some other term was used the disturbance was there nevertheless.

I use the term as it has been used before, I suppose, by everybody else, as meaning that form of mania in which the moral powers are affected, without there being any intellectual disturbance appreciable. That there may not be intellectual disturbance, in spite of our limited apprehension, I do not dispute. My meaning is, that there is none visible. All we see is moral impairment, and that is all we have a right to affirm the existence of.[14]

This discussion revealed for the first time those who supported Ray's position—Charles H. Nichols, of the Government Hospital for the Insane; John E. Tyler, of the McLean Asylum in Massachusetts; and Dr. J. Parigot, of Yonkers, New York. Nichols wrote:

I repeat: adopt what theory of metaphysics or psychology you will, whether you suppose that the faculties of the mind are distinct, and each is manifested through a different portion of the brain or the whole of it alike, or, on the contrary, that the mind is an indistinct entity, whose different modes of manifestation we call its faculties, I still see no reason why a portion or the whole of the brain may not be so disordered that the consequent deranged mental manifestations shall be confined to the individual's affective faculties, or, in other words, why the deranged mode of manifestation consequent upon disease of the organ or a portion of it, through which the manifestation takes place, should not be wholly affective or moral.[15]

According to Tyler the essense of moral insanity was a disease confined to the feelings without affecting the intellect. Parigot,

---

[12] Isaac Ray, "An Examination of the Objections to the Doctrine of Moral Insanity," *American Journal of Insanity*, XVIII (October 1861) 115.

[13] Discussion of paper previously presented by Andrew MacFarland entitled "Minor Mental Maladies," in *American Journal of Insanity*, XX (July 1863) 10-26, *American Journal of Insanity*, XX (July 1863) 63-106.

[14] *Ibid.*, p. 83.

[15] *Ibid.*, p. 67.

accepting the fundamental fact of moral insanity—a morbid condition of the feelings independent of the intellect—wanted, however, to substitute the term *diastrephia.*

Others of this period also followed Ray in his definition and defense of moral insanity. Amos Dean was a notable example. In his book on medical jurisprudence he reproduced Ray's classification—general moral mania and partial moral mania. Under the latter he placed "cleptomania," erotic mania, lying mania, pyromania, suicidal mania, and homicidal mania. (Moral insanity had already begun to proliferate, a condition we will note for the fifty years that follow.)[16] Theodore W. Fisher, assistant superintendent of the Boston Lunatic Hospital, accepted moral insanity, but preferred the term "affective insanity."[17] John Curwen, superintendent of the Pennsylvania State Lunatic Hospital, in his presidential address before the Medical Society of the State of Pennsylvania in 1869, endorsed moral insanity. He felt no hesitation in accepting a condition involving moral disorder without attendant intellectual "lesions":

It is to be carefully observed that this condition is not a steady growth from bad to worse, from a bad life and depraved habits to one much worse, but it is a total change of the whole conduct and character, that the man is as much the opposite of his former self in all his moral relations as it is possible for him to be, and that he now manifests traits of character and a course of conduct which no one who knew him before would ever have believed him capable of exhibiting. No evidence of delusion or other impairment of the intellectual faculties can be clearly discerned, unless we take it as an evidence of intellectual weakness that the man cannot see the exceeding incongruity between his present course of conduct and that which formerly rendered him so much honored and respected by a large circle of friends and acquaintances. . . . We will thus be led to admit distinctly a disorder of the moral powers, which may be called moral, emotional, or affective insanity, as the views of the person may dictate.[18]

[16] Amos Dean, *Principles of Medical Jurisprudence,* Albany and New York, 1850, pp. 495-516.

[17] Theodore W. Fisher, "Moral Insanity," *Boston Medical and Surgical Journal,* n.s. II, no. 8 (September 24, 1868) 114-116.

[18] John Curwen, "Presidential Address," *Transactions of the Medical Society of the State of Pennsylvania,* 1869, pp. 301-302.

J. William White, resident physician of the Eastern State Penitentiary in Philadelphia, in his report for the year 1874, conjectured upon the possible connection between physical causes of moral degeneracy and the evil propensities of habitual criminals. "Moral insanity" he used synonymously with "criminal neurosis."

Individuals born in good circumstances, having been carefully educated and surrounded by the protecting influences of home-life, frequently lose every correct feeling in regard to moral relations, while reason remains unimpaired, and the judgment on all other matters is thoroughly reliable.[19]

H. M. Bannister, co-editor of the *Journal of Nervous and Mental Disease*, and Charles H. Hughes, former superintendent and physician of the Missouri State Lunatic Asylum and lecturer on nervous diseases at the St. Louis Medical College, each endorsed "moral insanity," the latter feeling the name to be unfortunate. He suggested, instead, the term "affective insanity."[20]

In 1883 four works appeared bearing on insanity and its legal and medical relations.[21] One of these was by Edward C. Spitzka who, at the Guiteau trial two years before, had transmuted "moral insanity" into "moral imbecility" when he testified:

Some authors call that moral insanity which I term moral imbecility or moral monstrosity. By a moral monstrosity, I mean a person who is born with so defective a nervous organization that he is altogether deprived of that moral sense which is an integral and essential constituent of the normal mind, he being analogous in that respect to the congenital cripple who is born speechless, or with one leg shorter than the other, or with any other monstrous development that we now and again see.[22]

[19] J. William White, *Physician's Report, in Forty-Fifth Annual Report of the Inspectors of the State Penitentiary for the Eastern District of Pennsylvania*, 1875, p. 202.

[20] H. M. Bannister, "Moral Insanity," *Journal of Nervous and Mental Disease*, V (October 1877) 645-668; Charles H. Hughes, "Moral (Affective) Insanity," *Medico-Legal Journal*, II (1885) 22-52, 216-223.

[21] Allan McLane Hamilton, *Manual of Medical Jurisprudence*, New York, 1883, Wiliam A. Hammond, *A Treatise on Insanity in Its Medical Relations*, New York, 1883, Edward C. Mann, *A Manual of Psychological Medicine and Allied Nervous Diseases*, Philadelphia, 1883, Edward C. Spitzka, *Insanity*, New York, 1883.

[22] "Review of the Trial of Charles J. Guiteau," *American Journal of Insanity*, XXXVII (January 1881) 303-448.

Likewise in his book he restricted "moral insanity" to cases of feeble intelligence and called it "moral imbecility." Hamilton's objections to "moral insanity" will be noted later in this chapter in the discussion of the opponents of the doctrine. As for Hammond, while he would not permit himself the use of "moral insanity" as a term, he did draw up his own classification, placing in its stead the expression "emotional morbid impulses." He remarked that the "emotional morbid impulses" constituted a large and important part of that form of mental derangement described by Prichard as "moral insanity." Hammond declared that these impulses are what the prosecution witnesses at the Guiteau trial designated "wickedness," whereupon he takes them to task by observing that they have set themselves against the opinion of those European and American alienists most competent to judge. "Indeed," wrote Hammond, "the number of alienists who do not believe in the existence of emotional morbid impulses as a form of insanity is not much greater than the number of experts for the prosecution in the trial in question."[23] Among these impulses he recognized kleptomania, pyromania, homicidal mania, suicidal mania—all forms of irresistible impulses disposing to crime. Edward C. Mann in his treatise goes back to Prichard and Ray when he remarked that the great diagnostic mark of reasoning mania, or moral or affective insanity, was the absence of delusion. In such cases there was an entire change of character and habits evidenced by extraordinary conduct. Morbid impulses predominate while the intellect seems powerless to control.

In this connection, it is very interesting to note that moral degeneracy often follows as a sequence upon disease or injury to the brain. A severe attack of insanity sometimes produces the same effect, the intellectual faculties remaining as acute as ever, while the moral sense seems obliterated.[24]

Despite the confusion around the term "moral insanity" occasioned by the Guiteau trial there were still some who held to the term. A. B. Arnold, professor of clinical medicine at the

[23] William A. Hammond, op. cit., p. 432.
[24] Edward C. Mann, op. cit., p. 125.

College of Physicians and Surgeons in Baltimore, defined it as the morbid incapacity to resist evil impulses, whether it be due to congenital defect or from cerebral disease or brain injury.[25] We have cited William G. Stevenson's essay on criminality in the chapters on criminal anthropology, but it will not be amiss to note here that among other factors involved in criminal behavior he took into account a condition of moral deficiency:

Intelligence may be acute, the perceptive and reasoning faculties existing, it may be, in a high state of development. But with all this there is moral deficiency; a perversity of thoughts and desires, with violent passions, which being uncontrolled by the moral faculties (not necessarily because the perversities are greater than in other men, but because the moral force is less), there result immoral, criminal acts which are correct exponents of the organic cause by which and through which they alone exist.[26]

William P. Spratling, first assistant physician and pathologist at the New Jersey Insane Asylum at Morris Plains, in 1890, claimed that he established organic disease as a factor in moral insanity. In contrast to the true criminal he found the morally insane had a good intellect, and was ofttimes brilliant, but his moral powers were so low as to involve him in the foulest deeds.

Intelligence, with the morally insane, when exercised along the line of action he intends pursuing, or involuntarily pursues, does *not* teach him that what he would do, or is doing is *wrong*. His moral powers are dead. Intuitive moral feelings do not exist in his nature; and, for that reason he should *not* be held responsible for what is beyond his every effort to prevent. Then again, in other cases, the man who is morally insane, may *fully understand* that what he would do, or is doing, is wrong, and in violation of law and society; but he could not resist the impulse to do evil, because he undoubtedly is suffering from a *paralysis,* or *deficiency* of the *psychical inhibitory* forces, and absolutely without the slightest feeling of self-restraint, which he may honestly desire to exercise, he takes a false step. . . . With the ordinary criminal it is totally different. His intellect does not play him false. It permits him to always, under normal conditions, regulate his actions

[25] A. B. Arnold, "Moral Insanity," *Transactions of the Medical and Chirurgical Faculty of the State of Maryland,* 1887, pp. 120-125.
[26] William G. Stevenson, "Criminality," *Medico-Legal Journal,* V (1887-1888) 268.

in a manner that he reasons best for his purpose. His powers of self-restraint are not diseased.[27]

Like Spitzka several years before, I. N. Kerlin, director of the Pennsylvania Training School for the Feeble-Minded at Elwyn, converted moral insanity into moral imbecility by stressing the congenital origin of moral defect, but there is a strong suspicion that he also included the notion of mental defect in the term as well.[28] Insane criminals were classified into five categories by Julius B. Ransom, one of which was the phrenasthenic or psychopathic criminal, while another was the morally insane or reasoning phrenasthenic. The former was the man who acted by irresistible impulse, the latter he who acted without delusions but who had perverted sentiments and affections.[29]

Without using the term, Alonzo Richardson's description of a class of criminals conformed to it (Richardson was clinical lecturer on insanity at Starling Medical College, Columbus, Ohio, and formerly superintendent of the Columbus State Hospital). Persons of this class were of fair physical development, intellectually not enfeebled either congenitally or from acquired disease, but manifesting a total absence of the capacity to judge of the moral quality of their acts.[30] In his study of physical degeneracy Eugene S. Talbot also noted moral degeneracy, declaring that the person whom he called the moral imbecile had lost the last acquirement of the human race—the moral sense. Nor was the moral lunatic, as Talbot called him, far removed from the paranoiac.[31] W. Duncan McKim also saw the morally insane as an evidence of degeneracy, declaring that if a congenital structural abnormality underlay the moral defect the condition was known as moral idiocy, whereas it was moral insanity if the moral defect was a later development resulting

[27] William P. Spratling, "Moral Insanity," *Medico-Legal Journal*, VIII (1890) 220-226.

[28] I. N. Kerlin, "The Moral Imbecile," *Proceedings of the National Conference of Charities and Correction*, 1890, p. 245.

[29] Julius B. Ransom, "The Physician and the Criminal," *Journal of the American Medical Association*, XXVII (October 1896) 792.

[30] Alonzo B. Richardson, "The Relation of Criminality to Mental Defect," *Cleveland Medical Gazette*, XIII (December 1897) 75-89.

[31] Eugene S. Talbot, *op. cit.*

either from injury or degeneration of the brain. In either case the person was dangerous to the community.[32]

In 1904 a woman caused the deaths of an entire family by poisoning. When she was brought to trial, the prosecution and the defense agreed upon a committee of alienists to examine the prisoner and report upon her mental condition. In its report the committee found that she had acted without motive, fear, remorse, or guilt; that an irresistible propensity propelled her to crimes of arson and murder; that her mental state corresponded with a well-recognized form of mental defect of a moral type due to congenital degeneration, in which there was little or no intellectual disturbance apparent to the observer. She was found not guilty by reason of insanity and committed to the State insane hospital, whereupon Henry R. Stedman, a prominent psychiatrist, remarked:

Whatever view may be taken of this remarkable case, there can be no question that the moral monster thus far depicted is a striking illustration of so-called moral insanity, a condition described in most works by recognized authorities, from Prichard to Kraepelin and Wernicke, as a probable form of mental disease or defect. Its existence as a definite morbid condition has been repeatedly questioned, and its name criticised as inadequate and incorrect. "Moral insanity," however, has so far held its own that all alienists of today recognize that the term means a certain condition or kind of mental subnormality which is *sui generis*. It fits no other form of mental unsoundness. The progress of psychiatry has seen so many nosological terms discarded that is is remarkable that "moral insanity" should remain and flourish, thus demonstrating its practical utility as a term and its real value as a morbid mental condition.[33]

In order to establish the perspective of a century let us quote Stedman's definition, bearing in mind Pinel, Prichard, Ray, and Maudsley:

Moral insanity belongs to the group known as insanities of degeneration, and is better termed *degenerative insanity of the moral type*.

[32] W. Duncan McKim, *op. cit.*

[33] Henry R. Stedman, "A Case of Moral Insanity with Repeated Homicides and Incendiarism and Late Development of Delusions," *American Journal of Insanity*, LXI (October 1904) 286-287.

It should be exclusively reserved to designate a congenital, primary, constitutional and permanent mental condition affecting the moral nature and unassociated with evident impairment. These patients have good memory and understanding, ability to reason and contrive, much cleverness and cunning, and a general appearance of rationality, coexistent with very deficient control, absence of moral sense and human sentiments and feelings, perverted and brutal instincts, and propensities for criminal acts of various kinds which may be perpetrated deliberately and cleverly planned, yet committed with little or no motive and regardless of the consequences to themselvs and others. . . . They commit crime for crime's sake.[34]

When Stedman goes on to remark that these persons resembled the instinctive criminal of Lombroso, one is forcibly reminder that in the interval from 1835 when Prichard wrote, to 1904 when Stedman reported the current case, a whole school of criminal anthropology had developed, and had challenged all others for supremacy in the field of crime causation. In effect Stedman sought to reconcile the doctrine of moral insanity of the first third of the century with the degeneracy theories of the criminal anthropology school of the last third of the same century.

The doctrines of phrenology were being expounded by Gall at the turn of the same century that found Pinel introducing *manie sans delire*, the French terminology for moral insanity. Over a hundred years later we find an American physician, G. Frank Lydston, interpreting moral insanity in terms of Gall's phrenology, just as Stedman, in his definition of moral insanity, had gone back to Pinel. In 1904 Lydston wrote:

If there be aught of truth in Gall's theory of localization, it is not beyond the bounds of possibility that certain moral faculties are presided over by special cell areas, and that injury or disease of these centres may be productive of vicious or criminal impulses. That the posterior and middle lobes of the brain in general preside over the moral faculties of the mind, the anterior lobes being the intellectual inhibitory centres, is fairly well established. It follows, then, that diseases of what may be termed the moral centres, and disease of the inhibitory centres may alike produce moral perturbations.[35]

[34] Henry R. Stedman, *op. cit.*, p. 287.
[35] G. Frank Lydston, *The Diseases of Society*, Philadelphia, J. B. Lippincott Co., 1904, 155-156.

By defining moral insanity as a degeneration of the moral character without recognizable intellectual insanity, Lydston felt that it supported the view of special centers for the moral faculties.[36]

OPPOSITION TO MORAL INSANITY

By the middle of the 1880's, after a half century of controversy, the weight of opinion, lay and professional, was opposed to the term "moral insanity," although its use continued into the twentieth century. The testimony of the prosecution medical witnesses at the Guiteau trial in 1881 had overwhelmed the proponents of the doctrine. To gain some understanding of its repudiation it will be necessary to trace historically the opposition which led up to it.

Francis Wharton, an eminent member of the Philadelphia Bar, as early as 1855, in his famous work on mental unsoundness, could not accept moral insanity, *manie sans delire*, or instinctive madness, or the idea of irresistible impulse. To him they merely signified an "inefficiency of the intellectual force."[37] So cogent was Wharton's statement of the precedents against moral insanity, and so overwhelming was the body of the law represented therein, that American courts substantially followed Wharton's position, with only an occasional departure.

Although Dr. Amariah Brigham, superintendent of the New York State Lunatic Asylum and one of the founders and first editor of the *American Journal of Insanity*, held to the belief of irresistible impulse and moral insanity, nevertheless the *Journal*, after his decease in 1849, opposed and remained uninterruptedly opposed to the doctrine of moral insanity. The leading figure of the opposition was John P. Gray, who occoupied Brigham's former position as head of the asylum at Utica, and by virture thereof was editor of the *Journal*. No opportunity was lost to refute the doctrine, whether it was in comments on court trials, in comments on papers presented at the annual meetings of the Association of Medical Superintendents of American Institutions for the Insane, or in answer to articles, permitted to

[36] *Ibid.*, p. 158.
[37] Francis Wharton, *op. cit.*

be published, favoring moral insanity. In its pages opponents of the doctrine found ample space. An editorial, in 1858, denying the irresistibility of thieving, firing, or killing, remarked that the essential test was the capacity to distinguish between right and wrong: if a man knew the difference between right and wrong and persisted in doing the wrong, then obviously he was not an insane man, he was merely a bad man.[38] Andrew MacFarland precipitated the first extended discussion of the Association on the question when he insisted that there must always be a real intellectual disturbance in any form of insanity.[39] John P. Gray added that he had seen four to five thousand cases of the insane and had yet to find one case of moral insanity as described by the various writers on the subject. When Dr. Ranney asked Dr. Nichols for the difference between moral insanity and depravity, Dr. Nichols answered him:

It appears to me that when a person, possessing the power of controlling his actions, commits an act that he knows to be wrong, he sins, and his sin may well enough be called "moral depravity." But even if a person understands the sinfulness of the act he commits, or, knowing it to be wrong in its nature, is impelled to commit it by an uncontrollable feeling, or impulse, or delusion, caused by disease of the organ of the mind, it is then an act of insanity, and the actor is irresponsible.[40]

John Ordronaux, professor of medical jurisprudence in the Law School of Columbia College, objected to moral insanity because he could not accept a doctrine which called persons insane who were not characterized by delusions, hallucinations, or had suffered an organic brain change or other impairment of the intellect.[41] After quoting Ray's description of the morally insane, Ordronaux insisted:

[38] "Moral Insanity," *American Journal of Insanity*, XIV (April 1858) 311-322.

[39] Andrew MacFarland, "Minor Mental Maladies," *American Journal of Insanity*, XX (July 1863) 10-26.

[40] Charles H. Nichols, discussion of Andrew MacFarland's paper, *American Journal of Insanity*, XX (July 1863) 96.

[41] John Ordronaux, "History and Philosophy of Medical Jurisprudence," *American Journal of Insanity*, XXV (October 1868) 173-212.

The foregoing symptoms of moral insanity as given by Dr. Ray, are all striking delineations of what common sense, enlightened by revelation, would call *depravity*. Yet we are asked to believe that these signs constitute evidence of a form of insanity destroying human responsibility. The very conditions in fact which God thundered against, in the law given upon the Mount, and which the inspired Prophets, the Fathers of the Church, irrespective of denominational creeds, and learned divines and authoritative moralists have all agreed upon as constituting *sin*, the defenders of moral insanity term disease. They thus make it appear that the decalogue, and all human laws, are unjust because they visit penalties upon disease, and that in consequence there is no sin except in minor offenses. Under this new gospel petty-larceny is crime, while murder or arson are diseases;—and the more perfect in lying, stealing, cheating or murdering a man becomes, the more indubitably is he irresponsible.[42]

In a study of homicidal insanity consisting of sixty-seven cases subsequently committed to his asylum, John P. Gray, in 1875, affirmed that the insane act from motives, and that the delusion under which the mind acted could be ascertained. "The theory of impulsive acts, or impulsive insanity, finds no support in an analysis of clinical cases. Delusion is the motive, which in most cases controls the conduct of the insane."[43]

The controversy extended beyond the confines of the *Journal*. David Meredith Reese (author of *The Humbugs of New York*, a denunciation of animal magnetism, phrenology, homeopathia, quackery, etc.) reported unfavorably on moral insanity on behalf of a committee appointed by the American Medical Association in 1858. According to him the proponents of this docrtine derived their views from the peculiar teachings of phrenology, which recognized the instincts, moral propensities, and intellectual faculties as dependent upon certain portions of the brain.

It is only on the theory that the brain is a congeries of organs, each of which has its appropriate function, and severally developing in-

[42] John Ordronaux, "Moral Insanity," *American Journal of Insanity*, XXIX (January 1873) 321.
[43] John P. Gray, "Responsibility of the Insane—Homicide in Insanity," *American Journal of Insanity*, XXXII (October 1875) 154.

stinctive, moral, or intellectual results; and on the still bolder hypothesis that the organs of each separate function may be arbitrarily mapped out, or designated by the science, that this conception of moral insanity could ever have been engendered.[44]

Since the mind was the source of both the moral and intellectual developments, and since any disease of the brain, the organ of the mind, must affect the intellectual and moral functions, then, maintained Reese, there could be no insanity apart from disease of the brain. Here, and in other instances throughout this treatise, is to be found evidences of a controversy that loomed large during the nineteenth century. Were the causes of insanity psychic, i.e., moral, or were they somatic, i.e., physical? Without doubt this shift in emphasis from the moral to the physical is closely correlated with the rise of materialism during this period. The older metaphysical and theological speculations on the cause of mental disorder had given way to a modified version which stressed the moral factors. As the nineteenth century progressed even this proved unpalatable, and psychiatrists insisted upon finding actual changes that had taken place in the brain, either by injury or by disease, that would account for insanity. It remained for the next century to strike a balance somewhere between these two extremes.

Many years later James Hendrie Lloyd, an instructor in electro-therapeutics at the University of Pennsylvania Medical School, took the same position as Reese when he declared there was no moral "faculty" in the sense of its being a distinct agent, with its own powers and its own diseases, which may be affected without involving any of the other "faculties."[45] Others refused to accept moral insanity, as for instance John J. Elwell, a member of the Cleveland Bar, professor of medical jurisprudence at Ohio State University, Union Law College, and Western Reserve Medical College (and the author of a leading textbook on medical jurisprudence), Carlos F. MacDonald, and Clark Bell, for many years head of the Medico-Legal Society in New York

[44] David Meredith Reese, "Report on Moral Insanity in Its Relations to Medical Jurisprudence," *Transactions of the American Medical Association*, XI (1858) 725.

[45] James Hendrie Lloyd, "Moral Insanity—A Plea for a More Exact Pathology," *Journal of Nervous and Mental Disease*, XIII (November 1886) 681.

and editor of the later American editions of Taylor's *Medical
Jurisprudence,* the standard manual in England for many years.[46]
That the term had become the repository of doubtful or hard
cases was the objection Simon Herres citing the instance of Bruce
Thompson, the English prison physion who attributed so much
of human depravity in criminals to this form of mental disorder.[47] R. J. Patterson, like John P. Gray, rarely found a case
of moral insanity among asylum admissions, for in reporting to
the American Medical Association in 1877 he stated that of
43,705 admissions reported to him by various asylums there was
not a single case of moral insanity, while of 47,174 admissions
there were only twenty-two cases. He concluded that insanity
is both intellectual and emotional, that there was no such entity as
moral insanity.[48]

THE GUITEAU TRIAL

Perhaps no single event threw the doctrine of moral insanity
into the foreground as did the trial of Charles J. Guiteau for
the assassination of President Garfield in 1881.[49] Guiteau was
on trial for his life, and the main issue centered around his
responsibility—was he sane or was he insane at the time he
committed his act? Inevitably bound up with this was the question of whether such a disease entity existed as moral insanity.
From the time of its introduction in 1835 by Prichard, and its
promulgation three years later by Isaac Ray, the term "moral

[46] John J. Elwell, *Malpractice and Medical Evidence Comprising the Elements of
Medical Jurisprudence,* New York, 1st edition, 1859, 3rd, 1871; Carlos F. MacDonald,
"Case of Edmond J. Hoppin—Homicide Plea, Insanity," *American Journal of In-
sanity,* XXXIII (April 1878) 462-511; Alfred Swaine Taylor, *A Manual of Medical
Jurisprudence,* edited by Clark Bell in the 12th American Edition, 1897.

[47] Simon Herres, "On Moral Insanity," *Transactions of the Michigan State Medical
Society,* VII, no. 3 (1879), 418-425.

[48] R. J. Patterson, "Report on Moral Insanity," *Transactions of the American Medical
Association,* XXVIII (1877) 359-364.

[49] The trial showed that Charles Julius Guiteau was born in Illinois in 1841, and at
the age of nineteen had joined the Oneida Community in New York State. Four years
later he left the Community, without changing his views, in order to publish its doctrines
in his newly established *Theocrat.* From this time, 1865, until 1880, he was variously
lawyer, pamphleteer, and lecturer. Following Garfield's election in 1880, Guiteau, who
felt he had a part in it, deluged the President-elect with requests for a consular appointment. He persisted in his demands when Garfield became Prsident, and was finally
rebuffed by the Secretary of State, James G. Blaine. Guiteau shot the President July 2,
1881, the wound eventually proving fatal on September 19.

insanity" had been held in considerable distrust, suspicion, and even fear. Those who opposed the use of the term did so either on the ground that no such disability existed or that if it did it was not of such a character as to constitute an adequate defense in a criminal trial. There was very little acceptance of the term outside of the medical profession, and even among physicians themselves it was a minority-held conviction. In the Guiteau trial the medical witnesses called by the defense testified that Guiteau was insane; the prosecution medical witnesses that he was sane. Several of the defense witnesses testified that Guiteau's form of insanity was known as moral insanity. The prosecution witnesses denied the existence of moral insanity.

It will be well to consider the position of the defense witnesses, of whom the first was Dr. James G. Kiernan. Kiernan, who had been for eight years a practising physician and had given special study to mental diseases, was asked the following hypothetical question:

Assume it to be a fact that there was a strong hereditary taint of insanity in the blood of the prisoner at the bar; also that at about the age of thirty-five years his mind was so much deranged that he was a fit subject to be sent to an insane asylum; also that at different times from that date during the next succeeding five years he manifested such decided symptoms of insanity, without simulation, that many different persons conversing with him and observing his conduct believed him to be insane; also that during the month of June, 1881, at about the expiration of said term of five years, he honestly became dominated by the idea that he was inspired of God to remove by death the President of the United States; also that he acted upon what he believed to be such inspiration, and what he believed to be in accordance with the Divine will, in preparation for and the accomplishment of such a purpose; also that he committed the act of shooting the President under what he believed to be a Divine command which he was not at liberty to disobey, and which belief amounted to a conviction that controlled his conscience and overpowered his will as to that act, so that he could not resist the mental pressure upon him; also that immediately after the shooting he appeared calm and as one relieved by the performance of a great duty; also that there was no other adequate motive for the act than the conviction that he was executing the Divine will for the good of his country. Assuming all these propositions to be true, state whether, in your opinion, the prisoner was sane or insane at the time of shooting President Garfield.[50]

His answer was that, assuming all the propositions to be true, Guiteau was insane. Upon cross-examination Kiernan announced his belief in moral insanity, stating that insanity may exist without either delusion, hallucination, or illusion. Charles H. Nichols, who had been superintendent of the Government Hospital for the Insane and was at the time of the trial superintendent of the Bloomingdale Asylum, also answered to the hypothetical question that he believed Guiteau was insane; as did Charles F. Folsom, who for the past nine years had devoted special attention to mental diseases and at one time had been assistant in the McLean Asylum. Four other alienists in answer to the same hypothetical question declared Guiteau was unquestionably insane: William W. Godding, superintendent of the Government Hospital for the Insane; James H. McBride, superintendent of the Asylum for the Insane at Milwaukee; Walter Channing, who conducted a private asylum and who had at one time been assistant in the Asylum for Insane Criminals at Auburn, New York, and in the State Hospital at Danvers, Massachusetts; and Theodore W. Fisher, superintendent of the Boston Lunatic Hospital. Edward C. Spitzka, as noted in an earlier section of this chapter, had testified that Guiteau was insane and was also a moral imbecile, or rather a moral monstrosity.

To many of the prosecution witnesses moral insanity was simply wickedness; Guiteau was a sane man and responsible for his act. Among these witnesses was Allan McLane Hamilton, who had been connected with a hospital for epileptics and paralytics, had written a work on nervous diseases, and was to publish two years later his manual on medical jurisprudence. He declared Guiteau was sane, and in denying his belief in moral insanity, added that it was a convenient term for the excuse of acts committed as a result of anger and lust. A. E. MacDonald,

[50] "Review of the Trial of Charles J. Guiteau," *American Journal of Insanity*, XXXVIII (January 1882) 333.

superintendent of the New York City Asylum for the Insane and also professor of medical jurisprudence in the medical department of the University of New York, also testified that Guiteau was sane, and that moral insanity was but another name for wickedness or depravity. Indeed, said MacDonald, it was a term invented during the French Revolution to excuse the slaughter that took place. Insanity was not confined to the moral nature alone, he continued, nor was a man's brain divided into compartments which presided over certain actions and which could be diseased without the rest being affected. Randolph Barksdale, superintendent of the Central Lunatic Asylum at Richmond, Virginia, in holding Guiteau to be sane also denied the doctrine of moral insanity, as did John H. Callender, superintendent of the Tennessee Hospital at Nashville, and professor of physiology and diseases of the brain and nervous system at the University of Nashville and Vanderbilt University, who declared insanity was a physical disease of a physical organ in which the intellectual faculties were disturbed. Likewise Walter Kempster, superintendent of the Northern Hospital for the Insane in Wisconsin, disavowed his belief in moral insanity, declaring it to be a term which sought to excuse persons who had committed an outrageous act. The last of the medical witnesses for the prosecution was John P. Gray, superintendent of the New York State Lunatic Asylum at Utica, who maintained that Guiteau was sane. He asserted that he did not believe in moral insanity, that there could be no moral act without an intellectual operation, i.e., that the intellectual and the moral faculties are a unity, and that no disorder can come of the one without affecting the other. Furthermore, insanity was a disease of physical origin, and could not manifest itself through the moral nature only. The so-called moral insanities, he was convinced, were simply crimes, i.e., what others called kleptomania he called stealing, what to others was dipsomania was to him drunkenness, what pyromania was to others was incendiarism to him.

The Guiteau trial had given the death blow to the doctrine of moral insanity, despite the fact that its use occasionally continued into the twentieth century. Opponents of moral insanity prior to the trial were but the more convinced that no such disease classification existed, while the weight of medical testimony very considerably weakened the position of the proponents. Allan McLane Hamilton, in his manual on medical jurisprudence which appeared in 1883, ruled out moral insanity, monomania, and partial insanity, adding that we have no more right to use these terms than to speak of "partial" malaria or "partial" syphilis.[51] Even James G. Kiernan, a defense witness who announced his belief in moral insanity at the trial had, by 1884, modified his definition to include only cases in which the moral sense was congenitally absent or destructively involved by disease. Thus had the physical origin of mental disease prevailed. Kleptomania, for example, he no longer regarded as a form of moral insanity, it was a symptom designation rather than a disease designation. Kiernan even suspected mental enfeeblement in his modified definition and suggested the term "moral imbecility" to replace "moral insanity."[52] Another defense expert, Walter Channing, five years later, in reviewing the chapter on the relation of madness and crime in Stephen's *History of the Criminal Law in England*, denied moral insanity when he wrote:

That is, we believe that while cases may exist without delusion, strictly speaking, we feel sure that in any case of apparent moral insanity sufficient intellectual impairment will be found to constitute a true instance of complete insanity. There may be cases of insanity with the immoral elements most prominent, and these to us always correspond to the so-called "moral insanity." Unless something besides depravity exist, we cannot call a man insane.[53]

SUMMARY AND CONCLUSION

Initiated by Pinel, named by Prichard, articulated by Ray, outlawed by Wharton, denounced by Gray, moral insanity has had

---

[51] Allan McLane Hamilton, *op. cit.*, p. 20.

[52] James G. Kiernan, "Moral Insanity—What Is It?" *Journal of Nervous and Mental Disease*, XI (October 1884) 562.

[53] Walter Channing, "The Connection Between Insanity and Crime," *American Journal of Insanity*, XLII (April 1886) 471-472.

a varied, tenacious, and far from uneventful life. Beginning as *manie sans delire*, it has been identified by one writer or another and at one time or another as almost any form of mental abnormality—monomania, partial mania, dementia, dementia praecox, paresis, paranoia. Despite the efforts at exact definition, it has become the repository of the unclassifiable. Denied existence as a separate entity, it had been described as the condition precedent to the outbreak of one of the many insanities. By some it had been held to be the after-result of injury to, or degeneration of, the brain. Denied existence altogether, it had been called simply wickedness, perversity, depravity. Generally excluded from the textbooks of the twentieth century, it showed a strange pertinacity to appear in varied forms. As each form of mental disease became more sharply and precisely defined the residual had been labeled "moral insanity."

Tagged with the psychopathic by Ransom in 1896, it has never entirely escaped variations on that theme—psychopathic personality, psychopathic constitutional inferior, constitutional immorality, moral paretic. The morally insane was even converted into Lombroso's instinctive criminal, under the impact of the schools of criminal anthropology of the eighties and nineties. By the twentieth century there was the question whether the defective moral sense was congenital or acquired by deliberate choice. Charles W. Hitchcock, an asylum superintendent, called an individual who acquired his defective moral sense by deliberate choice a "psychopathic personality,"[54] while H. W. Wright, assistant alienist at the Bellevue Hospital in New York City, spoke of the constitutional inferior just as one had formerly described the morally insane.[55] For C. C. Wholey, assistant neurologist of the Western Pennsylvania Hospital at Pittsburgh, the test of moral insanity was the inherent deficiency of the moral sense; he insisted that it must not be applied to the inherently normal individual whose upbringing in an environment of poverty and

[54] Charles W. Hitchcock, "Imbecile, Criminal, or Both?" *American Journal of Insanity*, LXV (January 1909) 519-524.

[55] H. W. Wright, "The Problem of the Criminal in the Light of Some Modern Conceptions," *Journal of the American Medical Association*, LXI (December 13, 1913) 2119-2122.

vice had directed his conduct into the same channels as those spontaneously followed by the constitutional immoral.[56]

In his book, *The Individual Delinquent*, published in 1915, which marked a new era in our understanding of the offender, William Healy, founder and director of the Juvenile Psychopathic Institute in Chicago and later director of the Judge Baker Foundation in Boston, indicated that much of the confusion regarding the terms "moral insanity" and "moral imbecility" lay in the fact that different authors had been talking about different things.[57] Some sought an explanation by stating that the individual was insane, others that he was sane; some that the individual's behavior was due to congenital factors, others that it was due to the environment; some that he was characterized by mental deficiency, others that mentally he was unimpaired; some that his action was deliberate and by choice, others that he was irresistibly impelled; some that he was responsible, others that he was irresponsible; some that there was a separate moral faculty spatially located in the brain, others that the faculty psychology was impossible.

By the time Healy had written his eight-hundred-page work the term "moral insanity" had so far lost its original identity as defined by Prichard and Ray that it was used either not at all, or with what was taken to be its synonym—moral imbecility. Indeed Healy, when he converted moral insanity into moral imbecility, remarked:

When we began our work there was no point on which we expected more positive data than on moral imbecility. But our findings have turned out to be negative. We have been constantly on the lookout for a moral imbecile, that is, a person not subnormal and otherwise intact in mental powers, who shows himself devoid of moral feeling. We have not found one.[58]

Thus we are brought to moral imbecility, which will be discussed in the chapter on feeble-mindedness and crime.

[56] C. C. Wholey, "Cases of Moral Insanity Arising from Inherent Moral Defectiveness," *Journal of the American Medical Association*, LXII (March 21, 1914) 926-928.
[57] William Healy, *The Individual Delinquent*, Little, Brown & Co., Boston, 1915.
[58] *Ibid.*, p. 783.

IV

ALCOHOL AND DRUGS

THE use, or rather the misuse, of alcohol (and drugs) has been seized upon by many as an important factor in crime causation. Members of the medical profession, especially, have observed the physiological effects of alcohol upon the human system, and in turn have had their attention directed to its various manifestations, direct and indirect, in human behavior. Judges and lawyers also have been cognizant of the effects of alcohol on the actions of man and have been obliged to judge of these effects not physiologically but as they were evidenced in action. Both medicine and law have held that drunkenness was no excuse for crime. Their disagreement occurred in courts of law over the question of the mental state of the defendant. Traditionally, the physician has testified that where the use of alcohol has so affected an individual as to produce a diseased state of the mind, that person was not responsible for his actions. This rested upon the same premise as did exculpation on the grounds of insanity; indeed, it was the same premise—that the individual was not possessed of a mind capable of forming a criminal intent. When medicine and law could agree in a given case upon the diseased state of mind of the defendant, then there was no legal responsibility and the defendant was a candidate for the insane asylum or mental hospital. When, on the other hand, judge and jury held that the defendant was not a victim of a mental disease, but legally responsible, commitment to prison inevitably followed. In neither instance could medicine and law consent to the freeing of such individuals, being joined in their conviction that they were too great a menace to be at large in society. Much of the discussion which follows shall be on this question of the mental condition of the user of alcohol. The nub shall be: Did the use of alcohol (and drugs) produce a mental disease which in turn activated the individual to the commission of crime?

Among the first to recognize and distinguish the states of mind produced by alcohol was Benjamin Rush, preëminent American physician, teacher, and student of mental diseases, concerning whom D. Meredith Reese wrote in 1858:

That distinguished philosopher and philanthropist, Dr. Benjamin Rush, before the commencement of the present century, seems to have been the first to recognize that form of insanity, since called *dipsomania*, and, indeed, he preceded Pinel himself, in pleading for habitual drunkards, by ascribing their follies and crimes to *moral insanity*, which he defined as "derangement of the moral faculty, or morbid operations of the will." Hence, to rescue such from the penalties of the criminal law, he urged the opening of hospitals, or sober houses, for their physical restraint and moral treatment, alleging that they were as fit subjects for such sympathy, as other mad people. He declared all such to be monomaniacs, the victims of physical disease, which he, with philosophical accuracy, located in the brain. He taught that, although their drinking habits were the fruit of moral depravity at first, yet, after the brain itself had become diseased by this vice of indulgence, their continued drinking was the result of insanity.[1]

Reese's remarks were undoubtedly based on "An Inquiry into the Effects of Spirituous Liquors upon the Human Body, and Their Influence upon the Happiness of Society," first published by Rush in 1793. In this essay, Rush spoke of the use of liquors as causing men to violate promises and engagements, to be deficient in veracity and integrity, and finally to plunge them into crimes of a more heinous nature. Spirituous liquors, he claimed, filled our churchyards with premature graves, deranged and destroyed the intellectual powers, filled the sheriff's docket with executions, crowded hospitals with patients and jails with criminals.[2] In his revision of 1805 he noted the destructive effects of ardent spirits upon the mind, for he declared that they impaired the memory, debilitated the understanding, and perverted

---

[1] D. Meredith Reese, *op. cit.*, p. 730.

[2] Benjamin Rush, "An Inquiry into the Effects of Spirituous Liquors upon the Human Body, and Their Influence upon the Happiness of Society," *Medical Inquiries and Observations*, Philadelphia, II (1793) 57-82.

the moral faculties.[3] Finally, in his pioneer work on *Diseases of the Mind*, published in 1812, a year before his death, Rush reiterated that insanity may be induced by the excessive use of ardent spirits, culminating in a partial derangement of the moral faculties.[4]

Charles Caldwell, once a pupil, then a friend, and finally an antagonist of Rush, who had helped to organize the medical department of Transylvania University in Kentucky, shared his master's views when he declared, in 1832, that the drunkard was as truly a monomaniac as the one who was sound in other conceptions yet believed his feet and legs were made of glass or butter or his head of copper. Such a person could no more resist the propensity to drink than the other monomaniacs could dissolve the hallucinations that beset them. The more general and inveterate condition Caldwell called *mania a potu*.[5] Similarly Isaac Ray, in his *Medical Jurisprudence of Insanity*, published in 1838, recognized *mania a potu* (or delirium tremens), noting at the same time the effect of long continued use of alcoholic liquors upon the moral and intellectual powers. Of such a victim Ray observed that the moral powers were blunted, the great moral interests no longer kept hold on him, and the finer emotions deserted his nature. The victim also suffered hallucinations.

Under the influence of these terrible apprehensions, he sometimes murders his wife or attendant, whom his disordered imagination identifies with his enemies, though he is generally tractable and not inclined to be mischievous. After perpetrating an act of this kind, he generally gives some illusive reason for his conduct, rejoices in his success, and expresses his regret at not having done it before. So complete and obvious is the mental derangement in this disease, so entirely are the thoughts and actions governed by the most unfounded

[3] Benjamin Rush, "An Inquiry into the Effects of Ardent Spirit upon the Human Body and Mind with an Account of the Means of Preventing and of the Remedies for Curing Them," *Medical Inquiries and Observations*," Second Edition, Philadelphia, 1805, I, 335-371.

[4] Benjamin Rush, *Medical Inquiries and Observations upon the Diseases of the Mind*, Philadelphia, 1812.

[5] Charles Caldwell, "Thoughts on the Pathology, Prevention and Treatment of Intemperance, as a Form of Mental Derangement," *Transylvania Journal of Medicine and Associate Sciences*, V (July-September 1832) 309-350.

and absurd delusions, that if any form of insanity absolves from criminal responsibility, this certainly must have that effect.[6]

Indeed, Ray agreed with Rush that *mania a potu* was related to moral mania, particularly in view of its periodicity and uncontrollable and irresistible impulse. He cited examples from Esquirol depicting its irresistible and paroxysmal character.[7]

Amariah Brigham, superintendent of the New York State Lunatic Asylum at Utica, six years later, denied the plea of insanity to a person committing crime during voluntary intoxication, although he did accept the doctrine of irresponsibility in connection with crimes committed during *delirium tremens*.[8] His successor as superintendent and as editor of the *American Journal of Insanity*, John P. Gray, in 1857, was far less willing to grant the defense of drunkenness or dipsomania.[9] In his analysis of fifty-two cases of homicide in insanity he found but one instance of *mania a potu*.[10] In a case where the plea of dipsomania was interposed, Gray denied any evidence of insanity, declaring that even were dipsomania present he would not admit it as a disease. To him it was intemperance, not insanity.[11] During the next twenty years Gray had carried his earlier analysis of cases further, so that he then had fifty-eight homicides by insane men. One of these fifty-eight, as formerly, was a victim of *mania a potu*

[6] Isaac Ray, *Treatise on the Medical Jurisprudence of Insanity*, Boston, 1838, pp. 418-419.

[7] *Ibid.*, pp. 422-427.

[8] Amariah Brigham, "Definition of Insanity—Nature of the Disease," *American Journal of Insanity*, I (October 1844) 108-109.

[9] It will be apparent throughout this discussion that the moral sentiments of the writers often prevented them from exercising a scientific detachment. Thus Brigham, like many others, could not excuse the criminal acts of a man voluntarily intoxicated (no matter what the state of mind) although he could excuse the same acts if committed in a state of delirium tremens which might have been immediately precipitated by involuntary intoxication, but which condition resulted from a sustained period of voluntary intoxication. A doctrine of free will was reconcilable with insanity, but not with voluntary intoxication. No doubt much of the controversy over moral insanity centered around the question of free will. Certainly John P. Gray was a stout defender of man's free will choice, and a strong opponent of moral insanity.

[10] John P. Gray, "Homicide in Insanity," *American Journal of Insanity*, XIV (October 1857) 119-145.

[11] "Drunkenness and Crime," *American Journal of Insanity*, XXIV (April 1868) 489-491.

who had committed crime during a paroxysm of which he had no recollection. Other cases of delirium tremens Gray would not class as insanity, maintaining that one alleged lunatic feigned dementia after recovery, another was merely drunk, while all others were not insane.[12] D. Meredith Reese was just as opposed as Gray to moral insanity, and while he recognized that Rush might regard dipsomania as a form of moral insanity yet he, Reese, insisted that moral insanity was primarily a physical and secondarily an intellectual insanity. He distinguished between the delirium of recent intoxication which furnished no excuse to crime, and the insanity which accompanied a paroxysm of delirium tremens which both law and medicine regarded as a legitimate defense.[13]

"Oinomania" was the term used by George Cornell to describe what others called dipsomania. On Rush's authority he classed oinomania with moral insanity.[14] Others, Stephen Rogers,[15] C. B. Gilbert,[16] and James O'Dea,[17] used "methomania" to describe the insane condition involved in the irresistible desire to drink, although Gilbert had doubts of the existence of delusions and hallucinations. Rogers observed paroxysms and insane delusions with a liability to the commission of crime, while O'Dea (whose article was presented in 1868), regarded methomania as an adequate defense for crime. D. A. Morse, professor of nervous diseases and insanity at the Starling Medical College at Columbus, Ohio, shared with Gilbert, who held the chair of materia medica and therapeutics at the Detroit Medical College, the opinion that dipsomania (Gilbert thought methomania a misnomer) was not an insanity, on the ground that delusions, illusions, or hallucinations were absent.[18]

[12] John P. Gray, "Responsibility of the Insane—Homicide in Insanity," *American Journal of Insanity*, XXXII (July, October 1875) 1-57, 153-183.

[13] D. Meredith Reese, *op. cit.*, pp. 721-746.

[14] George Cornell, "Oinomania," *Cincinnati Lancet and Observer*, VI (March 1863) 156-159.

[15] Stephen Rogers,. "The Influence of Methomania upon Business and Criminal Responsibility," *Quarterly Journal of Psychological Medicine*, III (April 1869) 323-350.

[16] C. B. Gilbert, "Methomania," *Detroit Review of Medicine and Pharmacy*, VIII (June 1873) 248-257.

[17] James J. O'Dea, "Methomania," in *Medical Jurisprudence of Inebriety*, published by the Medico-Legal Journal Association, 1888, pp. 166-183.

Widespread opinion during this period of the seventies held that dipsomania (dipsomania and delirium tremens were used synonymously) was a form of insanity and hence a sufficient defense for crime. Paluel De Marmon,[19] Swan M. Burnett,[20] and I. D. Thomson, junior physician to the Mt. Hope Retreat and Insane Asylum,[20a] took this position. The latter classed it as one of the forms of moral insanity along with pyromania, erotomania, kleptomania, homicidal mania, and the like. All of these conditions had in common the fact that while the intellect recognized the wrong of the act to be committed and the patient would gladly avoid the act if he could, yet his volition was too feeble to resist the overwhelming influence of the impelling power.

In the whole field of the study of the inebriate and insanity, and the inebriate and crime, no one occupies a more prominent place than Thomas Davidson Crothers.[21] From the time of his first article in 1879 on the inebriate criminal, until 1914 when he wrote on the physical character of the crimes of the alcoholic, Crothers had been fighting to have the inebriate with an insane diathesis regarded in both law and medicine as an insane person. The usual type of inebriate criminal he felt to be a product very

---

[18] D. A. Morse, "Dipsomania and Drunkenness," *Transactions of the Twenty-Eighth Annual Meeting of the Ohio State Medical Society*, XXVIII (1873) 137-188.

[19] Paluel De Marmon, "Medico-Legal Considerations upon Alcoholism and the Moral and Criminal Responsibility of Inebriates," *Medical World*, I (December 1871) 201-223.

[20] Swan M. Burnett, "Dipsomania," *Transactions of the Tennessee Medical Society*, XIII (1875) 66-70.

[20a] I. D. Thomson, "Dipsomania, as Distinguished from Ordinary Drunkenness," *Transactions of the Medical and Chirurgical Faculty of the State of Maryland*, LXXXI (1879) 156-171.

[21] T. D. Crothers (1842-1918) received his medical training at Albany Medical College, after which he engaged in the practice of medicine until his appointment in 1874 as assistant physician to the New York State Inebriate Asylum at Binghamton. In 1876 he became superintendent of the Walnut Hill Asylum in Hartford, Connecticut, but when that institution closed from lack of State funds he organized the Walnut Lodge Hospital in Hartford, for the treatment of those addicted to the intemperate use of alcohol and opiates, and was for many years its superintendent. In 1887 he was one of the American delegates to the London International Congress for the Study of Inebriety. From 1876 until his death in 1918 he was editor of the *Journal of Inebriety*, the organ of the American Association for the Study and Cure of Inebriety. For many years he was secretary of the association. In 1908 he was professor of mental and nervous diseases and dean of the College of Physicians and Surgeons in Boston. He was president of the New York Medico-Legal Society in 1912.

largely of surroundings and accident, but he recognized a second
type that always exhibited early signs of physical degeneration
of the brain and nerve centers. This type was the born criminal
or inebriate, in which the criminal and insane diathesis was always
present.[22] Identifying the periodical inebriate possessed of delusions and hallucinations and evidencing impulses to kill, he insisted upon the fundamental insanity of this kind of person.[23] In
1889 he wrote:

If the drink craze was sudden, impetuous, and overwhelming, at its
onset, associated with delirium and often delusions, it is called dipsomania, a distinct form of insanity and irresponsibility. The victim is
controlled by a maniacal impulse, and is without clear conception or
control of his acts. He has a form of epilepsy and circular insanity
that cannot be mistaken. . . . If the act was done in the paroxysmal
stage of periodical inebriety or dipsomania there is strong probability
of insanity and irresponsibility.[24]

In a murder case which he reported, Crothers claimed the defendant's act was a natural sequence of his mental condition;
alcohol had added to the latent degeneration, thereby incapacitat-
ing the brain and impeding normal function.[25] In other criminal
offenses he recognized alcoholic trance, following which the
offender had no recollection of the nature of the acts he had
committed.[26] In pleading, as did Rush many years before, for
the inebriate hospitals to take the place of jails and prisons,
Crothers reaffirmed his own classification of 1879, dwelling
particularly upon the class of inebriates exhibiting criminal and
insane diathesis: "Such persons possess a distinct neurosis, which

[22] T. D. Crothers, "Inebriate Criminals," *Quarterly Journal of Inebriety*, III (June
1879) 129-146.
[23] T. D. Crothers, "A Case of Inebriety with Criminal Impulses," *Medical Record*,
XXIV (October 27, 1883) 457-459; also "Mania and Inebriety," *Medical Record*,
XXXII (September, 24, 1887) 421-422.
[24] T. D. Crothers, "The Question of Responsibility in Inebriety," *Alienist and
Neurologist*, X (January 1889) 47.
[25] T. D. Crothers, "Medico-Legal Problems of Inebriety," *Alienist and Neurologist*,
X (October 1889) 522-534.
[26] T. D. Crothers, "Alcoholic Trance in Criminal Cases," *Journal of the American
Medical Association*, XIV (April 5, 1890) 502-505; also "Some New Medico-Legal
Questions Relating to Inebriety," *Alienist and Neurologist*, XI (October 1890) 555-565.

manifests itself either in inebriety, insanity, epilepsy, criminality or pauperism; or, very commonly, two or more combined in one."[27]

In his book published in 1893, Crothers distinguished between inebriety and dipsomania, the latter term being used "to designate a large class of inebriates, in which the drink impulse comes on suddenly and after a time dies out, and is succeeded by a free interval. This has been truly termed a neurosis, which is practically another branch of the same family of epileptics."[28] The three forms of inebriety Crothers classed as the acute, the periodic, and the chronic, each of which was characterized by the complete absence of the moral nature. As to legal responsibility, he observed that the dipsomaniac may be irresponsible because of the imbecility of the will which so readily yields to the demands of the neurotic constitution. "All the laws and penalties which a State can enact against crime committed by the dipsomaniac will never prevent him, while at large, from committing murder, arson, or theft, or from taking his own life."[29] Here again Crothers was fighting the battle to have his own profession, as well as the law, recognize the likeness of dipsomania and insanity, for he remarked with reference to the law:

If I understand its meaning, the law discriminates between common drunkenness and dipsomania, but fails to recognize the likeness between dipsomania and insanity, or, in other words, it does not see a similarity between insanity from drink and insanity from other causes, though the manifestations may be similar. It assumes that the dipsomaniac is a voluntary *demon* or drunkard, and if he will, he may avoid the paroxysms that characterize the disease.[30]

Concerning crimes committed during a trance, Crothers observed that they may be either the acts of the epileptic or the

---

[27] T. D. Crothers, "Some Studies of Inebriate and Pauper Criminals," in *The Prevention and Repression of Crime, Being a Report of the Fifth Section of the International Congress of Charities, Correction and Philanthropy*, Chicago, June 1893, edited by Frederick H. Wines, 1894, pp. 10-27.

[28] T. D. Crothers, *The Disease of Inebriety*, New York, 1893, p. 29.

[29] *Ibid.*, p. 269.

[30] *Ibid.*, pp. 270-271.

alcoholic. If the latter, they may be the acts of the alcoholic dement, the sudden inebriate, the moral paralytic who drinks to excess, or the dipsomaniac and periodical inebriate. This was but the repetition of his argument published in 1890.

In an editorial in the *Quarterly Journal of Inebriety*, Crothers wrote specifically on the relation of inebriety to crime when he stated:

These defects are the essential factors of criminality. The senses send false impressions to the brain and the brain is unable to correct them, hence false thoughts, false acts, and abnormal conduct. Criminal acts come from inability to understand the relation of surroundings, and to adjust the conduct to the varying conditions of life. The criminal acts of the inebriate spring from this confusion of senses and judgment. Acts are misinterpreted, motives are ascribed to conduct that have no reasonable basis. Illusions and delusions come and go with increasing frequency, and finally become settled conceptions that are systematized and cannot be corrected. Delusions of sexual wrongs lead up to assaults and homicide; delusions of persecutions have the same ending; delusions of strength bring on reckless conduct and insane acts, together with unreasoning credulity and equally strange suspicion and want of confidence. Nearly all the crimes committed by inebriates are assaults against persons and delusions of ability to understand and act in relation to business and ethics along unusual lines of conduct. Such persons forge notes, misappropriate moneys, engage in dishonest transactions of every form, sustained by the delusion of superior skill to conceal it and ability to avoid legal consequences.[31]

In line with this was Crothers' strong conviction that since alcohol palsied the brain and made these offenders madmen, they were incapacitated to act sanely and hence could not be held legally responsible.[32]

In Crothers' second book on inebriety, published in 1911 (largely a restatement of his first book of 1893) he still regarded the disorder as a form of moral insanity, claiming that

---

[31] "Relation of Inebriety to Criminality," *Quarterly Journal of Inebriety*, XV (January 1893) 86.

[32] T. D. Crothers, "Should Inebriates Be Punished by Death for Crime?" *Charlotte Medical Journal*, VII (November 1895) 542-547.

alcohol first attacked the "moral" brain, and by cutting off some part of the higher brain, reduced the operation of the lower brain to the animal level.

The oft repeated statement that "inebriety is criminality," is true in a general sense, when criminality is understood as a course of conduct in which duty, right, and obligations to others are ignored. The inebriate has physically defective senses; he is not able to adjust himself to the outside world correctly, because his knowledge of its relations is imperfect. His power of reasoning is also deranged, because the impressions from without are faulty and the integrity of the normal action of the nervous system is impaired.[33]

Continuing in the same vein he added:

The coarser physical lesions in the inebriate are well recognized and can be traced in all cases. Beyond these, conduct indicates the higher moral defects and changes. Mental changes, as loss of pride, of character, or honor, respect for truth, of duty to others, low motives or no motives, extreme pessimism, are the first and common changes wrought by alcohol which lead up to criminal acts.[34]

Crothers' battle with the law to have the acts of the periodical inebriate accepted as stemming from the mind of an insane man had achieved little success by 1911, evidence of which may be found in his chapter entitled "Criminal Inebriates and Medico-Legal Superstitions." "Dipsomania" had well nigh dropped out of his vocabulary, being replaced by "periodical inebriate." Returning to his theme he remarked that all crime committed by inebriates and persons under the influence of spirits was the result of brain defects, brain unsoundness and weakness, and marked by illusions and hallucinations. This position was maintained in 1914, as indicated by his paper on the physical character of crimes of the alcoholic.[35]

As late as 1881 medical men like Theodore W. Fisher were still affirming the doctrine of Rush and Ray that dipsomania was a moral monomania of the same class as kleptomania or homicidal

[33] T. D. Crothers, *Inebriety*, Cincinnati, 1911, pp. 97-98.
[34] *Ibid.*, p. 98.
[35] T. D. Crothers, "The Physical Character of Crimes of the Alcoholic," *Bulletin of the American Academy of Medicine*, XV (February 1914) 33-40.

mania.[36] Edward C. Mann, too, held dipsomania to be a form of moral insanity, in which, while the person was aware that the act about to be committed was wrong, the control which the intellect exercised over the moral sense was overborne by the superior force derived from the disease.[37] The irresistible force of dipsomania was such that during the paroxysm the patient remained blind to all the higher emotions and pursued a course against which reason and conscience alike rebelled. There was a strong tendency to the commission of criminal acts which frequently was observed during trance states when the criminal impulse dominated the mind and actions. Mann was convinced that dipsomania was a valid form of mental disease—drunkenness being but one of its symptoms.[38]

Preferring the term "chronic alcoholic insanity," Edward C. Spitzka recognized the existence of a well-developed psychosis characterized by delusions and hallucinations under the influence of which crimes, often of a brutal nature, were committed.[39] Dipsomania he included in the category of the periodical insanities.

Rather than define dipsomania as an overpowering urge for intoxicating liquors, Thomas Lee Wright—another prolific writer in this field—maintained in 1885 that its essence was the overpowering desire for intoxication.[40] The effect of this was the depravity or total destruction of the moral nature. In addition to endorsing Crothers' position on the trance state in crimes of the alcoholic Wright insisted upon the delusional and hallucinatory nature of dipsomania, declaring it to be a true insanity and a valid defense in criminal actions.[41]

[36] Theodore W. Fisher, "Insane Drunkards," *Medical Communications of the Massachusetts Medical Society*, XII (1881) 315-335.

[37] Edward C. Mann, *Manual of Psychological Medicine, and Allied Nervous Diseases*, New York, 1883, p. 358.

[38] Edward C. Mann, "The Relation which Dipsomania Bears to Forensic Medicine," *Chicago Medical Journal and Examiner*, LIII (September 1886) 207-211.

[39] Edward C. Spitzka, *op. cit.*, p. 253.

[40] T. L. Wright, *Inebriism*, Columbus, 1885, p. 43.

[41] T. L. Wright, "The Inability to Discriminate Between Right and Wrong Disguised by Automatism," *Medical Record*, XXIV (July 14, 1883) 31-34; T. L. Wright, "The Disabilities of Inebriety—An Inquiry Respecting the Nature of Drunkenness, and of Its Responsibilities," *Journal of the American Medical Association*, XIV (March 8,

Needless to say, a problem of paramount importance in the relation of alcohol to crime lay in the determination of the responsibility of the offender. Thus Charles H. Hughes, in treating of the status of the inebriate in the courts, held that alcohol entailed disease of the brain as certainly as it vitiated morals and fostered vice.[42] Likewise Joseph Parrish, one of the leading students of inebriety in America in the late nineteenth century, who denied the causal relation between drunkenness and crime *except* by way of disease, said in 1889 that alcoholic inebriety was a disease which affected the nervous system chiefly, and in which the victim was controlled by an impulse beyond the reach of the human will. The criminal act was usually committed in a state of unconsciousness, and in a condition of irresponsibility.[43] Thomas B. Evans, the chairman of the section on medical jurisprudence of the American Medical Association, believed dipsomania to be a physical, corporeal disease, and in common with all forms of insanity, it was an extenuating factor in the commission of criminal activities.[44] The criminal inebriate, said L. D. Mason, consulting physician to the Inebriates Home, Fort Hamilton, Long Island, New York, should be dealt with like the criminal insane, criminal inebriety being a condition of monomania.[45] There was no crime in the calendar, he asserted, that the alcoholic maniac may not commit; his reason was temporarily dethroned, he was unconscious not only of the character of his acts, but of the acts themselves, and was therefore irresponsible. After

---

1890) 332-336; T. L. Wright, "Drunkenness and Its Criminal Responsibilities," *Quarterly Journal of Inebriety*, XII (October 1890) 345-351; T. L. Wright, "Observations on the Criminal Status of Inebriety," *Alienist and Neurologist*, XII (January 1891) 1-18; T. L. Wright, "The Equitable Responsibility of Inebriety," *Journal of Nervous and Mental Disease*, XVII (December 1892) 867-879.

[42] Charles H. Hughes, "The Status Ebrietatus in Our Courts," *Medico-Legal Journal*, V (1887-1888) 311-315.

[43] Joseph Parrish, "The Legal Responsibility of Inebriates," *Polyclinic*, VI (January 1889) 206-209.

[44] Thomas B. Evans, "The Responsibility of Dipsomaniacs," *Journal of the American Medical Association*, XIV (June 7, 1890) 809-812; also *Quarterly Journal of Inebriety*, XII (July 1890) 253-261.

[45] L. D. Mason, "The Absence of Reasonable Motive in the So-Called 'Criminal Acts' of the Confirmed Inebriate," *Journal of the American Medical Association*, XVII (November 21, 1891) 799-803.

remarking that the crimes of inebriety were seldom those of premeditation, malevolent reasoning, or of choice, William H.
Palmer added: "They are often unaccountable, are not excited by
natural or intelligible motives. They are the outcome of defect, of
incapacity, of an impulse called irresistible, because no inhibitory
or resistant force reacts against it."[46] On one of those rare occasions when a jurist permitted himself to write for a medical magazine, Martin A. Foran of the Cleveland Bench held that dipsomania, being a form of insanity, should be recognized as an
adequate plea in defense.[47] In a case where the defense of dipsomania was made successfully, James G. Kiernan remarked upon
the sufficiency of the plea and upon the fact that dipsomania was
a form of mental disease.[48] The classification of inebriates by
Charles L. Dana, an eminent neurologist, into the periodical inebriate, the pseudo-inebriate, the common drunkard, and the
victim of *mania a potu*[49] was subscribed to by Eugene S. Talbot
in his work on degeneracy, who considered dipsomania as one
of the periodical insanities—a periodical expression of degeneracy.[50] J. Sanderson Christison, who had been an assistant
physician at the New York City Lunatic Asylum, the Bellevue
Hospital, and the Wisconsin State Hospital for the Insane, maintained in his book on crime and criminals that inebriety was
frequently the cause of crimes of which the subject may not be
conscious. The condition of the mind on such occasions resembled
what was encountered in insanity or hypnosis, a condition suggesting the trance state mentioned by Crothers and other writers.
As in epilepsy, the alcoholic irritation seemed to involve the
higher centers of the brain, rather than the lower centers and
the spinal cord.[51] W. Duncan McKim agreed with Talbot as to

[46] William H. Parker, "Medico-Legal Status of Inebriety," *International Medical Magazine*, I (December 1892) 1175.

[47] Hon. Martin A. Foran, "Alcohol as a Defense for Crime," *Cleveland Medical Gazette*, XI (December 1895) 65-73.

[48] James G. Kiernan, "Dipsomania as a Defense for Crime," *Medicine*, II (July 1896) 563-569.

[49] Charles L. Dana, "Alcoholism in New York and the Classification of Inebriates," *American Journal of Insanity*, L (July 1893) 29-33.

[50] Eugene E. Talbot, *op. cit.*

[51] J. Sanderson Christison, *Crime and Criminals*, Chicago, 1899, pp. 25-26.

the degenerate character of the inebriate, holding dipsomania to be a form of insanity,[52] an opinion shared by Heinrich Stern.[53] Writing on the same subject, P. M. Lightfoot found the alcoholic possessed of delusions and hallucinations, and unable to distinguish between right and wrong.[54]

"Practically, then, inebriety means degeneracy, the subject being usually primarily defective in nervous structure and will power," said Lydston in his study of crime, in 1904.[55] Aside from physical degeneracy, he maintained, no cause is more potent in criminal behavior than inebriety, by reason of the disequilibrium in the nervous system which it produces. "Theft, murder, suicide, assault, sexual crime, indecency, sexual perversion—any or several of these may accrue from the action of alcohol on the nervous centers."[56] As for the true dipsomaniac, Lydston held him invariably to have criminal tendencies that might develop at any time; his criminality being of an explosive type, it was as likely to erupt as an epileptic seizure.[57]

Recognizing dipsomania as a valid defense for crime, Charles K. Mills, a celebrated neurologist, alienist, and teacher, in 1905 restricted its meaning to a form of impulsive insanity possessing an hereditary base (as did the Frenchman, Magnan, whom Mills followed). The true dipsomaniac was a neuropathic individual with an inherited insufficiency, who became a victim of obsessions and morbid impulses. At any time he was likely to commit homicide, theft, arson, sexual perversion, and assaults. The alcoholic somnambulist was given to stealing and killing; the alcoholic melancholic to suicide and murder; the alcoholic maniac to assaults and murder, and the victim of delirium tremens to assaults and murder.[58] Alfred Gordon, associate in nervous and mental

[52] W. Duncan McKim, *Heredity and Human Progress*, New York, 1901.

[53] Heinrich Stern, "Alcoholism and Crime—How We Should Deal with the Criminal Alcoholic," *Quarterly Journal of Inebriety*, XXIV (April 1902) 148-152.

[54] P. M. Lightfoot, "Alcoholism and Crime," *Quarterly Journal of Inebriety*, XXV (April 1903) 159-163.

[55] G. Frank Lydston, *The Diseases of Society*, Philadelphia, 1904, p. 200.

[56] *Ibid.*, p. 201.

[57] G. Frank Lydston, "Inebriety in Its Relations to Crime," *Journal of Inebriety*, XXX (Autumn 1908) 166-173.

[58] Charles K. Mills, "Some Forms of Insanity Due to Alcohol. Especially in Their Medico-Legal Relations," *American Medicine*, IX (February 11, 1905) 223-227.

diseases in Jefferson Medical College, Philadelphia, recognized acute and chronic alcoholism, with dipsomania as a variety of the chronic and characterized by paroxysmal imperative desires for alcohol. Being a constitutional disease there was no legal responsibility for criminal acts.[59]

To some, the chronic alcoholic was the most dangerous class of criminal, as for instance James May, medical member of the New York State Hospital Commission, who declared in 1912 that they often escape detection because they frequently show little amnesia or disorientation and learn to conceal their delusions. Their delusions were those of suspicion, infidelity, persecution, and electricity, and were very likely to eventuate in homicide, assault, and arson.[60] If crime was not the result of a physical defect, to what was it due? asked Edward Wallace Lee. In answer to his own question he declared that any pathological condition might be the exciting cause of a psychic neurosis that would lead to a disturbed physical change resulting in mental deterioration and acts of crime. Alcohol was the most potent factor in physical and mental degeneration and, by inference, in the production of crime.[61] Paul E. Bowers thought the dipsomaniac to be always a neurotic whose defects of the brain and central nervous system produced an insatiable, uncontrollable craving for alcoholic stimulants. In his discussion of alcoholic insanity and its rôle in criminal behavior, Bowers took account of the amnesia accompanying somnambulism, and stated that during these apparent dream states every conceivable crime may be committed. In delirium tremens the victim's delusions may drive him to murder, and often to suicide. The mental state of the chronic alcoholic is conducive to crime, for the moral sense is perverted, the will power is practically inert, and the individual becomes the abject slave of his own passions. His crimes may

---

[59] Alfred Gordon,. "Mental Responsibility in Acute and Chronic Intoxication with Alcohol and Other Drugs," *Old Dominion Journal of Medicine and Surgery*, VIII (May 1909) 305-316.

[60] James V. May, "Mental Diseases and Criminal Responsibility," *State Hospitals Bulletin*, V, n.s. (November 15, 1912) 339-371.

[61] Edward Wallace Lee, "Physical Defects as a Factor in the Cause of Crime," *New York Medical Journal*, C, (December 26, 1914), 1246-1251.

be those of petty thefts, larcency, forgery, rape, incest, sodomy, assaults, and homicides. The crimes of those suffering from alcoholic hallucinosis are likely to be homicide and homicidal attempts.[62]

Separate from those writers who described the direct connection between alcohol and crime, essentially through the channel of insanity, were those who dealt with the hereditary effects of alcohol. It is a familiar theme: alcoholism in the parent; crime, pauperism, and disease in the offspring. In a book published in 1872 on what he described as the dangerous classes of New York, Charles Loring Brace, a pioneer in the founding of the Children's Aid Society of New York in 1853, wrote that the indulgence of certain appetites (and he meant particularly the appetite for liquor) for two or more generations cultivated their strength until they came to exert an almost irresistible force which modified the brain and produced aberrational conduct.[63] The inebriate criminal, T. D. Crothers maintained in 1879, inherited an unbalanced organism, with a family history of insanity, epilepsy, inebriety, criminality, etc.[64] Four years later, after quoting William G. Stevenson on heredity and crime, he argued that the inebriety of the inebriate pauper was of the same order of neurosis as insanity, and depended upon some molecular change of nerve tissues, which, coming down from parent to child, fixed the moral and physical character of the child.[65] It may be recalled that in the discussion of the direct effects of alcohol upon crime it was observed that Joseph Parrish tended to minimize the rôle of inebriety as a direct causal factor in crime. He did, however, incline towards the acceptance of the doctrine of defective inheritance from alcoholic, insane, or epileptic parents. Indeed,

[62] Paul E. Bowers, *op. cit.*, pp. 69-75.
[63] Charles Loring Brace, *The Dangerous Classes of New York*, New York, 1872, p. 43.
[64] T. D. Crothers, "Inebriate Criminals," *Quarterly Journal of Inebriety*, III (June 1879) 136.
[65] T. D. Crothers, "Some Studies of Inebriate and Pauper Criminals," *The Prevention and Repression of Crime*, International Congress of Charities, Correction, and Philanthropy, 1893, p. 11.

Parrish insisted, there was a like inheritance of physical characters in criminals, lunatics, and dipsomaniacs.[66] Edward C. Mann
said that as a result of intemperance in the progenitors there
was transmitted to the offspring various forms of the neuroses,
which included dipsomania, epilepsy, chorea, insanity, or a proclivity to crime.[67] The inebriate whose actions culminated in terrible criminality was surely a victim of his ancestral nervous organization, according to J. S. Wight, professor of operative and
clinical surgery at the Long Island College Hospital and a member of the New York Neurological Society.[68] Insanity, inebriety,
and crime, these three, said Stevenson, were the results of
pathological conditions of nerve tissue. He introduced the notion
of "gemmules" (did not Charles Darwin also speak of gemmules
as a technique of hereditary transmission?) and maintained that
when they were transmitted they became active agents in the
formation of character.[69] The inebriate transmitted vices biologically which then found expression in the collateral degeneracies
of idiocy, lunacy, prostitution, and criminality, stated Hamilton
D. Wey, physician to the Elmira Reformatory, in his studies of
offenders in Elmira Reformatory.[70] George E. Dawson, fellow in
psychology at Clark University, confirmed this on the basis of his
study of juvenile delinquents in Massachusetts.[71] Similarly,
Henry E. Allison in 1896, in the light of his work with the
criminal insane, believed that insanity, epilepsy, and intemperance in the parents produced prenatal conditions whereby degenerative characters were fixed upon the offspring.[72] Crime in

[66] Joseph Parrish, *Alcohol Inebriety*, Philadelphia, 1883, p. 37.

[67] Edward C. Mann, *A Manual of Psychological Medicine, and Allied Nervous
Diseases*, Philadelphia, 1883, p. 356.

[68] J. S. Wight, "Plea for the Treatment of Criminals," *American Journal of
Neurology and Psychiatry*, II and III, (1884-1885) 128-140.

[69] William G. Stevenson, "Criminality," *Medico-Legal Journal*, V (1887-1888)
158-179, 257-282.

[70] *Seventeenth Year Book*, New York State Reformatory at Elmira, 1893, pp. 43-44;
Eighteenth Year Book, 1894, pp. 153-154.

[71] George E. Dawson, "A Study of Youthful Degeneracy," *Pedagogical Seminary*,
IV (December 1896) 249-253.

[72] Henry E. Allison, "Some Relations of Crime to Insanity and States of Mental Enfeeblement," *Journal of the American Medical Association*, XXVII (September 19,
1896) 646-647.

one of its medical aspects, he continued, might be regarded as in part the product of degeneracy caused by a bad and intemperate heredity operating in a bad environment. After considering the claims of environment as a productive agent in criminal behavior, Willis S. Anderson declared heredity to be the potent factor. He meant not that the parents have been actual criminals in a legal sense, but that the inebriate, the epileptic, the insane, the morally depraved, begat children who were deficient morally and who were prone to drift into criminal life without regard to environment.[73] Daniel R. Brower, professor of mental and nervous diseases at Rush Medical College, concurred in this when he held that the alcoholic, the narcotic, the epileptic, the neurotic, the hysteric, transmitted an unstable, irritable nervous system which diminished the power of inhibition.[74] According to Thomas Bassett Keyes, professor of suggestive therapeutics at the Harvey Medical College, Chicago, the greatest criminals were not the greatest drunkards, but in the majority of cases it would be found that they were the offspring of intemperate parents who sowed the seeds of crime by producing stock which was morally and physically degenerate.[75] Adopting the "born criminal" of Lombroso, M. P. E. Groszmann claimed that intemperate parentage played a fatal rôle in the production of the criminal neurosis.[76] Still another who asserted the degenerative effect of alcoholic parentage as shown by their debilitated, vicious, and criminal stock was August Drähms.[77] So held Louise G. Robinovitch, whose formula was: alcoholism in parents, crime in children.[78] Commenting upon the large percentage of cases in which parents were intemperate, S. Bloch in 1910 emphasized the likelihood of

[73] Willis S. Anderson, "The Study of Crime and Degeneration from a Medical Standpoint," *Transactions of the Michigan State Medical Society*, XX (1896) 363.

[74] Daniel R. Brower, "The Etiology and Treatment of Criminality," *Medico-Legal Journal*, XV (1897-1898) 361.

[75] Thomas Bassett Keyes, "Criminality and Degeneracy; Its Treatment by Surgery and Hypnotism," *Medico-Legal Journal*, XV (1897-1898) 369.

[76] M. P. E. Groszmann, "Criminality in Children," *Arena*, XXII (October 1899) 511-513.

[77] August Drähms, *op. cit.*, pp. 133-135, 180-187.

[78] Louise G. Robinovitch, "The Relation of Criminality in the Offspring to Alcoholism in the Parents," *Medico-Legal Journal*, XVIII (1900-1901) 341-351.

these begetting defective offspring such as epileptics, sexual perverts, idiots, and criminals.[79] Bernard Glueck cited a case (one of many in his study of the juvenile offender) which seemed to show the relation of alcoholism and habitual criminality. Glueck speculated on the basis of this case as to whether excessive use of alcohol should be considered a cause of the offender's degeneracy or its result. The entailment was hereditary, thought Glueck, because the father was a chronic alcoholic, the mother a neurotic, the maternal aunt insane, and an uncle a suicide.[80] While G. Milton Linthicum was concerned over the direct effects of alcohol in crime causation he was also aware of the rôle of alcoholic heredity, for he claimed that much of the degeneracy and crime in offspring derived from the alcoholism of the parent.

To prevent crime is to eliminate the criminal. To eliminate the criminal is to prevent his birth. To prevent his birth is to use every available means to have procreated normal brains. Normal brains are the offspring of normal fathers and mothers. While all crime, all immorality, all delinquency, are not the products of inebriety, it is the predominant factor and the one which if attacked will yield the greatest results.[81]

DRUGS

Drugs have been classed by many writers as narcotics along with alcohol, and have been alleged to be causative factors in abnormal behavior. Like alcohol, definite psychoses have been attributed to the use of drugs. Some writers have dwelt upon the immediate benumbing effects of drugs and upon the consequent behavior deviations. Still others have maintained that drugs, like alcohol, exercise an effect upon the offspring of narcotic parentage. Alonzo Calkins, in his book in 1871, wrote of opium and cannabis, making little mention of crime aside from suicide and infanticide.[82] According to H. H. Kane, superintendent of the De

---

[79] S. Bloch, "Psychological Study of Gangs," *Medical Record*, LXXVIII (September 17, 1910) 479.

[80] Bernard Glueck, "A Contribution to the Catamnestic Study of the Juvenile Offender," *Journal of the American Institute of Criminal Law and Criminology*, III (July 1912) 239-240.

[81] G. Milton Linthicum, "Inebriety and Crime," *Proceedings of the National Conference of Charities and Correction*, 1915, p. 410.

[82] Alonzo Calkins, *Opium and the Opium Appetite*, Philadelphia, 1871.

Quincey Home, Fort Washington, New York City, the long continued use of morphia in large amounts first affects the moral
nature, producing what can be termed a form of moral insanity.
Kane presented a case of a homicide by a physician who administered too much morphia, in which the physician's defense in
court was his own morphia mania or insanity.[83] Edward C.
Spitzka found a chronic form of opium insanity analogous to
chronic alcoholic insanity, in which there were delusions of persecution, and in which there was just as great likelihood of violent
and criminal behavior. In fact, he claimed, forms of alcoholic
mental derangement are imitated by the opium psychoses—the
opium delirium, the opium chronic delusional insanity, and the
opium maniacal furor.[84] Just as there was a periodical insanity
which he called dipsomania, so there was a morbid craving for
opium which was as distinct from the ordinary opium habit as
dipsomania was from inebriety.[85] When speaking of the irresponsibility of the dipsomaniac, Edward C. Mann recognized
that in like manner there may be a disordered impulse or craving
for opium, chloral, and other drugs, which dominate the character, and master the reason and the conduct.[86] Citing cases of
forgery, J. T. Eskridge, professor of mental and nervous diseases and of medical jurisprudence and dean of the medical
faculty of the University of Colorado, gave an instance of moral
imbecility complicated with the opium habit, in which he felt
there were definite kleptomaniac tendencies, the latter being for
him a recognizable form of mental disorder.[87] T. D. Crothers
entitled his book in 1893 *The Disease of Inebriety from Alcohol, Opium and Other Narcotic Drugs,* and discussed opium
inebriety, recognizing its rôle in criminal behavior. Almost ten
years later, in his *Morphinism and Narcomanias from Other*

[83] H. H. Kane, "Some Medico-Legal Aspects of Morphia-Taking," *Alienist and Neurologist,* III (July 1882) 419-433.

[84] Edward C. Spitzka, *op. cit.,* pp. 254-255.

[85] *Ibid.,* p. 271.

[86] Edward C. Mann, "The Relation which Dipsomania Bears to Forensic Medicine," *Chicago Medical Journal and Examiner,* LIII (September 1886) 207-211.

[87] Jeremiah T. Eskridge, "Report of Cases of Moral Imbecility, of the Opium Habit, and of Feigning, in which Forgery Is the Offense Committed," *Medical News,* LXII (January 14, 1893) 29-34.

Drugs, he mentioned the criminal assaults of the morphinist, adding that a moral palsy and paralysis of the will consisting in an inability to distinguish between right and wrong was observed to be present. The morphinist was a genuine lunatic, as much so as the dipsomaniac. Crimes of violence were rare because opium and morphine acted upon the brain and nervous system as a narcotic and a depressant, but crimes against the character and property of others were often found.[88] At another time, in 1911, he wrote:

In all probability the withdrawal of alcohol was followed by the secret use of some narcotic drugs for a long period of time, and the extraordinary conduct and criminal acts were due entirely to the degeneration of the brain, which began with alcohol and was intensified by drugs that were concealed.[89]

In the following year he stated that morphinists were seldom seen in courts for brutal crimes, like the alcoholic, although they were frequently charged as kleptomaniacs, and as aiders and abettors of crimes rather than as principals. They were victims of morbid impulses, their sense of right and wrong was weakened, they were susceptible to suggestion, suffered from masked delusions, and were characterized by the paralysis of the ethical brain and centers of volition.[90] G. Frank Lydston in 1904 confirmed the earlier statement of Eugene S. Talbot that opium seemed to be the Charybdis on which the human bark struck when escaping the Scylla of alcohol. Despite the relative infrequency of narcotic inebriety, Lydston maintained that it was a more important factor in the etiology of vice and crime than was generally supposed. The moral sense and the will were most seriously impaired, with accompanying delusions and hallucinations and consequent crimes. With hasheesh, the crimes were of an explosive and violent nature; with opium they were the crimes requiring deception and secretiveness such as forgery and swind-

[88] T. D. Crothers, *Morphinism and Narcomanias from Other Drugs,* Philadelphia, 1902.

[89] T. D. Crothers, *Inebriety,* Cincinnati, 1911, p. 357.

[90] T. D. Crothers, "Criminality and Morphinism," *New York Medical Journal,* XCV (January 27, 1912) 163-165.

ling; with cocaine the crimes were those in self-defense against an imaginary foe, often with homicidal impulses; with ether the crimes were most usually like those of the alcoholic; with chloral and the bromides the crimes were petty rather than crimes of impulse, although occasional suicidal impulses were observed.[91] The drug addict, said Charles K. Mills in 1905, committed crimes of every sort, from homicide and violent assault to petty larceny. Morphinists rarely committed crimes of violence unless suffering from delusions and hallucinations, or in trance states; their crimes included stealing, acting under false pretenses, passing bogus checks, and occasionally arson. Crimes of violence under delusions of persecution and in general delirium characterized the cocainist, while the combination of morphinism and alcoholism produced crimes of sexual immorality.[92] Still another wrote of the resemblance of drug psychosis to alcoholism, for Alfred Gordon noted the same mental deterioration as in alcoholism, the presence of delusions and hallucinations, and the lack of the capacity to distinguish between right and wrong. "Criminality," he added, "is a phenomenon of social pathology, and must therefore be studied from the standpoint of biological sciences."[93] Granting that of the crimes caused by the use of alcohol and drugs only two per cent were accountable to drugs, Edward Wallace Lee remarked: "From my present viewpoint I maintain that any pathological condition may be the exciting cause of a psychic neurosis that will lead to such a disturbed physical change as will result in mental deterioration and acts of crime."[94] Like many others Paul E. Bowers, in his book *The Relationship of Insanity to Crime*, published in 1915, considered drug effects, especially morphinism and cocainism, in his discussion of alcohol and crime. Five per cent of all the crimes of prisoners in his institution were due directly or indirectly to the use of drugs. The morphinist committed larceny, burglary, forgery, arson, blackmail, homicidal attempts, murder, and

[91] G. Frank Lydston, *op. cit.*, pp. 206-211.

[92] Charles K. Mills, "Morphinomania, Cocomania, and General Narcomania, and Some of Their Legal Consequences," *International Clinics*, I (1905) 159-176.

[93] Alfred Gordon, *op. cit.*, p. 316.

[94] Edward Wallace Lee, *op cit.*, p. 1249.

sexual crimes. With many of them were frequently delusions of persecution. Criminal manifestations among cocainists were essentially those of the morphinist, being if anything more profound in character. The paranoid state was also common among cocainists with consequent homicidal and suicidal attempts.[95]

For over a century the controversy had persisted whether or not alcohol was productive of vice or disease. In so far as it is the active agent in mental disease it has been dealt with as the subject matter of this chapter, for to that extent it has fallen legitimately into the discussion of biological theories of crime causation. This was early recognized by Benjamin Rush, who identified the mental disease as a form of moral insanity, and it was affirmed by Isaac Ray. Yet even when moral insanity had changed its form or had been abandoned, the conviction existed that the mental disorder deriving from the excessive use of alcohol was characterized by irresistible impulses, delusions, and hallucinations. Certainly in this wise it shared elements common to many forms of mental disease.

Variously known as *mania a potu*, chronic alcoholic insanity, oinomania, methomania, inebriety, delirium tremens, periodical insanity, it frequently was a precipitating factor in criminal behavior. Occasionally, too, it was held that the results might descend from generation to generation, appearing, if not as criminal behavior in the parent generation, then certainly as such in the offspring, according to the formula: alcoholism in the parent, criminality in the children.

Of the rôle of drugs in criminal behavior much the same may be said as was said of alcoholism. T. D. Crothers, who was more active than any other one man in interpreting the rôle of alcoholism in crime causation, included within his labors the field of drugs. Indeed, to many, the use of drugs was but a form of alcoholism, for others alcohol was a narcotic. Drug users, too, were characterized by delusions and hallucinations, and responded as if in answer to an irresistible impulse or to an imperative desire.

[95] Paul E. Bowers, *op. cit.*, pp. 72-75.

V

CRIMINAL ANTHROPOLGY I:
THE ANATOMY OF THE CRIMINAL

BEGINNINGS IN AMERICA

AT ONE time or another, attempts have been made to explain criminal behavior in terms either of the offender himself or of forces outside him. The former explanation has been developed chiefly by the criminal anthropologists, the latter by the sociologists. It was Lombroso who first gave substance to the formulations of criminal anthropology by his insistence upon the essentially atavistic nature of the criminal. Lombroso believed the criminal to bear the traits of his primitive ancestors; the criminal was morphologically a savage. Supporting this position was Bordier who examined the skulls of murderers, and Benedikt who studied the brains of beheaded criminals. Others, like Colajanni and Ferrero, stressed the psychic factor, dwelling on what may be termed the psychic atavism as being characteristic of the criminal and as the phenomenon which accounted for his criminal behavior. Allied with these theories was one which endeavored to explain criminal acts as a result of arrested development in the individual. Phylogenetically he had stopped in his development at a lower level of human evolution; ontogenetically this had taken place in childhood. With these few preliminary remarks let us turn to America to trace the influence of these ideas.

Perhaps one is surprised to find no mention of criminal anthropology in this country until E. P. Fowler's presentation of Benedikt in 1880, followed by his translation of Benedikt in the next year.[1] Until the time of this publication no treatment of criminal anthropology had appeared in the American literature.

[1] E. P. Fowler, "Are the Brains of Criminals Anatomical Perversions?" *Medico-Chirurgical Quarterly*, I (October 1880) 1-32.

The reason for this may be associated, perhaps, with the fact that American penology was very largely concerned with the incarceration of the criminal and the development of prison systems rather than with the study of the offender. The American penologist saw the incarcerated offender either as a victim of his heredity or of his environment; once having identified him in one or the other of these ways, the penologists' interest in crime causation ceased.

American criminal anthropology had no such original leaders as Rush and Ray. A scientific orientation around criminal anthropology still had to be achieved by 1890 despite the fact that Lombroso's first volume on criminal man had appeared more than two decades before. Indeed, when Robert Fletcher, president of the Anthropological Society of Washington, D.C., spoke, in 1891, on "The New School of Criminal Anthropology," he justified his recital of European works by declaring that nothing in the field of criminal anthropology had been published in the United States.[2] The first record of an American publication in this field was in 1888, when William Noyes, assistant physician at the Bloomingdale Asylum, New York, issued an uncritical adoption of the Lombrosian position.[3]

ATAVISM AND ARRESTED DEVELOPMENT

It was thus, practically, not until the last decade of the nineteenth century that theories of atavism and arrested development (and, as we shall see subsequently, of degeneration) came within the ken of American science. James Weir, in 1894, described the criminal as a savage in the midst of civilization; atavism had hurled him back thousands and thousands of years, placing him beside his pithecoid ancestor. Both morally and physically he was atavistic. "His emotions and desires, his responsibilities and religion are those of an autochthon, born and dead centuries and decades of centuries ago."[4] Seven years later,

---

[2] Robert Fletcher, "The New School of Criminal Anthropology," *American Anthropologist*, IV (July, 1891) 201-236.

[3] William Noyes, "The Criminal Type," *Journal of Social Science*, XXIV (April 1888) 31-42.

[4] James Weir, Jr., "Criminal Anthropology," *Medical Record*, XLV (January 13, 1894) 45.

August Drähms, chaplain of San Quentin prison, whose book carried an introduction by Lombroso, treated of the criminal as a moral anomaly, believing that he represented under modern conditions an instinctive savagery not yet eliminated by social evolution.[5] Atavism, or reversion to type, said G. Frank Lydston, was inseparable from the general law of evolution, and constituted the dynamics of crime. Whether associated with obvious physical reversions or not it was the dominant characteristic of the criminal.[6] Arthur MacDonald, in discussing the results of an investigation of sixty-five young criminals, insisted that their defects were those which were normal for lower races, and that the criminal was a reversion to a lower type.[7] "The child born centuries too late," was the term used by Thomas Travis, in 1908, to explain delinquency in those instances where juvenile delinquency could not otherwise be attributed to the environment.[8]

Others, such as G. Stanley Hall and his students in psychology, M. P. E. Groszmann, George Dawson, and Edgar James Swift, explained the criminal as an instance of arrested development. For instance, Dawson maintained that the persistence of the predatory instinct was the characteristic of the thief, an instinct normal among savages and semi-civilized peoples, but which, when found among contemporary peoples, stamped the offender as a person whose development had stopped at an earlier stage of human existence.[9] Speaking of the child, Dawson added that should the child's development cease at the stage

[5] August Drähms, op. cit., p. 59.

[6] G. Frank Lydston, The Diseases of Society, Philadelphia, 1904, pp. 75-79.

[7] Arthur MacDonald, Juvenile Crime and Reformation, Including Stigmata of Degeneration, Washington, D.C., 1908, p. 18.

Arthur MacDonald had been a specialist on the abnormal classes with the United States Bureau of Education from 1892 to 1904. He had previously studied in universities, both in America and Europe, and had published as early as 1893 a book on abnormal man and another on criminology. Repeatedly he had urged the Congress to establish a laboratory for the study of the criminal, pauper, and defective classes. His acquaintance with European literature on criminology and related subjects was extensive.

[8] Thomas Travis, The Young Malefactor, New York, 1908, pp. 97-99.

[9] George E. Dawson, "Psychic Rudiments and Morality," American Journal of Psychology, XI (January 1900) 181-224; M. P. E. Groszmann, "Criminality in Children," Arena, XXII (October 1899) 514; Edgar James Swift, "Some Criminal Tendencies of Boyhood: A Study in Adolescence," Pedagogical Seminary, VIII (March 1901) 65-91; G. Stanley Hall, Adolescence, New York, 1908.

when he is living over the instincts and habits of his animal and sub-human ancestors, he will be the typical delinquent. So also the inclination to assault and kill was explained in terms of an imperfectly developed human being in whom the psychical qualities of the animal or sub-human ancestors had persisted. He was not possessed of the moral sense of the civilized man, the moral sense which marked the culmination of the evolutionary process. Winfield Scott Hall, in 1914, joined in this general thesis.[10]

Philip Parsons, in his doctoral dissertation under the direction of Franklin H. Giddings at Columbia, while not fully accepting the atavistic theory did, however, offer his tentative conclusion that the criminal was an abnormal man, and that crime was the normal function of an abnormal man.[11]

This theory is based upon the same biological assumption as that of atavism, namely that numerous life germs or cells, or infinitesimal somethings which subsequently enter into the composition of the germ cells are transmitted for numerous generations. To these are added and with them transmitted new and more highly developed characters as the stock receives beneficent infusions of blood from advantageous crossings. But because of conditions under which the types bearing the older characteristics came into being, they are better fitted to survive and appear under conditions which are fatal to either the existence or the appearance of the newer or more highly developed ones. Thus it happens that under disturbed or unfavorable conditions the older types appear because of their fitness to do so. Thus the moral sense, which is perhaps the latest acquisition of the race, is not found in the criminal, or in a very low form only.[12]

DEGENERATION

While Morel originally (1857) regarded degeneration as a form of retrograde evolution, subsequent writers have modified it, often without being in agreement as to its exact definition. It was not restricted to criminal behavior, as instanced by Eugene

[10] Winfield Scott Hall, "The Relation of Crime to Adolescence," *Bulletin of the American Academy of Medicine*, XV (April 1914) 86-96.

[11] Philip A. Parsons, *Responsibility for Crime*, Columbia University Studies in History, Economics and Public Law, XXXIV, no. 3, New York, 1909.

[12] *Ibid.*, pp. 52-53.

S. Talbot's volume in 1898 which dealt with ethical degeneracy (crime, prostitution and sexual degeneracy, moral insanity, pauperism, and inebriety), intellectual degeneracy (insanities, neuroses, and epilepsies), sensory degeneracy (deaf-mutism, congenital color-blindness, smell abnormalities), nutritive degeneracy (goitre, cancer, gout, etc.), and local reversionary tendencies as mainfested in the teeth, jaws, palate, uteri, kidneys, liver, etc.[13] Specifically, Talbot found criminals to be a variety of the human species quite distinct from law-abiding men, forming a community which retrograded from generation to generation. The truth of the degeneracy doctrine, he claimed, had been forced upon him long before its popular apotheosis under Lombroso and Nordau.[14]

G. Frank Lydston, a collaborator of Talbot and a researcher and author in his own right, spoke of degeneracy as a degradation of development from the average normal type and as constituting the fundamental cause of the majority of crimes.

The essence of degeneracy is neuropathy—usually hereditary. Behind all processes of nutrition and growth is the physiologic architect, the nervous system. Through its trophic function the materials brought to the tissues are builded into cell and fibre. As is the integrity of the nervous system, so is the integrity of the structure built up through its influence.[15]

Later, he continued:

Inasmuch as tissue building depends upon the functional integrity of the nervous system, it is evident that degradation of development—i.e., degeneracy—has a neuropathic foundation. Whatever the exciting cause of a given social disease may be, the predisposing cause in the degenerate is a neuropathic constitution, giving rise to a perversion of formative energy which may be either in favor of or against a given structure. This neuropathic degeneracy is not necessarily ob-

[13] Eugene S. Talbot, op. cit.

[14] Talbot was trained in both medicine and dentistry, and had been for a number of years a professor of dentistry. In addition to this work on degeneracy (written at the invitation of Havelock Ellis for the Contempoary Science Series) which touched on social as well as physical aspects of degeneracy, he collaborated with Lydston on the study of the heads of criminals.

[15] The Diseases of Society, Philadelphia, J. B. Lippincott Co., 1904, p. 86.

vious; it may remain latent until some stress influence is brought to bear. The first debauch may demonstrate the existence of neuro-psychic degeneracy and develop inebriety in a person hitherto supposed to be perfectly normal. Temptation to crime may be followed by acts which show for the first time that the individual is a neuro-psychic degenerate.[16]

George E. Dawson based his study of juvenile delinquents upon the premise that the criminal was a victim of arrested development or of degeneracy, and that such imperfection or degeneration may be perpetuated in the offspring.

To the student of the defective and criminal classes, the theory of degeneration is at least profoundly interesting and suggestive. It proposes to bring crime, insanity, idiocy, and pauperism within the domain of law. These things cease to be accidents in nature or the results of satanic interference. They happen, as virtue, health, intelligence and prosperity happen, because some antecedent conditions have produced them. Would we know their proximate cause, we must look at the devitalized constitutions of men and women; at their diseased nervous systems and unstable brains; at their enfeebled intelligence, their blunted sensibilities, their impotent wills. Would we know a more remote cause, we must look at the gratification of appetites and passions that ought to have been controlled, or untoward circumstances that were beyond control, or a long process of ancestral decadence whose history may involve the mistakes and sins of many.[17]

Although disclaiming that crime was an atavism—a mere reversion to the once normal practices of our ancestors—or that there is a criminal type, recognizable simply by anatomical characteristics, W. Duncan McKim did admit that manifestation of ancestral ways was often an abnormality so incongruous with our present morals as to constitute crime, and added that the tendency to crime was essentially inborn.[18] This hereditary factor was the core of McKim's thesis, and involved essentially the transmission of degeneracy. Certain individuals inherited these weaknesses which constituted predispositions so that they succumbed to disease and crime which others—the normal—escaped.

[16] Lydston, *op. cit.*, p. 87.

[17] George E. Dawson, "A Study of Youthful Degeneracy," *Pedagogical Seminary,* IV (December 1896) 224.

[18] W. Duncan McKim, *op. cit.*

It may be well to recall McKim's schematization of criminality by which he subsumed it under the categories of abnormal tendencies and deficient self-restraint. Under the former he classed as degeneracy the congenital abnormal tendencies.

Defective conduct has its root in defective brain-action, which is dependent upon defective brain structure, and this may be congenital or acquired—usually through morbid tendencies transmitted by inheritance. Upon heredity, as already said, disease and degeneracy are, in very great degree, dependent; these are the roots from which spring abnormal tendencies and deficient self-restraint; criminality, then, the noxious flower of this twofold growth, is essentially a manifestation of heredity.[19]

A review of these attempted explanations of criminal behavior —atavism, its sub-category arrested development, and degeneration—reveals no clear-cut distinctions between them. Even Lydston scarcely succeeded in his effort to distinguish them when he wrote, in 1904:

The mistake is often made of confounding atavism with degeneracy pure and simple. They are not identical, although so closely related that the line of demarcation is not always clear. As already noted, degeneracy of brain may produce atavistic phychic phenomena even though there is no physical conformation corresponding with any distinct primitive human or lower animal type. Aberrations of cranial development may exist which in no wise present a type-resemblance to a primitive ancestral form. The difficulty of determining whether a given case of aberrant development of skull or brain, or other portions of the body, is due to vicious influences brought to bear upon the line of descent or upon the individual during uterogestation, or to a spontaneous harking back to primitive ancestral forms, is at once obvious. As a broad general proposition, atavism is not a cause of degeneracy, but degeneracy may cause what is in effect atavism. The animal-like traits of certain brain degenerates is a point in evidence.[20]

Frederick Howard Wines, like Charles R. Henderson,[21] found it impossible to accept the notion of a criminological type. He

---

[19] *Ibid.*, pp. 101-102.

[20] G. Frank Lydston, *op. cit.*, p. 77.

[21] Charles R. Henderson, professor of sociology at the University of Chicago, like Wines, was trained for the ministry. He was identified with charitable and penological interests in addition to his various editorial duties.

tried to differentiate atavism and the phenomena of pure inherit-ance from degeneration. The latter he held to be the result of causes operating in the present rather than in the past, being due as much, if not more, to environment as to heredity. He likened atavism to a line turned back upon itself, degeneration to a line bent downward at an angle, and arrested development to a line abruptly terminated.[22]

Vague and ill-defined as this may seem today, it is well to be reminded that the thought of that time centered around the proposition that the criminal was the product either of heredity or of environment. If one were committed to the former proposi-tion, as were the generality of physicians, then one proceeded to identify certain stigmata as evidence of criminality. Few writers differentiated stigmata of atavism from stigmata of degeneration, their sole concern being to identify these stigmata as characteris-tics of the criminal. It is in this form that their contributions shall be presented in the following section: first, the anatomical or structural characteristics, then the physiological or functional, with the sub-divisions of the physical and the psychical.

THE CRIMINAL BRAIN—ANATOMICAL OR STRUCTURAL

The discussion of the anatomical or structural characteristics of the criminal should begin quite naturally with the study of the criminal brain. The existence of such a separate type of brain was claimed by the Austrian psychiatrist Benedikt to be substan-tiated by research upon beheaded criminals. As reported by his American translator, E. P. Fowler, Benedikt held that the brains of criminals exhibited a deviation from the normal type and that criminals among the cultured races were to be regarded as an anthropological variety of their species. Benedikt, in a series of nineteen criminal brains, found deficiency of brain-substance and confluence of the fissures, the three most important fissures—the central (*sulcus centralis* or Rolando's fissure), third frontal (*sulcus frontalis perpendicularis*) and the parietal (*sulcus inter-parietalis*)—tending to unite with the Sylvian. From this he concluded that the conformation of the criminal brain was of the

---

[22] Frederick Howard Wines, *op. cit.*, p. 246.

relatively simple type observed in the Negro and other primitive races. Fowler was inclined to agree with Benedikt, but could not permit himself to go further than to ask:

If there exist physical causes for any type or types of crime, then evidently the criminal, if incited by a certain degree of specific provocation, will continue to commit crime until such physical cause shall have been cured by a continuous and judicious treatment. It hardly needs be added, that there would be great numbers of cases where the perverted anatomy could not be remedied, and where very little could be done beyond shielding such persons from provoking causes.[23]

May not the crimes of the "constitutional criminal" be the natural results of a lower animal type of brain which, from some cause, has thus developed in that particular individual of the human species, Fowler added.

Dr. Charles K. Mills, of Philadelphia, one of the most celebrated psychiatrists of his day, was familiar with the work of Benedikt and also had had the opportunity to examine the brains of the paupers and criminals found in the Philadelphia General Hospital (Blockley) where he was neurologist. Out of his experience he wrote, in 1882, that while he was not prepared to accept all of Benedikt's conclusions, he was satisfied that there was some truth in the principle which he had advanced.[24] In this article, a lecture delivered at the Philadelphia General Hospital in 1881, contrasting paralysis from cerebral disease with hysteroidal paralysis, he agreed with Benedikt that there were two types of brains—the normal separated-fissure type, and the confluent-fissure type.

Benedikt claims [wrote Mills], that he has found in examining a large number of brains from criminals, that instead of these fissures being separated, they are, in many instances, confluent. He makes the statement, which, from my study of the literature of the subject and my own experience (having examined forty to fifty brains for this point) I am compelled to doubt that it is a somewhat common

---

[23] E. P. Fowler, "Are the Brains of Criminals Anatomical Perversions?" *Medico-Chirurgical Quarterly*, I (October 1880) 20.

[24] Charles K. Mills, "The Brains of Criminals," *Medical Bulletin*, IV (March 1882) 57-60.

occurrence to find the fissure of Rolando running into the fissure of Sylvius. This is remarkable when it is rememberd that up to the publication of Benedikt's paper only four or five cases had been reported from all parts of the world; one of these by Dr. Parker, of this city, and one by myself, recorded by Dr. Parker in the Proceedings of the Academy of Natural Sciences. I have frequently seen the fissure of Rolando apparently running into the fissure of Sylvius. If you look at the brain before removing the pia mater, the two fissures will apparently run together; but on stripping off the membrane and examining carefully, you will find that the confluence is only apparent, and that just below the surface will be a little mass of convolution separating the two fissures.

I have, however, found in a number of instances in the examination of the brains from the pauper, vicious, and criminal classes, as represented in this hospital, in the insane department, and in other hospitals, that there is some truth in the statement, that these classes show a tendency to an excess of fissure development as compared with the development of convolution.

.   .   .   .   —   .   .   .   .   .   .

If further observations prove the correctness of Benedikt's statement, we shall certainly have made a great advance in the anatomical study of the brains of this class of mankind. . . . The ideal confluent-fissure-type brain of Benedikt may be represented by considering the fissures of the brain as watercourses. The fissures run into one another, so that if water were admitted it would flow from one fissure to the other over the whole surface of the brain. An examination of Guiteau's brain[25] may show that it is one of this confluent-fissure type.[26]

Writing five years later, Mills doubted whether the "criminal type" of brain could be separated from the brain found in idiocy, imbecility, paranoia, and other psychical degenerative states. He agreed with John G. Kiernan, another eminent neurologist, that between the true criminal type, the idiot, the imbecile, and the paranoiac, the psychological relations and anatomical bases were intimate and close.[27] Mills regarded it as "unphilosophical" to construct a theory of the anatomical basis of crime because crime

[25] Charles J. Guiteau was the assassin of President Garfield.

[26] Charles K. Mills, op. cit., pp. 58-59.

[27] Charles K. Mills, "Arrested and Aberrant Development of Fissures and Gyres in the Brains of Paranoiacs, Criminals, Idiots, and Negroes," Journal of Nervous and Mental Disease, XIII (September and October 1886) 523-550.

was technically a violation of the law, and anyone under sufficient stress was likely to become a criminal. However, "a certain number will always be found who are criminal as the result of their organization, because of retarded, defective, or aberrant brain development." Mills took cognizance of the objections of those who doubted whether any virtue is served by special studies of criminal brains, and at the same time admitted that Benedikt and his followers have erred in their assertion of an absolutely fixed type of criminal brain. He added that if we admit with the physiologists and anthropologists that a certain number of people were criminals as a result of inherited organizations, that very admission showed the necessity and the value of studies into the conditions of brain development.[28]

Benedikt's conclusions found confirmation in James Weir's studies of criminal brains. Weir examined twenty-three criminals' brains, twenty of whom were instinctive and habitual offenders. In nineteen of the brains he found marked abnormalities. In one, that of a negro hanged for murder, the cerebral fissures were highly confluent, and the cerebellum was not covered by the cerebrum. In two others there were very few convolutions, little depth, and little gray matter. All the brains were deficient in weight. Some of them had four anterior frontal convolutions, and one had fusion of the first and second convolutions, an abnormality which Weir considered peculiarly rare and striking. Most criminals he found to have shallow brain pans.[29]

In his study of degeneracy Talbot associated the criminal with the insane, the idiot, the imbecile, the feeble-minded, and others whom he designated as the degenerate class. In his chapter on the degeneracy of the brain he described some of the characteristics of the defective brains of members of these classes. These defects he enumerated as: 1. Atypical asymmetry of the cerebral hemispheres as regards bulk. 2. Atypical asymmetry in the gyral

[28] J. S. Wight, whom Mills quoted, testified to the defective neural organization of criminals, but his work will be considered in greater detail in the chapter on heredity. Edward C. Mann likewise remarked upon the deficient development of the brain of the criminal by showing that the cerebellum was not covered by the occipital lobes. His work on the criminal crania will be considered later in this chapter.

[29] James Weir, Jr., "Criminal Anthropology," *Medical Record*, XLV (January 13, 1894) 42-45.

development. 3. Persistence of embryonic features in the gyral arrangement. 4. Defective development of the great interhemispherical commissure. 5. Irregular and defective development of the great ganglia and of the conducting tracts. 6. Anomalies in the development of the minute elements or neurons of the brain. 7. Abnormal arrangements of the cerebral vascular channels. All these conditions, separately or in combination, were occasionally found in the brains of paranoiacs, moral imbeciles, criminals, deaf-mutes and other degenerates.[30]

A century after Gall's pioneer anatomical work on the human brain, G. Frank Lydston paid a belated homage in these words:

> The originality and boldness of Gall are shown by the striking fact that he was not only the father of psychology, cerebral anatomy, the cerebral localization, but the pioneer who foreshadowed the coming of modern criminology. . . . Modern criminology has, to be sure, not been so daring as Gall in the matter of cerebral localization, but its trend has been in the same direction, so far as criminal cranium and brain are concerned.[31]

Influenced by phrenological principles which he felt others had neglected or discarded erringly, Lydston placed particular stress upon the fore-brain, declaring it to be the seat of the inhibitory or control centers that enabled normal man to resist the primitive animal impulses which emanated from other parts of the organ. Disease, injury, or maldevelopment of certain portions of the brain produced a perturbation or loss of function in parts of the brain cells. These conditions, he continued, affecting certain cortical areas, also produced psychic aberrations, the character of which varied with the area affected. Lydston was not ready to make any final statements on the criminal brain, holding that not enough clinical and experimental evidence had been produced to warrant conclusions at the time of his writing. He attached no significance either to brain weight or brain size, asserting that the important feature of the brain was the development and complexity of the convolutions.

[30] Eugene S. Talbot, *op. cit.*, pp. 294-314.
[31] G. Frank Lydston, *op. cit.*, pp. 154-155.

THE CRIMINAL BRAIN NOT ESTABLISHED

During the period covered by this treatise (i.e., to 1915) the existence of the criminal brain was not proved, certainly not to the unanimous agreement of neurologists, pathologists, and other workers in the field of the abnormal. There was a caution mixed at times with skepticism, and at other times an outright denial. Francis X. Dercum, a noted Philadelphia neurologist, after examining the brain of a hanged murderer, wrote:

The writer refrains from making comments on the mental condition of such a brain. He does not, however, believe that any one with a full knowledge of the facts would predicate of such a brain a normal mind, and yet such an individual might be perfectly able to appreciate the consequences of crime, to differentiate between right and wrong, and to be, in the eyes of the law, a responsible individual. With this, however, the pathologist has nothing to do.[32]

Dr. H. H. Donaldson, professor of neurology at the University of Chicago, also examined the brain of a murderer—a specimen obtained from Dr. Van Gieson—but failed to find the confluent fissures as in the type described by Benedikt. "Undoubtedly," he said, "the criminal brain could be picked out of a mixed lot, but only by virtue of general characteristics, and there could be no certainty that all criminal brains could thus be selected."[33] In answer to the remarks of Donaldson, Mills stated that no one believed that all criminals presented a brain anatomy that would enable them to be arranged under a special type. Criminals belonged to a very different class. A criminal type of brain could be expected from those who were victims of a bad heredity or very early arrested development. Paranoiacs, idiots, imbeciles, criminals, and those generally who were victims of arrested or abortive development would probably present brain abnormalities even of a gross kind. Mills admitted that the brain which Dr. Donaldson exhibited seemed to him to show evidences of aberration, particularly in the parieto-occipital region.[34]

[32] Francis X. Dercum, "Description of the Brain of John M. Wilson, Hanged at Norristown," *Philadelphia Medical Times*, XVII (March 5, 1887) 368-371.

[33] H. H. Donaldson, "The Criminal Brain; Illustrated by the Brain of a Murderer," *Journal of Nervous and Mental Disease*, XIX (August 1892) 654.

[34] *Ibid.* Discussion following Dr. Donaldson's paper, pp. 655-656.

Nor could Abraham Jacobi, eminent medical teacher, editor, and practitioner, go so far as to believe in a special type of criminal brain. Crime, he held, was not an entity, but as manifold as human instincts or tendencies in general. In fact, many of the same changes which are claimed to be characteristic in the criminal may also be found in the insane.[35]

In his chapter on Criminal Anthropology, F. H. Wines strongly indicated his disbelief in the criminal type, whether it be of brain type, anatomical type, or physiological type. He was familiar with the work of Lombroso, Ferri, and Benedikt, but claimed that the biological and anthropological factors had been overstressed to the neglect of the sociological ones.[36]

August Drähms doubted, too, whether one should probe for the criminal brain, declaring that the relation of the brain to the criminal problem was inscrutable. He indicated that convolutions and gray matter were of far greater moment than brain size or brain weight, and criticized Benedikt for failing to establish a normal brain for comparison with the alleged criminal brain. In conclusion he remarked:

That defective brain organization and cranial asymmetry are sometimes closely interrelated with moral and mental degeneration, is undeniable; but that a causal relation is thereby proven to exist between such organic degeneration and the criminal propensity, or that mental alienation and moral defection necessarily verge one upon the other, is a position that cannot be maintained, and few would venture to affirm.[37]

After marking a post-mortem examination of two executed murderers, Edward Anthony Spitzka, teacher of anatomy at Jefferson Medical College in Philadelphia, and a son of Edward C. Spitzka, declared there was nothing about these brains to indicate abnormality. There was no grave defect or malformation, no tendency to the arcuate-fissuration type of carnivores, the cerebellum was not covered (as he claimed was artificially produced by Benedikt), the insulae were not exposed by defective

---

[35] Abraham Jacobi, "Brain, Crime and Capital Punishment," *Proceedings of the National Prison Association*, 1892, pp. 175-205.

[36] Frederick Howard Wines, *op. cit.*, pp. 229-265.

[37] August Drähms, *The Criminal*, p. 106. By permission of The Macmillan Co., publishers.

opercular development, the vermis was not hypertrophied, the cerebral fissures were not duplicated, and, he concluded, "there were none of the numerous 'stigmata' of development set up by Lombroso's followers in the Italian 'Uomo delinquente school.' "[38] Several years later the psychologist, Hugo Münsterberg, remarked succinctly: ". . . no one is predestined by his brain to the penitentiary."[39]

By the year 1910 there had been a general abandonment of the position that the criminal brain existed. As these thirty years are reviewed—beginning with the time of the introduction of Benedikt and Lombroso into America—it is evident that the doctrine of the separate type of criminal brain was never generally accepted. True, there was an honest difference of opinion by even the best informed (Donaldson and Mills), but not even Mills could fully endorse the doctrine although he believed that he had much evidence to support it. With the exception of several physicians who claimed to have identified the criminal brain among inmates, there was not a single American who unreservedly confirmed the findings of Benedikt. The tentative findings of Mills in the 1880's were never confirmed by him or by others during the later years. By 1910 the study of the criminal had shifted from the anatomy and physiology of the brain to the functioning of the human being as a whole.

Perhaps the most conclusive study which definitely disposed of the doctrine of the criminal brain was that of Charles W. McCorkle Poynter, published in 1912. Poynter, of the University of Nebraska, examined the brains of two bank robbers who had also committed a number of murders, both men having had previous criminal records. In the course of his report he also presented tables of variations of the brains of scholars, brains of inferior races, and the brains of criminals. Out of this mass of detail he reported that he could not find that criminals' brains showed anomalies and variations indicative of arrest of development or of atavism any more frequently than did the non-

[38] Edward Anthony Spitzka, "The Execution and Post-Mortem Examination of the Van Wormer Brothers at Dannemora," *Daily Medical Journal,* I (February 8, 1904) 1-2.

[39] Hugo Münsterberg, *On the Witness Stand. Essays on Psychology and Crime,* New York, 1908, p. 255.

criminal brain. No evidence, he declared, has ever been presented upon which to base the conclusion that the criminal brain as a whole is of a low order or of incomplete development.

A normal type does not exist, and consequently, a criminal type is impossible. But we may go farther and say that *not a single character reported from the brain of a criminal has been shown to have the remotest relation to his acts or habits of mind*. In the light of our present knowledge of variations, we must conclude that the two cases here presented, while representing two widely different types, are both free from evidence of inferiority and degeneration.[40]

Poynter admitted that the criminal brain exhibited a larger proportion of variations than the normal brain, but he denied that the individual variations were peculiar to the delinquents alone or that they were common to criminals. Granting the present incomplete knowledge of these variations, he declared that it could be positively stated that there was no criminal type of brain. He doubted that it could ever be possible to say from the macroscopic examination of the brain that it does or does not belong to a criminal. The connection between the structure of the brain and the psychic powers had not been established.

THE CRIMINAL CRANIUM

Having traced the investigations of the criminal brain, we now proceed to the problem of the criminal cranium. Whereas with the criminal brain it was chiefly the neurologist and pathologist who ventured an opinion, the situation with respect to the criminal cranium was quite the reverse. Anyone who had eyes to see felt qualified to discourse upon the form, size, and contour of the head of the criminal and to formulate his own scheme of classification.

One of the early textbook writers, Edward C. Mann, based a chapter entitled "The Psychology of Crime," almost entirely upon the researches of Benedikt.[41] The skull and brain, he held,

[40] Charles W. McCorkle Poynter, "Study of Cerebral Anthropology, with a Description of Two Brains of Criminals," *University Studies*, Lincoln, Nebraska, XII (October 1912) 409-410.

[41] Edward C. Mann, *A Manual of Psychological Medicine and Allied Nervous Diseases*, Philadelphia, 1883.

were closely interrelated, the pathological brain being identified with a skull development characterized by the shortening of the occiput, anterior vertex steepness, asymmetry and flattening of the occiput. Mann's conclusions may be represented as follows:

	Skulls of robber-murderers	Skulls of murderers from motive	Normal skulls
Brachycephalic occiputalis lacking in.	23%	45%	93.5%
Occipital flatness lacking in.........	16%	28%	58.0%
Asymmetry lacking in.............	10%	25%	68.0%

Hamilton D. Wey, one of the earliest original research workers in the medical departments of an American prison, while unable to accept the premise of the criminal brain, did, however, insist that the average criminal was hampered by a defective organization. During his service as prison physician at Elmira Reformatory under superintendent Z. R. Brockway the institutional reports revealed these early efforts to understand the behavior of the criminal. Wey's plea for the physical training of youthful criminals was a pioneer call from a pioneer institution, and grew out of his work as prison physician. Daily and intimate contact with the offender helped him to recognize certain peculiarities of mind and body that characterized those belonging to what he termed the "criminal class." Among the anomalies he noted was cranial asymmetry, which he declared to be a difference of degree only, rather than of kind. He did find the heads of thieves to be small, those of murderers to be large.[42] The existence of anomalies, wrote Abraham Jacobi, did not of themselves proclaim the criminal since some were to be found among the noncriminal, but where they were found in large numbers in the same individual it was a strong indication that such a person was a different kind of person—in short, a criminal. Among criminals he found that the head was more often brachycephalic than dolichocephalic, with pronounced prognathism, the underlying arches

[42] Hamilton D. Wey, "A Plea for Physical Training of Youthful Criminals," *Proceedings of the National Prison Association*, 1888, pp. 181-193; also "Criminal Anthropology," *Proceedings of the National Prison Association*, 1890, pp. 274-291.

of the frontal bones were often excessive, the bones in general thick, the occiput oblique. There was marked asymmetry of the head, with faulty development of the anterior portion. In criminals the head was either very small or very large. The heads of robbers were large, those of thieves small.[43] Confirmation of the size of criminals' heads was made by James Weir, who declared the average size was about that of normal people's heads, although among criminals there was a greater number of both large and small heads. In the case of the normal brachycephalic type of person, one found the criminal within that class to be pronouncedly so with similar cephalis index exaggerations in the other types. The oxycephalic or sugar-loaf form of head was characteristic of the instinctive criminal. A negro criminal's head was generally more dolichocephalic than the normal negro head.[44]

Another prison physician who examined his prisoners and found marked peculiarities was W. A. M'Corn of the Wisconsin State Prison at Waupun. While not willing to base a diagnosis of criminality upon the formation of the skull alone, he did observe that it was rare to find criminals with well-formed heads. Criminals, he noticed, were markedly oxycephalic as well as just the opposite, platycephalic. His Bertillon measurements on head form revealed the following: thieves, murderers (including homicides), sexual offenders, and fraud offenders were decidedly brachycephalic, being in excess of the normal limits in the case of thieves by 36%, of murderers by 9%, of sexual offenders by 14%, and of fraud offenders by 5%. Furthermore he found a very high proportion of these offenders to be scaphocephalic (keel-shaped) and oxycephalic (sugar-loaf or steeple shaped).[45] Certainly, wrote M'Corn, this must awaken the suspicion that criminals belong to the defective and degenerate class.

In contrast to M'Corn's conclusions (carefully based upon actual measurements) was the claim of J. B. Ransom that by placing his hand over the paracentral lobe, and without any prior

[43] Abraham Jacobi, *op. cit.*

[44] James Weir, Jr., *op. cit.*, p. 42.

[45] W. A. M'Corn, "Degeneration in Criminals As Shown by the Bertillon Syatem of Measurement and Photographs," *American Journal of Insanity*, LIII (July 1896) 47-56.

knowledge of the suspect's history, he could designate whether his crime had been either assault or homicide. If the right side of the cranium had a marked fullness over the paracentral lobe, indicating an excessive development of the right hemisphere of the brain over the left, then the possessor of such a cranium and of such a brain had impulses which led him toward homicide.[46] H. E. Allison, who saw a close degenerative resemblance between the criminal and the insane, believed that criminals, in common with the insane, exhibited marked asymmetry of the skull.[47]

Another original study of an inmate population, published at about the same time as M'Corn's, was George E. Dawson's of delinquent boys and girls. Again there was confirmation of the conclusion that heads of offenders, whether juvenile or adult, tended to be either unusually small or unusually large. Of the twenty-six boys he studied Dawson found 50% of them to have brachycephalic heads, 8% were dolichocephalic, while 42% were mesocephalic; among the twenty-six girls 68% were brachycephalic, none were dolichocephalic, and 32% were mesocephalic. Thus the heads of delinquents were either very wide or very narrow. Since the Indo-European type of head was mesocephalic, he concluded that the heads of these delinquent boys and girls deviated strongly from the normal. While the female head tended to be dolichocephalic normally, there was not a single one of the delinquent girls with a head of this type. Dawson even concluded that criminal women were more atavistic than men. Of the twenty-six boys studied, six had plagiocephalic (obliquity of the head) heads, two had platycephalic (flat) heads, one had a scaphocephalic (keel-shaped) head, one one had a hydrocephalic head; of the twenty-six girls five had plagiocephalic heads, two had platycephalic heads.[48]

Arthur Sweeney remarked, in connection with the relation

[46] Julius B. Ransom, "The Physician and the Criminal," *Journal of the American Medical Association*, XXVII (October 10, 1896) 790.

[47] H. E. Allison, "Insanity Among Criminals," *American Journal of Insanity*, LI (July 1894) 54-63; "Some Relations of Crime to Insanity and States of Mental Enfeeblement," *Journal of the American Medical Association*, XXVII (September 19, 1896) 646-650.

[48] George E. Dawson, "A Study in Youthful Degeneracy," *Pedagogical Seminary*, IV (December 1896) 232-233.

between crime and insanity, upon the marked irregularity of the skull with a greater development on one side than the other, the predominance of the parietal over the frontal region, excessive development of the supra-orbital ridge, and enlargement of the orbital cavity as being peculiar to the criminal more than in the case of the so-called normal person.[49] A year later Eugene S. Talbot devoted an entire chapter to the degenerate cranium in his work on degeneracy without mentioning the cranial characteristics of the criminal, but in a study published in the same year he drew attention to the marked dolichocephalism of the inmates of Pontiac and Elmira Reformatories in contrast to the mesocephalic population from which they were drawn. He also found a strong tendency toward oxycephalic head shape. Having found physical stigmata twice as numerous among these offenders as among those found in the non-criminal population, Talbot concluded that young criminals were, in the vast majority of cases, members of the degenerate classes. So handicapped were they by hereditary defects that they fell ready victims to criminal tendencies and environment.[50]

Although Arthur MacDonald's *Criminology* was dedicated to Lombroso in 1893, and although Lombroso's work was known to American students since the early 1880's, it was not until the opening of the twentieth century that the latter could acknowledge that his ideas had been fairly presented in America. The immediate occasion was his introductory statement in Drähms's book published in 1900, in which he stated: "I have not had the good fortune for some time to find an author who so thoroughly understands my ideas, and is able to express them with so much clearness, as the author of this book."[51] The only exception Lombroso took was to Drähms's statement that the American criminal differed in physiognomical type from his European contemporary: "This slight difference of opinion existing between

[49] Arthur Sweeney, "Crime and Insanity," *Northwestern Lancet*, XVII (May 15, 1897) 203-211.

[50] Eugene S. Talbot, "A Study of the Stigmata of Degeneracy Among American Criminal Youth," *Journal of the American Medical Association*, XXX (April 9, 1898) 849-856.

[51] August Drähms, *op. cit.*, p. xiii.

myself and the author, however, is insignificant as compared with the lucid exposition, the profound and original thought, with which the work is embellished."[52]

As part of his treatise on the criminal, Drähms discussed the cranial characteristics of the criminal as reflected in his own anthropometric studies of two thousand inmates, together with those of inmates of Elmira Reformatory and students of Amherst College, with the following results:[53]

Cephalic Index

Amherst Students....................	81.48
Elmira Inmates......................	79.00
San Quentin Inmates................	79.84
44 Murderers......................	83.51
33 Erotics........................	79.05
120 Robbers.......................	80.52
250 Recidivists...................	80.42
250 Single Offenders..............	80.52

Yet with all his anthropometric measurements Drähms found it impossible to admit the existence of the criminal type.

Drähms's *The Criminal* may be regarded with fairness as the first book on the American criminal that attempted an anthropological, biological, and psychological approach. Frances Kellor's *Experimental Sociology*, published in 1901, quite naturally stressed the sociological point of view since she was a student of the social sciences at the University of Chicago. However, it contained such a wealth of anthropological, biological, and psychological research material that it may with equal justice be called the second work on the American criminal.[54]

[52] *Ibid.*, *p.* xiv.

[53] *Ibid.*, p. 91. By permission of the Macmillan Co., publishers.

[54] Frances Kellor, *Experimental Sociology*, New York, 1901. While Arthur Mac-Donald's *Criminology* and his *Abnormal Man* antedated the publications of Drähms and Kellor, they were so laden with European material, and so lacking in original material on the American criminal that they hardly merit the distinction accorded to Drähms and Kellor. Talbot's *Degeneracy*, also antedating Drähms and containing material on the biologically degenerative aspects of criminality, cannot, because of lack of specificity of crime material, be classed with the work of Drähms and Kellor. The same conditions would disqualify Arthur MacDonald, and Charles Richmond Henderson, whose book on the dependent, defective, and delinquent classes appeared in 1893.

Miss Kellor was among the first research workers to go into the field for the study of her material (we must not, however, overlook the fieldwork of Richard Dugdale for his *Jukes,* nor that of Oscar McCulloch for his "Tribe of Ishmael"). Under the direction of the Department of Social Science of the University of Chicago she gathered material at first hand in the North and in the South on three groups: fifty-five white female students (as a control group) sixty white female criminals, and ninety Negro female criminals. She was cautious of the race factor, declaring that in the United States it was impossible to secure pure types, and hence the measurements of students and northern criminals by necessity included mixtures of Germans, Irish, Scotch, Welsh, Swedes, and English. Because of these mixtures the results of European investigators lose significance. Measurements of a member of a brachycephalic race might well show that brachycephalism was a criminal characteristic if he—the criminal —was compared with non-criminals of a dolichocephalic race. (This was done in one instance where measurements of Italians were applied to Negroes.) The tendency, Miss Kellor pointed out, was to underestimate the ethnic significance. This fact, substantiated by many other American investigators, as well as the fact that her study was the first of the American female criminal and of the Negro female criminal, justifies her work as a thoroughly original contribution.

By her measurements Miss Kellor demonstrated the following comparisons of students, white female criminals, and Negro female criminals with each other and with Lombroso's findings:

	Dolicho-cephalic	Meso-cephalic	Brachy-cephalic	Avg.
Students	30%	30%	40%	78.5
White Female Criminals	18%	31%	50%	80.5
Negro Female Criminals	27%	55%	17%	77.0
Prostitutes*	—	—	—	74.6
Felons*	—	—	—	80.2

* From Lombroso, cited by Kellor.

Commenting upon these measurements, she said:

These measurements show some interesting features, and psychological and sociological data throw some light upon them. The significant facts for cephalic indices are, large percentage of dolichocephalic students, of brachycephalic white criminals and of mesocephalic Negroes. The theory that savage races are dolichocephalic and that criminals are allied to them finds little support here. Negroes have been regarded as a pure dolichocephalic race. In the eight southern states visited, only Negroes under forty years of age were measured, and the investigator was compelled to take mixtures, so common was the infusion of white and Indian blood. This is changing the physical characteristics of Negroes.[55]

W. Duncan McKim, while denying a distinctive anatomical type, insisted that abnormalities of the cranium were exceedingly common, but qualified this by adding that there are many criminals of fine physique, attractive features, and pleasing manners.[56]

The controversy concerning the question whether it was the brain that determined the skull shape, or the skull that determined the dimensions of the brain, was carried on both in America and in Europe. By 1903 Robert Lamb, superintendent of the Dannemora State Hospital, New York (for the criminal insane), considered it settled that the skull was dependent upon the development of the cerebral cortex. The reason why the criminal skull was asymmetrical derived from the fact that portions of the cerebral cortex were over-developed at the expense of others.[57]

Perhaps the most extensive work on criminal crania was done by G. Frank Lydston who, as early as 1891 in collaboration with Talbot, published his first findings on habitual criminals and murderers at Joliet penitentiary. These findings were included in his book of addresses and essays in 1892, and were amplified in his book on the diseases of society in 1904.[58] One of the skulls

[55] *Ibid.*, p. 38. By permission of The Macmillan Co., publishers.

[56] W. Duncan McKim, *op. cit.*, pp. 159-160.

[57] Robert B. Lamb, "The Mind of the Criminal," *Proceedings of the American Medico-Psychological Association*, X (1903) 260.

[58] G. Frank Lydston and Eugene S. Talbot, "Studies of Criminals. Degeneracy of Cranial and Maxillary Development in the Criminal Class, with a Series of Criminal Skulls and Histories Typical of the Physical Degeneracy of the Criminal," *Alienist*

he examined and reported on in his chapter on criminal crania
in *Diseases of Society* was that of a Negro criminal of the petty
class who had committed suicide. Lydston pronounced this the
most marked specimen of the dolichocephalic cranium he had
ever seen, having a cephalic index of 59.9. The *tout ensemble* he
thought to be strongly suggestive of a reversion to the anthropoid
type, a characteristic which was often the distinguishing feature
of the degenerate Ethiopian skull, criminal or otherwise. Another
Negro skull belonging to a confidence operator and desperado
showed the characteristic dolichocephalic Negro type with an index of 71, together with an extraordinary thickness of the cranium. The next skull, again of a Negro (lynched for rape) was
characterized by this same massive thickness together with dis-
tortion, asymmetry, marked dolichocephalism, smallness of
frontal development, and enormous orbits. These peculiarities,
said Lydston, could not be accounted for solely on the basis of
accentuation of racial type, being, rather, atavistic, and to a certain degree degenerative, aberrations. A fourth skull had belonged to a half-breed Mexican and Negro of the petty criminal
type. It was markedly dome-shaped and extremely brachycephalic with an index of 98.1. Another mulatto, convicted of
attempted murder, presented the same kind of dome-shaped
brachycephalic cranium. Even after discounting the typical racial
features of another Negro, a five-year-old who had killed two
children, Lydston declared this head to be imperfectly developed
and animal-like. Another half-breed Negro head showed marked
brachycephalism, lack of frontal development, and a definite
dome-like structure. The skull of a train wrecker and murderer
was next exhibited and described as having an excessively developed occipital region, and a cephalic index of 77.8. The skull
of a burglar and desperado had pronounced defective frontal
development, with the cranium sub-microcephalic, massive prognathous jaws, huge supra-orbital ridge, all combining to give a
distinctly anthropoidal aspect. The next specimen, that of a
train wrecker, Lydston called one of the most interesting from
the point of view of degeneration and asymmetry. This cranium

and Neurologist, XII (October 1891) 556-612; G. Frank Lydston, *Addresses and Essays*, 2nd Edition, Louisville, Kentucky, 1893; G. Frank Lydston, *The Diseases of Society*, Philadelphia, 1904.

had a decidedly twisted appearance, with a cephalic index of 87.13. Other skulls presented were those of a prostitute with a decided dolichocephalic type of head, 67.9, but with unusual symmetry; an Indian prostitute with an index of 74.16 and marked symmetry; a murderer with marked dolichocephalism with an index of 70.6, marked asymmetry and moderate prognathism; and another murderer with decided asymmetry. Aside from the skulls Lydston produced photographs of living criminals with descriptions of their head forms, all of them abnormal to some degree, and exhibiting marks of degeneration.

He, too, was cautious of the race factor, pointing out that conditions in Europe were not a fair criteria for use in America. If it had been established that brachycephalism was characteristic of the criminal, then one should observe whether the criminals examined have belonged to a brachycephalic race. Lydston found another difficulty in securing normal standards by which to compare his findings; the offenders who were examined were usually the dregs of the crime class and could hardly be considered representative. Generally speaking, he found the criminal to have an inferior frontal development, with a tendency towards brachycephalism, with occipital development defective, and with extremes of cranial index. In races where brachycephalism was characteristic the offender was extremely so, in races where dolichocephalism predominated the criminal exemplified that quality in exaggerated form. His introductory statement may well serve as a concluding remark here:

The marked aberrance of type and asymmetry of the series of skulls and heads presented herewith are especially suggestive and striking, in view of the fact that they were not selected from a large number of skulls and subjects because of their deformity, but comprise the total number of a series of skulls placed in my hands, chiefly by nonscientists, who collected them solely because of the morbidly curious or historic interest attached to them by virtue of the crimes committed by their owners *in vivo*. The living subjects in the series also came under my observation incidentally. It is worthy of comment that even the remarkable series depicted in Lombroso's atlas does not present such remarkably aberrant types as does this series of studies.[59]

[59] G. Frank Lydston, *The Diseases of Society*, J. B. Lippincott Co., Philadelphia, 1904, p. 517.

Other writers mentioned cranial deformities as characteristic of the criminal type. Arthur MacDonald, in his petition to the national Congress for the establishment of a laboratory for the study of the criminal and defective classes in 1908, wrote of the defective head shape of young criminals.[60] Paul E. Bowers found, among other defects in criminals, malformations of the skull;[61] and Rock Sleyster, physician at the Wisconsin State Prison, stated that cranial asymmetry was unusually common among criminals.[62]

OTHER ANATOMICAL DEVIATIONS

We turn now to a further consideration of anatomical characteristics of the criminal other than cerebral and cranial. The opinion that the criminal bore in his physical make-up certain anomalies which were related to his abnormal behavior has been consistently held in America. While few went so far as to say that all peculiarities had a causal relation to delinquency, yet the combination of these anomalies and their presence in the particular individual stamped him as a deviation from the norm. Hamilton D. Wey, physician at Elmira Reformatory, for example, contended that the peculiarities of the body were an outward and visible sign of an inward "abbreviation," and that generally speaking the criminal was undersized, his weight was disproportionate to his height, and he had a tendency to flat-footedness.[63] Two years later he reported that the criminal's ears were voluminous longitudinally and transversely with a common tendency to be projecting; small ears were occasionally met, but large ones were more common. In crafty offenders Wey observed the yellow or gold irides in the eyes which lent them a snake-like appearance, full of finesse.[64]

[60] Arthur MacDonald, *Juvenile Crime and Reformation, Including Stigmata of Degeneration*, Washington, D.C., 1908, pp. 18-22.

[61] Paul E. Bowers, "Causes of Crime," *New York Medical Journal*, XCVIII (July 19, 1913) 128-131.

[62] Rock Sleyster, "The Physical Bases of Crime as Observed by a Prison Physician," *Bulletin of the American Academy of Medicine*, XIV (December 1913) 396-407.

[63] Hamilton D. Wey, "A Plea for Physical Training of Youthful Criminals," *Proceedings of the National Prison Association*, 1888, pp. 181-193.

[64] Hamilton D. Wey, "Criminal Anthropology," *Proceedings of the National Prison Association*, 1890, pp. 274-291.

Abraham Jacobi remarked upon the scantiness of hair and beard, the irregularity of the nose with an inclination to the one side, large lips, eyelids in close proximity to the nose, the iris usually defective, its color varying in the two eyes, the pupils not centrally located. In addition, the nails of the fingers and toes, the feet, and the genital organs were malformed. The club foot was frequent.[65] James Weir, too, remarked upon the criminal's ear, maintaining that he had never seen a large ear on an habitual thief nor a small ear on a murderer. The thief with murderous tendencies was reported to have especially elongated ears.[66]

Along with anomalies of the ears, H. E. Allison also remarked upon the peculiarities of the teeth, jaws, palate, and the sexual organs, adding, however, these precautions: that very often criminals were defective anatomically, but that it could not be predicted that every such person was of necessity and without choice a criminal.[67] Austin Flint, teacher of physiology at Bellevue Hospital Medical College (which he helped to found), author of works on physiology, visiting physician to the Matteawan State Hospital, and member of the New York Prison Association Executive Committee, who accepted with little reservation the findings of Lombroso, indicated nevertheless that he could not regard all abnormalities as the incontrovertible stamp of criminality, for he wrote:

Take, however, individual instances in which even a considerable number of these abnormalities exist. We may have a person with a marked peculiarity in skull formation, a heavy jaw, abundant red hair, scanty beard, diminished knee-jerk, defective sense of contact, acute vision, dull-hearing, taste, and smell, some muscular abnormality, and yet this person may pass through life honest and upright, showing no criminal tendency even when exposed to temptation and favored by opportunity; but it would be idle to say that, in a person who had committed a crime, physical abnormalities found to be more

[65] Abraham Jacobi, *op. cit.*

[66] James Weir, Jr., *op. cit.*, p. 42-45.

[67] H. E. Allison, "Insanity Among Criminals," *American Journal of Insanity*, LI (July 1894) 54-63; also "Some Relations of Crime to Insanity and States of Mental Enfeeblement," *Journal of the American Medical Association*, XXVII (September 19, 1896) 647-650.

frequent in the criminal than in the normal man, and particularly frequent in a certain class of criminals, may not be of great value in classifying the criminal, forming an estimate of his dangerous qualities and of the probability of reformation. A person may have the so-called insane ear or strikingly abnormal palate, great irregularities in the development of the teeth and an insane ancestry, and yet we must wait for positive evidence of insanity by word, deed or action before he can be pronounced insane. So physical abnormalities, even with criminal ancestry, are never in themselves absolute evidence of criminality.[68]

One of the most thoroughgoing studies made upon the delinquent was that of George E. Dawson, fellow in psychology at Clark University, under the direction of G. Stanley Hall.[69] Influenced by the success of evolutionary theories in biology, Dawson, in common with many others in the field of human behavior, felt that now there had been opened up the possibility of bringing human conduct, aberrant conduct in particular, under the domain of law. Crime, he felt, was not an accident; there were antecedent conditions to account for present behavior. To look for proximate cause, he held, we must study the devitalized constitutions of men and women, their diseased nervous systems and unstable brains, their enfeebled intelligence, their blunted sensibilities, their impotent wills.

Accordingly, Dawson studied twenty-six girls from the State Industrial School for Girls, and twenty-six boys from the Lyman School for Boys (both reform schools in Massachusetts). The girls had an average age of sixteen years, the boys of fifteen years, and were typical specimens of the following classes of offenders: thieves, incendiaries, assaulters, sexual offenders, general incorrigibles. For control groups he used similar groups from the public school children of Worcester, and in some instances used as standards the results of Bowditch on weights of Boston school children, of Porter on mean chest-girth of St. Louis children, and of Quetelet's anthropometric tables. Tests were made

[68] Austin Flint, "The Coming Rôle of the Medical Profession in the Scientific Treatment of Crime and Criminals," *New York Medical Journal*, LXII (October 19, 1895) 484.

[69] George E. Dawson, "A Study in Youthful Degeneracy," *Pedagogical Seminary*, IV (December 1896) 221-258.

as to vitality, head and face measurements, physical anomalies, sensory reaction, and mental reactions.

Compared with normal children the height of the boys was inferior by 9.9 centimeters (cms.) to the average of Boston boys of the same age, while that of the girls was inferior to the normal standard by 6.1 cms.; 92% of the boys and 86% of the girls fell below the normal standard by from 1 to 28 cms., while only 8% of the boys and 14% of the girls rose above the standard by from 1 to 9 cms. In weight, boys were inferior to the average normal by 5.93 kilograms (kgs.), while girls were superior by 0.55 kgs.; 84% of the boys and 37% of the girls were inferior to the normal average by 1 to 22 kgs., 12% of the boys and 59% of the girls were superior to the normal average by 1 to 13 kgs. This combination of low stature and heavy weight confirmed the findings of Formisari, Tarnowsky, and Lombroso, although the boys' results were at variance with the authorities cited by Lombroso.

In the section on cranial anatomy Dawson's material on the head form of the offender has already been presented, but it remains here to indicate his findings on facial and kindred features. As to facial index, both sexes had broader and shorter faces than the normal average. The facial index of the boys was 2.73% greater, and that of the girls 3.54% greater than the normal average. Of the boys 40%, and of the girls 44%, had exceptionally broad faces, that is, above 77; while only 8% of the boys and 4% of the girl had exceptionally narrow faces, that is, below 66. These results corroborated those of Ferri and L. Biliakow for males, and Tarnowsky for women. The boys committed for assault and incendiarism were found by Dawson to have the broadest faces, while the same held true for girls committed for stubbornness and unchastity. The author observed that the significance attaching to these measurements consisted in the fact that they constituted a deviation from the normal type since very broad or very narrow faces characterized the lower races, while the Indo-European face was medium in width. Perhaps, he suggested, the delinquent may either not have outgrown the infantile characteristics or his own race, or he may tend to revert to a lower race altogether.

Under stigmata of degeneracy, Dawson quoted the classification given by Adolph Meyer in the *American Journal of Insanity* for January 1896. Dawson reported facial asymmetry among 30.8% of the boys and 42.3% of the girls, which substantiated Lombroso's statistics of 25% and 33% respectively for men and women. Lombroso's norm of 6% for men and 0.1% for women was accepted as being average. Dawson found that 38.6% of the delinquent boys, and 34.6% of the delinquent girls, had deformed palates, which was almost twice as high as the normal given by Clouston. The former held that this relation of palatal deformity to crime was not accidental, evidencing the fact that the brain dominated skull growth and secondarily determined the shape of the upper maxillary bone and palate. Then since the brain derived its shape and size from the ancestry, and since faulty heredity will determine deficient brain, there followed a causal relation between poor nervous heredity and abnormal palate. As to other stigmata Dawson found 11.5% of the boys and 30.6% of the girls had prognathous jaws, which contradicted the commonly held opinion as to the prognathism of the criminal, since the normal percentage was 34; girls were entirely free of precocious wrinkles, bad eruptions, and unsightly birth marks, while boys had them in the following percentages respectively: 7.3, 15.4, and 3.8. None of the girls had protruding ears, while 34.6% of the boys did; 26.9% of the boys and 11.5% of the girls had asymmetrical ears; 38.6% of the boys and 42.3% of the girls had asymmetrical arms.

Degeneracy, whether in the insane, the idiot, or the criminal, showed itself, said Arthur Sweeney, not only in the mental operations but also in physical deformations of the body. In addition to cranial deformities he listed arrest or excessive development of the bones of the face, heavy and block-shaped jaws, high arched palate, receding lower jaw and forehead, handle-shaped ears, scanty beard, and early wrinkles.[70]

In the first work in America devoted entirely to the subject of degeneracy Eugene S. Talbot brought together and elaborated some of his earlier studies on criminal youth.[71] In the greater

---

[70] Arthur Sweeney, *op. cit.*   [71] Eugene S. Talbot, *op. cit.*

number of cases Talbot thought that crime was hereditary on the grounds that there existed such a great number of inheritable defects in criminals. The criminal was identified as having defective facial development with jaw and teeth deformities. In the case of 465 Pontiac Reformatory inmates, only 171 had normal jaws; in the case of 1,041 Elmira inmates, only 422 had normal jaws; while at Joliet prison, of 468 criminals only 164 had normal jaws. At Pontiac 342 boys had normal teeth, at Elmira 821 had normal teeth. Judged by the normal facial angles set by Camper measurements, most criminals were abnormal. In addition there were malformations of the nose, lips, eye, and ear.

The physician at Pontiac at the time of Talbot's studies was A. B. Middleton. This observer found the criminal characteristics to be so consistent that he offered the following statement with the assertion that the conclusions upon which it was based held true in ninety-eight out of every one hundred cases:

First.—Coarse features. *Second.*—High cheek bones. *Third.*—Thick, heavy and drooping eyebrows. *Fourth.*—Flat forehead. *Fifth.*—Coarse straight hair (among the whites only). These are about the first things a person notices peculiar about these boys, except the expression of guilt which is upon their faces. Next, by looking at them from behind, the very thick, large and heavy neck is very noticeable; the sterno-cleid-mastoid and trapezius muscles seem to be abnormally well developed in nearly every one. Then, from a side view of the neck and head, it will be noticed that the occipital bone seldom, if ever, projects very far past a line let fall parallel with the posterior surface of the neck, thus giving the head and neck a very straight and peculiar appearance, which is invariably the case among young criminals.[72]

[72] A. B. Middleton, "Characteristics of Criminals," *St. Louis Medical Era*, VIII (March 1899) 230-232. There were some exceptions to the tendency to accept too willingly the findings of European students. Among the earliest and most noteworthy (aside from the social scientists with whom we are not here concerned) was Ales Hrdlicka, a trained anthropologist, who studied the inmates of a juvenile asylum in New York. Writing in 1899 on the basis of first hand investigations, Hrdlicka found that although asylum children were somewhat smaller and lighter in weight than other children, the difference was more a matter of nutrition than of inherent physical inferiority. See Ales Hrdlicka: "Anthropological Investigations on One Thousand White and Colored Children of Both Sexes, the Inmates of the New York Juvenile Asylum." Supplement to the *Forty-Seventh Annual Report of the New York Juvenile Asylum,* 1899. He wrote: "If we consider the above data on the criminal and vicious children in

August Drähms did not confine his measurements to the criminal cranium. Comparing his own Bertillon measurements of white male convicts at San Quentin prison with similar measurements made by the Director of Physical Instruction and Sanitary Inspector of the Elmira Reformatory, and with the measurements of Amherst College students made by Dr. Hitchcock, he gave the following table:[73]

	College Students, Amherst College		2,000 Inmates, Elmira Reformatory		2,000 Prisoners, San Quentin	
	Metric	Continental	Metric	Continental	Metric	Continental
	mm.	in.	mm.	in.	mm.	in.
Stature height.......	1726	67.9	1694	66.7	1696	66.8
Outstretched arms....	1794	70.6	1740	68.4	1767	69.6
Right ear length......	....	....	61	2.4	62.4	2.5
Left foot length......	260	10.2	257	10.1	258	10.1
Middle finger length..	....	....	116	4.5	115	4.3
Left finger length.....	....	....	89	3.5	94	3.7
Left forearm.........	449	17.7	454	17.8	462	18.2
Cephalic length......	189	7.44	191	7.52	189	7.43
Cephalic width.......	154	6.1	151	5.9	151	5.9
Cephalic Index.......	81.48		79.00		79.84	

As to nasal index, Drähms found that among habitual criminals 44% possessed noses deviating to one side; among thieves 46% exhibited crooked noses, among sexual offenders 30%, and among homicides 42%. Other bodily signs characteristic of the criminal were prognathic jaw, large and projecting ears (among robbers 42% had large and projecting ears, among recidivists 71% had large ears and 57% projecting ears, among homicides 52% had large and 32% had projecting ears), greater orbital capacity, longer arms, left-handedness. The hands of assassins

---

the institution, and then compare them with similar data obtained from other groups of children here reported, we must come to the conclusion that the misbehaved children are not characterized as a class by any considerable physical inferiority, or by any great proportion of physical abnormalities; nor have I found that any particular atypical character could be said to be characteristic of this class of individuals." *Ibid.*, p. 73.

[73] August Drähms, *op. cit.*, p. 92. By permission of The Macmillan Co. publishers.

were short and large, those of thieves long and thin. Contrary
to other writers, Drähms believed the criminal to be heavier
and taller than normal men.

Commenting in summary fashion on this array of data concerning the physical attributes of the criminal, Drähms wrote:

This completes the criminal delineation in detail, as its subject
stands out in savage perspective from the canvas of anthropological
asymmetry—harsh in its discordant outlines; filled in with glaring
colors drawn from the pigments of a sedimentary humanity; abnormal, viewed as a whole; startlingly familiar upon closer inspection (though no less repugnant), its synthetic outline may yet be said
to rarely find its complete counterpart in actual flesh and blood. The
real man, as he exists, fits into the ideal prototype only piecemeal and
in fragmentary details.[74]

On the basis of her field studies Frances Kellor established
significant differences between white and Negro women criminals and a control group of white women students, which may
be summarized as follows:

	White Women Students	White Women Criminals	Negro Women Criminals
Nasal index...............	58.8	56.6	87.0
Length of ears—right......	56.0 mm.	57.0 mm.	57.0 mm.
Length of ears—left.......	56.0 mm.	58.0 mm.	56.0 mm.
Average mouth width......	48.0 mm.	46.0 mm.	50.0 mm.
Average lip thickness......	14.0 mm.	11.0 mm.	22.0 mm.
Height of forehead.........	66.0 mm.	60.0 mm.	65.0 mm.
Weight...................	124 lbs.	129 lbs.	*
Height...................	1651.0 mm.	1625.0 mm.	1600.0 mm.
Sitting height	866.0 mm.	870.0 mm.	825.0 mm.
Length of thumbs.........	59.0 mm.	59.0 mm.	63.0 mm.

* Not Obtainable.

There was evidently an inference of criminal causality here,
yet Miss Kellor urged caution in the interpretation of the data,
observing, for instance, that height and weight were somewhat
dependent upon racial and nutritional conditions. Furthermore,
there was need to consider the occupations of these offenders as
affecting such items as height and weight and certain muscle

[74] August Drähms, op. cit., pp. 121-122. By permission of The Macmillan Co.,
publishers.

measurements. To the usual conclusion that the hands and feet of criminals evidenced degeneracy Miss Kellor furnished a strong denial. She questioned Talbot's assertions that the flat foot was characteristic of savage races, to which criminals were closely allied. Rather some of her investigations showed that many of the best arches were observed among criminals, and that some of the most deficient were among students.[75]

To combat a prevalently held notion that all degenerates were criminals, Lydston argued that in some cases physical peculiarities had a practical bearing upon the scientific study of the criminal, while in others they were of no moment except as they bore upon the question of degeneracy as a whole. Crooked jaws, twisted heads, deformed ears (all of which he found in the criminals he examined) did not necessarily indicate a criminal. The degenerate may be a criminal, he may be an inebriate, he may be insane, or he may be a member of the social problem class. What Lydston insisted upon was that criminality may be but one of the many expressions of degeneracy.[76] Several years before, W. Duncan McKim had maintained that although criminals were physically defective by reason of abnormalities of jaws, teeth, nose, eyes, and ears, yet he denied that a distinctly anatomical type peculiar to criminals existed.[77]

Among the defects that Arthur MacDonald felt stamped the criminal as a reversion to a lower type were: arm reach greater than height, projection of lower jaw, defective palate, projecting ears, adherent ears, prominent cheek bones, defective teeth, occipital protuberances large, antitragus of ear large, helix of ear rudimentary or absent, thick lips, asymmetrical face, length of fingers greater than that of palm, nose crooked.[78]

Rock Sleyster, at the Wisconsin State Prison, regarded crime as a symptom of the offender's degeneracy, the criminal being a product of the same conditions that produced the insane, the epileptic, the feeble-minded, and other degenerates. The recidivist or habitual criminal at the State Prison, in whom he was

[75] Frances Kellor, *op. cit.*, pp. 35-49.
[76] G. Frank Lydston, *op. cit.*, pp. 86-88; 475-480.
[77] W. Duncan McKim, *op. cit.*, pp. 159-160.
[78] Arthur MacDonald, *op. cit.*, pp. 18-22.

particularly interested, showed marked physical inferiority. With an average of thirty-three years these criminals lacked 2.1 inches of height of the average Wisconsin boy just out of high school, lacked 2.5 inches of the average of Americans of their age, and lacked 2.7 inches of the average Harvard freshman reported by Professor Sargent. Common among them was the degenerate palate and ear, as well as facial asymmetry.[79]

Another prison physician, Paul E. Bowers of Indiana State Prison, while denying that the criminal was an anatomical type, did note anatomical defects in prisoners such as malformations of the teeth and palate, together with the Darwinian tubercle, the Morel ear, and prognathism. These denoted to Bowers the criminal's reversion to a more primitive type.[80]

[79] Rock Sleyster, *op. cit.*, pp. 396-407.
[80] Paul E. Bowers, "Causes of Crime," *New York Medical Journal*, XCVIII (July 19, 1913) 128-131; also "The Recidivist," *Journal of the American Institute of Criminal Law and Criminology*, V (September 1914) 404-415.

VI

CRIMINAL ANTHROPOLOGY II:
THE PHYSIOLOGY OF THE CRIMINAL

THE foregoing chapter traced the evidence pointing to an alleged anatomical criminal type. The task of the present chapter shall be to present the evidence which was adduced to demonstrate the existence of a criminal type with a physiological base. That which bore on the organization of the structure was discussed under anatomy, that which pertains to functioning shall be dealt herewith under physiology.

Considerable license shall be exercised in this chapter by employing a twofold classification of functioning. Concerning the first there can be little disagreement—the functioning of the organism on an organic level. Of the second, based on the assumption that psychological manifestations can be subsumed under physiology, there are valid grounds for dispute. Nevertheless this assumption will be made, that certain psychological manifestations have a physiological base in the functioning of the organism. With the larger question as to the criminal personality —organically causal or functionally causal—there always will be marked difference of opinion. For the social scientist the personality is essentially a social product, and the development of that personality a social process as well as the end of a social process. The non-social scientist places his emphasis particularly upon the organic base and is inclined to discount the rôle played by social action and interaction.

PHYSIOLOGICAL FACTORS
(a) Physical Attributes

Running through any discussion of characteristics of the criminal is the necessary distinction between the prisoner and the non-prisoner, between those characters or qualities derived from prison experience and those common to all offenders. The prison physician at Elmira Reformatory, Hamilton D. Wey, early made this distinction with respect to skin pallor and heart inhibition. At the same time he described the offenders at Elmira as having, at the period of adolescence, large prominent nipples surrounded by aureolae that were pigmented beyond what was usually seen in the male, and also as having mammary glands as large as a hickory nut, generally lateral, occasionally bilateral. Also "The genitals of this class were developed to a degree not altogether warranted by their years, but in accordance with the physiological law that use is a factor in structural amplification."[1] Two years later, at the 1892 congress of the same organization, the National Prison Association, Abraham Jacobi claimed goitre and rupture were often found among criminals. The veins were frequently dilated, and the vascular system functionally defective. Irritable heart, neuralgic headache, dizziness, fainting spells, convulsions, partial paralyses he found to be frequent occurrences.[2]

George E. Dawson, who it will be recalled, examined twenty-six boys and twenty-six girls in correctional institutions of Massachusetts, found the health of these children to be poor in comparison with that of normal children, although the institutional diet and régime undoubtedly were a factor in this condition.[3] The average mean chest-girth of the boys was 1.76 centimetres less than the normal average, and that of the girls 5.85 cms. less. Of the boys 70% and of the girls 73% were inferior to the normal average by from 1 to 15 cms., while 26% of the boys and 11% of the girls were superior. The average lung capacity of the boys was 154 cubic inches, as against 170 cu. in. among normal men. Although the ages of these boys ranged from sixteen to twenty-six years, the measurements indicated inferior lung capacity. In strength of grip the delinquent boy was inferior to the standard by .27 kilograms, and the girls by .87 kgs. Both sexes were inferior in 56% of the cases to the normal average by from 1.82 11.82 kgs., while 40% of the boys and 44%

[1] Hamilton D. Wey, "Criminal Anthropology," *Proceedings of the National Prison Association*, 1890, pp. 281-282.

[2] Abraham Jacobi, *op. cit.*, pp. 179-180.

[3] George E. Dawson, *op. cit.*, pp. 228-229.

of the girls were superior to the normal average by from 1.18 to 15.18 kgs.

As to sight, 32% of the boys and 20% of the girls had defective vision as compared with 18% among the normal group for boys and 24% for girls; 28% of the delinquent boys and 24% of the girls had defective hearing as opposed to 22.5% and 21.77% for normals; 32% of the boys and 44% of the girls showed normal sensitiveness of touch, 32% of the boys and of the girls showed a dull sense of touch, while 12% of the boys and none of the girls had delicate touch discrimination.[4]

That a definite connection between certain disease states and criminal behavior existed was the contention of J. B. Ransom. Out of 2,011 men examined by him upon their admission to prison, 239 had gross heart lesions and many others had more or less important ones.[5] Ransom estimated that 25% of all criminals would show diseases of the heart or of the great blood vessels. Meningitis, he held, was also a prolific cause of crime, especially of assault and homicide, by virtue of the formation of a thickened patch, a softened area, or a circumscribed adhesion. Such a condition was capable, as Ransom put it, of driving the unhappy to the most fiendish acts of violence, "as the spur to the horse, it urges on the diabolical impulse." Syphilis he also found to be an important cause of grave neurosis; among criminals a large percentage were syphilitic, with deposits of gummatous tumors which produced degeneracy of the brain tissues. Tuberculosis was also a factor in crime because of the presence of tubercular toxins circulating in the brain.[6]

In his "Short Notes in Anthropology," Hamilton D. Wey gave some indication of the material which he was to treat more fully two years later. In this latter report, which was his report to the superintendent, Z. R. Brockway, for the Twentieth Annual Report of the Elmira Reformatory, Wey, while refusing to admit

---

[4] George E. Dawson, *op. cit.*, pp. 231-243.

[5] J. B. Ransom, *op. cit.*

[6] It is significant in view of Ransom's position as a prison physician and of the period in which he practised—the end of the nineteenth century—to have him state: "The complete study and treatment of the criminal must ever be largely a sociologic one. . . . And gradually but surely the purely anthropologic study of the criminal has given place to a plainly more sociologic one based upon it." J. B. Ransom, *ibid.*, p. 793.

the criminal type, did recognize certain sense abnormalities, chest power of a low order, anomalies of circulation, nervous system imperfectly inhibited.[7] Among his nineteen tables there were some showing the relation between age and lung capacity, height and lung capacity, weight and lung capacity, age and strength of chest, age and strength of back, age and strength of legs, age and strength of arms, height and strength of chest, height and strength of back, height and strength of legs, height and strength of arms.

Eugene S. Talbot, too, remarked upon the low physical condition of criminals in reformatories as compared with healthy school children. The juvenile delinquents were puny, sickly, scrofulous, often deformed, sluggish, liable to fits, mean in figure, and defective in vital energy. In addition their complexion was bad, they had spinal deformities, and were likely to have club-foot, deaf-mutism, congenital blindness, and epilepsy.[8] In contrast to these descriptions of criminals is that of the prison physician, A. B. Middleton, who found inmates at Pontiac Reformatory healthy, with well-developed lungs and chest, although many of them had tobacco hearts.[9]

Among the feature which August Drähms noted were the coarse texture of the hair, rarity of baldness (2% of thieves, 13% of swindlers, and 19% of normals), thickness of eyebrows (especially in thieves), scantiness of beard in the male (with a tendency to the contrary in females), small and uneasy eyes (in the homicide cold, fixed and nystagmic, in the sexual offender generally light and projecting in their orbits), congestion of the eyelids (particularly in the case of the pronounced sexual offenders and congenital homicides). As to the general health of the criminal, Drähms held that his general vegetative functions exceeded those of the normal, while the muscular and osseous system was weak. The criminal was not long lived.[10]

On strength tests with the dynamometer Miss Kellor reported

[7] Hamilton D. Wey, "Short Notes in Anthropology," *Eighteenth Yearbook of the New York State Reformatory*, Elmira, New York, 1893, pp. 152-181; also "Notes and Observations," *Twentieth Yearbook*, etc., 1895, pp. 63-102, with nineteen tables.

[8] Eugene S. Talbot, *op. cit.*, pp. 18-19.

[9] A. B. Middleton, *op. cit.*, pp. 230-232.

[10] August Drähms, *op. cit.*, pp. 112-117.

the inferior performance of women criminals, white and Negro, in contrast to college students. Students recorded 71 pounds for the right arm and 60 for the left, white female criminals in the penitentiary tested 59 pounds right and 57 left, white female criminals in workhouse 53 right, 48 left, and Negro criminals 73 right and 69 left. The manometer used for chest strengths showed the average for students to be 166 pounds, for white criminals in the penitentiary 160, and for white criminals in the workhouse 113 pounds.[11]

G. Frank Lydston believed that the comparative study of the criminal and the normal man was one of the most difficult problems in science. He was particularly impressed with the sampling problem, pointing out that criminals in institutions were there by reason of their ill luck in getting caught, and that incarcerated criminals represented but a small, and not necessarily representative, proportion of the total population. Furthermore there was the difficulty of establishing normal standards for the comparison of physical and psychical anomalies. The criminal type might be paralleled by non-criminal degenerates.[12]

After making due allowance for insufficient data, superficial observations, and over-enthusiasm, the fact still remains that the born criminal is always, and the occasional criminal usually, a defective, and, like all other defectives, presents mental and physical aberrations that stamp him as abnormal. Criminal anthropology has not yet arrived at the point where arbitrary diagnoses or classifications of criminal types can be justified by the psychic and physical peculiarities of the criminal. In brief, the most that we have been able to do thus far is to stamp criminals as the vanguard of our vast army of degenerates, and to show that they are characterized by the psychic and physical anomalies of their congeners.[13]

Proceeding to the physical characteristics of the criminal, Lydston found a defective muscular system with marked lack of tone, defective chest development and stooped shoulders, and deficiency of the respiratory apparatus as characteristic features. Vascular and cardiac diseases were frequent, there were extensive

[11] Frances Kellor, *op. cit.*, pp. 46-47.
[12] G. Frank Lydston, *op. cit.*, pp. 476-516.
[13] *Ibid.*, pp. 479-480.

sexual anomalies in both male and female prisoners, with undescended testes and disproportionate size of penis and pronounced femininity in some males, and masculinity in some females, and with occasionally mammary enlargement and milk secretion in male criminals. Sexual criminals among males presented a sparseness of beard and body hair, while sexual criminals among females exhibited excessive hairy development.[14]

Among Wisconsin State Prison inmates Rock Sleyster found a deficiency in chest and expansion measurements, a subnormal temperature and a high pulse rate (except murderers, who had a normal temperature and pulse rate). The degenerate and subnormal were especially prone to diseases of the chest, they were characterized by pigeon breasts, poorly developed chests, and stoop-shoulders. Valvular heart lesions were common, while the rate of deaths from pulmonary and cardiac diseases was unusually high. Venereal diseases were extraordinarily common, but Sleyster thought this may be as much a symptom of degeneracy as a cause.[15]

With the continued use of the Juvenile Court in the first and second decade of the twentieth century and the establishment of medical services therewith, an increasing literature on the physical aspects of criminal behavior appeared. There was still occasional emphasis upon degeneracy, but generally speaking this was at a minimum, while the offender came to be regarded more as an individual than as the representative of a class. Edward F. Waite, a Judge of the District Court in Minneapolis, presented

[14] Although Lydston was one of the leading figures in criminal anthropology in America, he was neither unmindful of the extravagant claims made nor unsparing in his criticism of them. In one connection he wrote: "I have already stated that, in my humble opinion there has been much of rubbish in the alleged development of modern criminal anthropology. There has been a gathering of bricks by people who had no cement with which to put them together, and who could not build a house with them if they had the cement." In another place he added: "The foolishness that has been perpetrated in the name of criminal anthropology has perhaps added something to the gayety of nations, but it has done more to prejudice logical thinkers against a great principle,—i.e., the material factor in vice and crime." And finally, he remarked: "The form of the nose, color of skin, and peculiarities of the hair of criminals have received considerable attention, the labors of some scientists in these directions suggesting that the mountain of science sometimes labors and brings forth a mouse. Possibly future parturitions may develop more of importance, but it is well to remember that even scientists are not immune from monomania."

[15] Rock Sleyster, *op. cit.*

material which has been made available through the Court services showing that juvenile offenders had more physical defects than Minneapolis school children, while repeaters had more than first offenders.[16]

In the same symposium conducted by the American Academy of Medicine in 1913-1914, John H. Witter, formerly a probation officer and now a director of a boys' club, made his observation that an examination of children at the Chicago Detention home showed 204 carious teeth in the mouths of fifty-eight children, and that in 90% of the cases the teeth were almost wholly destroyed. Witter felt that there was a strong likelihood of irregular school attendance and truancy owing to ill health, and that truancy was often a prelude to juvenile delinquency. He cited the cases of four boys who had been delinquent through physical causes: one by reason of a head injury, another through feeblemindedness, a third because of eye strain, and the last owing to malnutrition.[17]

(b) Psychological Attributes

The present section will be concerned with a variety of attributes loosely subsumed under the psychological—ranging all the way from tattooing and left-handedness to reaction times and sensitiveness to pain. As is to be expected, it was the prison physician, and again Hamilton D. Wey of Elmira, who early brought to light his observations upon incarcerated offenders.[18] Tattooing, for instance, he found to be one of the characteristic expressions of the criminal, especially of the low-grade criminal. Not only was practically every part of the body tattooed, but every conceivable design was used, such as religious symbols, emblems

[16] Edward F. Waite, "The Physical Bases of Crime: From the Standpoint of the Judge of a Juvenile Court," *Bulletin of the American Academy of Medicine*, XIV (December 1913) 389-390.

[17] John H. Witter, "The Physical Basis of Crime from the Standpoint of the Probation Officer," *Bulletin of the American Academy of Medicine*, XV (April 1914) 102-104.

[18] Wey took over from the controversial field of biology the notion of the "sport," and asked in his report for 1895 whether criminals should not be regarded biologically as sports? His reference was not so much to behavior as to the structure and organization which underlay that behavior. With the biologists he regarded a sport as a spontaneous variation from the normal type which is not perpetuated.

of love, obscene legends, and animals of all kinds. Left-handedness was more common than among non-criminals.[19]

In testing his delinquent boys and girls from correctional institutions in Massachusetts, George E. Dawson observed the average mean reaction to pain on the part of the delinquent boy to be 3.73 kilograms greater than the normal average, while that of the girls was 1.64 kgs. greater than the normal average for girls; only 4% of the boys and 12% of the girls showed less sensitiveness to pain than normal children, while 92% of the boys and 80% of the girls showed greater sensitiveness, and 4% of the boys and 8% of the girls showed the same as the normal average. Dawson admitted his results were at variance with those of Lombroso's, but remarked that his findings were entirely consistent with the neurotic character of the delinquent, since a choreic boy or an hysterical girl will endure less pain than a healthy one. Furthermore, these delinquent children were in poorer health than the average normal child.[20]

On psychological tests the average of the Worcester school children was taken as 100%. In attention the average for delinquent boys was 78%, for delinquent girls 80%; in memory the average for boys was 99%, for girls 91%; in association the average for boys was 44%, for girls 113%. All these tests showed wide variations in accomplishment, some with very low averages (lower for delinquents than for normals) and some with very high averages (in the case of the delinquent girls some scored higher than normals).

Thus Dawson established, for himself and for his day, the inferiority of the delinquent. The delinquent, compared to the normal, was shorter in stature, lighter in weight, with diminished strength in the muscles of the hands, and with greater sensitiveness to pain. With the delinquent there was also a tendency towards smaller heads, broader faces, the general type

---

[19] Hamilton D. Wey, "Criminal Anthropology," *Proceedings of the National Prison Association*, 1890, p. 282; "Notes in Anthropology," *Eighteenth Yearbook of the New York State Reformatory*, Elmira, New York, 1893, pp. 170-173; "Observations and Notes," *Twentieth Year Book of the New York State Reformatory*, Elmira, New York, 1895, pp. 86-95.

[20] George E. Dawson, *op. cit.*, p. 232.

conforming to that of the lower races or that of the infantile period of our own race. Similarly he possessed more physical anomalies than did the normal person, chiefly of asymmetrical heads and faces, and deformed palates. He had more defects in sight and hearing, and a greater dullness in the sense of touch. Even in his mental reactions he was inferior, particularly with respect to attention, memory, and association.[21]

Eugene S. Talbot, who had classified the criminal as a degenerate, described him as stupid, liable to fits, irritable, violent, and too often quite incorrigible.[22] Daniel R. Brower, touching on the psychic side of the criminal, found him to be morally insensible, with lack of foresight, of a low grade of intelligence, possessed of vanity, egotism, and a victim of emotional insanity.[23] Brower also noted tattooing as common to criminals, as had also the two prison physicians, W. A. M'Corn and A. B. Middleton, before him.[24]

On the other hand, August Drähms declared no particular significance attached to tattooing, the practice not being peculiar to criminals alone, but fully as common with sailors and soldiers. He regarded it as the mark of the wanderer and idler the world over.[25] He did, however, subscribe to the moral insensibility of the criminal. Furthermore, the criminal was cruel, with lack of remorse as a logical corollary; he lacked conscience and foresight; he was mentally and emotionally unstable; he was vain; he was insensible to pain. Faithful to his pals, on other counts he was untruthful. His intelligence was of a low order. Blushing, which Drähms called nature's barometer of the sensibilities, was not a weakness of the criminal nature. Among ninety-eight young offenders 44% did not blush, and out of 122, 81% did not respond.[26]

In common with Brower, M'Corn, and Middleton, and with Lydston, who followed her publication by three years, Miss

---

[21] George E. Dawson, *op. cit.*, pp. 247-248.

[22] Eugene S. Talbot, *op. cit.*, pp. 18-19.

[23] Daniel R. Brower, "Medical Aspects of Crime," *Boston Medical and Surgical Journal*, CXL (June 15, 1899) 570-574.

[24] W. A. M'Corn, *op. cit.*, p. 51; A. B. Middleton, *op. cit.*, p. 232.

[25] August Drähms, *op. cit.*, p. 115.

[26] *Ibid.*, pp. 59-81.

Kellor held tattooing to be characteristic of the criminal. Students were not so decorated, in contrast to white and Negro female criminals.[27] On psychological tests which she made upon students and criminals she found no color blindness for students or criminals, although there was color weakness in both; strabismus, myopia, and hypermetropia appeared in all classes, as well as discrepancies between the eyes (for white criminals the right eye was better for 25%, the left for 16%, and the remainder showed equal or no defects). Auditory tests revealed that the average distance at which a stop watch could be heard (with cotton-stopped ears) for students was, in feet, 3.9 for right ear and 4 for the left; for criminals 4.7 for right and 5.4 for left; for Negroes 6.3 for right and 6 for left. Students showed marked defects to the extent of 22% of their number in contrast with 23% for white criminals and 11% of Negroes.

On dermal and muscular tests, criminals generally speaking were less sensitive to pain and touch than students. Olfactory tests showed that students had an error percentage of 47, white criminals in penitentiary 72, white criminals in workhouses 77, Negro criminals 56, tending to disprove that criminals have their olfactory senses better developed and hence are allied to the savage races. In gustatory tests there was practically no difference in the error percentage of students, white criminals, and Negro criminals. In hearing tests criminals were superior.

The psychological tests also revealed students to exceed criminals in memory, while Negro criminals scored lowest. On association tests criminals were inferior to students in rate of association, their associations had a narrower range, while their quality of thought reflected a lower moral, intellectual, and social grade.

The third group of tests (the first was physical, the second mental) was the psycho-physical. On the fatigue tests in this category it was found that white criminals and Negro criminals were equally susceptible to fatigue, while student susceptibility was greater. Criminals exceeded students in strength of pull. Coördination tests between hand and eye showed students rank-

[27] Frances Kellor, *op. cit.*, p. 48.

ing higher than Negro criminals and making fewer errors. In
another coördination test, students and white criminals were
more accurate than Negroes. Responses of the individual, as
measured by respiratory charts, to surprise, pain, odors, hate,
love, joy, modesty, vanity, fear, showed an inferiority on the
part of the criminal, white and Negro. Certainly, said Miss Kellor, criminals are not equipped for functioning as successfully
in response to outward forces as are those of more accurate per-
ceptions and judgments.[28]

Men who were brought into daily contact in their professional
work with what used to be called, in the "charitological" writings
of the 1880's and 1890's, the criminal and pauper classes, were
inclined to be rather forthright in their observations, taking little
refuge in citation from authority. Such a one was Henry M.
Boies, who wrote in 1893, out of his vast experience in prison
and institutional inspection work, that examination had undoubtedly shown the abnormality of all criminals. They, in common
with paupers, were the degenerate, imperfect, knotty, worm-
eaten, half-rotten fruit of the race.

They are human deformities and monstrosities, physically ill-
shapen, weak and sickly, with irregular features. They bear a sinister,
ignoble, and furtive expression. They have an unbalanced and distorted cranium, are of a low order of intelligence, apparently devoid
of the nobler sentiments; with a depraved if not utter absence of
moral sense or conscience. They are as abnormal and anomalous
mentally and morally, as physically, yet we know physical anomalies
often exist without psychical deformity, and moral obliquity or depravity is found in youth without outward evidence, though they
stamp their seal indelibly upon the physique before old age.[29]

In 1901 (Boies was a member of the Pennsylvania State Board
of Public Charities from 1887 to 1902) in addition to describing
them as physically deformed, defective, and undeveloped, they
were held to be psychically warped and depraved.[30]

According to W. Duncan McKim, the criminal had a sinister
look, was insensible to pain, was vain, cruel, and morally in-

---

[28] Frances Kellor, op. cit., pp. 50-78.
[29] Henry M. Boies, Prisoners and Paupers, New York, 1893, p. 172.
[30] Henry M. Boies, The Science of Penology, New York, 1901, pp. 23-24.

sensible.[31] On the other hand, R. T. Irvine at Sing Sing Prison, while noting that the criminal was vain, selfish, impure, self-indulgent, cowardly, impatient, bad-tempered, unstable, reckless, apathetic, self-conceited, fickle, wayward, and stupid, stated that he attached no special value to the list of these characteristics. Even though it was neither scientific nor exhaustive, yet he did find most of these characteristics to accompany degeneration, of which crime was but one of its many expressions.[32]

Perhaps few descriptions of the criminal were as full as Lydston's, given in his book on the diseases of society, published in 1904. As to muscular activity he found the criminal ordinarily sluggish and indolent, but capable upon occasion of extraordinary agility. Left-handedness he found to be common among the criminal population, as well as ambidexterity, with a greater strength in the left hand among criminals in contrast to the normal population. His relative insensitivity to pain ranked him among the lower savages and animals, but Lydston was not convinced of the reputed "disvulnerability" of criminals. As to intelligence, there was no set level among criminals, Lydston continued, some were stupid, some were highly ingenious, the degree of intelligence varying with the type of offender and his particular criminal skill. The American murderer had high intelligence, as might be expected from the fact that he was a criminal by impulse; very often he represented the type of sporadic criminality. The true criminal was a supreme egotist, without conscience or remorse. He was without courage, was emotionally unstable, was devoid of sentiment, was vain above all things. In short, the criminal, judged by his personality, was an atypical being.[33]

In describing degenerate and criminal children, G. Stanley Hall dealt with their neurotic character, their irritability, their vanity, lack of vigor, fluctuations in mood, sexual perversion at puberty, extreme shyness, and "dashing about like a ship without a rudder, fairly well if the winds be fair and the sea calm, but dependent on the elements for the character and the time of

[31] W. Duncan McKim, *op. cit.*, pp. 158-169.
[32] R. T. Irvine, "The Congenital Criminal," *Medical News*, LXXXII (April 18, 1903) 749-752.
[33] G. Frank Lydston, *op. cit.*, pp. 490-516.

the final wreck."[34] They easily become victims of insomnia, neurasthenia, hypochondria, neuroticism, hysteria, or insanity, and commit crime with less cause or provocation than other persons.

Paul E. Bowers described the physical characteristics of the criminal and then insisted that the physiological anomalies suggested the causes which produced defects in the psyche. He defined more clearly as psychic phenomena the exaggerated egotism of the criminal, his eccentricities, his ill-balanced mental activities, irritability, inability of continuous applicaton to mental or normal labor, emotional poverty, brutality, and fatalism.[35] In the next year (1914) Bowers, insisted upon these same physiological and psychic defects, adding to them moral anaesthesia and emotional instability, as well as tattooing (evidence of reversion to a more primitive order), and depraved aesthetic taste.[36]

THE PHYSIOGNOMY OF THE CRIMINAL

Around the turn of the nineteenth century in France Lavater studied the physiognomy of the criminal. No record of his influence in America exists, save through the work of the early phrenologists and the later findings of the criminal anthropologists. It was not until the influence of Lombroso was felt that there was anything more than the intuitive convictions of scholars and preachers that the criminal could be known by his facial features.

As in the case of so much of what has already been presented we must start with Hamilton D. Wey, of Elmira Reformatory, as he described the criminal he found in the reformatory. The asymmetrical head with facial lines coarse and hard was characteristic of the degenerative physiognomy.[37] Abraham Jacobi, too, in his study of the criminal, declared that physiognomic doctrines have a certain basis in fact.[38] Basing his studies upon Bertil-

---

[34] G. Stanley Hall, *Adolescence*, New York, 1908, I, pp. 335-337.

[35] Paul E. Bowers, "Causes of Crime," *New York Medical Journal*, XCVIII (July 19, 1913) 128-131.

[36] Paul E. Bowers, "The Recidivist," *Journal of the American Institute of Criminal Law and Criminology*, V (September 1914) 404-415.

[37] Hamilton D. Wey, "A Plea for Physical Training of Youthful Criminals," *Proceedings of the National Prison Association*, 1888, p. 183.

[38] Abraham Jacobi, *op. cit.*, pp. 179-180.

lon measurements and photographs of prisoners in the Wisconsin State Prison, M'Corn found definite features peculiar to the criminal.[39]

Concerning the physiognomy of the criminal Daniel R. Brower wrote emphatically:

The habitual criminal, who constitutes the great bulk of the class, is a biological study, and his anatomic, physiologic and psychologic nature demands our most careful investigation, in order that we may determine the ways and the means to settle the various questions to which he gives rise. There is a criminal physiognomy, by no means easy to describe, but the same, no matter whether seen in our jails or in the jails of any other country on the globe. Any physician, by looking at the face, without being able to describe its anatomic peculiarities, can reach conclusions, as Mantegazza writes, on five important problems: (1) The condition of health or of sickness; (2) the degree of beauty or of ugliness; (3) the moral worth; (4) the intellectual worth; (5) the race. The study of physiognomy, regarded as of such great importance by the physician of the last century, is too much neglected by the physician of today.[40]

August Drähms gave perhaps the most complete treatment of the criminal physiognomy of all American writers. In his chapter on the instinctive criminal he considered fully the facial angle of Camper, the facial index (breadth to length), the nasal index (breadth to length), the palatal index (width to length of palatal vault), the criminal jaw, the criminal ear, the hair of the criminal, eyebrows, beard, orbital index, and eyes, and came to the conclusion that there was a distinct criminal physiognomy.[41] Frances Kellor, on the other hand, doubted the existence of a physiognomical type of offender, declaring that theories of physiognomy contributed nothing to our understanding of causes of crime.[42]

Lydston also undertook to answer the question as to whether or not the criminal's appearance was different from that of other people.

[39] W. A. M'Corn, *op. cit.*
[40] Daniel R. Brower, *op. cit.*, p. 571.
[41] August Drähms, *op. cit.*, pp. 106-113.
[42] Frances Kellor, *op. cit.*, pp. 39-41.

Without claiming that the criminal presents characteristics that are pathognomic of his profession, or which would enable even the expert to pick him out on sight, I do not hesitate to express my belief that he presents, in general, characteristics of expression that distinguish him from the average of men.[43]

Lydston felt that vocational influences were exerted upon criminals just as they were upon other men. These influences, together with unconscious imitation and habit, were powerful factors in molding the criminal physiognomy. He was convinced that conformation and expression of face were shaped by, and often an index of, mental operations, and that the character of the emotions to which one was habitually subjected permanently modified the facial expression.[44]

CONCLUSION

Beginning belatedly and developing haltingly, criminal anthropology has run a course in America that has been marked by many contradictions. When the conclusions of Lombroso, Benedikt, and other European students of the criminal were introduced into America there was a general acceptance of them, but at the same time there was an occasional dissent. Perhaps this was inevitable since the circles to which such conclusions reached contained those very students who had shared in the controversies of the theories of biological and social evolution raging since

[43] G. Frank Lydston, *op. cit.*, p. 486.

[44] No discussion of American criminal anthropology would be complete without mention of the writings of other writers in the field whose main dependence was upon European works. These writers added little if anything to the store of original research on the criminal, but by their familiarity with the works of Europeans they brought to native writers the range and variety of foreign research. Chronologically they were: Robert Fletcher, "The New School of Criminal Anthropology," *American Anthroplogist*, IV (July 1891) 201-236; Arthur MacDonald, *Criminology*, 1893; *Abnormal Man*, 1893; *Education and Patho-Social Studies*, 1893; *Experimental Study of Children*, 1899; *Hearing on the Bill—H. R. 14798—to Establish a Laboratory for the Study of the Criminal, Pauper, and Defective Classes*, 1902; *A Plan for the Study of Man*, 1902; *Statistics of Crime, Suicide, and Insanity*, 1903; *Man and Abnormal Man*, 1905; *Juvenile Crime and Reformation*, 1908; Charles Richmond Henderson, *An Introduction to the Study of the Dependent, Defective and Delinquent Classes*, 1893; Austin Flint, "The Coming Rôle of the Medical Profession in the Scientific Treatment of Crime and Criminals," *New York Medical Journal*, LXII (October 19, 1895) 481-490; John J. Berry, "The Physical Basis of Crime," *Medical Age*, XIV (February 10, 1896) 72-77.

Darwin and Spencer had first enunciated them in the 1850's, 1860's and 1870's. The difference of opinion within the field of criminal anthropology largely centered around the question whether or not criminal man was a special kind of creation. For many it was impossible to admit that the criminal was a product of orderly evolution. These reasoned that there must be some explanation of this being who was a variant in the field of social behavior, and this explanation must lie in actual anatomical and physiological differences. As token of his difference the criminal was considered atavistic, a victim of arrested development or a product of degeneracy, or even biologically a sport. While one body of opinion held to differences in structure and functioning of the criminal's organism, another held equally determinedly to differences in structure and functioning of the criminal brain. For some the criminal had a characteristic head form and shape, and for others his variation from the normal was based upon his differences of body and brain as expressed in his functioning as a unique individual. The criminal reacted in certain ways as distinct from the normal man because, organically, he was that kind of being.

A review of criminal anthropology in America reveals nothing original in the early years with the possible exception of the work of Dr. Hamilton D. Wey at Elmira Reformatory; the early works were principally borrowing or translations from the European students. But as time went on, more and more Americans based their findings upon their first-hand contact with the criminal, inside and outside of prison. It was in this field that the prison physician made his greatest contribution. The record here begins in the last quarter of the nineteenth century with the Fowler translation of Benedikt and the researches of Wey, and concludes with the findings of Dr. William Healy which so decisively shifted attention from the anatomical to the psychological and social.

As the conclusions of the workers in the field of criminal anthropology are critically examined in the light of our knowledge of today it is perhaps too easy to demonstrate the inherent weaknesses of much of their work. Yet it is necessary, and is done with the suspicion that much of the research today may undergo the same scrutiny in the years to come. Perhaps most noticeable in the earlier works is the proneness to jump to causal conclusions where perhaps no causal relation existed. In some instances the differences between the criminal and the non-criminal are cited and the conclusion immediately arrived at that these differences are causal. In other cases there are conclusions drawn upon imperfect statistical samples, samples used without regard to the most fundamental axioms of statistics as to representativeness or adequacy. Finally, the commonest and most besetting error was the assumption of a unilateral and unifactoral explanation of criminal behavior. It remained for Dr. Healy to present evidence so convincing that future researchers can never go back to the days of simple explanation. Criminal behavior is complex, and requires for understanding more than a knowledge of head form, brain convolutions, or galvanometer reaction times.

VII

HEREDITY

THE IMPORTANT and predominating rôle of heredity in criminal behavior is a constant theme running through the works of the authors presented in these pages. Many of these give some consideration to the social or environmental factor, but the major emphasis of every author considered was upon the rôle of the factor immediately beyond the control of man—heredity. Criminal anthropologists in general have concluded their works with a brief acknowledgment of the fact that the surroundings had some influence upon man's conduct, but most of their work built up a stronger case for hereditary factors. This treatise is not concerned with the age-old controversy of heredity and environment, but rather it seeks to examine the thought in a period of American life which dealt with a biological, physiological, and anthropological approach. The relative merits of heredity and environment, of nature versus nurture, are not involved here.

At the outset it may be well to state that the theological doctrine of man's original sin constitutes a separate body of thought that is beyond the province of this work. Were the premise of man's original sin granted, there would be no need for this or any other treatise on criminal behavior; there would be no need for calling in the aid of the sciences of anthropology and biology; no need to study man's criminal behavior in relation to his functioning organism and his anatomical structure; no need to study him in relation to other men.[1]

The reports of the Eastern State Penitentiary may be taken as a starting point of what has become a very considerable body of knowledge. While, strictly speaking, penology is concerned with the disposition of the offender after commitment, significant

[1] For the purposes of the present work the modern definition of hereditary transmission is adopted. Wherever writers have described a transmission as congenital when the obvious meaning was hereditary, it will be interpreted as hereditary. Hereditary transmission is understood to be transmission through the germ plasm.

insight into the factors bringing the prisoner to prison has frequently come from penology. Opened in 1831, the Eastern State Penitentiary of Pennsylvania began a notable and far-reaching experiment in penology, and its uninterrupted annual reports from that date are a record of that experiment. Written by wardens chosen because of competency, and by inspectors with an extraordinary devotion to the problem of the prisoner, these early reports contained, in addition, the accounting of the physician and the moral instructor. The combined labors of these four public servants furnished a series of documents which are without equal in American penology.

Examining the early reports, one finds the moral instructor ascribing the chief cause of crime to "propensity." In his 1841 report he assigned it as the cause in 116 out of 400 cases; in 1842 it was responsible for 40 out of 110 cases; in 1843, 54 out of 132 cases; in 1844, 66 out of 156 cases; and in 1845, for 340 out of 962 cases. It may here be noted, parenthetically, that propensity has a strong phrenological tone; classifications that followed from 1856 to 1865 were unadornedly phrenological. Thus in 1856 the moral instructor designated under *Predominant Passions* the following:

Jealousy	.24%
Combativeness	3.38%
Amativeness	8.17%
Destructiveness	17.30%
Acquisitiveness	70.90%

In 1875 the report of the inspectors stated that the "crime cause" was either chronic, contagious, or constitutional; chronic as the result of social influences, contagious as the sudden, unexpected, and undeveloped criminal cause and effect, and constitutional as the consequence of inherited predisposition or tendency to commit acts in violation of the law.

That a tendency, predisposition to commit crime is hereditary, seems hardly to be doubted. It may arise from a lack of moral force to resist it, or that want of moral force may be more apparent from the low mental or physical forces which otherwise would counteract its development. It may be that there are peculiar inherited moral traits which do not animate the mind to a full comprehension of the motives and actions which are in themselves criminal.[2]

Frequently these reports contained tables showing the number of relatives of prisoners who were or had been in prison, as evidence of inborn criminality. The report for the year 1879 gave a table headed "Showing Hereditary Crime-Cause of Thirty-Seven Convicts in Confinement During 1878." The report demonstrated that of these thirty-seven every one had some relatives in prison. How irresistible, the report asks, must be the mental and moral tendencies of those who have been endowed with the evil and degenerated characteristics of several generations!

Again, there is an inherited trait or taint in many, which may possibly lead to the commission of crimes, a motor, as it were, that unconsciously impels those who suffer from this hereditary taint, to become criminals, and consort with the wicked class.

Children born of parents who are of the criminal class, or who are associates in vices, or in connection with the depraved class, a large and growing population, especially in cities, are predisposed to, if they do not inherit the moral defects of character that tend to crime.[3]

Beginning with 1880 the reports listed causes of crime, among which were given: "Hereditary and Association" and "Inherent Depravity." In 1881 the classification was "Hereditary," "Inherent Depravity," " Physical Disease." The 1887 report contained case histories of prisoners illustrating inherent depravity. "Hereditary crime-cause makes it next to impossible to prevent those who are afflicted by it from commiting crime. Inherent depravity and mental disease have like results."[4] In 1891 the report carried a table showing convicts received during the previous year who were on their third conviction. The crime-cause of these fourteen was "inherited depravity." Of the seven convicts on fourth conviction all were victims of "inherent depravity." In the following year there were thirty-two prisoners with

[2] Forty-Fifth Annual Report of the Board of Inspectors of the Eastern State Penitentiary of Pennsylvania, 1875, p. 52.

[3] Forty-Ninth Annual Report of the Board of Inspectors of the Eastern State Penitentiary of Pennsylvania, 1879, p. 16.

[4] Fifty-Seventh Annual Report of the Board of Inspectors of the Eastern State Penitentiary of Pennsylvania, 1887, p. 16.

third convictions whose crime-cause was "inherent depravity";
eleven who were fourth offenders and whose crime-cause was
"inherent depravity"; four who were serving their fifth terms
suffered from "inherent depravity"; one convict, serving his
sixth term, was also a victim of "inherent depravity," as was
also one prisoner serving his seventh term. Considerable concern was expressed over the repeated commitments of these
offenders:

The inherited cause of crime, or what is called "inherent depravity"
for want of a thoroughly critical analysis, produces results that seriously
imperil society. Reconvictions of these adult violators of law seem to
have no influence to prevent them from committing crime over and
over again without even a semblance of regret. They are without
moral force to restrain themselves; they are unable to resist. Crime
is a vocation they follow without considering the consequences. They
seem to be insensible to imprisonment. It represents no deterrent influences. When they come back to the penitentiary it is looked upon
by them as a matter of course. They regard it as an incident of their
persistent adherence to their business in life.[5]

These three categories were but a part of a larger number of
twenty-five causes listed in these reports, but they outweighed
proportionately all other of the twenty-two factors. While the
reports of any other penal institution in the United States might
be selected for our purpose, the reports of the Eastern State
Penitentiary of Pennsylvania perhaps best reflect the ideology
of that school of American penology which held to the Pennsylvania or solitary system. It must be remembered that these reports were primarily a presentation of the virtues of this system,
and a defense against its detractors and attackers, principally in
New York and Boston.[6]

[5] *Sixty-Third Annual Report of the Board of Inspectors of the Eastern State Penitentiary of Pennsylvania*, 1893, p. 104.

[6] The early leading figures in the Eastern State Penitentiary were the members of
the Society of Friends of Philadelphia, but in later years the control, lodged in a board
of inspectors, became diffused throughout the community. One of the ablest and most
devoted citizens of Philadelphia to give his time and talents to this enterprise was
Richard Vaux, who served on the Board of Inspectors from 1842 to 1895, the last
forty-three of the years as President. A reading of the annual reports together with the
writings of Vaux on "crime-cause" will bear evidence to the dominant rôle which he
played in the life of the institution and in the composition of the reports. Even after

This exposition of the reports of the Eastern State Penitentiary would be incomplete without mention of Richard Vaux's published work on "crime-cause." Vaux wrote in 1882:

The purpose of these remarks is to call attention to the cause of crime, the influences which exist to create it, and to those social conditions out of which it is produced, as well as to the fact that in many instances it is an inherited trait in the moral character of individuals, over which they exercise no preventive control, by reason of the want of that power of comprehension which subjects action to the government of moral dominion.[6a]

The list of crime causes are:

1. Hereditary and inherent depravity.
2. Insanity.
3. Association.
4. Compulsion of Social Forces.
5. Pauper training, by public institutions.
6. System of public school training.
7. Physical disease.
8. Family influences.
9. Amusements.
10. Want of home government.
11. Education, and weakness in moral power.
12. Laxity in the administration of the law.
13. The want of trade knowledge teaching.
14. The want of corrective treatment of vagrant youth.
15. Pauperizing the indigent and making criminals of neglected children.
16. The laxity of discipline, and the want of proper capacities in the police.

---

his death in 1895, his influence continued in the person of Warden Cassidy, although, it is true, to a diminished extent. With Cassidy's death in 1901 Vaux's influence grew still weaker. The twenty-five classifications of Vaux's and Cassidy's time were reduced by Cassidy's successor, Bussinger, to fifteen in 1902 and to six in 1903. With Bussinger's removal in 1903, the acting warden became Joseph Welch, formerly the moral instructor, and the categories were lessened to three—"Inherent Depravity," "Compulsion of Social Forces," and "Weakness in Moral Power." After 1904 the tables of crime-cause were not presented, and from that time on the reports are valueless so far as material on crime causation is concerned. See *Dictionary of American Biography*, XIX, 238.

[6a] Richard Vaux, *Short Talks on Crime-Cause and Convict Punishment*, Philadelphia, 2nd Edition, 1882, p. 47.

17. The want of rigid regulations as to taverns, etc.
18. Idleness, and the want of means to prevent it by some system of compulsory trade teaching.
19. The want of all incentives to learn trades.
20. Too much license and no repressive means to control self-will in the young.
21. The want of a perfected system of law to regulate minor offenses that are not in themselves more than venial.
22. The poor houses, almshouses, and institutions in which infant children are cared for.[7]

The confusion between crime and insanity occurred throughout the literature of both criminology and psychiatry, though to a lesser extent in the latter. As early as 1845, Amariah Brigham, editor of the *American Journal of Insanity,* took exception to an article published by the Pennsylvania Prison Society in which the words "prison" and "lunatic asylum" were placed in juxtaposition. The Prison Society replied in effect that it had intended no harm, whereupon Brigham undertook to enlighten them on the distinction between the criminal and the insane man.

We must consider them [the imprisoned criminals] for the most part objects of pity—the unfortunate inheritors from nature of tendencies to error, which instead of being repressed by proper education, have been strengthened by their social condition and the neglect of society.[8]

Brigham spoke in phrenological language of the small influence of the higher faculties, and of the great influence of the propensities.

So certain were some writers in the 1870's of the hereditable nature of crime that they attributed criminal behavior to the inheritance of "germs of crime," and "germs of insanity." These may be imbedded in the "ganglia and vital currents" of the sympathetic system. The author of a textbook on mental diseases, A. J. Davis, wrote in 1871:

Do not germs of insanity, and germs of crime, too, grow and incubate and come into action in accordance with fixed divine laws

[7] Richard Vaux, *op. cit.,* pp. 61-62.
[8] Amariah Brigham, " 'Journal of Prison Discipline,' and Lunatic Asylums," *American Journal of Insanity,* II (October 1845) 177.

and indispensable accompanying conditions? One mind may be fifty years, while another may require less than twenty, in bringing the inherited "germs of murder" into a state for their most violent manifestation. The same immutable rule will apply to every other phase of crime; also the various forms of insanity, matricide, the propensity to poison, or to commit suicide.[9]

A. J. Davis called them "germs of crime," while Charles Loring Brace, pioneer in child welfare work, called them "gemmules."

I have known a child of nine or ten years [said the latter] given up apparently beyond control, to licentious habits and desires, and who in all different circumstances seemed to show the same tendencies; her mother had been of similar character, and quite likely her grandmother. The "gemmules," or latent tendencies, or forces, or cells of her immediate ancestors were in her system, and working in her blood, producing irresistible effects on her brain, nerves, and mental emotions, and finally, not being met early enough by other moral, mental, and physical influences, they have modified her organization, until her will is scarcely able to control them and she gives herself up to them.[10]

Despite his belief in the possibility of reforming young offenders, Z. R. Brockway, a prison official, still held that there were hereditary factors involved in criminal behavior. He spoke of the paralytical or undeveloped state of the moral faculties of the mind as being transmitted from one generation to another through the physical or material organism. He cited the fact that a census of prisoners on a certain day showed that 28% of them have or have had relatives who are criminals.[11]

Speaking before the graduating class of the Cincinnati College of Medicine, J. A. Thacher, professor of principles and practice of medicine, observed that many men were controlled by a fault of organization which they could not help, a fault that carried them along captive in spite of themselves. There were moral

---

[9] A. J. Davis, *Mental Disorders; Or, Diseases of the Brain and Nerves, Developing the Origin and Philosophy of Mania, Insanity, and Crime, with Full Directions for Their Treatment and Cure.* New York, 1871, pp. 287-288.

[10] Charles Loring Brace, *op. cit.*, p. 44.

[11] Z. R. Brockway, "Prisoners and their Reformation," *Transactions of the International Penitentiary Congress*, 1872, pp. 612-623.

idiots just as there were intellectual imbeciles; there was a "congenital deficiency" which denied to man the sense of right. "That vice and crime are frequently the result of a faulty conformation is evident from the fact that they are often hereditary."[12]

Oliver Wendell Holmes, eminent in medicine and literature, presented in a non-medical publication in 1875 an extensive review of the work of M. Prosper Despine, *Psychologie Naturelle*, (1868). In Volume I, Despine expounded his general doctrine concerning the motives of human action, the degree to which they are ordered by the will or to which they are simply automatic. The second volume began with a consideration of mental alienation and imbecility, passed to the description and illustration of moral insanity and idiocy as seen in criminals, and concluded with certain clinical observations made upon parricides and homicides. The third and last volume studied the mental and moral conditions of infanticides, suicides, incendiaries, robbers, and others belonging to the medical study of criminals. Since the review was largely a succinct summary of Despine's material there was little of Holmes's original contribution save perhaps his stress upon the rôle of heredity when he wrote:

Now the observation of certain exceptional natures tends to show that a very large portion of their apparent self-determinations or voluntary actions, such as we consider that *we* should hold ourselves responsible for, are in reality nothing more nor less than reflex movements, automatic consequences of practically irresistible causes existing in the inherited organization and in preceding conditions.[13]

That crime and insanity may derive from common sources was an opinion held by many members of both the legal and medical professions, as well as by many of the lay population. That they were hereditarily transmissible was equally accepted. John Stolz, a practising physician, in his book on crime related a conversation between a doctor and a lawyer discussing a recent murder. The lawyer asked the doctor whether there was such a thing as a predisposition to steal, lie, etc., which could be trans-

[12] J. A. Thacher, "The Psychology of Vice and Crime," *Cincinnati Medical News*, II (March 1873) 101-117.

[13] Oliver Wendell Holmes, "Crime and Automatism," *Atlantic Monthly*, XXXV (April 1875) 469.

mitted from parent to child, and which would end in some terrible crime. The doctor, in reply, had not the slightest doubt of it. He had studied criminals and their histories, and had found nearly every case traceable to a "disreputable ancestry." Furthermore, said the doctor, the most eminent of the medical faculty, physiologists, and professors of mental science, nearly all agree that mind is a physical manifestation, and that it is governed by physical laws, and that all crime is the result of an organic or constitutional condition, favoring or producing discord among the faculties of the mind. Criminal action is the result. In fact, he continued, it is a settled truth that crime is the result of depravity, both physical and mental, and can be considered a species of insanity. Men commit crime from necessity or choice, the latter in obedience to a natural propensity.

It is a well-attested fact that persons acquire a sort of mania to lie, steal, etc., brought about by circumstances, most insidious, and over which they have no control; among which we mention parental transmission, associations, bodily habits, and influence of society in general.[14]

In refutation of this position came the word of one of the leading American alienists of the late nineteenth century, John P. Gray. Gray, it will be recalled, was the staunch foe of the doctrine of moral insanity. No man, he asserted, was compelled or impelled by natural or divine law to commit the sins of his fathers. No man was born a forger, a burglar, a thief, an assassin, a murderer, because his grandfather or father represented one or the other of these classes of criminals. This was no more true than to say that a man was born to be a shoemaker or a blacksmith merely because his parent or his grandparent was such by occupation.

Occupations or crimes that are found to run in families are simply the result of education and training. They are not born or inbred. It would not require much observation to show that the sons and daughters of such persons are not only destined by birth to the profession or pursuits of their fathers, but are often not inclined to them or competent for them. Good parents have children who grow up in

[14] John Stolz, *The Cause and Cure of Crime, with a Treatise on Capital Punishment*, Philadelphia, 1880, p. 52.

vice and crime, and criminal parents have children who grow up to the most exemplary lives.[15]

The remark of J. S. Wight that a man's reformation ought to have begun in his ancestors bore testimony to the stress which he placed upon heredity. Speculating upon the man who murders for no apparently understandable reason, he observed that the progenitors of the man had deformed heads and deficient brains, and had been surrounded by crime throughout their lives. Just as a man was color-blind, so this man was morally color-blind; could he be expected to appreciate whether actions were good or bad any more than the color-blind man could appreciate colors?

And this criminal will be in the manacles and fetters of his hereditary organization. He is, to be sure, born innocent and innoxious, but then he is the offspring of his ancestors, and their crimes culminate in him. He had no voice in the selection of his father and his mother; he was in no wise consulted. His ancestors did not transmit to him a moral nature.[16]

Many of the hereditarians, long before the days of the eugenists, were concerned with the quality of the race, and disturbed by the lack of prohibitions, on the part of the state, on the marriage of members of the criminal and other defective classes. It was their strong belief that criminals received their evil proclivities from their parents, that a thief transmitted a secretive, dishonest, sneaking disposition to his offspring, and that such a child came into the world ticketed, as J. H. Kellogg put it, "for the state prison by the nearest route."[17] Jennie M'Cowen, a practising physician, writing in the *Journal of Heredity* on heredity and its relation to charity work, seized the biblical explanation to describe the transmissibility of crime as the sins of the fathers being visited upon the third and fourth generation![18]

Many of those concerned believed crime to be a disease, a

<hr>

[15] John P. Gray, "Heredity," *American Journal of Insanity*, XLI (July 1884) 7-8.

[16] J. S. Wight, "A Plea for the Treatment of Criminals," *American Journal of Neurology and Psychiatry*, III (1884-1885) 134.

[17] J. H. Kellogg, *Plain Facts for Old and Young, Embracing the Natural History and Hygiene of Reproduction*, New Edition, Burlington, Iowa, 1886.

[18] Jennie M'Cowen, "Heredity in Its Relation to Charity Work," *Journal of Heredity*, I (January 1886) 48-49.

nervous disease, hereditary in character, originating in the nervous system or the brain. William G. Stevenson, in his elaboration of this theme, relied chiefly on the evidence of neural physiology. He accepted the testimony concerning the inheritance of many neurotic diseases, among which he listed chorea, hysteria, hypochondriasis, inebriety, insanity, and crime. Children whose parents have these disorders were more likely to develop neurotic disease than those whose parents are free from them, because they possessed a nervous organization predisposing to the appearance of ancestral vice. The form might differ in the transmission: what was chorea in the parent might be transformed into epilepsy in the offspring, insanity might be metamorphosed by transmission into crime, dipsomania, etc. To the question, "Why is one man a criminal?" Stevenson answered:

For the same reason that another is a moralist, or an honest, law-abiding citizen. Either an inherited organization having morbid antecedents gives the bias to development and action, or a constitution, originally well endowed, is so modified by morbid influences as to render possible subsequent moral alienation. Criminals are such, either because they inherit brain structure potentially incapable of generating moral faculties, or, through the influence of repressive environment, the development of mind does not evolve sufficient moral strength to guide and control the lower propensities of man's nature. In either case, however, criminals are, generally speaking, diseased elements, or members, of the body politic—born of it, belonging to it, and of necessity correlated with it in every stage of human evolution. Positively they are diseased in that, as a class, they bear evidence of bodily infirmity, neurotic diseases largely predominating, either in the milder types, or as epilepsy, inebriety, and insanity, which, with scrofulous and tuberculous development, determine with certainty the fact of bodily and nervous degeneration.[19]

Stevenson was in general agreement with those who held that inebriety, insanity, and criminality were correlatives of each other, and all of them hereditary. Criminals were products of our civilization, their crimes carried and assumed different forms under different stages of evolution. Having proved to his own

[19] William G. Stevenson, *op. cit.*, pp. 266-267.

satisfaction that crime sprang from "the secret forces of organization," and was but a symptom of moral alienation resulting from an inherited vice of character, over the origin of which the possessor had no control, Stevenson asked how such a person could do differently than he does. Forthwith came his own answer: "He who has no moral faculties cannot be held responsible for moral wrong-doing, and he who is morally dead through the vice of inherited nature is absolutely beyond the jurisprudence of penal retribution."[20]

Supertintendent Peter Bryce of the Alabama Insane Hospital, speaking before the National Conference of Charities and Correction, was just as certain as Stevenson (whom he quoted) that the lawbreaker acted in response to a force greater than his own which was not subject to his control, but he could not agree with those who held that this was a diseased condition. Deficient or undeveloped nerve centers did not constitute disease of the brain or insanity any more than a departure from some arbitrary standard of physical strength constituted disease of the muscles. Men varied in mental and moral qualities, he claimed, as they did in physical aptitudes, according to their constitutions. The important factor was the nervous structure. If that was imperfect as a whole or in any of its parts, there was a necessary departure from the normal mental and moral endowments. Not only were the organic peculiarities hereditary (a fact well established), but also the mental and moral.[21]

Approaching the criminal from the physiological point of view, R. E. M'Vey, professor of clinical medicine at the Kansas Medical College, found that the elements that made up the criminal character and determined the destiny of the individual were inherent in the tissues that made up his organism:

Where there is poverty of blood there will be instability of the brain and nervous structures with the vacillations in morality and industrial pursuits. The factor behind all forms of crime is instability of structure. The various forms of crime are but different mani-

[20] William G. Stevenson, *op. cit.*, p. 281.

[21] Peter Bryce, "Moral and Criminal Responsibility," *Proceedings of the National Conference of Charities and Correction*, 1888, pp. 75-91; also in *Alienist and Neurologist*, IX (1888) 428-448.

festations of instability of brain and nervous tissue, which leads to unstable habits and purposes. In the criminal the molecular changes in the brain are feeble, and impressions made upon it, by external excitations, are not transformed into thought with the same rapidity as in those whose molecular changes are more vigorous from the presence of blood, rich in nutritive material, from suitable food and regularity in eating and business habits.[22]

M'Vey contended that criminals were often the descendants of persons of unstable nervous elements and of those who were inebriates, epileptics, and of unsound mind.

The controversy as to the relative importance of heredity and education in criminal behavior was endless. Some believed that to open a school was to close a prison. Others, strongly influenced by the biological-hereditary school of thought, were convinced that though education was useful, yet after all what the individual received through inheritance was what decided his conduct. Sophia McClelland was of the latter opinion, remarking that nature was the stronger agency, just as poison was more active than its antidote. Murder and theft were just as subject to the law of heredity as were the physical propensities.[23] Two years later she was still concerned with the respective forces of heredity and environment, and still held to the predominant strength of heredity. She spoke of individuals with inherited incapacities such as morbid cravings, strong passions, and wills too feeble to resist temptation. Others had a brain so abnormal from inherited morbid conditions arising from various neurotic affections that they were unable to resist temptations from without or morbid impulses from within.[24]

Not all the offspring of a family suffering from pathological nervous systems would necessarily be criminal; one may be epileptic, another may have chorea, another may be insane. The last, said T. Marion Dunagan, may be affected with the worst of all diseases—crime. Let the insane man murder and his condition

[22] R. E. M'Vey, "Crime, Its Physiology and Pathenogenesis, How Can Medical Men Aid in Its Prevention?" *Kansas Medical Journal*, I-II (June 1890) 500.

[23] Sophia McClelland, "Hereditary-Criminality, etc., vs. Education," *Medico-Legal Journal*, VIII (1890) 16-41.

[24] Sophia McClelland, "Criminals the Product of Hereditary Degeneracy," *Medical Record*, XLII (July 23, 1892) 96-100.

is recognized at once; he is guarded with care and sent to a splendid asylum where no pains are spared to insure his comfort, and every effort is made to restore him to sound mental health. But not so for him who has the misfortune to fall a victim to crime.[25]

That like begat like, that imperfect seed in parentage would not produce perfect offspring, that certain inherited defects or deficiencies induced criminality—these, according to Boies, were laws of biology and as invariable as the law of gravitation. From criminals and paupers could only come more criminals and paupers.[26] This earlier thought was but the more strongly held by Boies eight years later when he elaborated it in his book purporting to be a scientific treatise on the science of penology. Figs could not grow from thistles, grapes from thorns, nor honest moral character from parents diseased with moral depravity.

The science of heredity makes it probable that not only the fifty to seventy-five per cent of criminal moral depravity which has been traced, but nearly every case of it is due to a diseased or disordered organism or function of organs, produced by ancestral influences. Good seed generates sound and healthy fruit, and imperfect parentage can only yield defective offspring.[27]

In the effort to build a science of penology Boies led up to certain theorems which in some instances he called positive laws of penology. In the first place, he maintained, criminality had one unfailing symptom—crime, the sum and substance of which was moral depravity. The positive deduction of penology was, therefore: *"That the cause of crime is the moral depravity of the criminal."*[28] Criminal moral depravity was a distinct and easily recognizable disease, it might be organic or functional, chronic or acute, inherited or casual, curable or incurable, like other human disease. The disease was characterized by a faulty relation between the selfish, egoistic, and altruistic instincts, wherein the

[25] T. Marion Dunagan, "A Few Facts Showing the Great Need of Physical Development and Physical Care to Lessen Crime and the Number of Criminals," *Memphis Medical Monthly*, X (August 1890) 350-354.

[26] Henry M. Boies, *Prisoners and Paupers*, New York, 1893.

[27] Henry M. Boies, *The Science of Penology*, New York, 1901, p. 49.

[28] *Ibid.*, p. 37.

just balance of control was lost. Whence flowed another theorem of penology: "*That criminality is a diseased condition of the human character.*"[29]

The non-medical person is intrigued with the technical terminology of the physician. The student of the social sciences envies the precision of the natural scientist's terms. The early stages of any discipline which aims to become scientific are characterized by this obsession with terms—for example, Lester F. Ward and early American sociology. Call crime a disease and it is not such an unnatural next step to use the language of the medical profession. Boies furnished such a good example for this phenomenon that an extensive quotation may be warranted:

> In diagnosing the causes of the disease of criminality in the individual, conciseness requires us to follow the analysis of the physician; even if we are compelled to use a technical nomenclature. Physicians recognize three kinds of causes of disease: the *procatarctic*, which is an antecedent condition of things outside of the principal cause, facilitating the production of the effect; the *proegumenal*, or that within the principal cause which either predisposes or directly excites it to action; and the *synectic*, or continent cause, which is the essence of the disease itself, considered as the cause of the symptoms.
>
> Applying these terms to our analysis we find that moral depravity or degeneracy may be denominated the synectic cause of criminality. This is an abnormal and unnatural condition of the organic structure of the human system, which necessarily produces faulty and erroneous function. This organic abnormality may be of the physical, mental, or moral system. Physical abnormality is the most readily discovered, and has received the most thorough scientific examination. Mental abnormality, which is also easily observed, varies like the physical in degree and intensity. It is an unsettled question whether mental or moral traits of character are transmitted independently by inheritance to the same extent as physical similarities, except as they depend upon and are governed by the physical constitutional inheritance. We know that intellectual characteristics depend upon the structure of the brain and nervous system which, like the rest of the physique, is greatly modified by heredity and environment. We know also that morality and honesty are associated with a healthy physique and an evenly balanced, properly cultivated brain; although we have not yet dis-

---

[29] *Ibid.*, p. 39.

covered the exact relations between the three elements of human nature. Some persons are by nature honest, upright, truthful. They have no disposition toward any form of vice. Others refrain from falsehood, dishonesty, and crime by constant struggle against temptation. Still others maintain a semblance of honesty from a regard for public reputation, without any principle on the subject; or with the belief that it is "smart" to use honesty and honor as cloaks wherewith to dupe their fellows, while they prey upon them. Next to these are the criminals who make crime a profession. . . . It is impossible to resist the conclusion, in view of these known facts, that these varieties of crime are due to natural predispositions, caused by peculiarities of the physical constitution. The synectic cause of criminality, is therefore, defective organism or function.

The proegumenal cause exists in the abnormal relations of the organs, or their unnatural operation. They are unbalanced, without their natural counterpoise of sound judgment. A predominance of the organs of selfish gratification and evil propensity over those of sound judgment and self-restraint predisposes to moral depravity and incites criminal action.

The procatarctic causes of moral depravity are those which produce the defective or diseased condition of the human organism, and its faulty functions. Such causes are inherited peculiarities, arrested development, deficient nutrition, and infection—translated into penological terms, heredity and environment. Faulty function results from the imperfect condition, or the disproportionate powers and relations of the organs, caused by defective birth or development.[30]

Many writers on crime were aware of the manifold factors involved in criminal behavior, and this included members of the medical profession despite their emphasis, generally speaking, upon the biological element. By the same token those outside the profession who stressed for the most part the social factors, were also aware that other elements entered into the situation. Frederick Howard Wines, an outstanding figure in the field of social work and penology, was most emphatic that crime sprang from no one source, that the causes were not mutually exclusive. He classified causes of crime into individual,

[30] Henry M. Boies, *The Science of Penology,* pp. 40-43. No other writer seems to have been so bold (or was it rash?) as Boies nor does any other appear to have followed him in his discussion of the procatarctic, proegumenal, and synectic causes of crime.

social, and cosmical. Cosmical causes were beyond the control of either the individual or the community—weather, etc. Social causes resided in the environment and in individual relationships. The physical seat of criminal impulse was in the nervous system, a product of heredity. These hereditary causes of crime were as completely beyond our control as the cosmical. But, for Wines, heredity was a continuing influence, with a future as well as with a past. He was skeptical of the belief of "some earnest and well-meaning people" who held that crime would be diminished considerably by perpetual isolation or by surgical operations. The criminal anthropological type upon which this assumption was made was certainly not proved, and again Wines repeated that "every crime is the result of a combination of causes, near and remote, direct and indirect, whose number and separate value cannot be fully calculated, and whose analysis is a task of almost infinite difficulty."[31] His strong Calvinistic leanings compelled him to declare that after all it was God, not man, who worked out the human destiny.[32]

Julius B. Ransom, the prison physician, believed that there was a born criminal who was an instinctive criminal, and who presented anomalies of organization and psychic aberration. These criminals took to crime as an occupation just as other men became mechanics or artisans. They were deficient in both moral and physical sensibilities, which was evidenced in their inability to see the evil side of a criminal act as well as in their indifference to consequences and their lack of feelings of remorse. These criminals were largely incapable of reformation or improvement, and it was from this class that the majority of incorrigibles came.[33]

Still another physician, W. S. Anderson, held that just as physical and mental peculiarities were transmitted from parent

[31] Frederick Howard Wines, op. cit., pp. 278-279.
[32] Wines's contribution to the history of American penology was of far greater moment than his contribution to crime causation, in which connection it is pertinent to observe that in the 1910 and 1919 editions of his *Punishment and Reformation* four of his original chapters were discarded: one on causes of crime, the second on the theory of punishment, the third on prevention of crime, and the fourth on the outlook for the future.
[33] J. B. Ransom, op. cit., pp. 792-793.

to child, so were moral and criminal tendencies. He denied that environment was the potent factor; rather actual criminal tendencies were transmitted. It is not that a parent must of necessity have been criminal in the legal sense, but that the inebriate, epileptic, insane, morally depraved parent would beget children who were deficient morally and were prone to drift into criminal life, without regard to environment.[34]

August Drähms, was convinced of the existence of the factor of heredity in criminal behavior. In the first of his three chapters on the instinctive criminal he treated of the psychological aspects, in the second the emphasis was upon the physiological characteristics, while the third chapter was entitled: "The Instinctive Criminal. His Origin. Heredity." It was in this chapter that he developed his thesis that man came into the world with certain mental and bodily qualities and endowments which gave a predisposing bent to his impulses and largely tended to shape his subsequent career. Heredity was the preëminent component, environment was only a modifying one.

No discussion of the rôle of heredity was possible around this period without taking into account Weismann's theory of the continuity of the germ plasm, as presented in his essays on heredity in 1891 and 1892. According to Weismann the germ plasm was distinct from the soma or body plasm, and was relayed from generation to generation relatively unchanged. This was in opposition to the Lamarckian doctrine of the transmissibility of acquired characters, and the view of Charles Darwin that gemmules were given off by the various organs into the blood, for which the germ cells had a special affinity. Neither Darwin's nor Lamarck's position was abandoned without a struggle, and it should be remarked that American students entered into the controversy, some with convictions on the one side and some on the other. Eugene S. Talbot, for example, could not surrender his Lamarckian views, holding in his volume on *Degeneration* (1898), that there was ample evidence to substantiate the inheritance of acquired characteristics. One has but to examine his chapter on "Heredity and Atavism" to realize his strong convictions on this point.

[34] W. S. Anderson, *op. cit.* p. 363.

Drähms, on the other hand, accepted Weismann in the main, but was puzzled by the question how certain characteristics originated in the germ plasm. When untroubled by these doubts Drähms believed in the inheritance of physiological, psychological, and psychical traits. Avarice in the parent led to theft in the child, sexual appetite in the parent might be transmitted, and in its degenerate form might curse the offspring with a life of lust and unnatural crime, not to speak of the propensity of rape. Instinctive homicidal proclivity, too, could descend from one generation to another. In summary, Drähms remarked:

In the light of these facts, thus intensely suggestive, the genetics of the instinctive criminal propension is not far to seek. In almost every instance it is the direct entailment of a precriminalistic stock whose antecedent moral ideals were low, and whose nature had already received the inviolable impress of the pregenital taint to be transmitted to the descendant with the unerring certainty characteristic of Nature in all her ways.

The burden with which the congenital offender comes already laden, and from which he draws his inspirational forces, is purely congenital. It is the product of entailed inheritance from ancestral germ-plasm out of whose mysterious depths they are evolved, possessing all the potency that molds the embryo into the image of the original, elaborating and imparting to it its very essence and individuality, even carrying in its current and inoculating that new life with the very germs of theft and murder already stirring in the blood of its progenitor ages back, and waiting but the call of opportunity to spring into sentient life in the scion, and expend itself at times in wanton joy at the incitation of the savage nature.

As if to further accentuate this law, and thus aggravate the case, all such as come under the ban instinctively seek a criminal environment in which to nourish and fructify the latent germ, thus complicating by so much the problem of Nature's struggle to perpetuate her biological ideals, good or bad, even to the "visiting of the iniquities of the fathers upon the children to the third and fourth generation."[35]

---

[35] August Drähms, *op. cit.*, pp. 141-143. By permission of The Macmillan Co., publishers. Quite certainly not all prison chaplains shared Drähms's emphasis on the biological factor in the analysis of crime and the criminal. Five years earlier J. H. Albert, chaplain of the Stillwater prison in Minnesota, had told the National Prison Association that he believed the doctrine of the instinctive criminal had been carried too far. In deploring the

W. Duncan McKim was another who believed that criminality had its real basis in heredity. By this he did not mean that an individual inherited an actual crime or crimes, but rather the tendency to crime. This tendency was inherent within the kind of brain inherited; a brain with an abundance of morbid desires with little power of restraint. Just what kind of brain this was McKim failed to state, but he did take occasion to deny the "criminal type" known by anatomical characteristics, as well as to deny the atavistic nature of crime. Yet at another place he wrote: "I think, that a manifestation of ancestral ways is often an abnormality so incongruous with our present morals as to constitute crime, and that the tendency to crime is essentially inborn."[36] He was so imbued with his belief in the inheritance of this tendency to crime and other social ills that he recommended euthanasia —a painless putting to death of the undesirable elements in society—as a condition of human progress.

The prison physician who observed thousands of prisoners could find the morbid inheritance of the offender in the brain, according to Robert T. Irvine of Sing Sing Prison, New York. He confirmed McKim, declaring that this brain, although to all appearances perfect, had a tendency to break down under circumstances which would not affect a person possessing a healthy mental endowment. "My own observations," he wrote in 1903, "which have been practically unlimited along lines of information connected with the male offender, have led me to believe, in the last few years, that criminal character depends in the first instance on heredity. Of course in this, as well as all other state-

---

fact that heredity had been drawn upon to account for almost everything in human nature, he expostulated with the criminal anthropologists as follows: "If a man lied, it was instinctive; if he got drunk, or stole, it was instinctive, hereditary. If he got into the penitentiary some wiseacre came up, squinted along one side of his head, squinted along the other side, looked profound, sat down and wrote instinctive. And then began to inquire who his grandmother was. A year or so ago I heard the criminal described. He might be known by his physical irregularities. His head was lopsided; nose not exactly on the medial line; the arm bones a little disproportioned; the fingers misshapen; toes deformed; and so on, until I began to wonder if it might not soon come to pass that we should need only to send out a few experts, with tape line and note book, and so find out who are criminals to be clapped into prison, and who are the good citizens to go free." J. H. Albert, "Barriers Against Crime," *Proceedings of the National Prison Association*, 1895, pp. 126-127.

[36] W. Duncan McKim, *op. cit.*, pp. 159.

ments made of this subject, let us remember that they are probably not absolutely accurate, but are mostly approximate to the truth. But in the generality of this conclusion I am satisfied to be at one with the greatest names of our profession as well as the deepest thinkers of all ages."[37] And again,

. . . so the born criminal is the product, mind and body, of the forces of heredity. Not only his body, but his mind is deeply impressed with the character of the parentage. And few indeed are the criminals who come to our prison at Sing Sing with minds that were at birth *tabula rasa*, whose mental powers at birth were not already thickly sown with seeds of crime—call them definite qualities, or for the greater part with first mental tendencies; when they reach us they are surely, for the most part, anthropologically and psychologically analogies of the congenital criminal.[38]

In his *Juvenile Crime and Reformation*, Arthur MacDonald classified criminals from adventure, criminals by nature, and criminals who were mentally weak, though not insane. The class of juvenile criminals who were so by nature lacked all moral feeling and remorse, were impulsive and did evil instinctively. He illustrated the hereditary cases by instances of murder by a twenty-one-year-old girl, a murder by a young boy, poisoning and incendiarism by a fifteen-year-old boy, attempted murder by a ten-year-old boy, and a murder by a boy of thirteen. In another section MacDonald presented cases of young murderers by nature, girl assassins, girl incendiaries, and young criminals with hereditary taint.[39]

Few writers held that the only factor in crime was heredity, for even those who placed much stress upon heredity took the environmental factors into account. Such was G. Frank Lydston, who, in his chapter on "Materialism versus Sentiment in the Study of the Causes and Correction of Crime." listed sixteen causes of crime of which ten were definitely environmental.[40] In

[37] Robert T. Irvine, "The Congenital Criminal," *Medical News*, LXXXII (April 18, 1903) 750.

[38] *Ibid.*, p. 750.

[39] Arthur MacDonald, *Juvenile Crime and Reformation, Including Stigmata of Degeneration*, Washington, D.C., 1908, pp. 26-51.

[40] G. Frank Lydston, *Addresses and Essays*, Louisville, 1892, pp. 93-107.

his *Diseases of Society*, published twelve years later, his revised list contained twenty causes of which at least fifteen could be considered environmental. Among his causes which were non-environmental were: 1. Hereditary influences. 2. Defective physique, hereditary or congenital, and imperfectly developed intellect. 3. Brain and nerve degeneracy, brain injuries. 4. Alcoholic and other forms of inebriety (which may also be social). 5. Mental disease. Lydston believed nerve degeneracy to be the primary factor in the causation of crime, and there was no doubt with him but that it was hereditary—"neuro-degeneracy of the parent criminal is the material basis of heredity in crime," was his way of putting it. Both the nervous system and the glandular system were affected by the processes of nutrition and growth, but if the quality of the food was poor, its quantity deficient, and its assimilation faulty, then both these systems were bound to suffer, resulting, in turn, in defective brain tissue. Hence it followed:

Whatever the exciting cause of a given social disease may be, the predisposing cause in the degenerate is a neuropathic constitution, giving rise to a perversion of formative energy which may be either in favor of or against a given structure. This neuro-psychic degeneracy is not necessarily obvious; it may remain latent until some stress influence is brought to bear. The first debauch may demonstrate the existence of neuro-psychic degeneracy and develop inebriety in a person hitherto supposed to be perfectly normal. Temptation to crime may be followed by acts which show for the first time that the individual is a neuro-psychic degenerate.[41]

It is to be expected that one who was working upon the hypothesis that crime is the normal function of an abnormal man would account for much of crime in terms of the hereditary factors. Philip Parsons, in his chapter on "Heredity and Environment," quoted a sufficient number of other writers to help substantiate his point as to the influence of heredity, alcoholic heredity, insane heredity, neurotic heredity, etc. In addition the "Tribe of Ishmael" and the "Jukes" were mentioned. He agreed with McKim that what was inherited was the tendency to crime, remarking, however, that what the individual is to be is deter-

[41] G. Frank Lydston, *op. cit.*, p. 87.

mined before the rôle of the environment comes into play. For certain persons crime will always be the rule, improve surroundings how we may. How can it be otherwise, Parsons asked, if it can be proved that crime is the normal function of an abnormal man?[42]

Several paragraphs must suffice for the miscellaneous contributions of those who incidentally touched upon matters of criminal behavior, but whose remarks were not extensive in nature. The neuropathic aspect of the individual was commonly dealt with. Horatio C. Wood, a distinguished Philadelphia physician and writer, believed the criminal a neuropath without the power to control his actions.[43] G. Frank Lydston and Hamilton D. Wey, we have already noticed, were of the same mind. Habitual criminals, said J. Sanderson Christison, an author of a book on criminals, and one who had been identified with the work of several insane asylums, were most commonly the offspring of neurotic parents.[44]

A study of one hundred recidivists, each at least four times convicted, by Paul E. Bowers revealed that fifty-six of them bore the burden of neuropathic taint in the form of an instability of the nervous system.[45]

Others believed the criminal to be a psychopath. Said A. Peskind: "A person born to offend society is not a normal man. The hereditary criminal is a psychopath and his dominant passion is the commission of crime."[46] Paul Bowers, already referred to, in addition to finding neuropaths in his study of recidivists also found seventeen out of one hundred to be psychopaths.[47]

Diathesis as applied by the physician to physical disease such as tuberculosis was a term occasionally used when speaking of crime. Unwilling to assert the direct inheritance of criminal traits,

[42] Philip A. Parsons, *Responsibility for Crime*, Columbia University Studies in History, Economics and Public Law, XXXIV, no. 3, New York, 1909, pp. 70-83.

[43] Horatio C. Wood, "Neuropathic Insanity and Its Relation to Crime," *Transactions of the Medical Society of the State of Pennsylvania*, XXIII (1892) 92-104.

[44] J. Sanderson Christison, *op. cit.*, p. 98.

[45] Paul E. Bowers, "The Recidivist," *Journal of the American Institute of Criminal Law and Criminology*, V (September 1914) 404-415.

[46] A. Peskind, "Heredity and Crime: Its Prevention and Treatment," *Cleveland Medical Gazette*, X (March 1895) 199.

[47] Paul E. Bowers, *op. cit.*, p. 407.

one could, by the use of the word "diathesis" imply the analogous nature of crime and disease. C. H. Reeve spoke of "a confirmed criminal diathesis, or any other case of abnormality, where hereditary transmission of a viscious condition may follow.[48] Others used synonymous expressions of tendency and predisposition. M. P. E. Groszmann said of the criminal by heredity that there could be a direct transmission of criminal tendencies, or a transmission of degenerative traits, either of which could develop into criminality in the children.[49] Criminal tendencies could be inherited and transmitted, said John B. Chapin, physician-in-chief and superintendent of the Pennsylvania Hospital for the Insane in Philadelphia,[50] as did also W. O. Henry, professor of orthopedic surgery and gynecology in the John A. Creighton Medical College, Omaha, Nebraska.[51]

Finally, there is a miscellaneous variety of explanations, such for instance as A. L. Clark's "that the offspring of criminals will follow in the footsteps of their ancestry and become criminals";[52] or J. H. McCassy's (formerly superintendent of the Kansas State Insane Asylum) that "crime, imbecility and insanity are due in 60 to 75 per cent of cases to heredity," and that "heredity is the great causal factor of crime."[53] R. B. Sellers stated that the stain of a criminal could be in a man's blood for generations back, lying dormant in his parents only to develop in him. "No factor in the causation of crime plays a more important rôle than does heredity."[54] For H. L. Appleton, president of the Tri-State Medical Society of Alabama, Georgia, and Tennessee, crime was a

---

[48] C. H. Reeve, "The Philosophy of Crime," *International Congress of Charities, Correction and Philanthropy*, 1893, p. 32.

[49] M. P. E. Groszmann, *op. cit.*

[50] John B. Chapin, "The Psychology of Criminals, and a Plea for the Elevation of the Medical Service of Prisons," *American Journal of Insanity*, LVI (October 1899) 317-326.

[51] W. O. Henry, "Relations of Disease, Crime and Vice," *Journal of the American Medical Association*, XXIV (March 2, 1895) 302-305.

[52] A. L. Clark, "Thoughts on Criminology," *Chicago Medical News*, XXX (February 1897) 41-44.

[53] J. H. McCassy, "How to Limit the Overproduction of Defectives and Criminals," *Journal of the American Medical Association*, XXXI (December 3, 1898) 1343-1347.

[54] R. B. Sellers, "The Etiology and Elimination of Crime," *Transactions of the Texas Medical Association*, XXXVI (1904) 314.

germ which could be inherited and transmitted from parent to child just as any other disease could be handed on.[55] G. Stanley Hall, one of America's pioneer psychologists and the author of the monumental volumes on adolescence, considered crime one of the diseases of society.[56] William H. Carmalt declared that criminals were the victims of an inherited vice; of an indisposition or inability to resist temptation; of an actual desire to do the wrong thing; of a more or less irresistible impulse to injure or inflict pain without any sort of provocation.[57] Seventy per cent of criminals were so by instinct, according to G. G. Marshall, who announced that "Of all the causes tending to produce the criminal character, one of the greatest and certainly to the medical profession, the most important, is heredity."[58] That crime was not handed down as such through the germ plasm from our ancestors was the position of Haldor Sneve, professor of mental and nervous diseases at the University of Minnesota, who presented the view that parental diseases which infected the growing foetus or infant predisposed to crime because of weakened mind.[59] Winfield Scott Hall, professor of physiology, Northwestern Medical School, was convinced that:

The immediate hereditary influences, from parents and grandparents, are perhaps no less potent in shaping the life of youth than are the influences already mentioned. That a criminal father should beget a child predestined to criminality is a foregone conclusion. The father exerts a hereditary influence equal to all the previous ancestors in the paternal line.[60]

Surely, this is Galton's law of ancestral inheritance! For I. L. Nascher there was a class of criminal acts due to inherent moral

[55] H. L. Appleton, "Crime, a Disease, with Some Suggestions for Its Cure," *Southern Medicine and Surgery*, IV (September 1905) 186-188.

[56] G. Stanley Hall, *op. cit.*, p. 406.

[57] William H. Carmalt, "Heredity and Crime, a Study in Eugenics," *Proceedings of the Connecticut State Medical Society*, 1909, pp. 240-282.

[58] G. G. Marshall, "The Disease of Criminality," *Vermont Medical Monthly*, XVIII (March 15, 1912) 56.

[59] Haldor Sneve, "Influence of Parental Diseases, Habits and Heredity upon Juvenile Crime," *Bulletin of the American Academy of Medicine*, XIV (October 1913) 359-368.

[60] Winfield Scott Hall, "The Relation of Crime to Adolescence," *Bulletin of the American Academy of Medicine*, XV (April 1914) 86-96.

defect or perversion which could not be eradicated because inherent within the individual.[61]

CONCLUSION

An examination of the American thought presented in the foregoing pages reveals a strong belief in the inheritance of crime. Yet here the agreement ends, for there is neither agreement as to what is inherited nor the means by which that inheritance takes place. For some it was the crime itself which was inherited, whereby the crime of the parent descended (chromosomally, as it were) to the child; for others what was inherited was a propensity, a tendency, a mental state predisposing to criminal behavior which was a part of the physical endowment. In both instances the transmission was biological, i.e., through the germ or soma plasm, but in the first instance the inference was that of germ-cell inheritance, while in the latter it was a somatic or body-cell inheritance. The difference lay in the expression of this inherited defect. In the one case the child who had received in his germ cells the criminal character of the parent was destined to become a criminal because the body cells would also have received the inheritance, while in the other case the child might be spared a criminal career if environmental conditions were favorable enough to counteract the criminal inheritance. Thus while a child might inherit from an insane, an epileptic, an inebriate, a neuropathic, a psychopathic parent, it was not *per se* impelled to crime unless the countervailing environmental influences proved ineffective.

In the earlier years there was a greater emphasis upon direct inheritance, which stressed the biological transmission to the entire exclusion of the environment, but with a broader understanding of the interrelationship of the biological and the environmental there was a growing acceptance of indirect inheritance. For the students of the subject whose works are here considered the problem remained basically a biological one, with a tendency, however, in the twentieth century, to recognize its complexity.

[61] I. L. Nascher, "Psychanalysis of Criminality," *American Practitioner*, XLVIII (May 1914) 233-238.

The influence of the theories of evolution, of mutation, of the principles of Mendelian inheritance, of the continuity of the germ plasm, and even of eugenics, is obvious. Physicians in the main, these writers had a grounding in the physical sciences, and were familiar with Lamarck and his theory of the inheritance of acquired characters (only a few, however, were inclined to adopt him uncritically), with Charles Darwin and Alfred Wallace and their theories of evolution (though here again, few retained Darwin's theory of pangenesis), with Mendel, DeVries, Tschermak, Correns, Weismann, and Thomas Hunt Morgan. For the most part their writ:ngs on the criminal were based on observations in medical practice, upon their reading of the works of students of crime (here and abroad), and, in some instances where their experiences as prison physicians brought them into contact with the convicted offender, upon first-hand study and observation.

It was really not until after the introduction of the juvenile court and later its accompanying clinic that any conclusions could be based upon a scientific analysis of the offender. The Juvenile Psychopathic Institute of Chicago furnished William Healy the opportunity to study one thousand juvenile recidivists in the clinic, and to give to the world *The Individual Delinquent*, which marked a new departure in the study and understanding of the offender. The year before the publication of *The Individual Delinquent*, in 1914, Healy and Edith R. Spaulding, the latter being resident physician at the Reformatory for Women in Massachusetts, issued a paper in which they denied that there was any evidence of the direct inheritance of criminalistic traits as such.[62] Of indirect inheritance of criminalistic tendencies they found ample evidence through such hereditable factors as epilepsy, insanity, feeble-mindedness, etc. It may be repeated here that many of the writers that have been considered in this treatise in most instances have been aware of this indirect inheritance and have placed crime as one of the degenerative diseases along with the others or as the product of the degenerative diseases. Crime to them was but one of the many effects of a vicious

[62] Edith R. Spaulding and William Healy, "Inheritance as a Factor in Criminality: A Study of a Thousand Cases of Young Repeated Offenders," *Bulletin of the American Academy of Medicine*, XV (February 1914) 4-27.

heredity, the same conditions which produce crime might just as well produce insanity, epilepsy, inebriety, feeble-mindedness, etc. Some called these degenerative diseases by various names—degenerative psychoses, neuropathic insanity, collateral degeneracies. By whatever name they were known they were still recognized as pathological and as factors in the production of the criminal. The trend toward recognition of the indirect rather than the direct inheritance of criminalistic factors was well on the way by the time Healy's work had appeared. The merit of his work lay in its thorough-going clinical study of a sufficiently large statistical sample to warrant definite conclusions. The clinic, a product of the belief that the proper study of the criminal man was the criminal man, came to deny the "born criminal." Is it not a queer twist of fate that this agency for the study of criminal man should have been one of the many influences that emanated from Lombroso who, with all his errors, opened a new era in criminology when he directed a world from the study of the crime to the study of the criminal. Healy's work was a continuation of that same Lombrosian spirit, fortunately implemented with twentieth-century tools.

VIII

HEREDITY:
THE JUKES

PERHAPS no one book in the field of criminology in America has lent itself to such partisan interpretation as has Richard Dugdale's *The Jukes,* published in 1877.[1] Unread, misread, or wilfully distorted, it has been used by hereditarians and environmentalists alike to assert and supposedly to prove their respective positions. It is therefore imperative at the outset to examine carefully Dugdale's work of 1877 in order to understand adequately the nature of his investigations and conclusions. At the beginning of his study Dugdale admitted that heredity and environment were the two limits within which the whole question of crime, its origin, its nature, and its treatment, was contained. His ideal objective, he maintained, was to determine how much crime resulted from heredity and how much from environment. At the conclusion of the second case he observed: "We have here an environment in three generations which corresponds to the

---

[1] Richard L. Dugdale (1841-1883) was a member of the executive committee of the New York Prison Association. In 1874 he was appointed a committee of one to inspect thirteen county jails in New York State, and it was out of this experience that he gathered material for his report on the "Jukes" family which he presented to the Prison Association as an appendix to the 1875 report. This report, together with further studies on criminals, was published two years later as *The Jukes,* with the sub-title *A Study in Crime, Pauperism, Disease and Heredity.*

Aside from his affiliation with the Prison Association, Dugdale was Secretary of the Section on Sociology of the New York Association for the Advancement of Science and Arts; Secretary of the New York Social Science Society, and of the New York Sociology Club; Treasurer of the New York Liberal Club; Vice-President of the Society for the Prevention of Street Accidents; Secretary of the Civil Service Reform Association; first Secretary of the Society for Political Education; a member of the American Social Science Association, of the American Public Health Association, of the American Free Trade League, of the Chamber of Commerce, and of the American Institute. There can be no gainsaying of the fact that for the period in which he lived and wrote his was an unusual competency for a work which Giddings called "the best example of scientific method applied to a sociological investigation." See *Dictionary of American Biography,* V, p. 493.

heredity; this environment forming an example to the younger generation which must have been sufficient, without heredity, to stimulate licentious practices."[2] Regarding prostitution in woman as the analogue of crime in man, Dugdale found that prostitution might become an hereditary characteristic, and might be perpetuated without the presence of a favorable environment to call it into activity, but he also added that in most cases the heredity was also accompanied by an environment which ran parallel to it. However, where the heredity and the environment were in the direction of harlotry, if the environment were changed at a sufficiently early period, the career of prostitution might be arrested and the sexual habits amended. Speaking specifically about crime Dugdale offered these conclusions:

1. That the burden of crime is found in the illegitimate lines.
2. That the legitimate lines marry into crime.
3. That those streaks of crime found in the legitimate lines are found chiefly where there have been crosses with X [X = relations by marriage of cohabitation].
4. That the eldest child has a tendency to be the criminal of the family.
5. That crime chiefly follows the male line.
6. That the longest lines of crime are along the line of the eldest son.
7. That crime, as compared to pauperism, is an indication of vigor.[3]

Since crime was an evidence of vigor to Dugdale, he held more of a brief for it than for pauperism. He stated that hereditary pauperism was more fixed than hereditary crime, and that the criminal was more amenable therefore to discipline. Similarly, criminal careers were more easily modified by environment because crime was an index of capacity, and wherever there was capacity, there environment was most effective in producing modifications of conduct. Dugdale was aware throughout his book that heredity and environment were interacting. On one occasion, concerning the formation of character, he wrote:

[2] Richard L. Dugdale, *The Jukes*, New York, 1877, p. 20.
[3] *Ibid.*, pp. 41-42.

Where there is heredity of any characteristic, it would seem there is a tendency, and it might almost be said, a certainty to produce an environment for the next generation corresponding to that heredity, with the effect of perpetuating it. Where the environment changes in youth the characteristics of heredity may be measureably altered.[4]

In the light of the diverse interpretations of *The Jukes* it seems well to make the following extensive quotation from Dugdale's tentative conclusions (Dugdale cautioned the reader repeatedly of the tentative character of his study, pleading that the preliminary generalizations should not be indiscriminately applied to the general question of crime, since his work was based mainly on blood relations living in a similar environment).

Where the organization is structurally modified, as in idiocy and insanity, or organically weak, as in many diseases, the heredity is the preponderating factor in determining the career, but it is, even then, capable of marked modification for better or worse by the character of the environment. In other words, capacity, physical and mental, is limited and determined mainly by heredity. This is probably because these cerebral conditions are fixed during the period of ante-natal organization.

2. Where the conduct depends on the knowledge of moral obligation (excluding insanity and idiocy), the environment has more influence than the heredity, because the development of the moral attributes is mainly a post-natal and not an ante-natal formation of cerebral cells. The use to which capacity shall be put is largely governed by the impersonal training or agency of environment.

3. The tendency of heredity is to produce an environment which perpetuates that heredity: thus, the licentious parent makes an example which greatly aids in fixing habits of debauchery in the child. The correction is change of environment. For instance, where hereditary kleptomania exists, if the environment should be such as to become an exciting cause, the individual will be an incorrigible thief; but, if, on the contrary, he be protected from temptation, that individual may lead an honest life, with some chances in favor of the entailment stopping there.

[4] *Ibid.*, p. 49.

4. Environment tends to produce habits which may become hereditary, especially so in pauperism and licentiousness, if it should be sufficiently constant to produce modification of cerebral tissue.

If these conclusions are correct, then the whole question of the control of crime and pauperism becomes possible, within wide limits, if the necessary training can be made to reach over two or three generations.

5. From the above considerations the logical induction seems to be, that environment is the ultimate controlling factor in determining careers, placing heredity itself as an organized result of environment. The permanence of ancestral types is only another demonstration of the fixity of the environment within limits which necessitate the development of typal characteristics.[5]

These conclusions (it must be repeated, tentatively offered by Dugdale), together with sixty-two pages of detailed text, must be studied carefully before one quotes Dugdale in support of the heritable nature of crime, or before one accepts the interpretation of another who may or may not have read the original work. Certainly Dugdale admitted both factors, but not one to the exclusion of the other.

Writing fourteen years after the publication of *The Jukes* Robert Fletcher, in his article on criminal anthropology in America, remarked that the evidence from *The Jukes* was so striking that it seemed impossible to doubt that the criminal propensities could be and were transmitted by descent.[6] Nathan Oppenheim, writing in 1896, declared the Jukes family to be a startling example of transmitted crime,[7] while George E. Dawson, in the same year, believed the statistical study of criminal heredity used with the Jukes family tended to establish the fact of a criminal neurosis, a position also adopted by M. P. E. Groszmann, who followed Dawson's article closely.[8] To Drähms, the

[5] Richard L. Dugdale, *op. cit.*, p. 57.

[6] Robert Fletcher, "The New School of Criminal Anthropology," *American Anthropologist*, IV (July 1891) 201-236.

[7] Nathan Oppenheim, "The Stamping Out of Crime," *Popular Science Monthly*, XLVIII (February 1896) 527-533.

[8] George E. Dawson, "A Study in Youthful Degeneracy," *Pedagogical Seminary*, IV (December 1896) 221-258; M. P. E. Groszmann, "Criminality in Children," *Arena*, XXII (October 1899) 509-555.

Jukes family offered convincing proof of the propagative power to criminality through the operation of what he termed the law of hereditary entailment.[9] Thomas Travis agreed with Dawson and Groszmann that crime or a neurotic tendency thereto could be transmitted by heredity.[10] The study of a number of families, such as the Jukes, convinced Philip Parsons of the importance of heredity and led him to remark: "It is generally conceded that we inherit tastes, habits, diseases, or tendencies to diseases, physical characteristics, etc., why not criminal tendencies as well?"[11]

There were others who were not content only to interpret the Jukes as illustrating the inheritance of crime, but who advocated asexualization of members of such families. As early as 1889 John Morris, president of the Maryland Medical and Chirurgical Faculty and of the Maryland Inebriate Asylum, contended that the criminal must be made a eunuch for society's sake, "if not for the sake of the kingdom of heaven." Certainly, he maintained, the state of New York would have been spared the expenditure of over a million dollars and six generations of paupers, idiots, thieves, and burglars if the first defective Jukes had been castrated.[12] This opinion was shared by William A. Hammond, who wished that castration had been practised on some of the early ancestors of the Jukes family.[13] Later, when vasectomy was introduced as the best surgical method of asexualization, many of its proponents cited the Jukes as convincing testimony to the expense, misery, and worthlessness which could have been spared had this simple operation been performed early enough. Such was the position of William J. Chandler, Judge Warren W. Foster, and G. Henri Bogart.[14]

[9] August Drähms, op. cit., p. 137.

[10] Thomas Travis, op. cit., pp. 153-154.

[11] Philip A. Parsons, op. cit., p. 79.

[12] John Morris, "Crime: Its Physiology and Pathenogenesis. How Far Can Medical Men Aid in Its Prevention?" Maryland Medical Journal, XX (April 27, 1889) 501-512.

[13] William A. Hammond, "A New Substitute for Capital Punishment and Means for Preventing the Propagation of Criminals," New York Medical Examiner, I (March 1892) 190-194.

[14] William J. Chandler, "Sterilization of Confirmed Criminals, Idiots, Imbeciles and Other Defectives by Vasectomy," Journal of the Medical Society of New Jersey, VI (December 1909) 321-326; Warren W. Foster, "Hereditary Criminality and Its

Just as there were those who interpreted the Jukes as a family which proved the hereditary character of crime and cited it as such, there were others in the medical profession (aside from the still larger number of social scientists and environmentalists, not here considered) who refused to accept the Jukes as an example of the proof of hereditary crime, claiming that both the factors of heredity and environment were involved in the lives of those folk. G. Frank Lydston claimed, in his discussion of the Jukes and of allied families, that the separation of the two influences of heredity and environment was a very difficult matter, since direct and even collateral members of the family were exposed to the same vicious environment during the plastic stage in the development of the brain. Granting the assumption of the proponents of heredity, practically all of the children of such parentage must of necessity grow up without moral sense:

A point worthy of attention is the fact that where vicious parentage is upon only one side, the child may present the traits of the normal parent. Heredity is not one-sided, as might be inferred from the writings of some criminologists. A unilateral heredity of good may offset an heredity that is bad upon the other side. Even where environment is unfavorable during growth and development, the child may still escape criminality.[15]

At another place Lydston held that the force of heredity was often discounted by environmental influences. A prison chaplain, J. H. Albert, admitting that a predisposition to crime might be born with a person, declared that under proper conditions it might not develop. Of the Jukes studies he wrote:

Old mother Jukes and her criminal progeny have ever been the clinching argument for instinctive crime. But mother Jukes and her children have committed vastly more crimes in the hands of the hereditarians, than they ever committed in actual life. It never seems to have

---

Certain Cure," *Pearson's Magazine*, XXII (November 1909) 565-572; G. Henri Bogart, "Asexualization of the Unfit," *Medical Herald*, XXIX (June 1910) 298-301.
    [15] G. Frank Lydston, *op. cit.*, p. 72.

occurred to these doctors, that this family might have been improved, if someone had taken them kindly and firmly in hand.[16]

Frances Kellor was critical of the usual interpretation of the Jukes family, for she remarked:

The Jukes family, investigated by Dugdale, and the Cretien family by Ribot are quoted daily in support of the theory of hereditary influence of crime. But writers have ignored the stress which Dugdale places upon environment. In the description of the first habitat, where the whole family of ten occupied one room and habits and modes of living were most disgusting and immoral, is given the key-note to the book. On almost every page occurs these significant statements: "The environment runs *parallel* with the heredity"; "environment *unknown*"; "environment unfavorable." In only one instance is a change to good environment shown and then the significant statement is that the woman married to a good industrious man was leading a good life. In the face of these facts where there was no opportunity for improvement, this can be no argument for heredity.[17]

In 1912, thirty-five years after Dugdale wrote, Henry H. Goddard, director of research of the Vineland Training School, in his own study of the Kallikaks (a family not unlike the Jukes) remarked:

So far as the Jukes family is concerned, there is nothing that proves the hereditary character of any of the crime, pauperism, or prostitution that was found. The most that one can say is that if such a family is allowed to go on and develop in its own way unmolested, it is pretty certain not to improve, but rather to propagate its own kind and fill the world with degenerates of one form or another. The formerly much discussed question of the hereditary character of crime received no solution from the Jukes family, but in the light of present-day knowledge of the sciences of criminology and biology, there is every reason to conclude that criminals are made and not born.[18]

[16] J. H. Albert, *op. cit.*, p. 127.

[17] Frances A. Kellor, *op. cit.*, p. 157. By permission of The Macmillan Co., publishers.

[18] Henry H. Goddard, *The Kallikak Family—A Study in the Heredity of Feeble-Mindedness,* New York, 1912, pp. 53-54. By permission of The Macmillan Co., publishers.

One must recognize, however, that Goddard's emphasis upon the rôle of feeble-mindedness as a causal factor in criminality was but an indirect claim that criminality was of an hereditary character, and his statement just reproduced must be interpreted in that light, especially since this significant sentence concluded his quotation: "The

ALLIED STUDIES OF DEGENERATIVE FAMILIES

There have been other studies of families purporting to show the hereditable nature of crime, among which should be mentioned the European study of the descendants of Ada Jurke, by Poellman of Bonn University, and that of the Chretien family by Ribot, both extensively quoted by students in the field in America. In this country the early studies were those of the Tribe of Ishmael by Oscar M'Culloch in 1888, the Smoky Pilgrims by Frank Blackmar in 1897.[19] Later *The Kallikaks* by Goddard appeared in 1912, together with *Hill Folk* by Davenport and Danielson, and *The Nam Family* by Estabrook and Davenport. In 1913 Elizabeth S. Kite, who worked with Goddard at Vineland, issued "The Pineys," while in 1916 appeared Estabrook's *The Jukes in 1915*.[20] Both the Reverend Oscar M'Culloch and Professor Blackmar were concerned primarily with the families in question as examples of social degradation, or deteriorating individuals in a social milieu, and only very incidentally with their relation to crime or to the inheritance of crime. Goddard's and Kite's works dealt with the relation of feeble-mindedness to crime, and of heredity to feeble-mindedness, while the volumes of Estabrook, Davenport, and Danielson was avowedly aimed to show the need for a study of eugenics, a movement getting under way toward the close of the first decade of the twentieth century.

CONCLUSION

Dugdale's pioneering study came at a time when the doctrines of biological and social evolution pervaded the scientific as well as the lay world. The factor of survival of the fittest was one ex-

---

best material out of which to make criminals, and perhaps the material from which they are most frequently made, is feeble-mindedness."

[19] Oscar M'Culloch, "The Tribe of Ishmael; A Study in Social Degradation," *Proceedings of the National Conference of Charities and Correction*, 1888, pp. 154-159; Frank W. Blackmar, "The Smoky Pilgrims," *American Journal of Sociology*, II (January 1897) 485-500.

[20] Henry H. Goddard, *op. cit.*; Charles B. Davenport and Florence H. Danielson, *Hill Folk*, Cold Spring Harbor, New York, 1912; Arthur H. Estabrook and Charles B. Davenport, *The Nam Family*, Cold Spring Harbor, New York, 1912; Elizabeth S. Kite, "The Pineys," *Survey*, XXXI (October 4, 1913) 7-13. Arthur H. Estabrook, *The Jukes in 1915*, Washington, 1916.

planation of the method of evolution which was seized upon and applied to the study of social phenomena. (By a strange irony, the Jukes, an "unfit" family, did survive!) It was perhaps inevitable that this explanation should be used for criminal behavior, possibly because it was so facile an explanation. Certainly, as first offered, it was uncritically accepted, elaborated, and still further propounded. Other families were traced until there was built up a fairly convincing case for the familial inheritance of crime.

At the same time other forces were working to compel a more scientifically tempered interpretation of such investigations, and to balance them with a consideration of the environmental conditions which were perpetuated through families and individuals, and tended to produce criminal behavior. At the same time the studies have also shown, by their limitations, the inadequacy and falsity of building a theory of crime causation upon them.

IX

HEREDITY:
HUMAN STERILIZATION

LONG before eugenics as a movement had gotten under way abroad or in this country there was a strong belief in some—perhaps in most—quarters that crime and the criminal character were inherited. The medical profession certainly shared this conviction, for the advocacy of surgical extirpation of the criminal came almost entirely from the physicians themselves.

Analysis of the literature of sterilization reveals three approaches, each with its own basic assumptions. One of these was obviously the punitive; the criminal ought to be punished by asexualization, especially for certain crimes. In the case of sex crimes the intent was evidently retributive, and only by implication served the purpose of cutting off the criminal strain. A corollary of this rested upon the narrow basis of social protection; that a released asexualized criminal was relatively harmless, since the destruction of his sexual powers deprived him of the virulent courage so essentially a part of the criminal. A second position was the therapeutic, which held that sterilization was beneficial to certain individuals—particularly those persons affected with mental disorders which prompted them to criminal acts. The third view—the eugenic—rested unmistakably on the premise that criminals begat criminals and that the most effective way to reduce and prevent criminality was to reach it at its biological source. The discussion which follows here will be chiefly around the third, rather than the first or second view.[1]

The first instance of the recommendation of asexualization of criminals in America came from Orpheus Everts, superintendent of the Cincinnati Sanitarium, in a lecture delivered in February

---

[1] It must be observed that in many instances the proposal to asexualize the criminal came not always because the offender was essentially criminal, but because the criminal was a member of the group so easily categorized in the past century, the defective classes.

1887, and published a year later.[2] Despite the title of the article—a penalty for crime and the reformation of criminals—Everts was concerned with the hereditary transmission of constitutional depravities. Sexual sterilization he deemed necessary to protect society from "the savages of civilization," i.e., the vicious, criminal, or defective classes.

The physical or structural, and consequently psychical, characteristics of the defective classes of society, manifested by well marked proclivities to mental disorder, vice or crime, developed under circumstances, often, to be regarded as unfavorable for such manifestations, are reproducible and being constantly reproduced, perpetuated, and multiplied with a tendency to exaggeration, by intermarriage of persons of like defects, according to the recognized laws, or uniformity of results, of activities of living matter, called heredity.[3]

Surgical asexualization, without naming the method, was Evert's proposal.

Castration for criminals was the avowed position of John Morris, president of the Maryland Inebriate Asylum.[4] He inquired how many criminals would have been prevented had the original progenitor of the Jukes family been emasculated. Reference to the Jukes and allied families in connection with asexualization was common. While Morris admitted that no man was born a criminal, he argued that some men were born with a temperament or constitution, which under certain circumstances made for the development of the criminal. It was the habitual criminal who must be deprived of the power to procreate—for society's sake as well as for the "sake of the kingdom of heaven." William A. Hammond, a medical teacher and alienist, likewise would have subjected the Jukes ancestors to castration, and would also use it as a substitute for the death penalty and life imprisonment, declaring it less cruel than the former and more efficacious than the latter.[5] A. C. Ames, too, conceived castration to be both a means to prevent the hereditary transmission of crime and a

[2] Orpheus Everts, "Asexualization, as a Penalty for Crime and the Reformation of Criminals," *Cincinnati Lancet-Clinic*, XX (March 1888) 377-380.

[3] *Ibid.*, p. 379.

[4] John Morris, *op. cit.*, pp. 48-69.

[5] William A. Hammond, *op. cit.*, pp. 190-194.

punishment.[6] To Henry M. Boies, a member of the Board of Public Charities of the State of Pennsylvania, the criminal was a horrid breed, only effectually stopped by castration, a procedure which obviated the necessity of the permanent seclusion which would be otherwise imperative.[7] "No fact is better established," said F. E. Daniel, editor of the *Texas Medical Journal*, "than that drunkenness, insanity, and criminal traits of character, as well as syphilis, consumption, and scrofula descend from parent to child."[8] He deplored the situation because no effort was being made to lessen the degrading effects of hereditary transmission of these vices. Castration, especially in sexual crimes, would be at once punitive, curative, and preventive; and he agreed with G. Frank Lydston that it would have a more powerful restraining effect on the rapist than hanging, burning at the stake, or electrocution. The influence of Everts upon Robert Boal was obvious, for the latter used Evert's title and entire paragraphs of his article in making his recommendation of emasculation for habitual criminals. Boal defined the habitual criminal as one possessed of an hereditary criminal taint exhibited through two or three generations.[9]

Titles of articles are misleading, as for instance, F. L. Sims's "Asexualization for the Prevention of Crime and the Propagation of Criminals" in which, like Hammond before him, he urged asexualization as a substitute for capital punishment and as a deterrent for Negro rape, rather than as an eugenic measure.[10] V. P. Armstrong, from Texas, held that there were brains which were distinctly criminal, and that the constitutional criminal should not be allowed to procreate: "There is a remedy for

[6] A. C. Ames, "A Plea for Castration as a Punishment for Crime," *Omaha Clinic*, VI (November 1893) 343-345.

[7] Henry M. Boies, *Prisoners and Paupers*, New York, 1893, p. 270.

[8] F. E. Daniel, "Should Insane Criminals, or Sexual Perverts, Be Allowed to Procreate?" *Medico-Legal Journal*, XI (1893-1894) 275.

[9] Robert Boal, "Emasculation and Ovariotomy as a Penalty for Crime and the Reformation of Criminals," *Transactions of the Illinois State Medical Society*, 1894, pp. 533-543.

[10] F. L. Sims, "Asexualization for the Prevention of Crime and the Propagation of Criminals," *Transactions of the Medical Society of the State of Tennessee*, 1894, pp. 100-114.

every murderer, thief, harlot, incendiary, rape-fiend, and habitual criminal that lives, and that remedy is emasculation."[11] For some writers, not all criminals merit asexualization. W. O. Henry suggested ovariotomy and testiotomy for sexual crimes alone, admitting, however, that parents transmitted tendencies to disease, crime, and vice.[12] As has been noted elsewhere, Austin Flint refused to accept physical abnormalities as absolute evidence of criminality, although he did speak of those of criminal ancestry and of the born criminal, and recommended sterilization.[13] E. Stuver held that asexualization, being both preventive and curative, should be applied to all hereditary and chronic criminals of both sexes, thereby reducing both disease and crime by removing the exciting cause—perverted sexual passions.[14] B. A. Arbogast declared that castration as a condition precedent to the release of all professional and confirmed criminals should be practised.[15] J. W. Frazier believed with the Austrian, Benedikt, in the criminal brain, and at the same time regarded crime as a disease to be extirpated in the individual by means of castration.[16]

In 1893 G. Frank Lydston of Chicago corresponded with Dr. Hunter McGuire of Virginia concerning asexualization, and recommended castration for those who had committed capital crimes and for criminals of the habitual class.[17] In a later article, dated 1896, he recommended asexualization of habitual criminals, certain murderers, and rapists, giving as his reason that the ap-

[11] V. P. Armstrong, "Crime, Disease and the Remedy," *Texas Health Journal*, VII (June 1895) 277.

[12] W. O. Henry, "Relations of Disease, Crime and Vice," *Journal of the American Medical Association*, XXIV (March 2, 1895) 302-305.

[13] Austin Flint, "The Coming Rôle of the Medical Profession in the Scientific Treatment of Crime and Criminals," *New York Medical Journal*, LXII (October 19, 1895) 481-490.

[14] E. Stuver, "Asexualization for the Limitation of Disease, and the Prevention and Punishment of Crime," *Journal of Materia Medica*, XXXIII (November 1895) 167-170.

[15] B. A. Arbogast, "Castration—The Remedy for Crime," *Denver Medical Times*, XV (August 1895) 55-58.

[16] J. W. Frazier, "Castration for Crime as Preventive and Curative Treatment," *Texas Medical Journal*, XI (March 1896) 498-503.

[17] "Sexual Crime Among the Southern Negroes," being Correspondence between Hunter McGuire of Virginia and G. Frank Lydston, of Chicago, in *Virginia Medical Monthly*, XX (May 1893) 105-125.

plication of this technique would serve as punishment, act as a deterrent to others, and would prevent the propagation of more criminals.[18] Since criminality was a disease of degeneracy and since the hereditary and incurable criminal would be certain to have criminal offspring, A. L. Clark felt that there was but one remedy, a remedy that struck at the root of the evil—castration.[19] Incorrigibles should suffer both imprisonment and castration, was the opinion of S. L. N. Foote.[20]

I claim these unfortunates can no more control their acts than they can their belief. . . . Acts are controlled by motives; and we must act in accordance with the strongest motive. We never act otherwise. Motives are the result of collateral circumstances, operating through the senses upon the cerebral organization. . . . And now, how came we by these peculiar organizations on which collateral influences operate so differently? Did we have any say as to what the configuration of our own heads or bodies should be? Did we form a prenatal resolution to be known as blondes or brunettes, six inches or six feet tall, wise or foolish, good or bad? A negative reply is unavoidable. All our features and faculties were predetermined at the instant of conception and by prior circumstances operating upon our ancestors, and subsequent circumstances operating upon them and us, over which we had no control. . . . Can we do anything to better the condition? . . . Though the past is fixed and unchangeable, the future is ours to control provided the motive exists; and motive or no motive, we determine what it shall be either blindly or intelligently. The first thing to do, is to arrest the propagation of criminals and imbeciles. Do you ask how this can be done? I will try and tell you. The laws of heredity are fixed and unchangeable as those of gravitation, heat, light, or any others known; and one of those is, that like begets like. "Do men gather grapes of thorns or figs of thistles?" Nay verily! But might we not as well expect this as expect high moral and intellectual endowment in the progeny of men and women steeped in crime and stupidity?[21]

[18] G. Frank Lydston, "Asexualization in the Prevention of Crime," *Medical News*, LXVIII (May 23, 1896) 573-578.

[19] A. L. Clark, "Thoughts on Criminology," *Chicago Medical Times*, XXX (February 1897) 41-44.

[20] S. L. N. Foote, "An Address on Crime and Its Prevention," *Kansas City Medical Index*, XVIII (July 1897) 243-245.

[21] *Ibid.*, pp. 243-244.

In 1899 appeared the first record of a proposal to sterilize criminals by vasectomy. By means of vasectomy the vas deferens is cut, and the ends tied so that spermatozoa are not permitted to escape into the seminal fluid. The operation is not serious, and requires, in the case of the male, only a local anaesthesia. The corresponding operation in the female is salpingectomy, whereby the ligation of the oviducts prevents the ovum from entering the uterus. Though not as simple as vasectomy, it is regarded as a relatively harmless operation. Prior to the invention of these two operative techniques, sterilization was accomplished by means of castration—in the male by removal of the testes (testiotomy), in the female, of the ovaries (ovariotomy).

It was A. J. Ochsner, chief surgeon of Augustana Hospital and of St. Mary's Hospital in Chicago, who published the first paper on vasectomy for criminals.[22] Accepting the statistics of E. Bleuler and Lombroso as well as others that three-fourths of all crimes were committed by habitual criminals, Ochsner held that if it were possible to prevent habitual criminals from having children, then crime would decrease considerably. After stating that a very large proportion of all criminals, degenerates, and perverts have come from parents similarly afflicted, he suggested vasectomy for the habitual criminal. Ochsner cited two of his cases in which he had performed vasectomies upon male patients (non-criminals) and deemed the operation simple, safe, sure, and admirably suited to replace castration in dealing with criminals.[23]

Following the introduction of this method in 1899, vasectomy replaced castration as a suggested method of dealing with the habitual, born, or instinctive criminal. Within the same year Daniel R. Brower denounced castration as too cruel, and observed:

The operation proposed by Dr. Ochsner, consisting in a resection of the vas deferentia, does not mutilate the person, it does not destroy

---

[22] A. J. Ochsner, "Surgical Treatment of Habitual Criminals," *Journal of the American Medical Association*, XXXII (April 22, 1899) 867-868.

[23] Although Ochsner's paper was the first publication in America on vasectomy, it was Dr. Harry C. Sharp, surgeon of the Indiana Reformatory in Indiana, who is credited with being the first to perform the operation upon criminals. Mention shall be made subsequently of Dr. Sharp's work and publications.

his sexual power, but it does prevent his power of propagation, and it is an operation attended with very little risk to life, and in my judgment it may be made a most useful agent in preventing an increase in criminals.[24]

Three years later, in 1902, Harry C. Sharp presented his first paper on vasectomy.[25] After quoting the labors of 'Galton and Ribot on heredity he deplored the rapid increase in the criminal and defective population, declaring that vasectomy was an effective method of combating such a situation. He recognized that Ochsner had performed vasectomy twice for diseases of the prostate, while he himself had performed forty-two vasectomies without impairment of sexual power of the subjects. In recommending vasectomy to the medical profession and at the same time enlisting their interest and support in the cause of sterilization of criminals and defectives Sharp stated:

Gentlemen, it is my judgment, founded on research and observation, that this is the rational means of eradicating from our midst a most dangerous and hurtful class. Too much stress cannot be placed upon the present danger to the race. The public must be made to see that radical methods are necessary. Even radical methods may be made to seem just if they are shown to be rational. In this we have a means which is both rational and sufficient. It remains with you—men of science and skill—to perpetuate a known relief to a weakening race by prevailing upon your legislatures to enact such laws as will restrict marriage and give those in charge of State institutions the authority to render every male sterile who passes its portals, whether it be almshouse, insane asylum, institute for the feeble-minded, reformatory, or prison. The medical profession has never failed in an attempt, and it will not fail in this.[26]

Thus the campaign had begun for a sterilization law, finding its first victory seven years later, in 1909, in the enactment by the State of Indiana of the first law in the United States providing for

[24] Daniel R. Brower, "Medical Aspects of Crime," *Boston Medical and Surgical Journal,* CXL (June 15, 1899) 574.
[25] Harry C. Sharp, "The Severing of the Vas Deferentia and Its Relation to the Neuropsychopathic Constitution," *New York Medical Journal,* LXXV (March 8, 1902) 411-414.
[26] *Ibid.,* pp. 413-414.

the operation of vasectomy upon male criminals and other defectives.

With a surgical invention that had changed the technique of sterilization and even rendered it more likely of acceptance, the conviction was strengthened that criminals sprang from criminals through the germ plasm. Thus Ellinwood expressed concern over the hereditary transmission of morbid and vicious propensities, particularly involving the sexual passions, and urged vasectomy for crimes of sexual passions and perversions.[27] L. A. Westcott, too, would subject the criminal to vasectomy so that he could not reproduce his own kind. If there be anything to the doctrine of heredity, Westcott argued, the criminal parent will transmit some, if not all, of his criminal tendencies to his children.[28] Jesse Ewell demanded that the sexual offender be castrated, both his ears cut off, and that then he be turned loose.[29] The intent here was unmistakeably punitive.[30]

Not only the physician, but also the student who approached the study of the criminal from the point of view of the social sciences, such as Travis, recommended sterilization for the hopeless criminal as well as for the natural criminal. Travis proposed both sterilization and isolation on a remote island.[31] M. E. Van Meter, although a physician, was strongly inclined to insist that crime had not only a legal definition but also a moral aspect—the begetting of offspring with an hereditary predisposition to criminality was perhaps more a moral than a legal con-

[27] C. N. Ellinwood, "Vasectomy: An Argument for Its Therapeutic Use in Certain Diseases and as a Means of Diminishing Crime and the Number of Criminals," *California State Journal of Medicine*, II (February 1904) 60-61.

[28] L. A. Westcott, "A Radical Treatment for the Prevention of Crime and Disease," *Medical Council*, X (September 1905) 330-332.

[29] Jesse Ewell, "A Plea for Castration to Prevent Criminal Assault," *Virginia Medical Semi-Monthly*, XI (January 1907) 463-464.

[30] It is but fair to note here that the feeling that rapists should be castrated was not only found in the South, but in the North as well. G. Frank Lydston of Chicago so recommended it as early as 1893, again in 1896, and for the third time in his book published in 1904. It should be observed that in 1904 Lydston urged vasectomy for other crimes, but still held to castration for rape. See G. Frank Lydston, *Diseases of Society*, Philadelphia, 1904, pp. 562-568.

[31] Thomas Travis, *The Young Malefactor, A Study in Juvenile Delinquency, Its Causes and Treatment*, New York, 1908, pp. 213-214.

cern. Such a crime—legal and moral—could be reached only by sterilization.[32]

The first compulsory sterilization law was enacted in Indiana in 1907. This statute provided for the sterilization of "confirmed criminals, idiots, imbeciles, and rapists," if, in the judgment of a committee of experts and the board of managers of the institution, procreation was inadvisable.[33] Dr. Harry C. Sharp, surgeon to the Reformatory, had been experimenting on the voluntary sterilization of inmates since the late 1890's, but it was not until after the practice was legalized and he had a sufficient number of cases with postoperative histories that he published his results. From 1899 to 1907 he had performed vasectomies on 465 cases with no unfortunate results. Of these cases one hundred and seventy-six had requested vasectomies.[34] There seems to be no question but that Sharp was the leading and most important figure in the early days of the movement to sterilize criminals by means of vasectomy. He as surgeon, and W. H. Whittaker as superintendent of the Indiana Reformatory, were the pioneers in this field, and it was largely through their efforts that Indiana passed its first sterilization law.

If Dr. Sharp was not his own propagandist (and he appears not to have been, judging by the paucity of his works) then that position must be awarded to G. Henri Bogart, a physician of Brookville, Indiana. Indeed, by his own statement he was the press agent for the movement. Acknowledging that Dr. Sharp was the originator of the operation of vasectomy for criminals, Dr. Bogart claimed that he (Bogart) published the first formal announcement of vasectomy as a legal means for controlling the growing danger of degeneracy and inherent criminality. This

---

[32] M. E. Van Meter, "A Plea for Sterilization as a Prevention for Crime and Disease," *American Journal of Dermatology and Genito-Urinary Diseases*, XII (July 1908) 288-295.

[33] This law was declared unconstitutional by the Indiana Supreme Court in 1921 on the ground that it denied the patient due process of law. A second law was passed in 1927 which is still in effect and valid.

[34] Harry C. Sharp, "Vasectomy as a Means of Preventing Procreation in Defectives," *Journal of the American Medical Association*, LIII (December 4, 1909) 1897-1902; also, "Rendering Sterile of Confirmed Criminals and Mental Defectives," *Proceedings of the Annual Congress of the National Prison Association*, 1907, pp. 177-185.

paper, which appeared in August 1908, cited the Indiana law as the first effort of an American commonwealth to apply medical emasculation to the prevention of crime, disease, and degeneracy. Bogart declared that during the first year of operation of the law there had been 296 perfect operations performed in state institutions.[35] In the following year, dealing with the same subject, he cited the horrible example of the Jukes, and speculated: "Try to compute the crime and sorrow and misery and suffering that would have been prevented had Max Jukes encountered Dr. Sharp, under Superintendent Whittaker's régime, before he opened the Pandora's box of evil. . . ."[36] The series of articles which came from Bogart's pen in the next few years emphasized and elaborated his fundamental points already presented: crime was hereditary, criminals should be vasectomized; the defective classes were breeding faster than the "upper" classes, the defective classes should be vasectomized. The editor of the *Texas Medical Journal*, Dr. F. E. Daniel, had already advocated castration for criminals in 1893. At his invitation Bogart published "Sterilization—the Indiana Plan," in the *Texas Medical Journal*, and followed it with "More on Vasectomy." Within six months of his first article it had been republished in identical form in the same journal because the editor declared the readers' demands had been so great that a reprinting was necessary. In addition to these two articles Bogart produced at least eight others within the next three years, all dealing with the same theme.[37]

During 1909 and 1910 there was a deluge of articles purport-

[35] G. Henri Bogart, "Restricting the Propagation of the Unfit," *Medical Council*, XIII (August 1908) 282-284.

[36] G. Henri Bogart, "Asexualization of Criminals by Severance of Vas Deferens," *Medical Council*, XIV (August 1909) 297.

[37] G. Henri Bogart, "A Plea for Double Vasectomy in Criminals and Those Mentally Deficient," *American Journal of Dermatology and Genito-Urinary Diseases*, XIII (May 1909) 221-224; "Asexualization of the Unfit," *Medical Herald*, XXIX (June 1910) 298-301; "Procreation Laws," *Medical Fortnightly*, XXXVII (September 1910) 348-350; "Sterilization—The Indiana Plan," *Texas Medical Journal*, XXVI (September 1910) 79-86; "More on Vasectomy," *Texas Medical Journal*, XXVI (January 1911) 239-242; "Sterilization of the Unfit," *Texas Medical Journal*, XXVI (February 1911) 279-286; "The Indiana Plan," *Medical Herald*, XXX (January 1911) 81-84; "Sterilizing the Unfit," *Texas Medical Journal*, XXVII (March 1912) 327-330.

ing to show cause why "the criminal and other members of the defective classes" should not be allowed to procreate. Early in 1909 William T. Belfield discussed the merits of castration, colonization, and vasectomy, and came to the conclusion that criminals should undergo vasectomy.[38] J. Ewing Mears, a Philadelphia physician intensely interested in race betterment (as were most of those who advocated any form of sterilization), recommended vasectomy for perverts and degenerates, idiots, imbeciles, epileptics, and the vicious insane, as well as for those criminals who practise sexual perversion and adnormal indulgences.[39] "Prophylaxis for both disease and crime is quite overshadowing the ancient custom of prescribing medicine and punishment," said Benjamin Ricketts, who suggested that, instead of administering a dose of punishment to the criminal, let him be sterilized.[40] W. J. Chandler was another of the many who had cited the Jukes as an example of hereditary crime and prescribed sterilization of the criminal for this evil.[41] Indiana's sterilization statute was cited by Earl E. Gaver, a physician from the neighboring state of Ohio, as an effective example for other states to follow.[42]

Few utterances on the sterilization of criminals aroused more discussion, pro and con, than did the remarks made by Judge Warren W. Foster, of the Court of General Sessions, of New York City. Writing in a popular magazine, *Pearson's*, in 1909, Judge Foster accepted the Lombrosian position that atavism was of preëminent importance in the causation of crime. He quoted G. Frank Lydston on the tenets of modern criminology, cited the Jukes as examples of the inheritance of crime, and concluded that there existed a class of criminals which could be called instinctive,

[38] William T. Belfield, "The Sterilization of Criminals and Other Defectives by Vasectomy," *Chicago Medical Reporter*, XXXI (March 1909) 219-222.

[39] J. Ewing Mears, "Asexualization as a Remedial Measure in the Relief of Certain Forms of Mental, Moral and Physical Degeneration," *Boston Medical and Surgical Journal*, CLXI (October 21, 1909) 584-586.

[40] Benjamin Merrill Ricketts, "Sterilization for Crime," *Medical Review of Reviews*, XV (November 25, 1909) 755-757.

[41] William J. Chandler, "Sterilization of Confirmed Criminals, Idiots, Imbeciles and Other Defectives by Vasectomy," *Journal of the Medical Society of New Jersey*, VI (December 1909) 321-326.

[42] Earl E. Gaver, "Procreation in Its Relation to Insanity, Crime and Degeneracy, with Suggestions of Remedy," *Ohio Medical Journal*, V (May 15, 1909) 257-263.

born, or congenital. Granting that heredity was the most potent
source of crime, and arguing that society should protect itself by
preventing the further breeding of criminals, Foster discussed
emasculation, regulation of marriage, segregation, and vasectomy.
Of these he regarded vasectomy as the best, and held it to be
the certain cure for hereditary criminality.[43] Burnside Foster, a
physician and no relation to the Judge Warren Foster just
named, writing two months later in the *St. Paul Medical Journal*,
of which he was editor, declared that a very large percentage of
habitual criminals, the degenerates and the sexual perverts, were
the offspring of parents of the same kind as themselves. Expressing approval of the Indiana law, he believed that since the large
class known as degenerates, which included the chronic insane,
the imbecile, the epileptic, the confirmed inebriate, the sexual
pervert, and the habitual criminal, were sure to beget and
procreate their kind, that some radical measure was needed. That
measure was sterilization by vasectomy.[44]

Burnside Foster's was but one of the many contributions which
appeared during the year 1910 advocating the sterilization of the
criminal. James Bloss stressed vasectomy as a prophylaxis rather
than as punishment,[45] while G. D. Lind observed that although
petty crimes had diminished, capital crimes had not and that
therefore the cause must lie in something which is inherited from
one's ancestors. To reach this something he proposed sterilization.[46] In the same year Carrington published the third of his
articles recommending sterilization of confirmed criminals.[47] In

[43] Warren W. Foster, "Hereditary Criminality and Its Certain Cure," *Pearson's Magazine*, XXII (November 1909) 565-572.

[44] Burnside Foster, "The Sterilization of Habitual Criminals and Degenerates," *St. Paul Medical Journal*, XII (January 1910) 29-34.

[45] James R. Bloss, "Sterilization of Confirmed Criminals and Other Defectives," *West Virginia Medical Journal*, IV (March 1910) 291-294.

[46] G. D. Lind, "What Can the Medical Profession Do to Prevent Crime?" *West Virginia Medical Journal*, IV (March 1910) 294-297.

[47] Charles V. Carrington, "Hereditary Criminals—The One Sure Cure," *Virginia Medical Semi-Monthly*, XV (April 8, 1910) 4-8. His earlier papers were: "Sterilization of Habitual Criminals," *Proceedings of the Annual Congress of the American Prison Association*, 1908, pp. 174-177; "Sterilization of Habitual Criminals," *Virginia Medical Semi-Monthly*, XIV (December 24, 1909) 421-422, and one a year earlier to which it closely corresponded entitled "Sterilization of Habitual Criminals, with Report of Cases," *Virginia Medical Semi-Monthly*, XIII (December 11, 1908) 389-390.

urging Virginia to pass a sterilization law like that of Indiana, he asserted that heredity was the greatest causal factor in crime, and that because of atavism, or the tendency to return to type, criminals must not be allowed to procreate. M. O. Shivers offered vasectomy as the surgeon's contribution in the treatment of criminals and defectives.[48] Others, such as J. M. Keniston, accepted Kraepelin's classification of the criminal as in the class of degenerates, sub-class of psychopathic personalities, and favored vasectomy as a method of ridding society of such defectives.[49] A. L. Parsons likewise contended that criminals were degenerates and that degeneracy had as a most potent causative factor an hereditary predisposition or tendency. Hence he approved of vasectomy, emphasizing, however, that its use was prophylactic rather than punitive.[50] On the other hand C. H. Preston, while he believed in asexualization, maintained that castration or vasectomy should be practised only on prisoners when there is a possibility of pardon or escape, for otherwise the vasectomized released prisoner would only spread disease—vasectomy permitting the power to debauch and infect.[51] He preferred castration for confirmed criminals and defectives. Speaking from his experience as a physician and from his four years as superintendent of Elmira Reformatory, Frank W. Robertson was convinced that the weight of opinion supported the hypothesis of the hereditary transmission of crime, and that vasectomy was the answer.[52] With a different experience—as professor of medicine at Johns Hopkins University—Llewellys F. Barker implied sterilization when he classed as social deteriorants and degenerates the criminal classes, the insane, the feeble-minded, the chronic inebriates, the habitual vagrants, the permanent pauper

[48] M. O. Shivers, "The Surgeon's Part in the Treatment of Criminals and Defectives," *Journal of the American Medical Association*, LIV (May 14, 1910) 1634.

[49] J. M. Keniston, "Defectives and Degenerates: A Menace to the Community," *Yale Medical Journal*, XVII (June 1910) 1-7.

[50] A. L. Parsons, "The Prophylaxis of Criminality," *American Practitioner and News*, XLIV (July 1910) 348-356.

[51] C. H. Preston, "Vasectomy. Its Ethical and Sanitary Limitations," *West Virginia Medical Journal*, V (July 1910) 16-18.

[52] Frank W. Robertson, "Sterilization for the Criminal Unfit," *American Medicine*, V, n.s. (July 1910) 349-361, also in a letter to the editor of the *Survey*, "Sterilizing of the Unfit," *Survey*, XXIV (August 20, 1910) 730.

class, the congenital deaf and dumb, and the sexual perverts.[53] And finally, for the year 1910, George Sehon, in submitting to the American Prison Association the report of the Committee on Prevention and Probation, stated there was no question as to the efficacy of sterilization as a preventive of delinquency. His only regret was its belated recognition and acceptance.[54]

In the next year, 1911, Hoag of Illinois cited with approval the Indiana sterilization legislation of 1907.[55] S. M. Jenkins of Oklahoma wanted Bogart to come from Indiana and to work for similar legislation in Oklahoma. Like many other ardent advocates of this form of social control, he wanted sterilization to be mandatory in every state institution for the confirmed criminal, the insane, the idiot, the imbecile, the feeble-minded, the epileptic, and the rapist.[56] In 1910-1911 New Jersey had enacted its sterilization law, and Orton, physician to the Rahway Reformatory in that state, recommended vasectomy for habitual criminals, and castration for rapists.[57] Malone Duggan also favored vasectomy for the criminal, the feeble-minded, the inebriate, the prostitue, and the sexual pervert, declaring all of them to be such because of direct inheritance.[58] Tom Williams citing Sharp's accomplishments in Indiana and Carrington's efforts in Virginia, favored a sterilization statute for his own state, Georgia.[59]

In the following year the discussion of and agitation for sterilization legislation continued. John N. Hurty, Health Com-

[53] Llewellys F. Barker, "On the Prevention of Social Deterioration and Degeneracy, Especially by Denying the Privilege of Parenthood to the Manifestly Unfit," *Maryland Medical Journal*, LIII (September 1910) 291-297.

[54] George L. Sehon, "Report of the Committee on Prevention and Probation," *Proceedings of the Annual Congress of the American Prison Association*, 1910, pp. 131-153.

[55] Junius C. Hoag, "The Relation of Vasectomy to Eugenics," *Chicago Medical Recorder*, XXXIII (January 1911) 1-17.

[56] S. M. Jenkins, "Sterilization of the Unfit," *Journal of the Oklahoma State Medical Association*, III (February 1911) 312-315.

[57] G. L. Orton, "The Procreative Regulation of Defectives and Delinquents," *Journal of the American Medical Association*, LVIII (June 29, 1912) 2021-2023.

[58] Malone Duggan, "The Surgical Solution of the Problem of Race Culture," *Texas State Journal of Medicine*, VII (July 1911) 87-89.

[59] Tom A. Williams, "The Sterilization of Degenerate Criminals," *Atlanta Journal-Record of Medicine*, LVIII (October 1911) 371-373.

missioner of Indiana, suggested sterilization after declaring that just as some men are born color-blind so others may be born morally color-blind. Carlos F. MacDonald, a noted American alienist, expressed approval of Hurty's thesis by adding that the individual with a criminal brain will beget offspring with criminal brains.[60] So too, Marshall, who spoke of the disease of criminality (believing 70 per cent of all criminals are so by "instinct") held that the reproduction of children by degenerates and incorrigibles should be prohibited.[61] E. F. Bowers cited the Jukes as exemplifying the inheritance of criminal traits, and favored Dr. Sharp's technique for criminals.[62] Paul E. Bowers, when citing the Jukes, realized the importance of recent studies of heredity as well. His own studies of six cases of inmates of the Indiana State Prison emphasized the factor of poor heredity. He fully supported the practice of vasectomy for all defectives, which included criminals.[63] On certain occasions a physician who favored sterilization was in a position to do more than simply to discuss or agitate for it. Such was the experience of Dr. Daniel Parker, who at one time was a county judge, and who in 1912 was a member of the Texas State Legislature. Dr. Parker had introduced a sterilization bill, but owing to political wrangles and, as he put it "to some extent my own inexperience," it died on the calendar. He was convinced from his study of heredity that crime was a species of insanity and was inherited, and that vasectomy was the most effective instrument in preventing its transmission. Like many of the eugenists before and since his time he deplored the modern methods of keeping alive the unfit and of allowing their strains to be perpetuated.[64] Likewise C. M. Clark held that depraved heredity was responsible for that great class of de-

[60] John N. Hurty, "The Sterilization of Criminals and Defectives," *Social Diseases*, III (January 1912) 1-47.

[61] G. G. Marshall, "The Disease of Criminality," *Vermont Medical Monthly*, XVIII (March 15, 1912) 54-59.

[62] E. F. Bowers, "Sterilization of Degenerate Criminals and the Insane," *Medico-Pharmaceutical Critic and Guide*, XV (May 1912) 177-179.

[63] Paul E. Bowers, "A Plea for Sterilization," *Dietetic and Hygienic Gazette*, XXVIII (September 1912) 585-589.

[64] Daniel Parker, "The Prevention of the Increase of Insanity, of the Procreation of the Congenitally Defective and of the Criminally Disposed," *Texas Medical Journal*, XXVIII (October 1912) 135-139.

fectives who carried in their train disease and crime. He agreed with W. Duncan McKim that crime was essentially inborn, and that vasectomy was necessary for idiots, imbeciles, epileptics, habitual drunkards, insane criminals, and other criminals who might be adjudged incorrigible.[65] D. H. Calder, superintendent of a state mental hospital, declined to accept all criminals as being hereditarily defective, but he did favor sterilization as a condition precedent to parole from penal institutions when, in the judgment of the state board of eugenics, sterilization was advisable. In addition he proposed that this state board of eugenics should act with the state board of health in connection with the public schools, the industrial school, schools for the deaf, dumb, and blind, the state hospital, and the state prison.[66]

A short time later, early in 1913, Dew concurred in such a procedure and recommended that his own state, Virginia, should also sterilize criminals as a prerequisite to liberation rather than keep them in perpetual segregation.[67] Rebecca George also dismissed segregation, as well as marriage regulation and emasculation (meaning castration) and endorsed vasectomy as being far more effective in eliminating the production of the criminal, the feeble-minded, the insane, and the epileptic.[68] W. O. Henry held that it was the duty of the state to sterilize certain elements of the population, among which are the criminal degenerates.[69] And finally for this year, 1913, Dr. Jordon, professor of histology and embryology at the University of Virginia, joined with others in classing the criminal with the unfit and recommending their sterilization.[70]

[65] C. M. Clark, "A Plea for Sterilization of Criminals, Epileptics, Imbeciles and Insane," *Northwest Medicine*, IV, n.s. (December 1912) 360-363.

[66] D. H. Calder, "Statutory Eugenics," *Northwest Medicine*, IV, n.s. (December 1912) 357-360.

[67] H. W. Dew, "Sterilization of the Feeble-Minded, Insane and Habitual Criminals," *Virginia Medical Semi-Monthly*, XVIII (April 1913) 4-8.

[68] Rebecca Rogers George, "Sterilization of the Unfit," *New England Medical Gazette*, XLVIII (September 1913) 466-473.

[69] W. O. Henry, "Duty of the State to Promote the Health of Its Subjects by Sterilizing the Insane, Criminal Degenerates, Inebriates and Other Habitual Drug Users, as Well as to Sterilize Its Confirmed Criminals for Social and Economic Reasons," *Medical Herald*, XXXII (September 1913) 321-329.

[70] H. E. Jordon, "Surgical Sex-Sterilization. Its Value as a Eugenic Measure," *American Journal of Clinical Medicine*, XX (December 1913) 983-987.

EUGENICS

Eugenics as a movement in its earlier days in America was very largely the work of Charles B. Davenport, who had been influenced by the pioneer work of Sir Francis Galton and Karl Pearson in England. In 1910 Davenport founded the Eugenics Record Office at Cold Spring Harbor, Long Island, New York, in connection with the Department of Genetics of the Carnegie Institution. A year later, in his book *Heredity in Relation to Eugenics*, he traced the inheritance of family traits, among them the hereditary criminal instincts.[71] Eight cases purporting to show the inheritance of criminal instincts were described by Davenport in this work. He was skeptical, however, of the effectiveness of asexualization. First of all he believed that the legislation providing for sterilization was based upon a false notion of heredity—the notion that parents transmitted their identical traits to their children. Traits, he insisted, were transmitted by means of the germ plasm, and parents and children may resemble each other in many respects because they carry to some extent the same germinal material. Speaking specifically of the feeble-minded, he observed that the children of a feeble-minded parent may bear normal children if mated to a normal individual, and that the children of this union in turn may, by uniting with other normals, produce normals, the feeble-minded strain remaining recessive. Secondly, he remarked that the laws defining classes to be sterilized were too vague in their description of these classes. He preferred castration to vasectomy since both licentiousness and disease might otherwise increase. Certainly castration for rapists would seem preferable to vasectomy. Perhaps, Davenport suggested, it might be better to segregate these classes—the feeble-minded, the epileptic, the insane, the hereditary criminals, and the prostitutes—throughout their reproductive period.

Several years earlier the American Breeders Association organized a committee of eugenics which consisted of David Starr Jordan, chairman, Alexander Graham Bell, Luther Burbank, W.

[71] Charles B. Davenport, *Heredity in Relation to Eugenics*, New York, 1911.

E. Castle, C. R. Henderson, A. Hrdlicka, V. L. Kellogg, Adolf
Meyer, J. Arthur Thomson, W. L. Tower, H. J. Webber, C. E.
Woodruff, F. A. Woods, and C. B. Davenport, secretary. In
reporting on the work of the committee in 1909 Davenport urged
the need for investigation, education, and legislation. It was as
a part of the legislative program that sterilization of idiots,
imbeciles, and dangerous criminals was recommended.[72]

Other eugenists of this period also favored sterilization,
notably H. H. Laughlin who, as superintendent of the Eugenics
Record Office at Cold Spring Harbor, was associated with Davenport. Speaking before the First National Conference on Race
Betterment, Laughlin recommended sterilization as follows:

These four agencies—education, legal restriction, segregation and
sterilization—complement one another in the order named. They are
a primary remedial value; if the first fails, apply the second; if it
also fails, apply the third; if segregation ceases and the two factors do
not deter from parenthood the potential parent of inadequates, apply
the fourth. To purify the breeding stock of the race at all costs is the
slogan of eugenics.[73]

OPPOSITION TO STERILIZATION

The proposals looking toward sterilization of criminals were
not without opposition. Some denounced them as being inhuman,
some as impractical, some as useless, and still others as irreligious,
and an impious denial of a God-given right.

While castration was still the only method available Mark
Millikin opposed it on humanitarian grounds.[74] The same is true
of Frederick H. Wines.[75] J. W. Lockhart asked what good it
would do. He answered his own question by stating that not
only would it do no good but would do irreparable harm.[76] A. C.

[72] Charles B. Davenport, *Eugenics*, New York, 1910, pp. 26-35.

[73] H. H. Laughlin, "Calculations on the Working Out of a Proposed Program of
Sterilization," *Proceedings of the First National Conference on Race Betterment*, 1914,
p. 478.

[74] Mark Millikin, "The Proposed Castration of Criminals and Sexual Perverts,"
Cincinnati Lancet-Clinic, XXXIII (August 1894) 185-190.

[75] Frederick H. Wines, *op. cit.*, pp. 296-297.

[76] J. W. Lockhart, "Should Criminals be Castrated?" *St. Louis Courier of Medicine*,
XIII, n.s. (October 1895) 136-137.

Corr took issue with Dr. Boal, denying the efficacy of castration, stating that the criminal tendency was the result of environmental influences.[77] In the following year, 1896, Corr again attacked Dr. Boal's position and cited the discussion of N. S. Davis of Chicago as follows:

I have seen nothing in my observations in human society to make me believe that human depravity is greatly ruled by simply the sexual organs in either sex. That they are capable of exerting a predominating influence in individual cases, as much and probably a great deal more owing to bad training, bad education, bad surroundings than to any inherent vice in these organs, is undoubtedly true, but whether they have any more tendency to produce crime than a man's stomach I very much doubt. I think it has been shown that a well developed dyspeptic is about as likely to go wrong as almost any other class we might enumerate. It is not, in my estimation, the fault of the organs that we propose to excise as much as it is the fault in the brain that accompanies them, and if you want to get rid of the tendency to crime you will have to excise some of the cells of the brain, if you can find the proper ones, instead of the sexual organs.[78]

Drähms attacked asexualization of criminals on the grounds that he opposed capital punishment—because it did not deter and because it was barbarous. "The doctrine of asexualization or the sterilization of criminals is amenable to much the same criticism. Its consideration scarcely deserves passing notice, and is but the whim of the impractical theorist."[79]

Though much of the force of the opposition to asexualization was dissipated when vasectomy was introduced, yet sufficient argument remained even after 1899. For Alfred Herzog, who was aroused by Judge Foster's article, "Hereditary Criminality and Its Certain Cure," vasectomy struck at the root of marriage and the family. Furthermore it was illegal to prevent conception.[80] In the four volumes which C. R. Henderson edited for the

[77] A. C. Corr, "Emasculation and Ovariotomy as a Penalty for Crime and as a Reformatory Agency," *Medical Age*, XIII (December 1895) 714-716.

[78] A. C. Corr, "Medical Aspect of Crime," *Journal of the American Medical Association*, XXVII (October 10, 1896) 788.

[79] August Drähms, *op. cit.*, pp. 361-362.

[80] Alfred W. Herzog, "Vasectomy—A Crime Against Nature," *Medico-Legal Journal*, XXVII (1909-1910) 150-158.

Eighth International Prison Congress in 1910, he presented the positions pro and con on the question of sterilization of criminals, in remarks prepared by J. B. Ransom, physician to Clinton Prison.[81] In Volume III of the same work Henderson observed that both the National Conference of Charities and Correction and the American Prison Association had considered the matters in their meetings without having committed themselves to policy. To Henderson the matter was open to "serious if not fatal objections."[82] Francis Barnes opposed the ethical right of the state to mutilate the individual, and raised the additional question as to where the line could be drawn. Furthermore, there was a much greater chance for the spread of venereal diseases.[83] Charles Nammack, professor of Clinical Medicine at Cornell University Medical College, declared that crime and criminality, being attributes of the mind, were not inherited, and hence he was opposed to sterilization of criminals. "They assume that man with a criminal mind has a criminal brain, and that he will beget offspring with criminal minds and criminal brains. Yet no examination of the brain of any criminal has ever shown why he was a criminal."[84] Prison physician Thayer of Clinton, New York, questioned the value of vasectomy as a factor in lessening crime because he considered criminality an acquired rather than an hereditary characteristic.[85] In his discussion of sterilization and segregation, H. H. Goddard, director of research at the Vineland Training School for the Feeble-Minded, declared it a mistake to extend vasectomy to criminals, because there was no proof that crime was hereditary. On the ground that the easiest material out of which to make criminals was the feeble-minded, he argued that the feeble-minded, rather than the criminal,

[81] Julius B. Ransom, "The Prison Physician and His Work," *Penal and Reformatory Institutions*, being Volume II of *Correction and Prevention*, Charities Publication Committee, New York, 1910, pp. 261-290.

[82] Charles R. Henderson, editor, *Preventive Agencies and Methods*, being Volume III of *Correction and Prevention*, New York, 1910, pp. 59-62.

[83] Francis J. Barnes, "Vasectomy," *New England Medical Monthly*, XXIX (December 1910) 454-458.

[84] Charles E. Nammack, "Is Sterilization of the Habitual Criminal Justifiable?" *New York Medical Record*, LXXIX (February 1911) 249.

[85] Walter N. Thayer, Jr., "What May We Do with Our Criminals?" *Survey*, XXIV (July 9, 1910) 587-589.

should be sterilized. He shared with others the misgiving that if criminals were sterilized there was a much greater probability that they will be promiscuous and thus spread venereal disease. Goddard believed the question to be one of segregation *and* sterilization, not segregation *or* sterilization.[86]

While some would agree to sterilization of all defectives and delinquents, there were others who reflected the editorial comment in the *Survey*, in 1912, to the effect that while the feebleminded and the insane might be sterilized, we were not yet willing to accept it for other classes such as the criminal.[87] In the following year H. H. Hart, of the Russell Sage Foundation, writing in the same journal, opposed sterilization, criticized Dr. Sharp, and declared that what was needed was improved custodial care.[88] According to H. Douglas Singer, director of the Illinois State Psychopathic Institute, the criminal could not be reformed by vasectomy. Since vasectomy was useless, then incarceration for life should be prescribed. If the criminal could improve, obviously there was no need for vasectomy. Furthermore, if criminals were vasectomized and liberated they complicated the problem of venereal infection.[89]

STERILIZATION LEGISLATION

A review of the literature of sterilization reveals an interesting and significant pattern. From the time of Evert's paper in 1888 until the close of the century there was a considerable conviction that crime was hereditary and that one effective, perhaps the most effective, way of reaching it was by castration. In 1899 vasectomy was developed, a method far simpler from every point of view, yet it was almost a decade before it obtained acceptance. Indeed, it was not until the first sterilization statute, in 1907,

[86] H. H. Goddard, "Sterilization and Segregation," *Bulletin of the American Academy of Medicine*, XIII (August 1912) 210-219.

[87] *Survey*, XXIX (December 21, 1912) 374-375.

[88] H. H. Hart, "A Working Program for the Extinction of the Defective Delinquent," *Survey*, XXX (May 24, 1913) 277-279; also "The Extinction of the Defective Delinquent. A Working Program," *Proceedings of the Annual Congress of the American Prison Association*, 1912, pp. 205-225.

[89] H. Douglas Singer, "The Sterilization of the Insane, Criminal and Delinquent," *Illinois Medical Journal*, XXIII (May 1913) 480-485.

that vasectomy really came out into the open. The general under-lying premise remained—that crime was inherited through the germ plasm, and that the prevention of procreation was the condition precedent to the elimination of crime in the individual and criminality in society. Vasectomy was seized upon by the hereditarians and the early eugenists, and pressure was exerted to have that premise written into the law of the states.

The first bill favoring human sterilization was introduced in Michigan in 1897, but failed of passage. In 1905 the Pennsyl-vania legislature passed the first bill of any state in the Union, but it was vetoed by the governor. It was not, therefore, until 1907, that the first law appeared when Indiana, on March 9, placed on its statute books a provision for the asexualization of con-firmed criminals, rapists, idiots, and imbeciles. Even though 1907 marked the first date of the legal provision for sterilization, it was a known fact that for many years there had been secret sterilization performed upon the inmates of state institutions. By June 1915, thirteen states had enacted sterilization laws. The lack of agreement and clarity as to whether individuals, classes of individuals, or offenses were to be reached by sterilization, or whether sterilization was intended to be eugenic, therapeutic, or punitive is indicated in the conflicting provisions as reflected in the laws themselves. Among provisions for sterilization of institu-tion inmates were those pertaining to criminals; in these thirteen statutes the following were named as subjects for asexualization: habitual criminals, those three times convicted of a felony, rapists, those twice convicted of sexual crimes, those convicted of carnal abuse of a female under ten years, and inmates of a prison deemed unimprovable, physically or mentally.

CONCLUSION

The biological and sociological evidence that has accumulated with the past two decades casts considerable doubt upon the tenets so quickly, so uncritically adopted, and so tenaciously held in the quarter century before. There is more unanimity today than ever before that criminality, per se, is not inherited, and that criminals, as criminals, should not be subjected to compulsory sterilization. Thus it is becoming accepted increasingly that crime is an evidence of maladjustment between the individual and society. There are soberer students of eugenics who are also recognizing that in some instances criminals are characterized by mental disorders or deficiencies and are recommending sterilization, not because the individuals are criminals, but because they are mentally diseased or deficient. Indeed, there is even a respectable opinion today which holds that a human sterilization program should provide for the sterilization of individuals, not of classes.

X

FEEBLE-MINDEDNESS

FOR centuries the category of insanity had included the mentally deficient—those variously called at one time or another feeble-minded, morons, idiots, imbeciles, simpletons, fools, etc. Too often these victims were as unsegregated as the insane, being indiscriminately lodged in prisons, jails, workhouses, poorhouses, and asylums. It was not until 1838 that the French alienist Esquirol, in his *Des Maladies Mentales*, distinguished mental defect from mental disease. He regarded idiocy—which until the twentieth century was used generically to represent what we today term feeble-mindedness—not as a disease, but a condition in which the intellectual faculties had never been manifested. This distinction was unknown in America until Isaac Ray presented it, in the same year as Esquirol, in his *Medical Jurisprudence of Insanity*. Nevertheless, though he recognized the practical distinction, idiocy still remained in his classification of insanity.[1] He differentiated those faculties which functioned abnormally subsequent to their development, which he classified as mainia and dementia, from those which either had never developed or were defective in development, in which case he classed them as idiocy and imbecility (idiocy and imbecility being merely differences in degree—the idiot being without semblance of reason, while the imbecile's development had been arrested at an early period of his existence).[2]

Concerning the relation of the imbecile to crime, Ray asked whether we could impute crime where there was neither inten-

---

[1] Another decade passed before this separation of the mentally defective from the mentally diseased was to become a reality, translated into separate custodial care. On October 1, 1848, Massachusetts set aside a wing of the Perkins Institution for the Blind as an experimental training school for the pauper and indigent idiots. Three years later the work was placed on a permanent basis and incorporated as the Massachusetts School for Idiotic and Feeble-Minded Youth. In July 1848, a private school was established in Barre, Massachusetts, for the "education and management of all children who by reason of mental infirmity are not fit subjects for ordinary instruction."

[2] Isaac Ray, *A Treatise on the Medical Jurisprudence of Insanity*, Boston, 1838, pp. 68-95.

tion nor consciousness of injury. The imbecile acted from an animal impulse and would as readily murder a fellow being as he would put to death a brute, being constitutionally unable to appreciate any difference in the moral character of the two actions. Furthermore, he knew no restraint, he was unable to feel benevolence and sympathy for his fellow men, was unable to grasp the notion of an Almighty Being, and was unable to see any connection between his crime and the penalty attached to it. Continuing, Ray remarked that the imbecile labored under no delusion, and yet he was without accountability. The strength and extent of his moral faculties could not be measured by his ability to perform routine mechanical tasks; his was not the intelligence to discern moral truth. Following these observations, Ray cited a case of a parricide by an imbecile, and noted that his proneness to mischief and cruelty at an early age pointed to an originally defective constitution unattended by any mania. Other cases of crimes committed by imbeciles were cited, Ray observing that there was a wretched class of men in whom mental imbecility was accompanied by more or less perversion of the moral faculties—a class whose only incentive was the satisfaction of animal passion.

It was Ray's opinion that even with this distinction between imbecility and insanity it was entirely possible, even probable, that the imbecile would not be legally responsible, because his mental powers were insufficient to entertain a criminal intent. While American courts had accepted this theoretical distinction between the imbecile and the insane man, they were unwilling to exculpate the offender on the grounds of his imbecility; indeed, they seemed the more ready to convict the imbecile for the very reason that he was not insane. Whereupon when in 1867 a court convicted Gregor MacGregor of murder, an article (quite certainly Ray's) in the *American Journal of Insanity* protested: "But he had not that degree of mental activity and energy which an enlightened common sense should deem necessary to a criminal intent."[3]

[3] Unsigned article, "Imbecility and Homicide: Case of Gregor MacGregor," *American Journal of Insanity*, XXIII (April 1867) 563.

A half century after Ray thus described certain imbeciles, Henry M. Hurd, superintendent of the Eastern Michigan Asylum, spoke of imbecility with moral perversion, a condition which Edward C. Spitzka, in 1883, had called moral imbecility.[4] Hurd, rather than use the term "moral insanity" which connoted normal mental development, described imbecility coupled with moral perversion in these words:

In these unfortunate persons there seems to be a normal, and in fact often an undue development of the perceptive faculties, emotions and organic impulses, and a corresponding deficiency of reasoning and inhibitory powers. In all persons of this class with whom I have come in contact the degree of mental development is about equal to that of a person of average mental capacity at puberty, and beyond this point the unfortunate moral imbecile never seems to go. Up to the age of puberty, for obvious reasons, their mental deficiencies are not apparent, but when they pass this age and begin to feel the stirring of physiological impulses their mental deficiency becomes patent to all. The more their characteristics are studied, the more evident it becomes that the apparent moral defect is really a mental deficiency.[5]

In this description Hurd was joined by Isaac N. Kerlin, head of the training school for the feeble-minded at Elwyn, Pennsylvania, who in his annual reports for 1884 and 1889, as well as in his address at the Annual Conference of Charities and Correction in 1890, had identified as a moral imbecile the individual who seemed to act without relation to the accepted moral values because of mental weakness. Kerlin recognized this person as not being insane, but as a member of that class of beings who shaded into crime on one side and idiocy on the other.[6] It was out of this degenerate stock—feeble-minded stock—that the criminal largely came, and the congenital criminal was simply a

[4] Henry M. Hurd, "Imbecility with Insanity," *American Journal of Insanity*, XLV (October 1888) 261-269; Edward C. Spitzka, *op. cit.*, p. 281.

[5] Henry M. Hurd, *op. cit.*, p. 267.

[6] Isaac N. Kerlin, *Thirty-Second Annual Report of the Pennsylvania Training School for Feeble-Minded Children*, Elwyn, 1884, p. 10; *Thirty-Seventh Annual Report*, etc., 1889, pp. 7-9; "The Moral Imbecile," *Proceedings of the National Conference of Charities and Correction*, 1890, pp. 244-250. Martin W. Barr, who succeeded Kerlin as head of Elwyn, claimed that Kerlin was the first to classify moral imbeciles as a distinct type.

moral imbecile, according to Martha Louise Clark, a teacher in an institution for the feeble-minded.[7]

That the criminal was regarded by numerous authorities as a product of degeneration, of which mental deficiency was often an element, was indicated in the chapters on criminal anthropology. Eugene S. Talbot, in his treatise on degeneration in 1898, placed the imbecile in the gap between the criminal and the idiot. After speaking of the idiot, he said:

At a still higher stage the imbecile may manifest destructive instincts, may steal without the signs of remorse displayed by a housebred dog, or may kill without recognizing the results of killing. The intellect may be comparatively developed in certain imbeciles in comparison with the ethical defects. For lack of proper associating fibers, the imbecile may be unable to acquire those higher associations constituting the secondary ego, in the most elevated sense. To this class ultimately belong the instinctive homicides, torturers, sexual criminals and thieves, so frequently found among the juvenile offspring of degenerate stock. In them the primary ego is strong, and the restraints of the secondary ego, which perceives the rights of others, weakened or completely absent. This class forms the germ of the congenital criminal whom no discipline can tame, and who is incapable of being taught the dangers of his procedures under the law of the land.[8]

For most writers on the subject of mental abnormality, mental deficiency was a valid part of their discussion, as instanced by Alonzo Richardson, who spoke of a class of persons in whom there was a natural tendency toward criminal conduct, and in whom the tendency was clearly the result of physical and natural defect or disease. In these individuals there was no power within them to prevent or to protect them from the execution of these tendencies. After discussing criminal acts arising from mental disease, he turned to the class in which criminal conduct was clearly the result of mental enfeeblement from birth, declaring a large proportion of criminals were of this class.[9]

What others had called moral imbecility, W. Duncan McKim,

[7] Martha Louise Clark, "The Relation of Imbecility to Pauperism and Crime," *Arena*, X (November 1894) 788-794.

[8] Eugene S. Talbot, *op. cit.*, p. 317.

[9] Alonzo B. Richardson, *op. cit.*, pp. 75-89.

in 1901, called moral idiocy, a condition wherein the person suffered from an inherited defect of brain and was incapable of appreciating the distinction between right and wrong, or of exercising restraint in any form. The difference between this and moral insanity, according to McKim, was a matter of acquirement—moral insanity was induced by injuries or degenerative processes, while moral idiocy was due most frequently to ancestral insanity, drunkenness, or epilepsy.[10] Martin W. Barr, chief physician of the Pennsylvania Training School for Feeble-Minded Children, at Elwyn, identified among his population a certain number who were marked by "degeneration of the psychic forces," and perversion or complete absence of the moral sense. These he called, after his predecessor Kerlin, moral imbeciles, classifying them as the low-grade or cruel and bestial type, the middle grade characterized by an absence of altruism and constantly infringing the rights of others, and the high grade whose mental powers were subordinated wholly to a perverted moral sense.[11]

Ever since the time when Isaac Ray wrote on imbecility and crime, there had been need for a more accurate classification of the person of limited mental capacity who committed criminal acts. Such a classification was provided in the year 1908, separately, by Drs. Walter E. Fernald and Charles W. Burr; the former being superintendent of the Massachusetts School for the Feeble-Minded, the latter professor of mental diseases at the University of Pennsylvania, both members of the American Medico-Psychological Association. It was at the 1908 meeting of this body that Fernald presented his paper on "The Imbecile with Criminal Instincts." Anticipating H. H. Goddard, he held that every imbecile, especially the high-grade one, was a potential criminal who needed only the proper environment and opportunity for the development and expression of his criminal tendencies. In the nineteen cases of imbeciles from the Massachusetts School for the Feeble-Minded he found unmistakable mental deficiency and evidence of criminal nature, as judged by

[10] W. Duncan McKim, op. cit.
[11] Martin W. Barr, Mental Defectives, Philadelphia, 1904, pp. 129-130, 264-281.

the offense. Indeed, these might well be called cases of moral imbecility, for Fernald claimed to have found no case of moral imbecility which was not a case of true imbecility. Furthermore, Fernald asked, is not there a close resemblance between the imbecile and the instinctive criminal of Lombroso? Is not the typical instinctive criminal of Lombroso a typical adult imbecile of middle or high grade, plus opportunity and experience in the community? Do they not have a common heredity, and similar evidences of degeneration—anatomical, physiological, and psychical?[12] Dr. Burr described the imbecile with criminal instincts to have a history such as this:

. . . either he never develops normally, mentally, or morally, or, after some acute infectious disease or a serious head injury during the earlier developmental stage of life, he shows marked defect. He can no longer concentrate the mind, is cruel and brutal, sexually passionate and perverted, lies and steals and mayhap murders and shows no remorse for his conduct. He is nonsocial and tyrannical and sometimes cowardly. He cannot acquire the rudiments of book learning. His moral deficiency often becomes more marked at or soon after puberty. These defectives are not all equally deficient. One meets with examples of every degree from slight to severe.[13]

It was this class as described by Fernald and Burr about whom Charles W. Hitchcock was uncertain when he presented his paper at the same meeting as Fernald. Hitchcock was not certain whether the man he had examined was an imbecile, a criminal, or both. Dr. Norbury, in the discussion which followed, declared him to be the moral imbecile described many years before by Kerlin, while Dr. Bancroft insisted, in effect, that Kerlin's moral imbecile, Fernald's and Hitchcock's man were one and the same.[14] The same might well be said of the forty cases of girls committed to the New York Training School who mere mentally deficient and were without moral sense, cited by Hortense

[12] Walter E. Fernald, "The Imbecile with Criminal Instincts," *Proceedings of the American Medico-Psychological Association*, 1908, pp. 363-381.

[13] Charles W. Burr, "Imbecility and Crime and the Legal Restraint of Imbeciles," *Pennsylvania Medical Journal*, XI (June 1908) p. 696.

[14] Charles W. Hitchcock, "Imbecile, Criminal, or Both?" *Proceedings of the American Medico-Psychological Association*, 1908, pp. 263-272.

Bruce.[15] Thus it will be seen that the feeble-minded offender had achieved some degree of classification and differentiation so that by the first decade of the twentieth he was recognized in prisons, in training schools, and in the population at large. In 1911, largely through the efforts of Walter E. Fernald, Massachusetts authorized separate custodial provision for these delinquents (although it was not until 1922 that the provision actually became effective).

FEEBLE-MINDEDNESS IN THE PENAL POPULATION

A concomitant aspect of this movement for the classification of the feeble-minded criminal was the analysis of the penal population on the basis of intelligence of inmates. From the earliest of these studies it was assumed and then "proved by estimates" that a large proportion of the prison and correctional school population was feeble-minded, with the inference that their feeble-mindedness was a causal factor in their criminality.[16] Among the first of these estimates of the intelligence of incarcerated offenders was that given by Franklin Niebecker, superintendent of the House of Refuge at Glen Mills, Pennsylvania, in 1901, in an address before the National Conference of Charities and Correction. On the basis of conversation with each boy committed, his school record upon admission and one year later, the visiting agent's report of his home, and the history of the boy at the time of commitment, Niebecker reported that one hundred consecutive admissions were decidedly below the standard of boys in the public school system of Philadelphia: 35% of the institution boys were below normal.[17] In the next year Dr. Frank L. Christian, senior physician at Elmira Reformatory, stated in his annual report that of the 811 inmates admitted during the year 130 (16%) were diagnosed as mentally de-

[15] Hortense V. Bruce, "Moral Degeneracy," *Journal of Psycho-Asthenics*, XIV (September 1909) 39-47.

[16] One of the few dissenting voices was that of G. Frank Lydston, who in 1904 declared that while the born criminal might lack intelligence, yet there was reason to believe that other criminals were of normal if not, in many cases, of superior intelligence. G. Frank Lydston, *The Diseases of Society*, pp. 496-498.

[17] Franklin H. Niebecker, "The Mental Capacity of Juvenile Delinquents," *Proceedings of the National Conference of Charities and Correction*, 1901, pp. 262-268.

fective.[18] Perhaps the first breakup of this group of mental defectives to be found in a prison was that made by J. W. Milligan, physician to the Indiana State Prison. Speaking before the National Prison Association in 1906 he declared that of the 926 inmates of the Indiana State Prison, 114, or 12%, were mental defectives. Of these 114 mental defectives sixty-nine were insane, ten were epileptics, sixteen had an epileptic history or had had epileptoid attacks, five were feeble-minded, and fourteen were degenerate and abnormal. Accepting five of this 114 as feebleminded, we have a percentage of a trifle over 4. (This is the year 1906; it will of interest to compare this figure with those far higher to be published within the next decade.)[19] In remarking upon this figure of 12% of mental defectives, Amos Butler, secretary of the Board of State Charities of Indiana, pointed to the fact, in 1907, that one-fifth of the population of Elmira Reformatory was feeble-minded, while the proportion in the Indiana Reformatory was 21%.[20] Butler did not doubt that feeble-mindedness was a prolific source of crime.

Examination of the population of a reform school was demanded frequently for practical purposes such as classification, or for parole release. On the basis of such a study of 1,186 girls at the State Industrial School at Lancaster, Ohio, and of the 1,625 boys at the Lyman School for Boys (also in Ohio), reported by Elizabeth Evans and Mary Dewson, it was found that 5.7% of the girls were feeble-minded and required custodial care, while 22.3% were sub-normal but might be tried on parole. Among the boys only fifty or about 3% were feeble-minded or sub-normal.[21] On the basis of psychological studies of memory and tests of tactual impressions, criminals rated far below students, according to Hugo Münsterberg, psychologist at

[18] Frank L. Christian, *Physician's Report, Twenty-Seventh Annual Report of the New York State Reformatory* at Elmira, 1902, pp. 56-76.

[19] J. W. Milligan, "Mental Defectives Among Prisoners," *Proceedings of the National Prison Association*, 1906, pp. 195-205.

[20] Amos Butler, "The Burden of Feeble-Mindedness," *Proceedings of the National Conference of Charities and Correction*, 1907, pp. 1-10.

[21] Elizabeth G. Evans and Mary W. Dewson, "Feeble-Mindedness and Juvenile Delinquency," *Charities*, XX (May 2, 1908) 183-191.

Harvard University, who stated that of two hundred "criminal boys" examined, 127 were deficient in their general make-up, either in the direction of hysteric emotion or of epileptic disturbance. While mental inferiority would not force a person to steal or to commit a crime, nevertheless criminals were recruited especially from the mentally inferior—"that is the only true core of the doctrine of the born criminal."[22]

GODDARD AND THE BINET-SIMON TESTS

Prior to 1910 all estimates of the proportion of mentally deficient in penal and correctional institutions were based upon psychological studies of memory and association, or upon the guesses of administrators, physicians, or teachers within these institutions. It was not until Henry H. Goddard had brought from Europe knowledge of Binet's work that there was any comparable standard by which to judge mental ability. In 1908 Goddard had mentioned the Binet-Simon tests in a paper he published in the *Training School,* the magazine issued by the institution at Vineland. In January 1910 there appeared the translation of Binet's scale, and by September Goddard had reported on his classification of four hundred feeble-minded children according to the Binet scale. The next year Goddard and a research assistant, Helen F. Hill, presented the first study of delinquents ever made in America when they reported on tests given to twelve inmates of the New Jersey State Hospital for the Insane. Of the twelve inmates tested, with chronological ages ranging from eleven to fifty years, ten were rated feeble-minded and two insane; while of the ten alleged to be feeble-minded four were of the eight-year-old level, four others had nine-year-old minds, one had a ten-year-old mind, and the last one had a twelve-year-old mind. The authors commented to the effect that the feeble-minded were not able to compete in the struggle for existence, and that when they were left to their own devices to make a living in the world they almost inevitably fell into crime or pauperism.

[22] Hugo Münsterberg, *On the Witness Stand,* New York, 1908, pp. 242-245.

We have mentioned elsewhere that of twenty-five children at Vineland who have manifested tendencies that would make them criminals if they were responsible, at least twenty show the mentality of nine or ten. This can hardly be accidental. There must be some peculiar stress to which children of this age are liable, or some relationship between criminal tendencies and this arrest of development at about nine. The fact that practically the same result is found in these two widely separated groups must be significant.[23]

Three months later Goddard and Hill again reported on Binet tests given to delinquents, this time to fifty-six girls ranging in age from fourteen to twenty years, who were on probation. Using, rather arbitrarily, as their criterion of feeble-mindedness the performance of twelve years of age, the authors concluded that fifty-two of the fifty-six girls were feeble-minded.[24] Speaking before the 1911 National Conference of Charities and Correction, Goddard declared that 25% of delinquents were mentally defective. Indeed, he said, all mental defectives would be delinquents in the very nature of the case, did not some one exercise care over them.[25] In 1912 Goddord published the famous study of the Kallikaks, in the course of which he questioned the hereditability of crime by stating that there was every reason to conclude that criminals were made and not born. Granting that criminals were made, the material—the best material—out of which to make criminals, and perhaps the material from which they were most frequently made, was feeble-mindedness. Goddard even hazarded the opinion that Lombroso's criminal types may have been types of feeble-mindedness on which criminality was grafted by the circumstances of their environment.[26]

The introduction of the Binet scale stimulated a tremendous activity in the testing of inmates of penal and correctional institutions with a view to distinguishing the normal from the sub-

[23] Henry H. Goddard and Helen F. Hill, "Feeble-Mindedness and Criminality," *Training School*, VIII (March 1911) 6.

[24] Henry H. Goddard and Helen F. Hill, "Delinquent Girls Tested by the Binet Scale," *Training School*, VIII (June 1911) 50-56.

[25] Henry H. Goddard, "The Treatment of the Mental Defective Who Is Also Delinquent," *Proceedings of the National Conference of Charities and Correction*, 1911, pp. 64-65.

[26] Henry H. Goddard, *The Kallikak Family—A Study in the Heredity of Feeble-Mindedness*, New York, 1912, p. 59.

normal mentally. The Binet scale as revised by Goddard classified those who were four or more years retarded as being at the twelve-year-old level or lower, and hence feeble-minded. But before the use of the Binet scale had become widespread, the *Training School* (presumably Goddard) had made inquiry of reformatories and industrial schools, by questionnaire, as to the number of inmates considered mentally defective. Thirty-four replies from twenty-seven superintendents, representing 13,188 cases, averaged 14.5% feeble-minded. The range of variation was from 0% to 41% feeble-minded.[27] In contrast to this were the test results published by Goddard and Mrs. E. Garfield Gifford on a random selection of one hundred boys and girls appearing before the Newark Juvenile Court, whose offenses were serious enough to warrant detention by the court. Of these one hundred children, sixty-six were feeble-minded.[28] In commenting upon the same set of facts which he presented in the *Journal of the American Institute of Criminal Law and Criminology*, Goddard remarked that the proportion of feeble-mindedness among adult criminals was at least as high as 25%, and that this number had become criminals because they were feeble-minded and unable to do right.[29] Goddard carried the same percentage—25—for the prison population before the American Prison Association.[30] By 1914, when his book on feeble-mindedness had appeared, Goddard was surer that the percentage was nearer 50 than 25. On page 9 of this volume he listed the estimates of sixteen reformatories and institutions for delinquents ranging from 28 to 89%, again emphasizing the relation between the feeble-minded and the criminal.

The hereditary criminal passes out with the advent of feeble-mindedness into the problem. The criminal is not born; he is made.

[27] "Estimated Number of Feeble-Minded Persons in State Reformtories and Industrial Schools," *Training School*, IX (March 1912) 8-10.

[28] Mrs. E. Garfield Gifford and Henry H. Goddard, "Defective Children in the Juvenile Court," *Training School*, VIII (January 1912) 132-135.

[29] Henry H. Goddard, "The Responsibility of Children in the Juvenile Court," *Journal of the American Institute of Criminal Law and Criminology*, III (September 1912) 365-375.

[30] Henry H. Goddard, "Feeble-Mindedness and Crime," *Proceedings of the American Prison Association*, 1912, pp. 353-357.

The so-called criminal type is merely a type of feeble-mindedness, a type misunderstood and mistreated, driven into criminality for which he is well fitted by nature. It is hereditary feeble-mindedness, not hereditary criminality that accounts for the conditions. We have only seen the end product and failed to recognize the character of the raw material.[31]

And again:

Every feeble-minded person is a potential criminal. This is necessarily true since the feeble-minded lacks one or the other of the factors essential to a moral life—an understanding of right and wrong, and the power of control.[32]

In his contribution to the symposium under the direction of the American Academy of Medicine, Goddard affirmed his 50% estimate by remarking that one is not far wrong in holding to 50% of prison and reformatory population as being feeble-minded; one is absolutely safe in saying 25% are feeble-minded.[33]

In *The Criminal Imbecile* published the next year the percentage was still 50%. In this volume containing the histories of three men who had committed homicides, Goddard strengthened his thesis of the relation of feeble-mindedness to crime (in individual instances) and gave support to the concept offered earlier by Fernald and Burr of the imbecile with criminal instincts. Noteworthy too, is the fact that these were the first court cases in which the Binet-Simon tests were admitted in evidence (1914). In one instance the jury acquitted on the ground of criminal imbecility, the tests showing the sixteen-year-old defendant to have the mentality of a child of ten years; in the second instance the defendant was convicted of first degree murder, the jury being unwilling to accept the defense of imbecility; while in the third, the conviction of second degree murder resulted (Oregon having abolished the death penalty a

---

[31] Henry H. Goddard, *Feeble-Mindedness, Its Causes and Consequences*, New York, 1914, p. 8. By permission of The Macmillan Co., publishers.

[32] Henry H. Goddard, *op. cit.*, p. 514. By permission of The Macmillan Co., publishers.

[33] Henry H. Goddard, "Relation of Feeble-Mindedness to Crime," *Bulletin of the American Academy of Medicine*, XV (April 1914) 105-112.

month previous, only a second degree verdict could be rendered),
the jury again being disinclined to recognize the mental age of
this twenty-four-year-old man as being that of a child of nine
years.[34]

Enough has been written to indicate the specific contribution
of Goddard to the thinking on the relation between feeble-
mindedness and crime, and to give some perspective to that
period which marked the introduction of the Binet-Simon tests
into America. Within a decade many of Goddard's assumptions
and dogmatic claims were to be overruled, other studies were to
show the need for revision of his estimates, but even beyond these
there remained the fact that for the first time, through Goddard's work, we possessed a tool and a technique for measuring
normality and subnormality.

THE BINET AND OTHER TESTS IN CORRECTIONAL AND
PENAL INSTITUTIONS

It has already been observed that with the advent of the
Binet tests there was a pronounced effort on the part of officials
dealing with delinquents and criminals—courts, psychological
clinics, reform schools, reformatories, and prisons—to determine
the mental capacity of their charges. A list of these early studies
was given by Goddard in his book on feeble-mindedness, and
it will be recalled that the percentages of feeble-mindedness in
the populations tested ranged from 28 to 89. In the present
discussion those studies which appeared before 1915 will be reviewed in order to note the extraordinary direction which this
new technique gave to our thinking on the subject of feeble-
mindedness and criminal behavior, as well as to indicate the
variations in the tests themselves and the differences of interpretation.

The first of the Binet test results was reported by Frank
Moore, superintendent of the New Jersey Reformatory, before
the National Conference of Charities and Correction in 1911.
Covering a period of eighteen months admissions, the tests re-

---

[34] Henry H. Goddard, *The Criminal Imbecile*, New York, 1915; see also P. M. Kerr,
"The Mental Status of Roland P.," *Alienist and Neurologist*, XXXVI (May 1915)
131-154.

vealed 46% of these admissions to be feeble-minded.[35] In the following year the physician to the same institution, G. L. Orton, showed that of six hundred admissions of young men during two years 48% of them were feeble-minded.[36] If the Binet scales in themselves were conclusive, said Katherine Bement Davis, head of the New York State Reformatory for Women, the one hundred white admissions tested by Jean Weidensall (who, according to Dr. Davis, studied Goddard's methods) in the Reformatory showed not one case of normal mentality, for not a single inmate tested higher than the twelve-year-old level although they ranged in physical age from sixteen to twenty-nine years.[37] Likewise 116 prostitutes committed from New York City to the same reformatory tested below the twelve-year level.[38] Of sixty girls examined by Louise Morrow and Olga Bridgman at the State Training School for Girls at Geneva, Illinois, in 1912, six were normal, fourteen were retarded from one to three years, while the remainder were retarded from four to thirteen years.[39] Two years later in the same institution Olga Bridgman reported 89% of 118 consecutive admissions were retarded three or more years, and hence by the commonly accepted standard of the Binet tests of that day (although Goddard insisted on four years retardation) were mentally defective.[40]

Even though the Binet test seemed the especial tool of the psychologist (did not Goddard say that the more skilled the psychologist the higher would be the scores of feeble-mindedness?) yet not a few of the institution physicians made use of

[35] Frank Moore, "Mentally Defective Delinquents," *Proceedings of the National Conference of Charities and Correction*, 1911, pp. 65-68.

[36] G. L. Orton, *op. cit.*, pp. 2021-2023.

[37] Katherine Bement Davis, "Feeble-Minded Women in Reformatory Institutions," *Survey*, XXVII (March 2, 1912) 1849-1851.

[38] Katherine Bement Davis, "A Study of Prostitutes Committed from New York City to the State Reformatory for Women at Bedford Hills," Chaper VIII, pp. 163-252, in George J. Kneeland, *Commercialized Prostitution in New York City*, New York, 1913.

[39] Louise Morrow and Olga Bridgman, "Delinquent Girls Tested by the Binet Scale," *Training School*, IX (May 1912) 33-36.

[40] Olga Bridgman, "Delinquency and Mental Deficiency," *Survey*, XXXII (June 13, 1914) 302.

them. For instance, William G. Eynon, who was attending physician at the New York House of Refuge in 1913, tested four hundred boys aged eight to twenty years, and reported 37% normal, 2% above normal, and 61% below normal.[41] Supplementing the Binet-Simon tests with those devised by William Healy, E. F. Green, physician to the Minnesota State Reformatory at St. Cloud, found that of 250 inmates about 36% were average or above, 59% were morons (by Goddard's definition, who introduced the term into the literature, a mental age of from eight to twelve years), and 5% imbeciles with mental ages ranging from five to seven years.[42]

Margaret Otis, resident psychologist at the New Jersey State Home for Girls and guest psychologist at the Vineland Training School under Goddard in 1912-1913, tested 172 girls, of whom she found 75% defective (scores below the twelve-year level), and 25% presumably normal.[43] Using William Stern's concept of the Intelligence Quotient, which had been recently introduced into the United States, H. M. Jennings and A. L. Hallock examined twenty boys and six girls of the George Junior Republic, supposedly an institution for normal delinquent children, and found ten of them scoring 77 or below. Thus on the basis of Stern's classification of 80-84 as doubtful, 71-77 as moron, and 62-71 as imbecile, about 38% were rated as moron or below.[44] Another definition of mental ability in relation to Intelligence Quotient, Kuhlmann's, held the imbecile to have an I.Q. of 63-71, the moron 71-77, the doubtful 80-84, and the normal 90 and over (the I.Q. being the chronological age divided into the mental age, with the exception that all chronological ages over sixteen years are treated as 192 months). On this basis

[41] William G. Eynon, "The Mental Measurement of Four Hundred Juvenile Delinquents by the Binet-Simon System," *New York Medical Journal*, XCVIII (July 26, 1913) 175-178.

[42] E. F. Green, "Report of Physician and Psychologist on the Reformatory Population at St. Cloud, Minnesota," *Journal of the American Institute of Criminal Law and Criminology*, IV (September 1913) 420-421.

[43] Margaret Otis, "The Binet Tests Applied to Delinquent Girls," *Psychological Clinic*, VII (October 15, 1913) 127-134.

[44] H. M. Jennings and A. L. Hallock, "Binet-Simon Tests at the George Junior Republic," *Journal of Educational Psychology*, IV (October 1913) 471-475.

David S. Hill, director of the division of educational research of the public school system of New Orleans, reported forty-four delinquent boys, or about 70% of those tested, who were below an I.Q. of 90, and of whom fifteen were below 70.[45] If Goddard's figure of four or more years of retardation be accepted as the criterion of feeble-mindedness, then, said Emile Renz and Mary Storer, who examined one hundred admissions to the Girls' Industrial School in Ohio, about 59% are feeble-minded. George S. Addams, E. J. Emerick, and H. H. Drysdale quoted this same study in substantiation of their thesis of the tie-up between feeble-mindedness and crime. Renz thought that perhaps 36% of feeble-mindedness among delinquents may be the conservative figure.[46] William J. Hickson, as director of the Psycopathic Laboratory of the Municipal Court of Chicago, examined 245 boys referred by the Boys' Court and found about 85% to be distinctly sub-normal.[47] Rudolph Pintner, of the Psychology Department of Ohio State University, in the same year, 1914, presented the test results of one hundred children in the Juvenile Court of Columbus, Ohio, who were held in the House of Detention awaiting hearing or disposition of the Court. On the basis of 3.1 or more years retardation, 46% were rated feeble-minded, while if these ratings were translated in terms of I.Q., 57% would be feeble-minded.[48] Early in 1915, with the aid of the Goddard revision of the Binet scale and of the Goddard form-board, H. B. Hickman, principal of the school department of the Indiana

[45] David S. Hill, *An Experimental Study of Delinquents and Destitute Boys in New Orleans*, New Orleans, June 1914.

[46] Emile Renz, "A Study of the Intelligence of Delinquents and the Eugenical Significance of Mental Defect," *Training School*, XI (May 1914) 37-39; Mary Storer, "The Defective Delinquent Girl," *Journal of Psycho-Asthenics*, XIX (September 1914) 23-30; George S. Addams, "Defectives in the Juvenile Court," *Training School*, XI (June 1914) 49-54; E. J. Emerick, "The Defective Delinquent in Ohio," *Journal of Psycho-Asthenics*, XIX (September 1914) 19-22; H. H. Drysdale, "The Problem of the Feeble-Minded, the Insane and the Epileptic," *Cleveland Medical Journal*, XIV (October 1915) 672-683.

[47] William J. Hickson, "The Defective Delinquent," *Journal of the American Institute of Criminal Law and Criminology*, V (September 1914) 397-403.

[48] Rudolph Pintner, "One Hundred Juvenile Delinquents Tested by the Binet Scale," *Pedagogical Seminary*, XXI (December 1914) 523-531.

Boys' School, found that of 229 admissions in 1914, 166 or 72% were three or more years retarded and hence feeble-minded; of these 166 boys 45 or 27% were imbeciles with mental ages of three to eight years.[49] E. A. Doll, of the department of Research of the Vineland Training School, in his supplementary analysis of Hickman's study, found that of the feeble-minded 82% were morons.[50] Another guest psychologist, Clinton P. McCord, who was at Vineland Training School in 1910, recorded a study of fifty prostitutes and wayward girls whose average mental age was ten years, while their chronological ages ranged from twenty-two to forty-one years; 54% were below the ten-year-old mental level.[51] Testing 250 cases in the Juvenile Court of Denver, C. S. Bluemel found 32.5% feeble-minded, as defined by three or more years of retardation. Probationers were feeble-minded in 6% of the cases, boys in the State Industrial School in 18%, and girls in the State Industrial School in 55% of the cases.[52] According to Lillian Streeter, speaking before the National Conference of Charities and Correction in 1915:

Another study was made of the mental grade and sex of the 147 boys and girls at the State Industrial School. These tests were given by one of the assistants at the State School for Feeble-Minded, a trained young woman of much experience. Of the total number of 147 children, only three were found normal, all boys. Of the 34 girls, one was backward, 33 were feeble-minded. Of the 113 boys, 87 were feeble-minded, 23 backward, and 3 normal, the summary of all the children showing 98% feeble-minded and backward, 2% normal. Surely no one can doubt that it is from the feeble-minded children of New Hampshire that her criminal classes are recruited.[53]

[49] H. B. Hickman, "Delinquent and Criminal Boys Tested by the Binet Scale," *Training School*, XI (January 1915) 159-164.

[50] E. A. Doll, "Supplementary Analysis of H. B. Hickman's Study of Delinquents," *Training School*, XI (January 1915) 165-168.

[51] Clinton P. McCord, "One Hundred Female Offenders. A Study of the Mentality of Prostitutes and 'Wayward Girls,'" *Training School*, XII (May 1915) 59-67.

[52] C. S. Bluemel, "Binet Tests on Two Hundred Juvenile Delinquents," *Training School*, XII (December 1915) 187-193.

[53] Lillian C. Streeter, "The Relation of Mental Defect to the Neglected, Dependent, and Delinquent Children of New Hampshire," *Procedings of the National Conference of Charities and Correction*, 1915, pp. 340-352.

TESTS OTHER THAN THE GODDARD REVISION

There is every reason to believe that all of the above results were secured by the use of the revision of the Binet-Simon scales as prepared by Goddard for American use. In some instances they were given by members or former members of the Vineland Training School staff, in others they were published in the bulletin, *Training School*, and in the remainder it stands fair to believe that were another scale than Goddard's used, that fact would have been mentioned. However, it was not long before other tests were devised by workers in the field, one of the earliest being that of William Healy and his collaborators at the Psychopathic Institute in Chicago. In her study of 106 delinquent girls Anne Burnett used the psychological tests developed by Healy and Grace Fernald. Admitting that the number was too small to admit of statistical conclusions it was noted that:

It at once appears that twenty-six of the group, or about 25 per cent, were mentally dull enough to come below the class which is designated as distinctly poor in mental ability. In other words, one quarter of the whole number were distinctly below par from the standpoint of mental powers.[54]

The Healy tests were again used, this time in 1915 by Edith Spaulding, resident physician of the Massachusetts Reformatory for Women, together with the Binet-Simon tests, and other psychological and psychiatric tests. Of the four hundred reformatory women examined, one group comprising 26.8% of the total showed slight mental abnormality and according to Dr. Spaulding might, in other classifications, be called the highest grade of feeble-minded, while 16.8% were in the marked mental defect group—the so-called morons with a mental age from seven to twelve years. Four women included in this category could be adjudged imbeciles.[55]

[54] Anne Burnett, "A Study of Delinquent Girls," *The Institution Quarterly*, III (June 30, 1912) 51.

[55] Edith R. Spaulding, "The Results of Mental and Physical Examinations of Four Hundred Women Offenders—With Particular Reference to Their Treatment During Commitment," *Journal of the American Institute of Criminal Law and Criminology*, V (January 1915) 704-717.

Other workers dealing with adult offenders found the commonly used Binet scale not adaptable for their purposes, and in many instances were compelled to modify it, or to use another modification, or to devise testing methods of their own. This was the problem with H. Douglas Singer, director of the State Psychopathic Institute, and George W. Ordahl, State psychologist of Illinois, who in 1915 examined fifty men in the State prison. Five of these men were considered "stupid" by the prison officials, five were considered intellectually bright; twenty were consecutive admissions, and the remaining twenty were taken at random from the prison population. The investigators used the Binet-Simon tests, together with certain tests devised by Kuhlmann (Director of Psychological Research at the State School for Feeble-Minded at Fairbault, Minnesota), by Terman of Stanford University, and by Ordahl. Of the fifty men 28% were rated feeble-minded because they were below the ten-year-age level. Of forty-nine women tested, 10% were held to be feeble-minded.[55a]

Another revision of the Binet scale was Terman's of Stanford University (which has since come to be accepted as the standard revision) which J. Harold Williams used with 150 delinquent boys in the Whittier State School, California, in 1915. These delinquents, who, with a median chronological age of sixteen and one half years scored a median mental age of twelve and one-half years, revealed 28% of their number as being definitely feeble-minded, and another 25% border-line. Later in this same year Williams also applied the Stanford revision to four hundred boys at the same school, and found 36% of them feeble-minded and 25% borderdline. According to Williams, feeble-mindedness accounted for one-third of all offenses committed by juvenile delinquents.[56]

There had been considerable question about the validity of

[55a] H. Douglas Singer and George W. Ordahl, "A Study of Prisoners at the Joliet Penitentiary," *The Institution Quarterly*, 1915, pp. 19-24; also in *The Delinquent*, V (September 1915) 1-6.

[56] J. Harold Williams, *A Study of 150 Delinquent Boys*. Stanford University, Bulletin No. 1, February 1915; *Defective, Delinquent and Dependent Boys*, Whittier State School, California, December 1915.

the Binet-Simon scale, which regarded any child as feeble-minded who did not measure up mentally to within four years of his chronological age. In 1915 Thomas H. Haines, clinical director of the Ohio Bureau of Juvenile Research, undertook to compare the relative ratings of the Binet scale—the Year Scale—with the Yerkes-Bridges—the Point Scale. One thousand admissions (671 boys and 329 girls) to the State Industrial schools were tested, and when scored by the Year Scale 57% were feeble-minded; whereas, when tested by the Point Scale (which considered a child feeble-minded who scored less than 75% of the average performance of his chronological age) only 29% of them were feeble-minded.[57] In another instance the Yerkes-Bridges Point Scale was used to examine criminals at the Massachusetts State Prison, while the Binet-Simon scale was used, supplementarily, when the diagnosis on the Point Scale was uncertain. Of the forty-seven cases referred for psychological examination because mental deficiency was suspected, C. S. Rossy noted that twenty-three, or approximately 50%, were diagnosed as feeble-minded, with five on the border line. When fifty-three additional examinations were made, bringing the total to one hundred, the proportion of feeble-mindedness had fallen to 29%, the borderline proportion remaining about the same, 11%.[58]

Finding neither the Binet, the Healy, nor the Fernald tests suitable for examining the adult offender, V. V. Anderson, director of the Psychopathic Laboratory of the Municipal Court of Boston, in 1914 set up other tests for comparative purposes with the Binet, and found about 30% mentally defective. When this sample of 100 cases of adult offenders was increased to 350 (140 men and 210 women) the proportion of feeble-mindedness re-

[57] Thomas H. Haines, *Mental Examination of Juvenile Delinquents*, Ohio Board of Administration, No. 7, December 1915; "Point Scale Ratings of Delinquent Boys and Girls," *Psychological Review*, XXII (March 1915) 104-109.

[58] C. S. Rossy, "First Note on a Psychological Study of the Criminals at the Massachusetts State Prison," *Collected Contributions from the State Board of Insanity and the State Institutions for Mental Disease and Defect*. Boston, 1915, Third Series, pp. 377-381; "Second Note on a Psychological Study of the Criminals at the Massachusetts State Prison," *Collected Contributions from the State Board of Insanity and the State Institutions for Mental Disease and Defect*. Boston, 1915, Third Series, pp. 523-529.

mained about the same. Anderson noted the significant difference that women offenders were more likely to be feeble-minded
than were men offenders. Among the women 40.95% were
mental defectives. Impressed as he was by the large number of
adult offenders, men and women, who were feeble-minded,
Anderson was also compelled to observe that the constitutional
psychopath (the individual not defective in intelligence, not
psychotic, but nevertheless so disorganized as a personality that
he finds it impossible to adjust to his social environment) constituted as great a proportion as did the feeble-minded. A year
later, in 1915, he deprecated reports of 89% of feeble-mindedness
among court or prison cases as being contrary to common sense
and experience. He placed the proportion between 10 and 30%,
but added that too many borderline cases were included in the
feeble-minded category. A reliable analysis would show many
of these to be psychopaths.[59]

OTHER ESTIMATES OF FEEBLE-MINDEDNESS IN THE
CRIMINAL POPULATION

In addition to the test results mentioned above there have been
other estimates, some based upon tests not specified, and others
based upon no test, but being sheer guesswork. Among the early
studies—1911—was that of Ernest K. Coulter, clerk of the Children's Court of New York County, in which it was stated that
of 108 cases referred by the Court to Dr. Max G. Schlapp, director of the Clearing House for Mental Defectives in New York
City, thirty, or about 28% were mentally defective.[60] Four years
later Dr. Schlapp diagnosed 171 of 520 cases (33%) which had
been sent to him by various courts for examination, as morons
and imbeciles.[61] Frank L. Christian, physician and, in 1912,

[59] V. V. Anderson, "An Analysis of One Hundred Cases Studied in Connection with
the Municipal Courts of Boston," *Boston Medical and Surgical Journal*, CLXXI
(August 27, 1914) 341-346; "The Laboratory in the Study and Treatment of Crime,"
Boston Medical and Surgical Journal, CLXXI (November 19, 1914) 803-808; "A
Proper Classification of Borderline Mental Cases Among Offenders," *Boston Medical
and Surgical Journal*, CLXXIII (September 23, 1915) 466-469.

[60] Ernest K. Coulter, "Mentally Defective Delinquents and the Law," *Proceedings
of the National Conference of Charities and Correction*, 1911, pp. 68-70.

[61] Max G. Schlapp, "The Mentally Defective as Cases in the Courts of New York
City," *Medical Record*, LXXXVII (February 27, 1915) 337-341.

assistant superintendent of the Elmira Reformatory, declared
that an examination of over 14,000 inmates of Elmira showed
that 42% were mentally defective.[62] While the officials of Elmira in 1901 had considered 20% of their population to be
mentally defective, by 1912 this figure had increased to 42%;
not, asserted Dr. Christian, because the mental capacity of the
inmates had decreased, but because of improved examinations
used by the physicians.[63] Lilburn Merrill, director of diagnosis
of the Seattle Juvenile Court, estimated twenty-seven boys and
girls out of 421 court cases (for the year 1912) to be feeble-
minded, while twenty-eight additional were classed as mentally
backward.[64] However, when a Juvenile Court Judge of Minneapolis cited the fact that an expert psychologist of the Seattle
Juvenile Court reported 18.5% of the delinquency with which
it dealt to be attributable to mental defect, the statement is misleading unless it is clear what is meant by mental defect. The
same Judge, Edward F. Waite, reported that the examination,
by Professor Miner of the University of Minnesota, of one
hundred consecutive cases of the more serious types of offenders
showed about 25% to be mentally retarded three or more years.[65]
Having arrived at the conclusion that one-half of the population
of the Indiana State Reformatory, of which he was associate
superintendent and director of research, was feeble-minded,
Rufus von KleinSmid maintained that mental defect was the
real, fundamental, efficient cause of the greater proportion of
crime.[66] Paul E. Bowers examined one hundred recidivists and
found 23% to be feeble-minded, and although he believed feeble-
mindedness to play a very considerable rôle in criminal behavior,

[62] Frank L. Christian, "Mental Defectives Among Delinquents," *Sixth Annual Report
of the State Probation Commission*, Albany, New York, 1912, pp. 208-222.

[63] Frank L. Christian, "The Defective Delinquent," *Albany Medical Annals*, XXXIV
(May 1913) 276-285.

[64] Lilburn Merrill, "The Clinical Classification of Delinquent Children According
to Causative Pathology," *Annual Report of the Seattle Juvenile Court*, 1913, p. 45.

[65] Edward F. Waite, "The Physical Bases of Crime: From the Standpoint of the
Judge of a Juvenile Court," *Bulletin of the American Academy of Medicine*, XIV
(December 1913) 388-395.

[66] Rufus Bernhard von KleinSmid, *Preliminary Report of the Department of Research,
Indiana Reformatory, from Its Inception in 1912 to the Close of the Fiscal Year*, 1914;
also "Some Efficient Causes of Crime," *Proceedings of the First National Conference on
Rase Betterment*, 1914, 532-542.

he was inclined to depreciate the extravagant claims of many psychological testers of the immediate, causative relation between feeble-mindedness and crime.[67]

Heretofore the tests which have been reported on have been largely modifications of the Binet-Simon—either Goddard or Stanford—or have been the Yerkes-Bridges, and in some instances the adaptations of such workers as Healy and Kuhlmann. Presumably they have been individually administered. A test of a different kind was given in 1914 by W. H. Pyle to a group of 240 inmates of the State Industrial Home for Girls at Chillicothe, Missouri. It consisted of substitution, invention, free association, opposites, logical and rote memory, ink-blots tests, together with two Ebbinghaus tests. On the basis of this group test Pyle reported about two-thirds of the delinquent girls to be below normal mentally, many of them high-grade morons. He was convinced there was a close relation between feeble-mindedness and crime.[68]

There were some who contented themselves with general statements about the relation between feeble-mindedness and crime, or who were willing to accept the statements of others. Anne Moore, making a survey for the Public Education Association of New York in 1911, found a close relation between feeble-mindedness and crime,[69] as did also Siegfried Bloch.[70] According to Max Schlapp the feeble-minded child was a potential criminal and might at any time commit a crime.[71] Frank Woodbury, secretary of the Committee on Lunacy of the Board of Public Charities, Philadelphia, believed that feeble-mindedness bore just as intimate a relation to crime as did insanity.[72] Frank

[67] Paul E. Bowers, "The Recidivist," *Journal of the American Institute of Criminal Law and Criminology*, V (September 1914) 404-415.

[68] W. H. Pyle, "A Study of Delinquent Girls," *Psychological Clinic*, VIII (October 15, 1914) 143-148.

[69] Anne Moore, *The Feeble-Minded in New York*, Published by the New York State Charities Association, 1911.

[70] Siegfried Bloch, "Delinquent Children from a Medical Standpoint," *American Journal of Obstetrics*, LXIII (May 1911) 917-926.

[71] Max G. Schlapp, "Feeble-Minded Boys and Crime," *Survey*, XXVII (March 2, 1912) 1846-1849.

[72] Frank Woodbury, "The Relation Between Crime and Insanity," *Journal of the American Institute of Criminal Law and Criminology*, IV (July 1913) 282-284.

W. Robertson warned of the rising danger of the feeble-minded having criminal tendencies,[73] while Haldor Sneve warned of the morons who composed one-half of our reformatory and prison population.[74] To Paul E. Bowers the recidivist was more or less mentally defective; habitual criminality being an expression of a condition of psycho-physical pathology.[75] To Victor Vaughan, president of the American Medical Association and dean of the Ann Arbor Medical College, every feeble-minded person was a potential criminal;[76] while to Charles R. Henderson most criminals were physically and mentally inferior, the mental subnormality being causally related to some deep anatomical and physiological defect.[77] Although denying that crime was hereditary, as so many had done, A. H. Cook concluded, however, that 20% of all crime was due to an hereditary predisposition to feeble-mindedness.[78]

THE MORAL IMBECILE—CONCLUDED

In the forepart of this chapter reference was made to mention of moral imbecility by Spitzka, Kerlin, and Barr, and of the criminal imbecile by Fernald and Burr, following which the historical survey was interrupted by the consideration of the tremendous vogue of the mental tests beginning with Goddard after 1908. Here the historical sequence is taken up again to carry it to the year 1915. Already the offender had been identified as an imbecile, and as insane, but it remained for Charles H. Hughes in 1911 to propose the insanity of imbecility. In this instance a commission had found a defendant, who had committed an homicide, to be of unsound mind. In reporting the

---

[73] Frank W. Robertson, "Crimes of the Adult from the Standpoint of the Alienist," *Bulletin of the American Academy of Medicine*, XIV (December 1913) 408-411.

[74] Haldor Sneve, *op. cit.*, pp. 359-368.

[75] Paul E. Bowers, "The Recidivist," *Journal of the American Institute of Criminal Law and Criminology*, V (September 1914) 404-415.

[76] Victor C. Vaughan, "Crime and Disease," *Proceedings of the American Prison Association*, 1914, pp. 292-301.

[77] Charles Richmond Henderson, "Physical Basis of Criminality," *Bulletin of the American Academy of Medicine*, XV (April 1914) 97-101.

[78] A. H. Cook, "The Innocent Criminal," *Southern Medical Journal*, VII (September 1, 1914) 717-723.

case, Hughes declared that it was an instance of a delusional change of character engrafted on or evolved from a restricted or imbecile state of brain and associated mind.[79]

It was Martin Barr who earlier outlined the low, middle, and high grade moral imbecile, and it was to the last that Walter E. Fernald applied the term "defective delinquent." The defective delinquent referred to the members of that class of delinquents whose mental lack was relatively slight, though unmistakable. In fact Fernald found a close resemblance between the defective delinquent and the instinctive criminal.

Every feeble-minded person, especially the high grade imbecile, is a potential criminal, needing only the proper environment and opportunity for the development and expression of his criminal tendencies. The unrecognized imbecile is a most dangerous element in the community. There are many crimes committed by imbeciles for one committed by an insane person. The average prison population includes more imbeciles than lunatics.[80]

Another Fernald, Guy, resident physician of the Massachusetts Reformatory, identified the defective delinquent, and attempted to differentiate him from delinquents in general by psychological tests. He characterized the defective delinquent as one who was smart enough to get into trouble, but not smart enough to keep out of it.[81] It was this class of offenders, unable to support themselves and not amenable to reform, which constituted the recidivist group.[82] Mentally deficient, possessing physical stigmata of degeneracy, neither insane nor idiot—such was Frank L. Christian's description of the defective delinquent as he had seen him in his experience as physician and assistant superintendent of Elmira Reformatory.[83] For Franklin C.

[79] Charles H. Hughes, "Imbecility and the Insanity of Imbecility or Dementia Praecox Before the Law," *Alienist and Neurologist*, XXXII (February 1911) 66-96.

[80] Walter E. Fernald, "The Burden of Feeble-Mindedness," *Medical Communications of the Massachusetts Medical Society*, XXIII (1912) 7.

[81] Guy G. Fernald, "The Defective Delinquent Class. Differentiating Tests," *American Journal of Insanity*, LXVIII (April 1912) 523-594.

[82] Guy G. Fernald, "The Recidivist," *Journal of the American Institute of Criminal Law and Criminology*, III (March 1913) 866-875.

[83] Frank L. Christian, "The Defective Delinquent," *Albany Medical Annals*, XXXIV (May 1913) 276-285.

Paschal, psychologist of the Indiana Reformatory, the core of the moral imbecile group was the feeble-minded offender.[84]

By 1915 the reaction against the vague and varying classifications of the defective delinquent had set in. V. V. Anderson identified at least five different categories of defective delinquents as commonly found in the literature and practice. Out of this confusion of borderline cases he chose to distinguish three distinct types: 1. The mental defectives, being so defective in mentality as to be unable to measure up to the standards of normal social organization; 2. Psychopaths, being so unstable and poorly balanced in mentality as to be continually liable to impulsive conduct and thus incompletely socialized; 3. The mental delinquent who was neither defective nor psychopathic in mentality, whose mental condition was acquired rather than innate, and who was reformable. Only one of these, the mental defectives, would Anderson call the defective delinquent.[85]

SUMMARY AND CONCLUSION

A backward glance over the record gives evidence of the strong conviction that feeble-mindedness plays a very efficient rôle in the production of criminal behavior. It may be imbecility coupled with insanity, it may be mental deficiency associated with physiological defects and the stigmata of degeneracy, it may be unadulterated feeble-mindedness, but in whatever form it is to be found, it is at the heart of the problem. As the Lombrosian concept of physical types declined, this concept of the mental type came to replace it. It is perhaps no accident that in England Goring was disproving and replacing Lombroso's anthropological type with a mental type at the same time that we in America were preoccupied with the mental status of the delinquent, and Goddard was writing that the so-called criminal type was merely a type of feeble-mindedness. Was not the person of arrested mental development merely the analogue of the physiologically

---

[84] Franklin C. Paschal, "The Feeble-Minded and Delinquent Boy," *Indiana Bulletin of Charities and Correction*, March 1915, pp. 68-73.

[85] V. V. Anderson, "A Proper Classification of Borderline Mental Cases Among Offenders," *Boston Medical and Surgical Journal*, CLXXIII (September 23, 1915) 466-469.

arrested person of the earlier schools of criminal anthropology?

In a previous chapter it was noted how moral insanity had taken on various meanings in the course of a hundred years. Moral imbecility, without the ancient lineage of moral insanity, also had its varied interpretations, misinterpretations, and reinterpretations. Beginning in the 1880's as "moral imbecility" (mental enfeeblement which vitiated moral judgment) as distinct from "moral insanity," it early became tinged with insanity, was variously called "moral idiocy" and "moral degeneracy," and by 1908 had been renamed "imbecility with criminal instincts" (with which Goddard's later "criminal imbecility" was synonymous). In 1912 the "moral imbecile" was known as the "defective delinquent," and finally by 1915 as the "mental defective." William Healy had converted "moral insanity" into "moral imbecility," but had been unable to find a single instance of such in his thousand delinquents. Indeed, his doubt that there was such a thing as a separate moral faculty subject to impairment was exactly the position taken by V. V. Anderson, who had proposed the term "mental defective." Said Anderson:

In fact we have come to realize that our moral judgments are inextricably mixed up with social judgments; that general intelligence, learning, experience, etc., are brought into play in the exercise of every moral judgment; that millions of brain processes are involved in every thought and act, and conduct is an expression of the whole machinery at work; that there is no ground for the presupposition of a separate sense that sits in judgment, approving or disapproving our actions. In short, a mentality incapable of forming moral judgments is likewise incapable of forming normal judgments along other lines, and is (ipso facto) a defective mentality, and is demonstrable by a thorough examination of general intelligence, judgment, reasoning capacity, etc. These are mental defectives, and not moral imbeciles.[86]

More than a word remains to be said of the psychological tests used to examine delinquents and criminals, especially since conclusions were so readily arrived at purporting to prove the inherent and inevitable causal connection between mental de-

[86] *Ibid.,* p. 467.

ficiency and crime. While the test results dealt with in the foregoing pages were but a minor fraction of an almost countless number in the period which followed the introduction of the Binet-Simon tests in 1908, they nevertheless constitute a body of conclusions that must be reckoned with in any treatment of the rôle of feeble-mindedness in criminal behavior.

At the outset of any critique of the mental tests the question must be raised whether any intelligence test of this or even a later period has conclusively proved that it perfectly measures intelligence. Much of the universal validity of these tests depends upon the extent to which they have taken the varying cultural elements and patterns into account. Furthermore, they have not always overcome the language differences in individuals which may be unrelated to their intelligence. In addition even the non-language, or "performance" tests have failed to equalize those elements which make for one person scoring relatively high on language tests, and low on performance tests, and vice versa. There are still other factors entering into the determinations of test results which may vary considerably and must be taken into account, such as situations under which the test is taken, emotional make-up and attitudes of the person tested.

There is good reason to believe that these criteria were not always observed in this early period of testing. Not even the relative objectivity, which was one of the ultimate achievements of the tests, characterized them during this period, for it was the boast of more than one proponent of the tests that the scores decreased with the increased skill of the examiner. When, for example, the questionnaire returns from penal and correctional institutions reveal feeble-mindedness ranging from no cases to 89% it must be patently clear that that very fact invalidates the returns and the methods by which the estimates were arrived at.

There also remains constant throughout this period the error of defining feeble-mindedness purely in psychological terms, rather than interpreting it in its social setting. The environmental demands made upon the person, whether delinquent or at the moment non-delinquent, whether incarcerated or in the community, are elements which must be considered when arriving at a definition of feeble-mindedness.

A further analysis of this period up to 1915 reveals the tendency toward conclusional thinking. The mere fact that a certain selected group of the population—delinquents or criminals—contained one-third who tested feeble-minded (granting for the moment the validity of the test) was deemed sufficient to warrant the deduction that the cause of crime in this one-third was feeble-mindedness. When this proportion mounted higher and higher, the more certain became the conviction that feeble-mindedness was the cause of crime. Indeed, it was even maintained that the feeble-minded criminal was the "born criminal."

We come to the year 1915. For decade after decade feeble-mindedness has been linked with criminal behavior; for some, even many, it was *the* causal factor. The feeble-minded person was even denied moral judgment. A reaction was setting in, here and there workers were questioning this position; but a world war and a decade of steady development in mental testing knowledge and technique intervened before we effected a redefinition of the relation between feeble-mindedness and crime. That redefinition was given tremendous impetus by the pioneering research of William Healy, and amplified by him and others who shared in the psychiatric advance that continues from that day to this. It is but fitting that this chapter and this treatise should close with Healy's name, for it was he who, like Lombroso more than a half century before, closed one era of criminology to open the next.

XI

CONCLUSION

IDEAS, as J. B. Bury has said, have their intellectual climate. Theories of crime causation in the nineteenth century did not develop in isolation or in a vacuum. Their cultural setting included advancements in biology, in medicine, in psychiatry, in psychology, and in sociology. In these disciplines were found the scientific or quasi-scientific explanations of man, his body, his mind, his actions, his society. It was inevitable that man's behavior—especially his criminal behavior—should come within the province of specialists in these fields.

Phrenology appeared in America at a time when men were turning from the concepts of the metaphysician and the theologian to the concepts of the scientist. These early scientists were chiefly physicians who, in the light of the knowledge of their day, based their explanation of human behavior upon their understanding of the anatomy and physiology of the human body. The original anatomical researches of Gall at the beginning of the nineteenth century had furnished a short-lived foundation for phrenology in Europe. By the time Charles Caldwell had imported it into America phrenology had become the victim of popularizers, such as Spurzheim and George Combe, and was content with merely the pretensions of a scientific basis. After two decades of controversy it had failed to prove its case and had lost the endorsement of those few eminent physicians who had once supported it. In the field of criminal behavior it had relied upon its propensities and its organs of destructiveness, amativeness, secretiveness, and philoprogenitiveness without at the same time being able to account for cases in which such organs were fully developed and yet from which no criminal behavior resulted. Furthermore, it failed to account for those instances in which offenders were convicted of crime who did not possess the phrenological cranial attributes. Phrenologists, despite their pretensions, were not able to distinguish the criminal from the non-criminal; phrenology was effective neither in the diagnosis nor in the treatment of the criminal. When it encountered an exact and critical analysis in the first half of the nineteenth century it was effectually banished from scientific consideration. A generation that was witnessing the change of medicine from an old art into a new science, a generation that in repudiating the monistic pathology of Benjamin Rush had characterized his medical essays as "utter nonsense and unqualified absurdity" was little inclined to favor a "system" of phrenology.

The doctrine of moral insanity gained its early acceptance largely through the personality of Isaac Ray, although its history is inevitably bound up with developments in the field of psychiatry from the time of Pinel to Kraepelin. It was not until the end of the eighteenth century that demonology gave way before the beginnings of a scientific psychiatry; that the medical point of view prevailed over the theological. Pinel's description of the more common types of mental disease on the basis of their symptoms was of a very general and approximate character and necessitated subsequent refinement.

Following Pinel there were attempts to find local lesions in order to distinguish the various manias, just as in general medicine (behind which psychiatry usually lagged) there had been, previously, the breaking down of the general fevers into specific ones—typhoid, typhus, and the like. Clinical pathological correlations began to replace symptomatic classifications. Neurologists, and particularly neural surgeons, succeeded in time in discovering somatic lesions so that reclassification was possible upon that basis of about half the known cases of mental disease. Later, when the bacteriologists contributed their researches on the spirochete, a still finer formulation was achieved. These advances stimulated further research for physical "causes" of delusions, etc., but such efforts were singularly discouraging and fruitless. By 1900 the search for these causes had shifted from a somatic to a psychic orientation, an orientation which had shown some promise in the second quarter of the ninteenth century.

Toward the latter part of the nineteenth century Kraepelin achieved a nosography based upon etiological distinctions which served for a time to bring order out of chaos. His early work under Wundt and his subsequent experience had convinced him that mental abnormality could be studied experimentally and would yield to quantitative description.

American students were acquainted with these developments and ofttimes shared in them. From the time when Benjamin Rush studied abroad down to the present generation of American psychiatrists and neurologists there has been considerable infusion of thought from abroad. This has been related to our own experience with the mentally diseased and those behavior deviates who are classified as criminals. Furthermore, the early emphasis of medical leaders such as Rush on the relation of mental disorder to behavior aberrations did much to lay the foundation for similar studies which continued through William Healy up to the present day.

These classification efforts and studies of mental disorder and crime were of practical importance in the Euro-American culture. In America it is possible to recognize the tremendous concern of the judiciary, of prison administrators, of the lay public even, over the question of culpability—that is, criminal responsibility. Psychiatrists and other physicians were responsive to this concern, as reflected in their work and publications of the past century. Refinement yielded to still further refinement, nosologies comprising hundreds of mental disorders were broken down to simpler systems, but throughout them all ran a common recognition of the need to differentiate, wherever possible, the mentally diseased from the criminal.[1]

An historical analysis of the rôle of feeble-mindedness in

[1] It should be noted that much of the early work of psychiatrists was custodial in nature. Many psychiatrists, compelled by the prevailing culture setting, were more often keepers than clinicians. Detention and custody preceded study and research. Several hospitals which were first founded around 1750 were not utilized for research until over three-quarters of a century after their establishment. Similarly asylums, founded around 1800, were not used for clinical purposes for another three-quarters of a century. It is common knowledge that the primary emphasis in prisons for the first century and a half of their existence has been custodial. Will the experience of hospitals and asylums some day be followed by prisons?

criminal conduct reveals two outstanding influences—the rise of eugenics and the development of psychological testing. Strikingly enough Goddard's study of feeble-mindedness and his identification of the moron appeared at about the same time as Davenport's work on eugenics (equally significant was the publication in 1913 of Goring's *The English Convict*) although in each instance considerable preliminary spade work had been done by other students in the field. The eugenists and the psychological testers seemed to confirm each others' findings and the conclusions therefrom. The early psychological testers had proved to their own satisfaction that most criminals were feeble-minded; their supplementary studies, such as that of the Kallikaks, showed that feeble-mindedness and, by implication, criminality were inherited. The eugenists with their investigations into "degenerate" families were equally convinced that criminal character was passed on through the germ plasm. Up to 1915 there was a widespread vogue and acceptance of these conclusions, but after the publication of Healy's intensive case studies of a thousand delinquents in 1915, the psychological testing of over a million American army recruits in 1917, and a decade of further experimentation in psychometrics, there was far less willingness to accept conclusions which had been so assertively maintained and yet so inadequately grounded.

The prelude to the conclusions of the eugenists was the century-old claim of the hereditarians. Insisting, if not upon the inheritance of a separate moral faculty, at least upon the inheritance of moral character, these hereditarians were convinced that crime was essentially inborn. This had been a part of theological doctrine since the first days of the Colonies, and was intrinsic in the attitudes and beliefs of the community as a whole. The physician, prison officers, the prison overseer or trustee shared this ideology inherent in the culture of seventeenth-, eighteenth-, and nineteenth-century America. It was not until research into the mechanisms of inheritance by the biologists weakened these "cultural compulsives" that any considerable revision of these ideas was accomplished. Furthermore, the rise of a school which centered upon the effect of the man-made environment on human behavior served to replace a philosophy of biological determinism with one culturally conditioned. Out of this process has come a recognition of the complementary aspects of the two—of the biological and the cultural factors. Accompanying this has been a shift from a belief in the inheritance of "gemmules" or "germs" of crime to a conviction that a biological individual becomes a socialized person through the integrations which arise out of the interplay of the biological endowment in cultural situations.

Criminal anthropology was a derivative of the theory of biological determinism, yet it never attained considerable proportions in America until after the importation, through translation, of Benedikt's work on the criminal brain. Its world-wide prominence, chiefly through the influence of Lombroso and his Italian followers, secured it a ready audience in America for the three decades beginning in the 1880's. A willingness to entertain its tentative premises and to conduct further research upon the prison population by such men as Mills, the neurologist, and Wey, the prison physician, did much to give impetus to criminal anthropology in America. It was sustained for years by the findings of prison physicians, of some few anthropologists, and of the many uncritical, both lay and professional, who accepted unquestioningly the claims of the current foreign literature. The publication in 1913 of Goring's *The English Convict*, coincident with a tremendous activity in psychological research in America, was more decisive perhaps than any other factor in undermining belief in a criminal anthropological type. It is not irrelevant to repeat here that a criminal with certain mental characteristics (according to Goring in England, Goddard in America) had replaced the physical type.

If any one fact stands out concerning the explanations which flourished during the period of a century or more in America, it was the fact that there was no one school, no one theory, of crime causation which was indigenous to America. This is not to say that there was a lack of theories, but rather that the abundance of theories was taken over from the European scene. The answer for this may be found principally in the nature of the American culture in the nineteenth century. A continent still had to be mastered, a nationhood achieved (Benjamin Rush, for example, had signed the document bringing the United States into being) a societal organization to be effected. The problem of a new nation and of new states were practical problems; hence the earliest theories and practices centered around the disposition of the offender rather than around causation. It is perhaps no accident that America's contribution to the problem of the criminal lay in penology—in the Pennsylvania system, for example. The emphasis was upon administration rather than upon investigation. So long as a prison could be adequately administered it was sufficient to accept the prevailing and accepted beliefs of accountability.

Another aspect of the American character of this period was its strong sense of individuality. What contributions there were during the nineteenth century were individual ones; there was no coherence, no whole. There was, for instance, nothing like the "Italian school" or the "French school" in which centered a body of scholars having substantially the same points of view, and to which common contributions could be made.

Nor were there any specialized journals to serve as clearing houses for students of criminology. Such writings as there were lay scattered throughout the literature—chiefly medical—and received only such fragmentary examination and criticism as the occasional interest of the busy physician or teacher could muster. There were no congresses until the 1870's, yet even after the organization of the National Prison Association the emphasis at annual meetings lay in problems of practical penology rather than of crime causation. Much the same was true of the work of the prison societies and their publications. Furthermore, no specialization existed in institutions of higher education. Neither courses in forensic medicine nor in medical jurisprudence in medical or law schools were concerned with anything more than description and classification. Departments of sociology, in the few schools in which they existed, considered crime and the criminal as social problems, and were content to have a bowing acquaintance with the current beliefs of criminal anthropology, or to disregard or dismiss all other aspects save the environmental.

There were other considerations which account for our borrowings from Europe and our failure to originate theories of crime causation here. A common base united Europe and America which transcended even language and political differences. The culture of both was sufficiently alike to permit an easy diffusion. Implicit and explicit in their common culture was a conviction that man was a free-will agent, that he knew the difference between right and wrong, that he was morally responsible for his actions. Furthermore, according to a common Calvinistic theology, man was born in sin; no theory of crime causation could be simpler than that.

If one more bit of evidence be necessary to understand the ease of borrowing from European sources, it may be found in the relatively advanced state of science and particularly of medicine in Europe. American students inevitably were drawn to European centers of science and medicine (Rush, like most of the early American physicians and teachers, had received his medical training abroad). It naturally followed that they and their students in turn became heavy debtors to European science.

American journals naturally reflected this influence. Many of them carried leading articles by European authorities, while others were composed as miscellanies, carrying a liberal and varied assortment of European reprints and notes. Finally, American books carried extensive quotations and citations from abroad. When it is realized that much of the early literature was of this nature, and in addition that many European books appeared under American editorship, it is possible to understand the all-pervasive influence of European thought in America.

The borrowings and diffusions have been interpreted with regard to teachers and the journals. The influence of administrators has been noted. It remains to mention for the moment the rôle of the occasional polemical writer and of the student who was convinced of the rightness of his position and adhered to it with unswerving tenacity. The oustanding polemicist was unquestionably Charles Caldwell, and while phrenology suffered eclipse before his death, nevertheless by his attacks and defenses he compelled its examination. Others who persisted in their convictions were, outstandingly, Isaac Ray, Amariah Brigham, T. D. Crothers, Hamilton D. Wey, G. Frank Lydston, G. Henri Bogart, Paul Bowers, and H. H. Goddard. It is not too much to say that these men played a more than ordinary part in the dissemination of their ideas, and contributed greatly to the dynamic ferment of American scientific thought in the field of crime causation.

The rôle of the physician in this ferment is unmistakable. Indeed, he was the dynamic agent. It was he, from the dawn of medicine in America up to the present day, who kept alive the spirit of science. Not only did he preserve and add to existing knowledge—for his field touched all borders of science—but he helped to maintain and extend the methodology of science. Practically all of the men whose contributions are embodied in this treatise were physicians, and they were representative of the vital interest which the profession as a whole had in human affairs. The contributions of physicians in other fields of science bears added testimony to this important fact. What other scientists there were held academic posts in universities or in certain of the government bureaus.

In the light of the intellectual equipment of the present day, it is profitable to examine those developments of the past century which have affected one or another of the theories of crime causation. The first of these is the trend in neurology and psychiatry toward a more refined classification. As token of this it may be noted that Kraepelin's nosology of the 1880's shows as marked divergencies from that of Rush as the modern does from that of Kraepelin. The discussion of insanity and moral insanity in this chapter attempts to state this succinctly.

Inextricably bound up with this, indeed basic to it, has been the increasing emphasis upon the social, i.e., cultural, component in human behavior. Inherent in the definition of mental disease in 1915 (Healy), more so than in 1880 (Kraepelin) or 1810 (Rush) is the element of the social situation, the recognition that mental abnormality is defined within the limits of a contemporary behavior pattern rather than in relation to an abstraction. The increasing attention given by anthropologists and sociologists to forms of social organization other than their own resulted in greater understanding of the process by which the group defines the behavior of individuals. Psychiatrists, especially, have not been unaffected by these studies of varying cultures and have interpreted deviational behavior, whether it be mental disease or crime, within the limits of the social setting.

A second development in the field of science and of scientific methodology has been the introduction and extensive use of the individual case history. Physicians may well object that their method has always been the case-history method. But it was not until the time of Kraepelin that any systematic effort was made to utilize the life history of the patient to its fullest possibility. Kraepelin was aided in his etiological analysis of mental disease by the careful observation of large numbers of cases and by his study of the patient's life history. His method consisted of an examination of the patient's life history from a long-range point of view, i.e., longitudinal, as well as from a cross-sectional view. This concept and the use of the life history as subsequently elaborated by psychiatrists, sociologists, and social case workers (so well exemplified in Healy's *Individual Delinquent*) has permitted a clearer insight into the developmental history of the individual and hence a truer understanding of present attitudes and behavior. Together with the insight gained from anthropological studies it has emphasized the uniqueness of behavior deviations, and at the same time has illustrated their common distribution among all peoples. With this knowledge available it was no longer possible for the serious student to construct a monistic system of crime causation. The essential contribution of the individual case history has been one of methodology—of furnishing a technique or means whereby the dynamic rôle of the human personality could be perceived in its interaction with other personalities operating in a dynamic rather than in a static environment.

Still a third development has been the discoveries made by the biologists and the psychologists. The identification of the mechanisms by means of which biological inheritance takes place, and the description of that process, rank among the greatest and most far-reaching of scientific discoveries. The implications, once the work of Mendel was revived and confirmed by later biologists, of such a doctrine were revolutionary in a world that heretofore had naïvely accepted the Garden of Eden and man's original sin, and had based a philosophy of behavior upon it.

When, for example, the facts supporting the theory of the continuity of the germ plasm were established, the doctrine of man's original sin was scientifically invalidated. A biology and a psychology (even a sociology) which accepted the differential nature of the germ plasm and the somatoplasm questioned seriously any claims for the inheritance of separate moral faculties, evil dispositions, or criminal characters. The psychologists, early grounded in biology and physiology, had insisted that human behavior was fundamentally causal, that is, behavior responded to antecedent causes. They also recognized differences between human beings and regarded these differences as a matter of degree rather than of kind. Another of their contributions was the measurement of capacity (innate) and achievement (acquired). Finally, it should be recognized that throughout its period of growth the predominant emphasis of psychology has been that of experimentation, which has not been unfelt in allied fields devoted to the study of human behavior.

The psychoanalysts, by their own distinctive methods, have endeavored to discover the motivating forces at work in the human personality. The earlier failure of the medical profession to find somatic bases for mental diseases had convinced the psychoanalysts of the need for a psychic pathology and etiology. Aiming to be neither experimental nor quantitative, they have been avowedly empirical in their procedure, relying chiefly upon the basic device of free association in dealing with autobiographical material. In probing below the surface of neurotic symptoms, they have found in the operation of the unconscious mind additional substantiation for a causal interpretation of behavior. It is they, perhaps more than any other single group, who have gone farthest in uncovering and distinguishing the underlying dynamisms of the unconscious life.

The last great development pertinent to an understanding of

behavior has been the phenomenal rise of the science of statistics and the widespread use of statistical techniques. Basic to such a science was the consideration of the factors of selection and sampling with a view to representativeness, as well as a recognition of the necessity for a control group or norm. These essentials of statistical method, together with the application of the fundamental theory of probability, had to be satisfied before any valid deductions could be drawn either from one case or from a multitude of cases. An earlier knowledge and a correct utilization of statistical technique by physicians and others would have precluded much of the fallacious thinking which characterized the studies of prisoners of the last century. No descriptions, for instance, could have been made of the criminal population based upon inferences drawn from an examination of fifteen offenders in prison. Concomitant with the extension of statistical procedure has been the growth of a scientific interpretation of statistics, an objectification that denied to the researcher the luxury of conclusional thinking, i.e., of using hypotheses as conclusions and then proceeding to "prove" them.

The history of any scientific theory is a history that is affected by strong personalities as well as by other realities in their cultural settings.[2] The history of biological theories of crime causation in America serves to illustrate this. Strong characters were attracted to the formulation of hypotheses of criminal behavior and were ready to defend these against all attacks. Thus Rush, Ray, Caldwell, Gray, Wey, Lydston, and Goddard (to mention but a few) were willing to stake their reputations upon the construction of a theory and to devote their energies to its defense. The century in which they lived and the very nature of their subject propelled the proponents of any theory into controversy. Indeed even theories in the milder and more neutral fields such as physics and chemistry had to undergo this same searching scrutiny. In the final analysis the strength of any theory was dependent upon the facts which supported it. If the theories could not stand up in the face of the facts it was the theories and not the facts which underwent change.

[2] See: Bernhard J. Stern, *Social Factors in Medical Progress*, New York, 1927.

One final word: There is need to evaluate the contributions of the physicians and others of this period who contributed to our understanding of crime causation in the light of the knowledge and experience of their day. If they were in error at times, it was the error which they shared with their generation. It was, for example, the error of Benjamin Rush with his pathology of one fever and consequent heroic treatments of blood-letting and purging. Yet in his day he was acclaimed the greatest physician his country had ever known. It is easy for physicians and even the lay student of today to perceive the folly of Rush's beliefs, but it is no diminution of Rush's stature when we interpret them in historical perspective. Likewise, it is no great feat to show the error of the students of crime causation of the nineteenth century, and to indicate how the researches of Healy and others have disproved old theories. Rather must we comprehend that today's science could not have been built save for the science of yesterday.

By 1915, with the aid of these developments, a more scientifically adequate understanding of crime causation was possible. We had come a long way from the time when the madman was indistinguishable from the criminal, from the time when it was held that the shape of the skull or of the brain determined criminal or non-criminal behavior, from the time when it was believed that there was a fixed criminal anthropological type, from the time when it was maintained that individuals inherited crime through the germ plasm, from the time, even within our own day, when it was asserted that every feeble-minded person was a criminal or a potential criminal.

Today we believe that criminal behavior indicates a difference, a difference not of kind, but a difference of degree. Today we have better resources for understanding the meaning of crime and the criminal; we stand ready to conceive of the criminal as a biological product as well as a product of the environmental forces around him. Modern criminological research now reveals him not as a composite of traits, which when added together become the criminal personality, but rather as a functioning, integrated personality.

BIBLIOGRAPHY

Note

BIOGRAPHIES of a number of the writers here considered may be found in the *Dictionary of American Biography*, volumes I to XX, 1928-1936; Index, 1937, Scribners, New York. The following biographical sources may be consulted also:

Atkinson, William B.: *Physicians and Surgeons of the United States*. Robson, Philadelphia, 1878.

Gross, Samuel D.: *Lives of Eminent American Physicians and Surgeons of the Nineteenth Century*. Lindsay, Philadelphia, 1861.

Henry, Frederick P.: *Standard History of the Medical Profession of Philadelphia*. Goodspeed, Chicago, 1897.

Kelly, Howard A.: *A Cyclopedia of American Medical Biography*, Saunders, Philadelphia, 1912.

Stone, R. French: *Biography of Eminent American Physicians and Surgeons*. Carlon and Hollenbeck, Indianapolis, 1894.

Thacher, James: *American Medical Biography*. Richardson & Lord and Cottons & Barnard, Boston, 1828.

Watson, Irving A.: *Physicians and Surgeons of America*. Republican Press Association, Concord, 1896.

Williams, Stephen W.: *American Medical Biography*. Merriam, Greenfield, Mass., 1845.

BOOKS

Allport, Gordon W.: *Personality: A Psychological Interpretation*. Holt, New York, 1937.

American Neurological Association: *Eugenical Sterilization*. Macmillan, New York, 1936.

Barr, Martin W.: *Mental Defectives*. Blakiston, Philadelphia, 1904.

Bell, Clark: *Medico-Legal Studies*. 1-8. Medico-Legal Journal Ass'n. 1889-1906. New York.

—— *Medical Jurisprudence of Inebriety*. Medico-Legal Journal Association, New York, 1888.

Benedikt, Moriz: *Anatomical Studies on the Brains of Criminals*. Translated by E. P. Fowler. Wood, New York, 1881.

Bibliography on Eugenics and Related Subjects. New York Senate Document, #42, volume XIX, Part II, 1915.

Blondel, Charles: *La Psycho-Physiologie de Gall.* Felix Alcan, Paris, 1914.

Boardman, A.: *A Defense of Phrenology.* Kearny, New York, 1847.

Boies, Henry M.: *Prisoners and Paupers.* Putnam, New York, 1893.

—— *The Science of Penology.* Putnam, New York, 1901.

Boring, Edwin G.: *A History of Experimental Psychology.* Century, New York, 1929.

Bowers, Paul E.: *Clinical Studies in the Relationship of Insanity and Crime.* Michigan City, Indiana, 1915.

Brace, Charles Loring: *The Dangerous Classes of New York.* Wynkoop and Hallenback, New York, 1872.

Bronner, Augusta F.: *A Comparative Study of the Intelligence of Delinquent Girls.* Teachers College, Columbia University, New York, 1914.

Bunnell, Ada, and Cook, W. Burt: *Bibliography of Medical Serial (Bunnell) with Bibliography of Medical Jurisprudence (Cook).* New York State Library, Bibliography #47, University of the State of New York, 1910.

Caldwell, Charles: *Autobiography of Charles Caldwell.* Lippincott, Grambo and Co., Philadelphia, 1855.

—— *Elements of Phrenology.* Skillman, Lexington, Kentucky, 1824.

Calkins, Alonzo: *Opium and the Opium Appetite.* Lippincott, Philadelphia, 1871.

Capen, Nahun: *Reminiscences of Dr. Spurzheim and George Combe.* Fowler and Wells, New York, 1881.

Chandler, Joseph R.: *Outlines of Penology.* James B. Chandler, Philadelphia, 1875.

Christison, J. Sanderson: *Crime and Criminals.* J. S. Christison, Chicago, 1898.

Combe, George: *Essays on Phrenology.* Carey and Lea, Philadelphia, 1822.

—— *Notes on the United States of America During a Phrenological Visit in 1838-1839-1840.* 2 Volumes, Carey and Hart, Philadelphia, 1841.

Cook, W. Burt: see Bunnell, Ada.

Cooper, Thomas: *Tracts on Medical Jurisprudence.* Webster, Philadelphia, 1819.

Crothers, T. D.: *The Disease of Inebriety from Alcohol, Opium, and Other Narcotic Drugs*. Treat, New York, 1893.

—— *Inebriety*. Harvey, Cincinnati, 1911.

—— *Morphinism and Narcomanias from Other Drugs*. Saunders, Philadelphia, 1902.

Danielson, Florence H. and Davenport, Charles B.: *The Hill Folk*. Cold Spring Harbor, New York, 1912.

Davenport, Charles B.: *Eugenics*. Holt, New York, 1910.

—— *Heredity in Relation to Eugenics*. Holt, New York, 1911.

Davies, Stanley P.: *Social Control of the Mentally Deficient*. Crowell, New York, 1930.

Davis, Andrew J.: *Mental Disorders: Or Diseases of the Brain and Nerves, Developing the Origin and Philosophy of Mania, Insanity, and Crime, with Full Directions for Their Treatment and Cure*. American News Co., New York, 1871.

Dean, Amos: *Lectures on Phrenology*. Oliver Steele, and Hoffman and White, Albany, 1834.

—— *Principles of Medical Jurisprudence*. Gould, Albany and New York, 1850.

Denys, Frederick W.: *Lombroso's Theory of Crime*. Helmles, Nyack-on-Hudson, no date.

Deutsch, Albert: *The Mentally Ill in America*. Doubleday, Doran, New York, 1937.

Drähms, August: *The Criminal: His Personnel and Env.ronment*. Macmillan, New York, 1900.

Dugdale, Richard: *The Jukes, A Study in Crime, Pauperism and Heredity*. Putnam, New York, 1877.

Estabrook, Arthur H.: *The Jukes in 1915*. Carnegie Institution, Washington, 1916.

—— and Davenport, Charles B.: *The Nam Family*. Cold Spring Harbor, New York, 1912.

Echeverria, M. G.: *On Epilepsy*. Wood, New York, 1870.

Ellis, Havelock: *The Criminal*. Scribner and Welford, New York and London, 1890.

Elwell, John J.: *Medico-Legal Treatise on Malpractice and Medical Evidence Comprising the Elements of Medical Jurisprudence*. Voorhies, New York, 1860.

Ewell, Marshall D.: *A Manual of Medical Jurisprudence*. Little, Brown, Boston, 1887.

Fowler, O. S. and L. N.: *Phrenology Proved, Illustrated and Applied*. Fowler and Brevoort, Philadelphia; N. Fowler, New York, 1839.

—— *Practical Phrenology*. Fowler, New York and Philadelphia, 1840.

Gall, Franz Joseph: *Craniologie, ou Découvertes Nouvelles, Concernant le cerveau, Le Crâne, et les Organes*. Nicolla, Paris, 1807.

—— *Sur les Fonctions du Cerveau et sur celles de Chacune de ses Parties, Avec des Observations sur la Possibilité de reconnoitre les Instincts, les Penchants, les Talents, ou les Dispositions Morales et Intellectuelles des Hommes et des Animaux, par la Configuration de leur cerveau et de leur tête*. Baillière, Paris, 6 volumes, 1822-1825.

—— and Spurzheim, John Gaspar: *Anatomie et Physiologie du Système Nerveux en General et du Cerveau en Particulier. Avec des Observations sur la Possibilité de Reconnoitre Plusiers Dispositions Intellectuelles et Morales de l'Homme et des Animaux, par la Configuration de leur Têtes*. Volume I-IV Schoell, Paris, 1810-1819.

—— *Recherches sur le Système Nerveux en General, et sur celui du Cerveau en Particulier*. Schoell, Paris, 1809.

Goddard, Henry Herbert: *The Criminal Imbecile*. Macmillan, New York, 1910.

—— *Feeble-Mindedness*. Macmillan, New York, 1914.

—— *The Kallikak Family*. Macmillan, New York, 1912.

Goodman, Nathan G.: *Benjamin Rush: Physician and Citizen*. University of Pennsylvania Press, Philadelphia, 1934.

Green, Sanford, M.: *Crime, Its Nature, Causes, and Treatment and Prevention*. Lippincott, Philadelphia, 1889.

Grimes, J. Stanley: *A New System of Phrenology*. Steele, Buffalo; Wiley and Putnam, New York, 1839.

Groszmann, M. P. E.: *The Exceptional Child*. Scribners, New York, 1917.

Hall, G. Stanley: *Adolescence*. Two volumes, Appleton, New York, 1908.

Hamilton, Allan McLane: *Manual of Medical Jurisprudence*. Bermingham, New York, 1883.

Hammond, William A.: *Insanity in Its Relation to Crime*. Appleton, New York, 1873.

—— *A Treatise on Insanity in Its Medical Relations.* Appleton, New York, 1883.

Harrison, George Leib: *Chapters on Social Science.* Privately printed, Philadelphia, 1877.

Haskins, R. W.: *History and Progress of Phrenology.* Wiley and Putnam, New York, Steele and Peck, Buffalo, 1839.

Hasse, Adelaide: *Index of Economic Material in Documents of the States of the United States.* Carnegie Institution, Washington, D.C., 1907-1922.

Healy, William: *Case Studies of Mentally and Morally Abnormal Types.* Harvard University Printing Office, Cambridge, 1912.

—— *Delinquency and Crime in Relation to Mental Defect or Disorder* in *Modern Treatment of Mental and Nervous Diseases,* edited by White and Jeliffe, volume I, Lea and Febiger, Philadelphia, 1913.

—— *The Individual Delinquent.* Little, Brown, Boston, 1915.

Henderson, Charles Richmond: *An Introduction to the Study of the Dependent, Defective and Delinquent Classes.* Heath, Boston, 1893.

—— Editor, *Correction and Prevention.* 4 volumes, Russell Sage Foundation, New York, 1910.

—— *The Cause and Cure of Crime.* McClurg, Chicago, 1914.

Hill, David S.: *An Experimental Study of Delinquent and Destitute Boys in New Orleans.* Commission Council, New Orleans, Louisiana, 1914.

Hochstein, Irma: *Bibliography on Sterilization of Criminals.* Wisconsin Library Commission, Legislative Reference Department, 1913.

Hurd, Henry M.: *The Institutional Care of the Insane in the United States and Canada.* 4 volumes, Johns Hopkins Press, Baltimore, 1917.

Jastrow, Joseph: *The Story of Human Error.* Appleton-Century, New York, 1936.

—— *Wish and Wisdom.* Appleton-Century, New York, 1935.

Jones, Silas: *Practical Phrenology.* Russell, Shattuck and Williams. Boston, 1836.

Kellogg, John Harvey: *Plain Facts for Old and Young.* I. F. Segner, Burlington, Iowa, new edition, 1886.

Kellor, Frances A.: *Experimental Sociology.* Macmillan, New York, 1901.

Key, Wilhelmine E.: *Feeble-Minded Citizens in Pennsylvania*. Public Charities Association of Pennsylvania, Philadelphia, 1915.

KleinSmid, R. B. von: *Preliminary Report of the Department of Research of the Indiana Reformatory*. Jeffersonville, Indiana, 1914.

Kneeland, George J.: *Commercialized Prostitution in New York City*. Century, New York, 1913.

Kuhlmann, Augustus Frederick: *A Guide to Material on Crime and Criminal Justice*. Wilson, New York, 1929.

Kurella, Hans: *Cesare Lombroso. A Modern Man of Science*. Rebman, New York, 1910.

Landman, J. H.: *Human Sterilization: The History of the Sexual Sterilization Movement*. Macmillan, New York, 1932.

Laughlin, H. H.: *Eugenical Sterilization in the United States*. Municipal Court, Chicago, 1922.

—— *Report of the Committee to Study and to Report on the Best Practical Means of Cutting Off the Defective Germ Plasm in the American Population*. Eugenics Record Office, Bulletin, no. 10 a, 1914.

List of Bibliographies on Crime and Criminals. United States Library of Congress, Division of Bibliography, Washington, D.C., 1922.

List of Works in the New York Public Library Relating to Criminology. Bulletin of the New York Public Library, XV, May, 1911, 259-317.

Lydston, G. Frank: *Addresses and Essays*. Renz and Henry, Louisville, Kentucky, second edition, 1892.

—— *The Diseases of Society*. Lippincott, Philadelphia, 1904.

MacDonald, Arthur: *Abnormal Man*. United States Bureau of Education, Washington, D. C., 1893. (Bibliography.)

—— *Criminology*. Funk and Wagnalls, New York and London, 1893. (Bibliography.)

—— *Education and Patho-Social Studies*. Government Printing Office, Washington, 1896.

—— *Experimental Study of Children, Including Anthropometrical and Psycho-physical Measurements of Washington School Children, and a Bibliography*. Government Printing Office, Washington, 1899.

—— *Hearing on Bill (H. R. 14798) to Establish A Laboratory for the Study of the Criminal, Pauper, and Defective Classes.* Government Printing Office, Washington, 1902. (Bibliography.)

—— *Juvenile Crime and Reformation.* Government Printing Office, Washington, 1908. (Bibliography.)

—— *Man and Abnormal Man.* Senate Document No. 187, 58th Congress, 3rd Session, Government Printing Office, Washington, 1905.

—— *Senate Document No. 400 (57th Congress, 1st Session) A Plan for the Study of Man.* Government Printing Office, Washington, 1902. (Bibliography.)

—— *Statistics of Crime, Suicide, Insanity, and Other Forms of Abnormality, and Criminological Studies.* Government Printing Office, Washington, 1903. (Bibliography.)

—— *Study of the Criminal, Pauper, and Defective Classes,* Government Printing Office, Washington, 1908. (Bibliography.)

Mann, Edward C.: *Manual of Psychological Medicine and Allied Nervous Diseases.* Blakiston, Philadelphia, 1883.

McKim, W. Duncan: *Heredity and Human Progress.* Putnam, New York, London, 1901.

Medical Jurisprudence of Inebriety. Medico-Legal Journal Publishing Co., New York, 1888.

Mears, James Ewing: *Problems of Race Betterment.* Dornan, Philadelphia, 1910, second edition.

Michael, Jerome, and Adler, Mortimer: *Crime, Law and Social Science.* Harcourt, Brace, New York, 1933.

Miller, D. R.: *The Crime Classes—Causes and Cures.* United Brethren Publishing Co., Dayton, Ohio, 1903.

Moore, Anne: *The Feeble-Minded in New York.* New York State Charities Association, New York, 1911.

Mosby, Thomas Speed: *Causes and Cures of Crime.* C. V. Mosby, St. Louis, 1913.

Mumford, James Gregory: *Narrative of Medicine in America.* Lippincott, Philadelphia, 1903.

Münsterberg, Hugo: *On the Witness Stand.* McClure, New York, 1908.

New York State Commission to Investigate Provision for the Mentally Deficient. (Bibliography on Eugenics) New York Senate Document #42, 1915.

Nordenskiöld, Erik: *The History of Biology.* Tudor, New York, 1935.

Norris, George W.: *Early History of Medicine in Philadelphia.* Collins, Philadelphia, 1886.

Norsworthy, Naomi: *The Psychology of Mentally Deficient Children.* Columbia University Monograph, New York, 1906.

Ordronaux, John: *Jurisprudence of Medicine.* Johnson, Philadelphia, 1869.

Park, Roswell: *An Epitome of the History of Medicine.* Davis, Philadelphia, 1897, 1898, 1899.

Parmelee, Maurice: *The Principles of Anthropology and Sociology in their Relations to Criminal Procedure.* Macmillan, New York, 1908.

Parrish, Joseph: *Alcoholic Inebriety, from a Medical Standpoint, with Cases from Clinical Records.* Blakiston, Philadelphia, 1883.

Parsons, Philip A.: *Crime and the Criminal.* Knopf, New York, 1926.

—— *Responsibility for Crime.* Columbia University Studies in History, Economics and Public Law, XXXIV, no. 3. New York, 1909.

Peirce, B. K.: *A Half Century with Juvenile Delinquents.* Appleton, New York, 1869.

Prichard, James Cowles: *A Treatise on Insanity and Other Disorders Affecting the Mind.* Sherwood, Gilbert and Piper, London, 1835.

Ray, Isaac: *Contributions to Mental Pathology.* Little, Brown, and Co., Boston, 1873.

—— *Mental Hygiene.* Ticknor and Fields, Boston, 1863.

—— *A Treatise on the Medical Jurisprudence of Insanity.* Little and Brown, Boston, 1838.

Reeve, Charles H.: *The Prison Question.* Knight and Leonard, Chicago, 1890.

Rush, Benjamin: *Medical Inquiries and Observations.* Volume II, Second Edition, J. Conrad & Co., Philadelphia, 1805.

—— *Medical Inquiries and Observations Upon the Diseases of the Mind.* First Edition, Kimber and Richardson, Philadelphia 1812.

—— *Sixteen Introductory Lectures, to Courses of Lectures Upon the Institutes and Practice of Medicine.* Bradford and Innskeep, Philadelphia, 1811.

Sachs, B.: *Insanity and Crime*. In Volume II, *A System of Legal Medicine*, by Hamilton, Allan McLane, Treat and Co., New York, 1900.

Sampson, M. B.: *Rationale of Crime*. From the Second London Edition, with Notes and Illustrations by E. W. Farnham, Matron of Mount Pleasant Prison. Appleton, New York and Philadelphia, 1846.

Select List of References on the Sterilization of Criminals. United States Library of Congress, Washington, 1913.

Sellin, Thorsten, and Shalloo, J. P.: *A Bibliographical Manual for the Student of Criminology*. Philadelphia, 1935.

Shryock, Richard Harrison: *The Development of Modern Medicine*. University of Pennsylvania Press, Philadelphia, 1936.

Spitzka, Edward C.: *Insanity, Its Classification, Diagnosis and Treatment*. Bermingham, New York, 1883.

Spratling, William P.: *Epilepsy and Its Treatment*. Saunders, Philadelphia, 1904.

Spurzheim, John Gaspar: *A View of the Elementary Principles of Education*. Marsh, Capen and Lyon, Boston, 1832.

Stolz, John: *The Cause and Cure of Crime*. Potter, Philadelphia, 1880.

Talbot, Eugene, S.: *Degeneracy; Its Causes, Signs and Results*. Scribners, New York, 1898.

Travis, Thomas: *The Young Malefactor, A Study in Juvenile Delinquency, Its Causes and Treatment*. Crowell, New York, 1908.

Vaux, Richard: *Short Talks on Crime Cause and Convict Punishment*. Second Edition, Philadelphia, 1882.

Wallin, J. E. Wallace: *Problems of Subnormality*. World Book Co., New York, 1917.

Warner, Amos G.: *American Charities*. Crowell, New York, 1894.

Wharton, Francis: *A Monograph on Mental Unsoundness*. Kay and Brother, Philadelphia, 1855.

White, William A.: *Outlines of Psychiatry*. New York Journal of Nervous and Mental Disease Publishing Co., New York, 1907.

—— and Jeliffe, Smith Ely: *Modern Treatment of Mental and Nervous Diseases*. Lea and Febiger, Philadelphia, 1913.

Wigmore, John H.: *A Preliminary Bibliography of Modern Criminal Law and Criminology*. Gary Library of Law, Northwestern University, Bulletin #1, Chicago, 1909.

Williams, J. Harold: *Defective, Delinquent and Dependent Boys.* Department of Research, Whittier State School, December, 1915, California.

—— *A Study of One Hundred and Fifty Delinquent Boys.* Research Laboratory of the Buckel Foundation, Department of Education, Stanford University, California, February, 1915.

Wines, Frederick Howard: *Punishment and Reformation.* Crowell, New York, 1895.

—— *The Prevention and Repression of Crime.* Being a Report of the Fifth Section of the International Congress of Charities, Correction and Philanthropy, Chicago, June, 1893. Johns Hopkins, Press, Baltimore, 1894.

Winship, Albert E.: *Jukes-Edwards: A Study in Education and Heredity.* Myers, Harrisburg, 1900.

Woodward, Samuel B.: *Reports and Other Documents Relating to the State Lunatic Hospital.* Boston, 1837.

Wright, Carroll D.: *Outline of Practical Sociology.* Longmans, Green, New York, 1899.

Wright, Thomas Lee: *Inebriism—A Pathological and Psychological Study.* Hubbard, Columbus, Ohio, 1885.

Young, Kimball, editor: *Social Attitudes.* Chapter XV (357-375) by E. H. Sutherland on *Mental Deficiency and Crime.* Holt, New York, 1931.

PERIODICAL LITERATURE

Aaron, Eugene M.: "Recent Researches in Criminology." *Scientific American Supplement,* XXXIII, June 18, 1892, 13727-13729.

Abbott, A.: "The Physiology of the Rogue." *Sanitarian,* XX, April, 1888, 289-303.

Adams, Chauncey: "Insanity in Its Relation to Crime." *Medical Times,* XXVIII, November, 1900, 321-324; XXIX, January, 1901, 5-8.

Addams, George S.: "Defectives in the Juvenile Court." *Training School,* XI, June, 1914, 49-54.

—— "Relation of Feeble-Mindedness to Delinquency." *Report of the Commissioner of Education,* 1913, Volume I, 494-496.

Albert, J. H.: "Barriers Against Crime." *Proceedings of the National Prison Association,* 1895, 126-134.

Alexander, Harriet C. B.: "The Degenerate and Crime." *Women's Medical Journal,* XXV, December, 1915, 263-269, (Bibliography).

—— "Legal Aspects of Epilepsy." *Alienist and Neurologist,* XXVII, May, 1906, 170-188.

—— "Physical Abnormalities of Prostitutes." *Medical Standard,* XIV, August, 1893, 43-45.

Allison, Henry E.: "Defective Inmates of Penal Institutions." *Proceedings of the National Prison Association,* 1904, 292-302.

—— "Hospital Provision for the Insane Criminal." *American Journal of Insanity,* LX, July, 1903, 111-121

—— "Insanity Among Criminals." *American Journal of Insanity,* LI, July, 1894, 54-63.

—— "Insanity and Homicide." *American Journal of Insanity,* LV, April, 1899, 627-638.

—— "On Motives which Govern the Criminal Acts of the Insane." *American Journal of Insanity,* XLIX, October, 1892, 192-205.

—— "Some Relations of Crime to Insanity and States of Mental Enfeeblement." *Journal of the American Medical Association,* XXVII, September 19, 1896, 646-650.

—— "What Constitutes an Insane Criminal and What Status Does He Occupy?" *Albany Medical Annals,* XVIII, December, 1897, 569-582.

Ames, A. C. "A Plea for Castration, As a Punishment for Crime." *Omaha Clinic,* VI, November, 1893, 343-345.

Anderson, C. H.: "Are Criminals Insane Individuals?" *Illinois Medical Journal,* XXV, April, 1914, 227-229.

Anderson, V. V.: "An Analysis of One Hundred Cases Studied in Connection with the Municipal Criminal Courts of Boston." *Boston Medical and Surgical Journal,* CLXXI, August 27, 1914, 341-346.

—— "The Laboratory in the Study and Treatment of Crime." *Journal of the American Institute of Criminal Law and Criminology,* V, March, 1915, 840-850; also in *Boston Medical and Surgical Journal,* CLXXI, November 19, 1914, 803-808.

—— "A Proper Classification of Borderline Mental Cases Among Offenders." *Boston Medical and Surgical Journal,* CLXXIII, September 23, 1915, 466-469.

Anderson, W. S.: "The Study of Crime and Degeneration from a Medical Standpoint." *Transactions of the Michigan State Medical Society*, XX, 1896, 357-364.

Andrews, Judson B.: "The Case of Peter Louis Otto. A Medico-Legal Study." *American Journal of Insanity*, XLV, October, 1888, 207-219.

—— "A Medico-Legal Case—The People vs. William Manley." *American Journal of Insanity*, XLVII, October, 1890, 152-165.

Appleton, H. L.: "Crime, A Disease, with Some Suggestions for Its Cure." *Southern Medicine and Surgery*, IV, September, 1905, 186-188.

Arbogast, B. A.: "Castration—The Remedy for Crime." *Denver Medical Times*, XV, August, 1895, 55-58.

Armstrong, V. P.: "Crime, Disease and the Remedy." *Texas Health Journal*, VII, June, 1895, 275-281.

Arnold, A. B.: "Moral Insanity." *Transactions of the Medical and Chirurgical Faculty of the State of Maryland*. 1887, 120-125.

"Asexualization of Criminals and Degenerates." *Michigan Law Journal*, VI, December, 1897, 289-315.

Babcock, W. L.: "A Case of Moral Insanity." *State Hospitals Bulletin* (Utica, New York) I, 1896, 120-124.

Bannister, H. M.: "Moral Insanity." *Journal of Nervous and Mental Disease*, IV, October, 1877, 645-668.

Barker, Lewellys F.: "On the Prevention of Racial Deterioration and Degeneracy, Especially by Denying the Privilege of Parenthood to the Manifestly Unfit." *Maryland Medical Journal*, LIII, September, 1910, 291-297.

Barnes, Francis J.: "Vasectomy." *New England Medical Monthly*, XXIX, December, 1910, 454-458.

Barr, Martin W.: "The Career of a Moral Imbecile." *Alienist and Neurologist*, XXXII, November, 1911, 573-592.

Batten, S. Z.: "The Redemption of the Unfit." *American Journal of Sociology*, XIV, September, 1908, 233-260.

Bauer, J. L.: "The Analysis of a Crime." *St. Louis Medical and Surgical Journal*, LXVIII, October, 1895, 201-210.

Beach, C. E.: "Sterilization of Criminals, Idiots, and Insane." *Lawyer and Banker*, IV, June, 1911, 212-218.

Belfield, William T.: "The Sterilization of Criminals and Other Defectives by Vasectomy." *Chicago Medical Reporter*, XXXI, March, 1909, 219-222.

Bell, Clark: "Delirium Tremens and the Law." *Quarterly Journal of Inebriety*, XV, January, 1893, 51.

—— "Heredity." *Medico-Legal Journal*, XV, 1897-1898, 224-228.

—— "Madness and Crime." *Medico-Legal Journal*, II, 1884-1885, 339-365; discussion, 394-414, 417-431, 446-449.

Bell, John: "On Phrenology, or the Study of the Intellectual and Moral Nature of Man." *Philadelphia Journal of the Medical and Physical Sciences*, IV, 1822, 72-113.

Bentley, Madison: "The Psychological Antecedents of Phrenology." *Psychological Monographs*, XXI, 1916, 102-115.

Berry, John J.: "The Physical Basis of Crime." *Medical Age*, XIV, February 10, 1896, 72-77.

Bissell, Helen W.: "Insane and Criminal Women." *Northwestern Lancet*, XVII, May 15, 1897, 211-212.

Blackmar, Frank W.: "The Smoky Pilgrims." *American Journal of Sociology*, II, January, 1897, 485-500.

Bloch, Siegfried: "Delinquent Children from a Medical Standpoint." *American Journal of Obstetrics*, LXIII, May, 1911, 917-926.

—— "Psychological Study of Gangs." *Medical Record*, LXXVIII, September 17, 1910, 477-487.

Bloss, James R.: "Sterilization of Confirmed Criminals and Other Defectives." *West Virginia Medical Journal*, IV, March, 1910, 291-294.

Bluemel, C. S.: "Binet Tests on Two Hundred Juvenile Delinquents." *Training School*, XII, December, 1915, 187-193.

Blumer, G. Alder: "A Half-Century of American Medico-Psychological Literature." *American Journal of Insanity*, LI, July, 1894, 40-50.

Boal, Robert: "Emasculation and Ovariotomy as a Penalty for Crime and the Reformation of Criminals." *Transactions of the Illinois State Medical Society*, 1894, 533-543.

Bogart, G. Henri: "Asexualization of the Criminal by Severance of the Vas Deferens." *Medical Council*, XIV, August, 1909, 296-297.

—— "Asexualization of the Unfit." *Medical Herald*, XXIX, June, 1910, 298-301.

—— "The Indiana Plan (Vasectomy)." *Medical Herald*, XXX, January, 1911, 81-84.

—— "More on Vasectomy." *Texas Medical Journal*, XXVI, January, 1911, 239-242.

—— "A Plea for Double Vasectomy in Criminals." *American Journal of Dermatology and Genito-Urinary Diseases*, XIII, May, 1909, 221-224.

—— "Procreation Laws." *Medical Fortnightly*, XXXVIII, September, 1910, 348-350.

—— "Restricting the Propagation of the Unfit." *Medical Council*, XIII, August, 1908, 282-284.

——"Sterilization—The Indiana Plan." *Texas Medical Journal*, XXVI, September, 1910, 79-86.

—— "Sterilization of the Unfit." *Texas Medical Journal*, XXVI, February, 1911, 279-286.

——"Sterilizing the Unfit." *Texas Medical Journal*, XXVII, March, 1912, 327-330.

Bohannon, E. W.: "A Study of Peculiar and Exceptional Children." *Pedagogical Seminary*, IV, October, 1896, 3-60.

Bowers, E. F.: "Sterilization of Degenerate Criminals and Insane." *Medico-Pharmaceutical Critic and Guide*, XV, May, 1912, 177-179.

Bowers, Paul E.: "Causes of Crime." *New York Medical Journal*, XCVIII, July 19, 1913, 128-131.

—— "Clinical Study of the Habitual Criminal." *Proceedings of the American Prison Association*, 1914, 281-292.

—— "Constitutional Immorality." *Illinois Medical Journal*, XXV, April, 1914, 230-236.

—— "Criminal Anthropology." *Journal of the American Institute of Criminal Law and Criminology*, V, September, 1914, 358-363.

—— "A Plea for Sterilization." *Dietetic and Hygienic Gazette*, XXVIII, September, 1912, 585-589.

—— "Prison Psychosis—A Pseudonym." *American Journal of Insanity*, LXX, July, 1913, 161-173.

—— "The Recidivist." *Journal of the American Institute of Criminal Law and Criminology*, V, September, 1914, 404-415.

—— "The Relation of Prison Life to the Development of Insanity Among Prisoners." *International Clinics*, IV, (22nd. Series) 1912, 273-281.

Brady. E. F.: "Emotional Insanity." *Clinical Reporter*, XIII, February, 1900, 45-50.

Branth, J. H.: "Physical Defects and Crime." *New York Medical Journal*, C, December 26, 1914, 1251-1252.

Bridgman, Olga: "Delinquency and Mental Deficiency." *Survey*, XXXII, June 13, 1914, 302.

—— "Mental Deficiency and Delinquency." *Journal of the American Medical Association*, LXI, August 16, 1913, 471-472.

Brigham, Amariah: "Crime and Insanity." *American Journal of Insanity*, IV, July, 1847, 67-72.

—— "Definition of Insanity." *American Journal of Insanity*, I, October, 1844, 97-116.

Brockway, Z. R.: "The Physical Basis of Crime—Viewed from the Prison." *Bulletin of the American Academy of Medicine*, XIV, December, 1913, 412-423.

Bronner, Augusta F.: "A Research on the Proportion of Mental Defectives Among Delinquents." *Journal of the American Institute of Criminal Law and Criminology*, V, November, 1914, 561-568.

Brower, Daniel R.: "Etiology and Treatment of Criminality." *Medico-Legal Journal*, XV, 1897-1898, 361-365.

—— "Medical Aspects of Crime." *Boston Medical and Surgical Journal*, CXL, June 15, 1899, 570-574; also *Journal of the American Medical Association*, XXXII, June 10, 1899, 1282-1287.

—— "Suggestions on the Limitations and Treatment of Juvenile Criminals." *Journal of the American Medical Association*, XXXI, December 3, 1898, 1333.

Brown, Philip K.: "Neurotic Basis of Juvenile Delinquency." *Journal of the American Medical Association*, LVIII, January 20, 1912, 184-186.

Brown, Sanger: "Responsibility in Crime from the Medical Standpoint." *Popular Science Monthly*, XLVI, December, 1894, 154-164.

Bruce, Hortense: "Moral Degeneracy." *Journal of Psycho-Asthenics*, XIV, September, 1909, 39-47.

Bryce, Peter: "Moral and Criminal Responsibility." *Proceedings of the National Conference of Charities and Correction*, 1888, 75-91; also *Alienist and Neurologist*, IX, 1888-1889, 428-448.

Bullard, William N.: "The Moral Responsibility of the Habitual Criminal." *New York Medical Journal*, LXXXI, January 7, 1905, 31-32.

Burnet, Anne: "A Study of Delinquent Girls." *Institutional Quarterly*, III, June 30, 1912, 47-53.

Burnett, Swan M.: "Dipsomania." *Transactions of the Tennessee Medical Society*, XIII, 1875, 66-70.

Burr, Charles W.: "Imbecility and Crime and the Legal Restraint of Imbeciles." *Pennsylvania Medical Journal*, XI, June, 1908, 695-701.

Burr, G.: "Distinction Between Disease and Morbid Anatomy of Disease Applied to Inebriety." *Proceedings of the American Association for the Cure of Inebriety*, V, 1875, 71-84.

Butler, Amos: "The Burden of Feeble-Mindedness." *Proceedings of the National Conference of Charities and Correction*, 1907, 1-10.

Buttolph, H. A.: "On the Phrenology of the Brain and Its Relations In Health and Disease to the Faculties of the Mind." *American Journal of Insanity*, XLII, January, 1886, 277-316.

—— "The Relation Between Phrenology and Insanity." *American Journal of Insanity*, VI, October, 1849, 127-136.

Calder, D. H.: "Statutory Eugenics." *Northwest Medicine* (n.s.) IV, December, 1912, 357-360.

Caldwell, Charles: "New Views on Penitentiary Discipline and Moral Education and Reformation of Criminals." *Phrenological Journal* (Edinburgh), VII, 1831-1832, 384-410, 493-517.

—— "Phrenology Vindicated." *Annals of Phrenology*, I, October, 1833, 1-102.

—— "Phrenology Vindicated." *Transylvania Journal of Medicine and Associate Sciences*, VIII, July, 1835, 301-393.

—— "Phrenology Vindicated Against the Charges of Fatalism." *American Phrenological Journal and Miscellany*, II, December, 1839, 98-110.

—— "Thoughts on the Most Effective Condition of the Brain as the Organ of the Mind, and on the Modes of Attaining It."

American Phrenological Journal and Miscellany, I, August, 1839, 393-430.

—— "Thoughts on the Pathology, Prevention and Treatment of Intemperance, as a Form of Mental Derangement." *Transylvania Journal of Medicine and Associate Sciences,* V, July-September, 1832, 309-350.

—— "Thoughts on the Structure and Dependencies of the Science of Medicine." *Transylvania Journal of Medicine and Associate Sciences,* II, August, 1829, 305-331.

—— "Thoughts on the True Connexion of Phrenology and Religion." *American Phrenological Journal and Miscellany,* I, June, 1839, 324-330.

—— "Thoughts on the True Mode of Improving the Condition of Man." *Transylvania Journal of Medicine and Associate Sciences,* VI, January-March, 1833, 5-46.

Carmalt, William H.: "Heredity and Crime: A Study in Eugenics." *Proceedings of the Connecticut Medical Society,* 1909, 240-282. (Bibliography.)

Carrington, C. V.: "Hereditary Criminals—The One Sure Cure." *Virginia Medical Semi-Monthly,* XV, April, 8, 1910, 4-8.

—— "Sterilization of Habitual Criminals." *Proceedings of the American Prison Association,* 1908, 174-177.

—— "Sterilization of Habitual Criminals." *Virginia Medical Semi-Monthly,* XIV, December, 24, 1909, 421-422.

—— "Sterilization of Habitual Criminals, With Report of Cases." *Virginia Medical Semi-Monthly,* XIII, December, 11, 1908, 389-390.

"Case of Patrick Maude, Executed for the Murder of His Sister." *American Journal of Insanity,* XVI, April, 1860, 484-486.

"Case of Perrine D. Matteson, Indicted for Murder in the First Degree, Plea, Insanity." *American Journal of Insanity,* XXXI, January, 1875, 336-344.

Chamberlain, A. F.: "Some Recent Anthropometric Studies." *Pedagogical Seminary,* VIII, June, 1901, 239-257.

Chandler, W. J.: "Sterilization of Confirmed Criminals, Idiots, Imbeciles, and Other Defectives by Vasectomy." *Journal of the Medical Society of New Jersey,* VI, December, 1909, 321-326.

Channing, Walter: "The Connection Between Insanity and Crime." *American Journal of Insanity,* XLII, April, 1886, 452-472.

—— "The Mental Status of Czolgosz, Assassin of McKinley." *American Journal of Insanity*, LIX, October, 1902, 231-278.

—— "Stigmata of Degeneration (Case of Amos D. Palmer)." *American Journal of Insanity*, LVI, April, 1900, 613-624.

Chapin, John B.: "Fifty Years of Psychiatry." *American Journal of Insanity*, LXI, January, 1905, 399-416.

—— "The Psychology of Criminals, and a Plea for the Elevation of the Medical Service of Prisons." *American Journal of Insanity*, LVI, October, 1899, 317-326.

Christian, Frank L.: "The Defective Delinquent." *Albany Medical Annals*, XXXIV, May, 1913, 276-285.

—— "Physician's Report." *Twenty-Seventh Annual Report of the New York State Reformatory at Elmira*, 1902, 56-76.

—— and Zeigler, L. M.: "Mental Defectives Among Delinquents." *Sixth Annual Report of the State (New York) Probation Commission*, 1912, 208-222.

Clark, A. L.: "Thoughts on Criminology." *Chicago Medical Times*, XXX, February, 1897, 41-44.

Clark, C. M.: "A Plea for the Sterilization of Criminals, Epileptics, Imbeciles and Insane." *Northwest Medicine*, IV (n.s.), December, 1912, 260-263.

Clark, Daniel: "Crime and Responsibility." *American Journal of Insanity*, XLVII, April, 1891, 496-506.

Clark, Martha Louise: "The Relation of Imbecility to Pauperism and Crime." *Arena*, X, November, 1894, 788-794.

Clarke, S. T.: "Case of Pierce—Plea, Insanity." *American Journal of Insanity*, XXVIII, January, 1872, 399-409.

Clum, A.: "Epilepsy and Its Relation to Insanity and Crime." *Cleveland Medical Gazette*, X, September, 1895, 513-526.

Clymer, Meredith: "Epilepsy and the Criminal Law." *Medical Gazette*, VI, May 27, 1871, 356-359.

—— "On the Mental State of Epileptics and Its Medico-Legal Relations." *Medical Record*, V, October 1, 1870, 363-366; November 1, 1870, 409-413.

Coates, Benjamin H.: "Comments on Some of the Illustrations derived by Phrenology from Comparative Anatomy." *Philadelphia Journal of the Medical and Physical Sciences*, VII, 1823, 58-80.

Conklin, William J.: "The Relations of Epilepsy to Insanity and Jurisprudence," *Transactions of the Ohio State Medical Society*, 1871, 251-295.

Cook, Abner H.: "The Innocent Criminal." *Southern Medical Journal*, VII, September 1, 1914, 717-723.

Cooke, Robert G.: "The Responsibility of Epileptics." *Albany Medical Annals*, XVIII, October, 1897, 471-476.

Coriat, Isadore: "Mental Condition of Juvenile Delinquents." *Psychological Clinic*, I, October 15, 1907, 125-137.

Cornell, George: "Oinomania." *Cincinnati Lancet and Observer*, VI, March, 1863, 156-159.

Corr, A. C.: "Emasculation and Ovariotomy as a Penalty for Crime and as a Reformatory Agency." *Medical Age*, XIII, December, 1895, 714-716.

—— "A Medical Aspect of Crime." *Journal of the American Medical Association*, XXVII, October 10, 1896, 786-788.

Coulter, Ernest K.: "Mentally Defective Delinquents and the Law." *Proceedings of the National Conference of Charities and Correction*, 1911, 68-70.

Cowles, E.: "Advancement of Psychiatry in America." *American Journal of Insanity*, LII, January, 1896, 364-386; also *Proceedings of the American Medico-Psychological Association*, II, 1895, 47-70.

Crafts, Leland W.: "A Bibliography on the Relations of Crime and Feeble-Mindedness." *Journal of the American Institute of Criminal Law and Criminology*. VII, November, 1916, 544-554.

—— and Doll, Edgar A.: "The Proportion of Mental Defectives Among Juvenile Delinquents." *Journal of Delinquency*, II, May, 1917, 119-150.

Crane, Harry W.: "Criminal Psychology." *Psychological Bulletin*, IX, December 15, 1912, 451-453.

"The Criminal Class and the So-Called Criminal Type." *Journal of the American Medical Association*, LVI, January 21, 1911, 201-202.

"Criminal Lunacy—Case of John Haddock." *American Journal of Insanity*, XI, April, 1855, 365-382.

Crothers, T. D.: "Alcoholic Trance in Criminal Cases." *Journal of the American Medical Association*, XIV, April 5, 1890, 502-505.

—— "A Case of Inebriety with Criminal Impulses." *Medical Record*, XXIV, October 27, 1883, 457-459.

—— "Criminality and Morphinism." *New York Medical Journal*, XCV, January 27, 1912, 163-165.

—— "Criminality from Alcoholism." *Journal of the American Institute of Criminal Law and Criminology*, IV, March, 1914, 859-866.

—— "Inebriate Criminals." *Alienist and Neurologist*, III, January, 1882, 66-84.

—— "Inebriate Criminals." *Quarterly Journal of Inebriety*, III, June, 1879, 129-146.

—— "Mania and Inebriety." *Medical Record*, XXXII, September 24, 1887, 421-422.

—— "Medico-Legal Problems of Inebriety." *Alienist and Neurologist*, X, October, 1889, 522-534.

—— "Morphinism and Crime." *Alienist and Neurologist*, XXII, April, 1901, 325-331.

—— "The Physical Character of Crimes of the Alcoholic." *Bulletin of the American Academy of Medicine*. XV, February, 1914, 33-40.

—— "Psychoanalysis of Criminality." *American Practitioner*, XLVIII, May, 1914, 228-233.

—— "The Question of Responsibility in Inebriety." *Alienist and Neurologist*, X, January, 1889, 45-52.

—— "The Relation of Inebriety to Criminality." *Quarterly Journal of Inebriety*, XV, January, 1893, 85-86.

—— "Review of the Otto Case." *American Journal of Insanity*, XLV, January, 1889, 435-442.

—— "Should Inebriates Be Punished by Death for Crime?" *Charlotte Medical Journal*, VII, November, 1895, 542-547.

—— "Some New Medico-Legal Questions Relating to Inebriety." *Alienist and Neurologist*, XI, October, 1890, 555-565.

—— "Some Studies of Inebriate and Pauper Criminals." *International Congress of Charities and Correction*. Fifth Section, 1893, 10-27.

Cumston, Charles Greene: "Pregnancy and Crime, a Medico-Legal Study." *Medico-Legal Journal*, XXI, 1903-1904, 333-347.

Curwen, John: "Presidential Address (Moral Insanity)." *Transactions of the Medical Society of Pennsylvania*, 1869, 287-304.

Daly, P.: "Insanity in its Relation to Crime." *Proceedings of the National Prison Association* (Transactions of the Fourth National Congress), 1876, 386-395, 565-567.

Dana, Charles L.: "Alcoholism in New York and the Classification of Inebriates." *American Journal of Insanity*, L, July, 1893, 29-33.

—— "On the New Use of Some Older Sciences—Degeneration and Its Stigmata." *Medical Record*, XLVI, December 15, 1894, 737-741.

—— "Mental Tests." *Medical Record*, LXXXIII, January 4, 1913, 1-10.

Daniel, F. E.: "Castration as a Treatment for Crime, Not as a Punishment." *Journal of the American Medical Association*, XXVI, February, 1896, 239.

—— "Should Insane Criminals or Sexual Perverts be Allowed to Procreate." *Medico-Legal Journal*, XI, 1893-1894, 275-292.

Davenport, Gertrude: "Hereditary Crime." *American Journal of Sociology*, XIII, November, 1907, 402-409.

Davis, Charles Gilbert: "Psychology of Crime and Criminals. and the Stigmata of Degeneration." *Case and Comment*, XIX, May, 1913, 820-826.

Davis, Katherine Bement: "Feeble-Minded Women in Reformatory Institutions." *Survey*, XXVII, March, 2, 1912, 1849-1851.

Dawson, George E.: "Psychic Rudiments and Morality." *American Journal of Psychology*, XI, January, 1900, 181-224.

—— "A Study in Youthful Degeneracy." *Pedagogical Seminary*, IV, December, 1896, 221-258.

Dawson, William W. J.: "Care of Feeble-Minded as a Preventive of Crime." *National Conference of Charities and Correction*, 1905, 529-530.

Denton, A. N.: "The Duality of Mind: Insanity and Vice and Criminal Responsibility." *Texas Medical News*, VI, February, 1897, 157-164.

Dercum, Francis X.: "Description of the Brain of John M. Wilson, Hanged at Norristown." *Philadelphia Medical Times*, XVII, March 5, 1887, 368-371.

Dew, H. W.: "Sterilization of the Feeble-Minded, Insane and Habitual Criminals." *Virginia Medical Semi-Monthly*, XVIII, April, 1913, 4-8.

Doll, Edgar A.: "Supplementary Analysis of H. B. Hickman's Study of Delinquents." *Training School*, XI, January, 1915, 165-168.

—— "A Working Bibliography of Feeble-Mindedness and Related Subjects." *Training School*, X, May, 1913, 40-43, 61-63.

—— see Crafts, Leland W.and Doll, Edgar A.

Donaldson, H. H.: "The Criminal Brain; Illustrated by the Brain of a Murderer." *Journal of Nervous and Mental Disease*, XIX, August, 1892, 654-656.

Down, Edwin A.: "The Sterilization of Degenerates." *Proceedings of the Connecticut State Conference of Charities and Correction*, 1910, 158-166.

Draper, J.: "Responsibility of the Insane." *American Journal of Insanity*, XL, October, 1883, 113-126.

Drew, Charles A.: "Signs of Degeneracy and Types of Criminal Insane." *American Journal of Insanity*, LVII, April, 1901, 689-698.

Drucker, A. P.: "A Study of One Hundred Juvenile-Adult Offenders in the Cook County Jail, Chicago, Illinois." *Journal of the American Institute of Criminal Law and Criminology*, IV, May, 1913, 47-57.

"Drunkenness and Crime." *American Journal of Insanity*, XXIV, April, 1868, 489-491.

Drysdale, H. H.: "The Problem of the Feeble-Minded, the Insane and the Epileptic." *Cleveland Medical Journal*, XIV, October, 1915, 672-683.

Dugdale, Richard: "Origin of Crime in Society." *Atlantic Monthly*, XLVIII, October, 1881, 452-462; December, 1881, 735-746; XLIX, February, 1882, 243-251.

Duggan, Malone: "The Surgical Solution of the Problem of Race Culture." *Texas State Journal of Medicine*, VII, July, 1911, 87-89.

Dunagan, T. Marion: "A Few Facts Showing the Great Need of Physical Development and Physical Care to Lessen Crime and the Number of Criminals." *Memphis Medical Monthly*, X, August, 1890, 350-354.

Dyett, A. R.: "The Medical Jurisprudence of Inebriety." *Medico-Legal Journal*, V, 1887-1888, 305-310.

Eastern State Penitentiary of Pennsylvania, Annual Reports, 1829-1915.

Echeverria, M. G.: "Criminal Responsibility of Epileptics, as illustrated in the Case of William Montgomery." *American Journal of Insanity*, XXIX, January, 1873, 341-425.

—— "On Epileptic Insanity." *American Journal of Insanity*, XXX, July, 1873, 1-51.

Ellinwood, C. N.: "Vasectomy, An Argument for Its Therapeutic Use in Certain Mental Diseases and as a Means of Diminishing Crime and the Number of Criminals." *California State Journal of Medicine*, II, February, 1904, 60-61.

Elwell, J. J.: "Epilepsy as a Defense for Crime." *Medico-Legal Journal*, VIII, 1890-1891, 55-64.

—— "Guiteau—A Case of Alleged Moral Insanity." *Alienist and Neurologist*, IV, April, 1883, 193-201.

—— Beard, George M., Seguin, E. C., Jewell, J. S., Folsom, Charles F.: "The Moral Responsibility of the Insane." *North American Review*, CXXXIV, January, 1882, 1-39.

Emerick, E. J.: "The Defective Delinquent in Ohio." *Journal of Psycho-Asthenics*, XIX, September, 1914, 19-22.

—— "The Segregation of the Defective Classes." *Proceedings of the National Education Association*, 1912, 1290-1296.

Eskridge, J. T.: "Report of Cases of Moral Imbecility, of the Opium Habit and of Feigning, in which Forgery Is the Offense Committed." *Medical News*, LXII, January, 14, 1893, 29-34.

"Estimated Number of Feeble-Minded Persons in State Reformatories and Industrial Schools." *Training School*, IX, March, 1912, 8-10.

Evans, Elizabeth G., and Dewson, Mary W.: "Feeble-Mindedness and Juvenile Delinquency." *Charities and the Commons*, XX, May, 2, 1908, 183-191.

Evans, T. H.: "The Epileptic Criminal; With Report of Two Cases." *Medical Record*, LXVII, February, 25, 1905, 295-296.

Evans, Thomas B.: "The Responsibility of Dipsomaniacs." *Quarterly Journal of Inebriety*, XII, July, 1890, 253-261.

Everts, Orpheus: "Are Dipsomania, Kleptomania, etc., Pyromania, etc., Valid Forms of Mental Disease?" *American Journal of Insanity*, XLIV, July, 1887, 52-59.

—— "Asexualization, as a Penalty for Crime, and Reformation of Criminals." *Cincinnati Lancet-Clinic*, XX (n.s.), March, 1888, 377-380.

—— "Degeneracy." *American Journal of Insanity*, LVII, July, 1900, 117-125.

Ewell, Jesse: "A Plea for Castration to Prevent Criminal Assault." *Virginia Medical Semi-Monthly*, XI, January, 1907, 463-464.

Eynon, W. G.: "Mental Measurements of Four Hundred Juvenile Delinquents by the Binet-Simon System." *New York Medical Journal*, XCVIII, July, 26, 1913, 175-178.

—— "Some Observations of the Juvenile Delinquent From a Medical Standpoint." *Pediatrics*, XX, July, 1908, 447-454.

Falret, Jules: "Moral Insanity." *American Journal of Insanity*, XXIII, January, 1867, 407-424; April, 1867, 516-546.

Farrar, C. B.: "Some Origins of Psychiatry." *American Journal of Insanity*, LXIV, January, 1908, 523-552; LXV, July, 1908, 83-101; LXVI, October, 1909, 277-294.

Fernald, Guy: "The Defective Delinquent Class—Differentiating Tests." *American Journal of Insanity*, LXVIII, April, 1912, 523-594.

—— "The Recidivist." *Journal of the American Institute of Criminal Law and Criminology*, III, March, 1913, 866-875; also *Proceedings of the American Prison Association*, 1912, 149-162.

Fernald, Walter E.: "The Burden of Feeble-Mindedness." *Medical Communications of the Massachusetts Medical Society*, XXIII, 1912, 1-17.

—— "The Imbecile with Criminal Instincts." *American Journal of Insanity*, LXV, April, 1909, 731-749; also *American Medico-Psychological Association Proceedings*, 1908, 363-381: also *Journal of Psycho-Asthenics*, XIV, September-December, 1909, 16-38.

Fish, A.M.: "Older Tenets and Newer Theories." *Proceedings of the American Prison Association*, 1909, 153-160.

Fisher, Theodore W.: "Insane Drunkards." *Medical Communications of the Massachusetts Medical Society*, XII, 1881, 315-335.

—— "Moral Insanity." *Boston Medical and Surgical Journal*, II (n.s.), September, 24, 1868, 114-116.

—— "New England Alienists of the Last Half Century." *Proceedings of the American Medico-Psychological Association*, I, 1894, 156-166; also *American Journal of Insanity*, LI, October, 1894, 161-170.

—— "Paranoia in Relation to Hallucination of Hearing, with Two Cases of Medico-Legal Interest." *American Journal of Insanity*, XLV, July, 1888, 18-31.

Fletcher, G. J.: "The New School of Criminal Anthropology." *American Anthropologist*, IV, July, 1891, 201-236.

Flint, Austin: "The Coming Role of the Medical Profession in the Scientific Treatment of Crime and Criminals." *New York Medical Journal*, LXII, October, 19, 1895, 481-490.

Flint, Austin: "Natural History of Crime." *Transactions of the American Medical Association*, XXVI, 1875, 121-123.

Folsom, Charles F.: "Case of Charles F. Freeman, of Pocasset, Massachusetts." *American Journal of Insanity*, XL, January, 1884, 353-363.

—— "The Case of Guiteau, Assassin of the President of the United States." *Boston Medical and Surgical Journal*, CVI, February 16, 1882, 145-153.

Foote, S.L.N.: "An Address on Crime and Its Prevention." *Kansas City Medical Index*, XVIII, July, 1897, 243-245.

Foran, Martin A.: "Alcohol as a Defense for Crime." *Cleveland Medical Gazette*, XI, December, 1895, 65-73.

Forster, Thomas: "Sketch of the New Anatomy and Physiology of the Brain and Nervous System of Drs. Gall and Spurzheim, Considered as Comprehending a Complete System of Phrenology." *Pamphleteer*, V, February, 1815, 219-244.

Foster, Burnside: "The Sterilization of Habitual Criminals and Degenerates." *St. Paul Medical Journal*, XII, January, 1910, 29-34.

Foster, Warren W.: "Hereditary Criminality and Its Certain Cure." *Pearson's*, XXII, November, 1909, 565-572.

Fowler, E. P.: "Are the Brains of Criminals Anatomical Perversions?" *Medico-Chirurgical Quarterly*, I, October, 1880, 1-32.

Frazier, J. W.: "Castration for Crime as a Preventive and Curative Treatment." *Texas Medical Journal*, XI, March, 1896, 498-503.

Furness, W. J. and Kennon, B. R.: "The Legal Responsibility in Epilepsy." *State Hospitals Bulletin*, II, 1897, 66-77.

Gault, Robert H.; "The Physician in the Service of Criminology." *Bulletin of the American Academy of Medicine*, XIV, October, 1913, 351-358.

Gaver, E. E.: "Procreation in Its Relation to Insanity, Crime and Degeneracy, with Suggestions of Remedy." *Ohio Medical Journal*, V, May 15, 1909, 257-263.

George, Charles E.: "Sterilization of Criminals, Idiots, and Insane." *Central Law Journal*, LXXV, August, 1912, 92-94.

George, Rebecca: "Sterilization of the Unfit." *New England Medical Gazette*, XLVIII, September, 1913, 466-473.

Gifford, E. G. and Goddard, H. H.: "Defective Children in the Juvenile Court." *Training School*, VIII, January, 1912, 132-135.

Gilbert, C. B.: "Methomania." *Detroit Review of Medicine & Pharmacy*. VIII, June, 1873, 248-257.

Glueck, Bernard: "A Contribution to the Catamnestic Study of the Juvenile Offender." *Journal of the American Institute of Criminal Law and Criminology*, III, July, 1912, 220-244.

—— "A Contribution to the Study of Psychogenesis in the Psychoses." *American Journal of Insanity*, LXVIII, January, 1912, 371-429.

—— "Head Injury and Syphilis as a Cause of Crime." *Bulletin of the American Academy of Medicine*, XV, June, 1914, 156-163.

—— "A Study of 608 Admissions to Sing Sing Prison." *Mental Hygiene*, II, January, 1918, 85-151.

Goddard, Henry, H.: "The Binet-Simon Tests of Intellectual Capacity." *Training School*, V, December 1908, 3-9.

—— "Feeble-Mindedness and Crime." *Proceedings of the American Prison Association*, 1912, 353-357.

—— "Feeble-Mindedness and Criminality." *Training School*, VIII, March, 1911, 3-6.

—— "Four Hundred Feeble-Minded Children Classified by the Binet Method." *Journal of Psycho-Asthenics*, XV, September, 1910, 17-30.

—— "Relation of Feeble-Mindedness to Crime." *Bulletin of the American Academy of Medicine*, XV, April, 1914, 105-112.

—— "The Responsibility of Children in the Juvenile Court." *Journal of the American Institute of Criminal Law and Criminology*, III, September, 1912, 365-375.

—— "Sterilization and Segregation." *Bulletin of the American Academy of Medicine*, XIII, August, 1912, 210-219.

—— "The Treatment of the Mental Defective Who Is Also Delinquent." *Proceedings of the National Conference of Charities and Correction*, 1911, 64-65.

—— "Two Thousand Normal Children Measured by the Binet Measuring Scale of Intelligence." *Pedagogical Seminary*, XVIII, June, 1911, 232-259.

Goddard, Henry H., and Hill, Helen, F.: "Delinquent Girls Tested by the Binet Scale." *Training School*, VIII, June, 1911, 50-56.

—— —— "Feeble-Mindedness and Criminality." *Training School*, VIII, March, 1911, 3-6.

Goddard, Henry H., see Gifford, E. G., and Goddard, Henry H.

Godding, W. W.: "A Judicial Advance—The Daley Case." *American Journal of Insanity*, XLV, October, 1888, 191-206.

Goldsmith, W. B.: "A Case of Moral Insanity." *American Journal of Insanity*, XL, October, 1883, 162-177.

Goler, G. W.: "The Juvenile Delinquent, Causes That Produce Him." *Proceedings of the National Conference of Charities and Correction*, 1896, 352-367.

Goodhart, S. P.: "Forensic Import of Psychic Epilepsy." *Medical Times*, XXXVII, May, 1909, 143-144.

Gordon, Alfred: "Mental Responsibility in Acute and Chronic Intoxication with Alcohol and Other Drugs." *Old Dominion Journal of Medicine and Surgery*, VIII, May, 1909, 305-316.

Gorton, D. A.: "Moral Insanity." *American Medical Monthly*, XVI, April, 1898, 56-64; June, 1898, 81-92; August, 1898, 201-208.

Graham, J. T.: "The Criminal Insane." *Medico-Legal Journal*, X, 1892-1893, 202-206.

Gray, John P.: "Heredity." *American Journal of Insanity*, XLI, July, 1884, 1-21.

—— "Homicide in Insanity." *American Journal of Insanity*, XIV, October, 1857, 119-145.

—— "Responsibility of the Insane—Homicide in Insanity." *American Journal of Insanity*, XXXII, July, 1875, 1-57; October, 1875, 153-183.

Green, E. F.: "Report of Physician and Psychologist on the Reformatory Population at St. Cloud Minnesota." *Journal of the American Institute of Criminal Law and Criminology*, IV, September, 1913, 420-421.

Groszmann, M. P. E.: "Criminality in Children." *Arena*, XXII, October, 1899, 509-525; November, 1899, 644-652.

Groszmann, W. H.: "The Atypical Child." *Bulletin of the American Academy of Medicine*, VIII, April, 1907, 76-88.

Grover, G. W.: "Psychological Studies of Criminals." *Medico-Legal Journal*, XVI, 1898-1899, 67-78.

Grube, R. H.: "Sterilization of Defectives for the Betterment of the Human Race." *Ohio State Board of Health Bulletin*, I, August, 1911, 250-252.

Guiteau-Review of the Trial of. *American Journal of Insanity*. XXXVIII, January, 1882, 303-448.

Haigh, T. D.: "Some of the Medico-Legal Aspects of Inebriety." *North Carolina Medical Journal*, XXIII, June, 1889, 413-420.

Haines, T. H.: "Mental Examination of Juvenile Delinquents." *Ohio Board of Administration*, Publication, #7, December, 1915.

―― "Point Scale Ratings of Delinquent Boys and Girls." *Psychological Review*, XXII, March, 1915, 104-109.

Hall, W. S.: "Relation of Crime to Adolescence." *Bulletin of the American Academy of Medicine*, XV, April, 1914, 86-96.

Hammond, William A.: "A New Substitute for Capital Punishment and Means for Preventing the Propagation of Criminals." *New York Medical Examiner*, I, March, 1892, 190-194.

―― "Madness and Murder." *North American Review*, CXLVII, December, 1888, 626-637.

―― "Reasoning Mania; Its Medical and Medico-Legal Relations. With Special Reference to the Case of Charles J. Guiteau." *New York Medical Gazette*, IX, March 18, 1882, 123-130.

―― "A Problem for Sociologists." *North American Review*, CXXXV, November, 1882, 422-432.

Harris, William T.: "The Philosophy of Crime and Punishment." *Proceedings of the National Prison Association*, 1890, 222-239, 240-241.

Hart, Hastings H.: "The Extinction of the Defective Delinquent." *Proceedings of the American Prison Association*, 1912, 205-225.

―― "A Working Program for the Extinction of the Defective Delinquent." *Survey*, XXX, May, 24, 1913, 277-279.

Hatch, Henry: "Crime and Criminals. And What Shall Be Done with the Latter?" *Physician and Surgeon*, XXVII, March, 1905, 108-112; also *Proceedings of the National Prison Association*, 1904, 302-307.

Hawley, Donley C.: "Heredity and Environment as Causes of Delinquency and Crime." *Bulletin of the American Academy of Medicine*, VII, August, 1906, 533-545.

Hay, Walter: "Moral Insanity." *Journal of the American Medical Association*, I, October, 27, 1883, 482-486.

Healy, William: "Epilepsy and Crime. The Cost." *Illinois Medical Journal*, XXIII, February, 1913, 193-199.

—— "The Individual Study of the Young Criminal." *Journal of the American Institute of Criminal Law and Criminology*, I, May, 1910, 50-62.

—— "Mental Defects and Delinquency." *Proceedings of the National Conference of Charities and Correction*, 1911, 59-63.

—— "Mentally Defective and the Courts." *Journal of Psycho-Asthenics*, XV, September, 1910, 44-57.

—— "Present Day Aims and Methods of Studying the Offender." *Bulletin of the American Academy of Medicine*. XIV, October, 1913, 342-350.

—— and Spaulding, Edith R.: "Inheritance as a Factor in Criminality." *Bulletin of the American Academy of Medicine*, XV, February, 1914, 4-27.

Henderson, Charles Richmond: "The Physical Basis of Criminality." *Bulletin of the American Academy of Medicine*, XV, April, 1914, 97-101.

Henry, W. O.: "The Duty of the State to Protect the Health of Its Subjects by Sterilizing the Insane, Criminal Degenerates, Inebriates and Other Habitual Drug Users, as Well as to Sterilize Its Confirmed Criminals for Social and Economic Reasons." *Medical Herald*, XXXII, September, 1913, 321-329.

—— "Relations of Disease, Crime and Vice." *Journal of the Medical Association*, XXIV, March 2, 1895, 302-305.

Herres, Simon: "Moral Insanity." *Transactions of the Michigan State Medical Society*, VII, 1879, 418-425.

Hershey, O. F.: "Criminal Anthropology." *Criminal Law Magazine and Reporter*, XV, July, 1893, 499-504; September, 1893, 658-663; November, 1893, 778-784.

Herzog, Alfred W.: "Vasectomy—A Crime Against Nature." *Medico-Legal Journal*, XXVII, 1909-1910, 150-158.

Heym, Albrecht: "Epilepsy in Its Forensic Aspect." *Chicago Clinic*, XII, September, 1899, 344-346.

Hickman, H. B.: "Delinquent and Criminal Boys Tested by the Binet Scale." *Training School*, XI, January, 1915, 159-164.

Hickson, William J.: "The Defective Delinquent." *Journal of the American Institute of Criminal Law and Criminology*, V, September, 1914, 397-403.

Hitchcock, Charles W.: "A Case of Dementia Praecox of Medico-Legal Interest." *American Journal of Insanity*, LXII, April, 1906, 615-626.

—— "Imbecile, Criminal or Both?" *American Journal of Insanity*, LXV, January, 1909, 519-524; also *Proceedings of the American Medico-Psychological Association*, 1908, 263-272.

Hoag, Junius C.: "Relation of Vasectomy to Eugenics." *Chicago Medical Recorder*, XXXIII, January, 1911, 1-17; also *Illinois Medical Journal*, XIX, March, 1911, 280-300.

Holmes, Bayard: " The Sources of the Defective, Dependent and Delinquent Classes." *Bulletin of the American Academy of Medicine*, I, October, 1894, 562-572.

Holmes, Oliver Wendell: "Crime and Automatism." *Atlantic Monthly*, XXXV, April, 1875, 466-481.

"Homicide in Which the Plea of Insanity was Introduced. Trial of Joseph J. Brown." *American Journal of Insanity*, XIII, January, 1857, 249-259.

"Homicidal Insanity." *American Jurist and Law Magazine*, XVI, January, 1837, 315-323.

"Homicidal Insanity. Case of Nancy Farrer." *American Journal of Insanity*, XII, April, 1856, 316-334.

Howard, E. H.: "Insane Family Groups with Criminal Tendencies." *State Hospitals Bulletin*, I, 1896, 349-351.

Howard, William Lee: "Alcoholic Maniacal Epilepsy: Transitory Disturbance of Consciousness Mediating Criminal Acts." *Maryland Medical Journal*, XXXVI, April 10, 1897, 466-469.

—— "Hypnotism and Crime, a Reply to Mr. Thomson Jay Hudson." *New York Medical Journal*, LXI, March 9, 1895, 298-300.

Hrdlicka, Ales: "Anthropological Investigations on One Thousand White and Colored Children of Both Sexes, the Inmates of the New York Juvenile Asylum." *Forty-seventh Annual Report of the New York Juvenile Asylum*, 1899, Supplement, 1-81.

Hudson, Thomson Jay: "Hypnotism and Crime." *New York Medical Journal*, LXI, May 11, 1895, 590-592.

—— "Hypnotism in Its Relations to Criminal Jurisprudence." *New York Medical Journal*, LXI, January 26, 1895, 106-109.

Hughes, Charles H.: "Imbecility and the Insanity of Imbecility or Dementia Praecox Before the Law." *Alienist and Neurologist*, XXXII, February, 1911, 66-96.

—— "Moral (Affective) Insanity." *Alienist and Neurologist*, III, January, 1882, 1-14; V, April, 1884, 297-314; also *Medico-Legal Journal*, II, 1885, 22-52, 216-223.

—— "A Case of Psycho-Sensory (Affective or Moral) Insanity." *Alienist and Neurologist*, VI, April, 1885, 229-233.

—— "Moral Insanity, Depravity and 'The Hypothetical Case.'" *Alienist and Neurologist*, II, 1881, 13-19.

—— "State of Missouri vs Anton Holm. Murder in the First Degree." *American Journal of Insanity*, XXXI, October, 1874, 254-263.

—— "The Status Ebrietatus in our Courts." *Medico-Legal Journal*, V, 1887-1888, 311-315.

—— Godding, W. W., Goldsmith, W. B.: "Report on Bibliography." (Insanity—Guiteau Trial.) *Alienist and Neurologist*, IV, October, 1883, 655-674.

Hughes, Marc Ray: "Society and Its Degenerates." *Alienist and Neurologist*, XXVII, February, 1906, 63-66.

Humphrey, Seth K.: "Parenthood and the Social Conscience." *Forum*, XLIX, April, 1913, 457-464.

Humphrey, T. C.: "The Asexualization of Criminals." *Proceedings of the Oregon Medical Society*, 1897, 53-55.

Hurd, Henry M.: "Imbecility with Insanity." *American Journal of Insanity*, XLV, October, 1888, 261-269.

—— "Psychiatry in the Twentieth Century." *Albany Medical Annals*, XXIII, March, 1902, 125-136.

Hurty, John N.: "The Sterilization of Criminals and Defectives." *Social Diseases*, III, January, 1912, 1-47.

Hutchinson, Woods: "Our Human Misfits." *Everybody's Magazine*, XXV, October, 1911, 517-529.

"Imbecility and Homicide. Case of Gregor MacGregor." *American Journal of Insanity*, XXIII, April, 1867, 547-563.

"Inebriety, Relation of, to Criminality." *Quarterly Journal of Inebriety*, XV, January, 1893, 85-86.

Irvine, Robert T.: "The Congenital Criminal." *Medical News*, LXXXII, April 18, 1903, 749-752.

Jacobi, Abraham: "Brain, Crime and Capital Punishment." *Proceedings of the National Prison Association*, 1892, 175-205.

Jarvis, Edward: "Criminal Insane." *American Journal of Insanity*, XIII, January, 1857, 195-231.

—— "Mania Transitoria." *American Journal of Insanity*, XXVI, July, 1869, 1-32.

Jenkins, S. M.: "Sterilization of the Unfit." *Journal of the Oklahoma State Medical Association*, III, February, 1911, 312-315.

Jennings, H. M., and Hallock, A. L.: "Binet-Simon Tests at the George Junior Republic." *Journal of Educational Psychology*, IV, October, 1913, 471-475.

Jones, E. E.: "The Feeble-Minded and Delinquent Girl." *Indiana Bulletin of Charities and Correction*, March, 1915, 74-79.

Jordon, H. E.: "Surgical Sex-Sterilization. Its Value as a Eugenic Measure." *American Journal of Clinical Medicine*, XX, December, 1913, 983-987.

Kain, John H.: "On Intemperance Considered as a Disease and Susceptible of Cure." *American Journal of the Medical Sciences*, II, August, 1828, 291-295.

Kane, H. H.: "Some Medico-Legal Aspects of Morphia Taking." *Alienist and Neurologist*, III, July, 1882, 419-433.

Karpas, Morris J.: "Criminology from the Standpoint of the Psychiatrist." *New York Medical Journal*, CIII, February, 1916, 246-249.

—— "Psychic Constitutional Inferiority." *New York Medical Journal*, XCVII, March, 22, 1913, 294-298.

Keedy, Edwin R.: "Sterilization of Habitual Criminals, and Feeble-Minded Persons." *Illinois Law Review*, V, April, 1911, 578.

Kellor, Francis A.: "Criminal Anthropology in Its Relation to Criminal Jurisprudence." *American Journal of Sociology*, IV, January, 1899, 515-527; March, 1899, 630-648.

—— "Criminal Sociology: The American vs the Latin School." *Arena*, XXIII, March, 1900, 301-307.

Keniston, J. M.: "Defectives and Degenerates: A Menace to the Community." *Yale Medical Journal*, XVII, June, 1910, 1-7.

—— "Recollections of a Psychiatrist." *American Journal of Insanity*, LXXII, January, 1916, 465-479.

Kennon, B. R., see Furness, W. J., and Kennon, B. R.

Kerlin, Isaac N.: Annual Reports of the Pennsylvania Training School for Feeble-Minded Children. Elwyn, Pa. Thirty-Second Report, 1884. Thirty-Seventh Report, 1889.

—— "The Moral Imbecile." *Proceedings of the National Conference of Charities and Correction*, 1890, 244-250.

—— "Moral Imbecility." *Philadelphia Medical Times*, XVII, April, 1887, 485-487.

Kerr, P. M.: "The Mental Status of Roland P." *Alienist and Neurologist*, XXXVI, May, 1915, 131-154.

Keyes, Thomas B.: "Criminality and Degeneracy; Its Treatment by Surgery and Hypnotism." *Medico-Legal Journal*, XV, 1897-1898, 366-374. (Bibliography.)

Kiernan, James G.: "The Case of Guiteau." *Chicago Medical Review*, IV, December 5, 1881, 544-545.

—— "Dipsomania as a Defense for Crime." *Medicine*, II, July, 1896, 563-569.

—— "Epileptic Insanity." *American Journal of Insanity*, LII, April, 1896, 516-529.

—— "Kleptomania and Pyromania." *Alienist and Neurologist*, XXXIII, May, 1912, 147-161; November, 1912, 373-389.

—— "Medico-Legal Relations of Epilepsy." *Alienist and Neurologist*, V, January, 1884, 12-32.

—— "Moral Insanity—What Is It?" *Journal of Nervous and Mental Disease*, XI, October, 1884, 549-575.

Kinne, L. G.: "Prevention of Propagation and Increase of Defectives, Delinquents and Criminals." *Bulletin of Iowa Institutions*, IV, 1902, 89-105.

Kirkbride, F. B.: "A Review of Two Investigations on the Defective and Delinquent." *Survey*, XXVI, April, 22, 1911, 164-168.

Kite, Elizabeth S.: "The Pineys." *Survey*, XXXI, October 4, 1913, 7-13.

—— "Responsibility and Crime—A Study and Interpretation of the Later Works of Alfred Binet." *Proceedings of the American Prison Association*, 1913, 330-345.

Klein, Philip: "Has Goring Disproved the Existence of the Stigmatised Criminal?" *Survey*, XXXIV, May, 22, 1915, 179-180.

KleinSmid, R. B. von.: "Some Efficient Causes of Crime." *First International Conference on Race Betterment*, 1914, 532-542.

Kline, Linus W.: "Truancy as Related to the Migratory Instinct." *Pedagogical Seminary*, V, January, 1898, 381-420.

Kohs, Samuel C.: "The Problem of the Moral Defective." *Training School*, XI, April, 1914, 19-22.

Kraus, William C.: "The Stigmata of Degeneration." *American Journal of Insanity*, LV, July, 1898, 55-88.

Kress, D. H.: "Alcohol and Moral Degeneracy." *Journal of Inebriety*, XXX, Autumn, 1908, 182-190.

Lamb, Robert B.: "The Criminal from a Medical Point of View." *American Journal of Obstetrics*, LXIII, April, 1911, 767-769.

—— "The Mind of the Criminal." *Proceedings of the American Medico-Psychological Association*, X, 1903, 259-267.

Laughlin, H. H.: "Calculations on the Working Out of a Proposed Program of Sterilization." *Proceedings of the First National Conference on Race Betterment*, 1914, 478-494.

Lea, H. C.: "Increase of Crime and Positive Criminology." *Forum*, XVII, August, 1894, 666-675.

Lee, Edward Wallace: "Physical Defects as a Factor in the Cause of Crime." *New York Medical Journal*, C, December, 26, 1914, 1246-1251.

Lightfoot, P. M.: "Alcoholism and Crime." *Quarterly Journal of Inebriety*, XXV, April, 1903, 159-163.

Lind, G. D.: "What Can the Medical Profession Do to Prevent Crime?" *West Virginia Medical Journal*, IV, March, 1910, 294-297.

Lindsay, H. A.: "The Sterilization of Certain Degenerates." *Bulletin of Iowa Institutions*, XIV, 1912, 52-60.

Lindsey, Edward: "The International Congress of Criminal Anthropology." *Journal of the American Institute of Criminal Law and Criminology*, I, November, 1910, 578-583.

Linthicum, G. Milton: "Inebriety and Crime." *Proceedings of the National Conference of Charities and Correction*, 1915, 407-411.

Lloyd, James Hendrie: "Moral Insanity—A Plea for a More Exact Cerebral Pathology." *Journal of Nervous and Mental Disease*, XIII, November, 1886, 669-685.

Lockhart, J. W.: "Should Criminals Be Castrated?" *St. Louis Courier-Medicine*, XIII, October, 1895, 136-137.

Lydston, G. Frank: "Asexualization in the Prevention of Crime." *Medical News*, LXVIII, May 23, 1896, 573-578.

—— "A Contribution to the Hereditary and Pathological Aspect of Vice." *Chicago Medical Journal and Examiner*, XLVI, February, 1883, 131-148.

—— "Inebriety in Its Relations to Crime." *Journal of Inebriety*, XXX, Autumn, 1908, 166-173.

—— "Some General Considerations of Criminology." *Proceedings of the National Prison Association*, 1896, 347-363.

—— "A Study of a Series of Degenerate and Criminal Crania." *Chicago Medical Recorder*, I, (n.s.), May, 1891, 203-224.

—— and McGuire, Hunter: "Sexual Crimes Among Southern Negroes." *Virginia Medical Monthly*, XX, May, 1893, 105-125.

—— and Talbot, Eugene S.: "Studies of Criminals." *Alienist and Neurologist*, XII, October, 1891, 556-612.

MacDonald, Arthur: "Digests of Criminological Literature." *American Journal of Psychology*, III, January, 1890, 114-126; April, 1890, 219-240; September, 1890, 385-397.

—— "Principles of Criminal Anthropology." *Alienist and Neurologist*, XXXVI, February, 1915, 1-6.

—— "Statistics of Physical Measurements and Anomalies of Criminals." *Alienist and Neurologist*, XXXIII, February, 1912, 31-68.

—— "Studies of Juvenile Delinquents." *Medical Record*, LXXII, July 20, 1907, 101-103.

MacDonald, Carlos F.: "Case of Edward J. Hoppin—Homicide Plea, Insanity." *American Journal of Insanity*, XXXIII, April, 1878, 462-511.

—— "The Legal versus the Scientific Test of Insanity in Criminal Cases." *American Journal of Insanity*, LVI, July, 1899, 21-30.

—— "Trial, Execution and Autopsy and Mental Status of Leon F. Czolgosz." *American Journal of Insanity*, LVIII, January, 1902, 369-386; also *Journal of Mental Pathology*, I, December, 1901-January, 1902, 179-194.

MacFarland, Andrew: "Minor Mental Maladies." *American Journal of Insanity*, XX, July, 1863, 10-26.

Makuen, G. H.: "Some Measures for the Prevention of Crime, Pauperism and Mental Deficiency." *Bulletin of the American Academy of Medicine*, V, August, 1900, 1-15.

Mann, Edward C.: "The Attitude of Legal Medicine vs the Disease of Alcoholic Inebriety." *Medico-Legal Journal*, V, 1887-1888, 397-402.

—— "The Relation Which Dipsomania Bears to Forensic Medicine." *Chicago Medical Journal and Examiner*, LIII, September, 1886, 207-211.

Marmon, Pauluel De: "Medico-Legal Considerations upon Alcoholism and the Moral and Criminal Responsibility of Inebriates."
Medical World, I, December, 1871, 201-223.

Marshall, G. G.: "The Disease of Criminality." *Vermont Medical
Monthly*, XVIII, March 15, 1912, 54-59.

Mason, L. D.: "The Absence of Reasonable Motive in the So-Called
'Criminal Acts' of the Confirmed Inebriate." *Journal of the
American Medical Association*, XVII, November 21, 1891,
799-803.

May, James V.: "Mental Diseases and Criminal Responsibility."
State Hospitals Bulletin, V, November 15, 1912, 339-371.

McBride, James H.: "The Mental Status of Guiteau—A Review."
Alienist and Neurologist, IV, October, 1883, 543-565.

McCassy, J. H.: "How to Limit the Overproduction of Defectives
and Criminals." *Journal of the American Medical Association*,
XXXI, December 3, 1898, 1343-1347. (Bibliography.)

McClelland, Sophia: "Criminals the Product of Hereditary Degeneracy." *Medical Record*, XLII, July 23, 1892, 96-100.

—— "Heredity—Criminality, etc., vs Education." *Medico-Legal
Journal*, VIII, 1890-1891, 16-41.

McCord, Clinton: "One Hundred Female Offenders—A Study of
the Mentality of Prostitutes and Wayward Girls." *Training
School*, XII, May, 1915, 59-67; also *Journal of the American
Institute of Criminal Law and Criminology*, VI, September,
1915, 385-407.

M'Corn, W. A.: "Degeneration in Criminals as Shown by the
Bertillon System of Measurement and Photographs." *American
Journal of Insanity*, LIII, July, 1896, 47-56.

M'Cowen, Jennie: "Heredity in Relation to Charity Work." *Journal
of Heredity*, I, January, 1886, 48-49.

McCulloch, Oscar C.: "The Tribe of Ishmael—A Study in Social
Degradation." *Proceedings of the National Conference of
Charities and Correction*, 1888, 154-159.

McGuire, Hunter, and Lydston, G. Frank: "Sexual Crimes Among
Southern Negroes." *Virginia Medical Monthly*, XX, May,
1893, 105-125.

M'Vey, R. E.: "Crime: Its Physiology and Pathenogensis. How
Can Medicine Aid in Its Prevention?" *Kansas Medical Journal*,
I-II, June, 1890, 499-504.

Mears, J. Ewing: "Asexualization as a Remedial Measure in the Relief of Certain Forms of Mental, Moral and Physical Degeneration." *Boston Medical and Surgical Journal*, CLXI, October 21, 1909, 584-586.

Merrill, Lilburn: "The Clinical Classification of Delinquent Children According to Causative Pathology." *Annual Report of the Seattle Juvenile Court*, 1913.

Metzger, Butler: "The Insane Criminal." *American Journal of Insanity*, LVIII, October, 1901, 309-314.

Meyer, Adolph: "A Review of the Signs of Degeneration." *American Journal of Insanity*, LII, January, 1896, 344-363.

Meyer, Herman H. B.: "List of References on Sterilization of Criminals." *Special Libraries*, V, 1914, 23-32.

Middleton, A. B.: "Characteristics of Criminals." *St. Louis Medical Era*, VIII, March, 1899, 230-232.

Milligan, J. W.: "Mental Defectives Among Prisoners." *Proceedings of the National Prison Association*, 1906, 195-205.

Millikin, Mark: "The Proposed Castration of Criminals and Sexual Perverts." *Cincinnati Lancet-Clinic*, XXXIII, (n.s.), August, 1894, 185-190.

Mills, Charles K.: "Arrested and Aberrant Types of Fissures and Gyres in the Brains of Paranoiacs, Criminals, Idiots and Negroes." *Journal of Nervous and Mental Disease*, XIII, September-October, 1886, 523-550.

—— "Benjamin Rush and American Psychiatry." *Medico-Legal Journal*, IV, December, 1886, 238-273.

—— "The Brain of a Negro Murderer." *Proceedings of the Pathological Society of Philadelphia*, XI, 1881-1883, 215-216.

—— "The Brains of Criminals." *Medical Bulletin*, IV, March, 1882, 57-60.

—— "The Case of Joseph Taylor, An Insane Prisoner Convicted of Murder in the First Degree." *Journal of Nervous and Mental Disease*, XI, October, 1884, 589-602.

—— "Morphinomania, Cocomania, and General Narcomania and Some of Their Legal Consequences." *International Clinics*, I, 1905, 159-176.

—— "Reflections on Criminal Lunacy with Remarks on the Case of Guiteau." *Transactions of the Medical Society of the State of Pennsylvania*, 1882, 55-80.

—— "Some Forms of Insanity Due to Alcohol, Especially in Their Medico-Legal Relations." *American Medicine*, IX, February 11, 1905, 223-227.

Miner, James B.: "The Scientific Study of Juvenile Delinquents in Minneapolis." *Journal of the American Institute of Criminal Law and Criminology*, III, January, 1913, 781-782.

Miner, Maude: "Reformatory Girls." *Charities and Commons*, XVII, February, 1907, 903-919.

Moore, Frank: "Mentally Defective Delinquents." *Proceedings of the National Conference of Charities and Correction*, 1911, 65-68.

"Moral Insanity." *American Journal of Insanity*, XIV, April, 1858, 311-322.

—— *American Journal of Insanity*, XX, July, 1863, 63-107.

—— *American Journal of Insanity*, XXIII, January, 1867, 407-424; April, 1867, 516-546.

Morris, John: "Crime: Its Physiology and Pathenogensis. How Far Can Medical Men Aid in Its Prevention?" *Maryland Medical Journal*, XX, April 27, 1889, 501-512; also *Transactions of the Medical and Chirurgical Faculty of Maryland*, 1889, 48-69.

Morrow, Louise, and Bridgman, Olga: "Delinquent Girls Tested by the Binet Scale." *Training School*, IX, May, 1912, 33-36.

Morse, D. A.: "Dipsomania and Drunkenness." *Transactions of the Ohio State Medical Society*, XXVIII, 1873, 137-188.

Morse, E. S.: "Natural Selection and Crime." *Popular Science Monthly*, XLI, August, 1892, 433-446.

Munroe, J. P.: "The Problem of Defective and Delinquents." *Journal of Pedagogy*, XX, June, 1910, 160-175.

Mulhall, Edith F.: "Crime and Mental Deficiency." *Training School*, X, October, 1913, 86-87.

Münsterberg, Hugo: "Hypnotism and Crime." *McClures*, XXX, January, 1908, 317-322.

Myers, Worthington: "Dipsomania." *Medical and Surgical Reporter*, XXXIX, November 30, 1878, 461-464.

Nascher, I. L.: "Psychanalysis of Criminality." *American Practitioner*, XLVIII, May, 1914, 233-238.

Nammack, C. E.: "Is Sterilization of the Habitual Criminal Justifiable?" *New York Medical Record*, LXXIX, February, 1911, 249-250.

Newkirk, H. D.: "The Relation of Physical Defect to Delinquency with Special Reference to the Hennepin County Juvenile Court." *Bulletin of the American Academy of Medicine*, XV, February, 1914, 41-46.

New York State Reformatory at Elmira. Annual Year Book.

Seventeenth Year Book, 1893, 43-44.

Eighteenth Year Book, 1894, 153-154.

Twentieth Year Book, 1896, 20-43, 62-103.

Nichols, Charles H.: "The Case of Charles Sprague." *American Journal of Insanity*, VI, January, 1850, 254-263.

Niebecker, Franklin H.: "On the Mental Capacity of Juvenile Delinquents." *Proceedings of the National Conference of Charities and Correction*, 1901, 262-268.

Noble, C. P.: "The Law of Degeneracy and Its Relation to Medicine." *New York Medical Journal*, XCII, December 24, 1910, 1261-1266.

North, Charles H.: "Insanity Among Adolescent Criminals." *American Journal of Insanity*, LXVII, April, 1911, 677-686.

Noyes, William B.: "The Criminal Equivalent of Insanity." *Medical News*, LXXXI, October 11, 1902, 679-683.

—— "The Criminal Type." *Journal of Social Science*, XXIV, April, 1888, 31-42.

Oberndorf, C. P.: "Constitutional Abnormality." *State Hospitals Bulletin*, II, March, 1910, 814-826.

Ochsner, A. J.: "Surgical Treatment of Habitual Criminals." *Journal of the American Medical Association*, XXXII, April 22, 1899, 867-868.

O'Dea, James J.: "Methomania." *Papers of the Medico-Legal Society*, 1888, 166-183.

Oppenheim, Nathan: "The Stamping Out of Crime." *Popular Science Monthly*, XLVIII, February, 1896, 527-533.

Ordronaux, John: "Case of Isabella Jensch—Epileptic Homicide." *American Journal of Insanity*, XXXI, April, 1875, 430-442.

—— "Case of Jacob Standerman." *American Journal of Insanity*, XXXII, April, 1876, 451-474.

—— "History and Philosophy of Medical Jurisprudence." *American Journal of Insanity*, XXV, October, 1868, 173-212.

—— "Moral Insanity." *American Journal of Insanity*, XXIX, January, 1873, 313-340.

Orton, G. L.: "The Procreative Regulation of Defectives and De-linquents." *Journal of the American Medical Association*, LVIII, June 29, 1912, 2021-2023.

Osborne, A. E.: "Responsibility of Epileptics." *Medico-Legal Journal*, XI, 1893-1894, 210-220.

Otis, Margaret: "The Binet Tests Applied to Delinquent Girls." *Psychological Clinic*, VII, October 15, 1913, 127-134.

Palmer, William H.: "Medico-Legal Status of Inebriety." *International Medical Magazine*, I, December, 1892, 1172-1177.

Parker, D.: "The Prevention of the Increase of Insanity, of the Procreation of the Congenitally Defective and of the Criminally Disposed." *Texas Medical Journal*, XXVIII, October, 1912, 135-139.

Parker, Edward Harper: "Heredity as a Factor in Pauperism and Crime." *Transactions of the Medical Society of the State of New York*, 1877, 158-171.

Parrish, Joseph: "The Legal Responsibility of Inebriates." *Polyclinic*, VI, January, 1889, 206-209.

―― "The Medical Jurisprudence of Inebriety." *Quarterly Journal of Inebriety*, X, 1888, 1-7; also *Medico-Legal Journal*, VI, 1888-1889, 37-43.

Parsons, A. L. "The Prophylaxis of Criminality." *American Practitioner and News*, XLIV, July, 1910, 348-356.

Paschal, Franklin C.: "The Feeble-Minded and Delinquent Boy." *Indiana Bulletin of Charities and Correction*, March, 1915, 68-73.

Patterson, R. J.: "Report on Moral Insanity." *Transactions of the American Medical Association*, XXVIII, 1877, 359-364.

Peskind, A.: "Heredity and Crime: Its Prevention and Treatment." *Cleveland Medical Gazette*, X, March, 1895, 199-204.

Peterson, Frederick: "Craniometry and Cephalometry in Relation to Idiocy and Imbecility." *American Journal of Insanity*, LII, July, 1895, 73-89.

―― "The Stigmata of Degeneration." *State Hospitals Bulletin*, I, 1896, 310-329.

Peyton, David C.: "Material of Clinical Research in the Field of Criminology." *Proceedings of the American Prison Association*, 1914, 255-267.

"Phrenological Examination of Prisoners." *American Phrenological Journal and Miscellany*, III, November 1840, 83-85.

Phrenology: "Character of La Blanc—Murderer." *American Phrenological Journal and Miscellany*, I, December, 1838, 89-96.

"Character of Tardy the Pirate." *American Phrenological Journal and Miscellany*, I, January, 1839, 104-113.

"Examination of a Skull." *American Phrenological Journal and Miscellany*, II, June, 1840, 427-428.

"Phrenological Developments of Fieschi; Who Attempted to Murder the King of France." *American Phrenological Journal and Miscallany*, I, August, 1839, 438-440.

"Phrenological Developments and Character of James Eager." *American Phrenological Journal and Miscellany*, VII, August, 1845, 263-268.

"Phrenological Developments and Character of William Miller, Who Was Executed at Williamsport, Pa., July, 27th, 1838, for the Murder of Solomon Hoffman." *American Phrenological Journal and Miscellany*, I, May, 1839, 272-286.

"Phrenological Developments and Character of Peter Robinson, Who Was Executed April, 16th, at New Brunswick, New Jersey, for the Murder of A. Suydam, Esq." *American Phrenological Journal and Miscellany*, III, July, 1841, 452-459.

Pintner, Rudolph: "One Hundred Juvenile Delinquents Tested by the Binet Scale." *Pedagogical Seminary*, XXI, December, 1914, 523-531.

Poynter, C. W. M.: "A Study of Cerebral Anthropology, with a Description of Two Brains of Criminals." *University (Nebraska) Studies*, XII, 1912, 345-400. (Bibliography.)

Preston, C. H.: "Vasectomy: Its Ethical and Sanitary Limitations." *West Virginia Medical Journal*, V, July, 1910, 16-18.

Punton, J.: "The Medico-Legal Aspects of Criminology." *Kansas City Medical Index-Lancet*, August, 1910, XXXIII, 247-252.

Pyle, W. H.: "A Study of Delinquent Girls." *Psychological Clinic*, VIII, October 15, 1914, 143-148.

Quantz, J. O.: "Dendro-Psychoses." *American Journal of Psychology*, IX, July, 1898, 449-506.

Quimby, Isaac N.: "Alcoholic Anaesthesia: A Factor in Crime." *Medico-Legal Journal*, XIII, 1895-1896, 194-204.

—— "Alcohol and Tobacco." *Medico-Legal Journal*, XIII, 1895-1896, 191-193.

Ransom, Julius B.: "The Physician and the Criminal." *Journal of the American Medical Association*, XXVII, October 10, 1896, 788-796.

Ray, Isaac: "Epilepsy and Homicide." *American Journal of Insanity*, XXIV, October, 1867, 187-206.

—— "An Examination of the Objections to the Doctrine of Moral Insanity." *American Journal of Insanity*, XVIII, October, 1861, 112-138.

—— "Homicide and Suspected Simulation of Insanity." *American Journal of Insanity*, XXXI, October 1874, 240-253.

—— "Insanity and Homicide." *American Journal of Insanity*, XII, January, 1856, 205-212.

—— "Life and Trial of Abner Baker, jr." *American Journal of Insanity*, III, July, 1846, 26-35.

—— "Trial of Furbush." *American Journal of Insanity*, IX, January, 1852, 151-166.

Reese, David Meredith: "A Report on Moral Insanity in Its Relations to Medical Jurisprudence." *Transactions of the American Medical Association*, XI, 1858, 721-746.

Reeve, Charles H.: "The Philosophy of Crime." *International Congress of Charities, Correction and Philanthropy*, (Fifth Section), 1893, 28-47.

Reid, Thomas J.: "Congenital Criminality and Its Relation to Insanity." *Northwestern Lancet*, XVII, March 1, 1898, 110-113.

Renz, Emile: "A Study of the Intelligence of Delinquents and the Eugenical Significance of Mental Defect." *Training School*, XI, May, 1914, 37-39.

Report of Committee on Colonies for and Segregation of Defectives. *Proceedings of the National Conference of Charities and Correction*, 1903, 245-254.

Reynolds, C. E.: "A Case of Moral Insanity Benefited by Craniometry." *Southern California Practitioner*, XXIX, May, 1914, 139-145.

Richardson, Alonzo B.: "The Relation of Criminality to Mental Defect." *Cleveland Medical Gazette*, XIII, December, 1897, 75-89.

Ricketts, Benjamin Merrill: "Sterilization for Crime." *Medical Reviews of Reviews*, XV, November, 1909, 755-757.

Riegel, Robert E.: "Early Phrenology in the United States." *Medical Life*, XXXVII, July, 1930, 361-376.

—— "The Introduction of Phrenology to the United States." *American Historical Review*, XXXIX, October, 1933, 73-78.

Robertson, Frank W.: "Crimes of the Adult from the Standpoint of the Alienist." *Bulletin of the American Academy of Medicine*, XIV, December, 1913, 408-411.

—— "Sterilization for the Criminal Unfit." *American Medicine*, V, (n.s.), July, 1910, 349-361.

—— "Sterilizing of the Unfit." *Survey*, XXIV, August, 1910, 730.

Robinovitch, Louise G.: "The Relation of Criminality in the Offspring to Alcoholism in the Parents." *Medico-Legal Journal*, XVIII, 1900-1901, 341-351.

Rodgers, A. S.: "Discussion of 'The Mentally Defective and the Courts.'" *Journal of Psycho-Asthenics*, XV, September, 1910, 57-60.

Rogers, Stephen, "The Influence of Methomania upon Business and Criminal Responsibility." *Quarterly Journal of Psychological Medicine*, III, April, 1869, 323-350.

Rossy, C. S.: "First Note on a Psychological Study of the Criminals at the Massachusetts State Prison." *Collected Contributions from the State Board of Insanity and the State Institutions for Mental Disease and Defect*, Third Series, 1915, 377-381.

—— "Second Note on a Psychological Study of the Criminals at the Massachusetts State Prison." *Collected Contributions from the State Board of Insanity and the State Institutions for Mental Disease and Defect*, Third Series, 1915, 523-529.

Rowland, Eleanor: "Report of Experiments at the State Reformatory for Women at Bedford Hills." *Psychological Review*, XX, May, 1913, 245-249.

Sabine, G. K.: "The Medico-Legal Relations of Alcoholism—Its Pathological Aspects." *Boston Medical and Surgical Journal*, CIII, September 2, 1880, 221-224; CVII, November 16, 1882, 460-463.

Scarcy, J. T.: "The Relation of Alcohol to Crime in Alabama." *Transactions of the Medical Association of Alabama*, 1891, 320-333.

Schlapp, Max G.: "Feeble-Minded Boys and Crime." *Survey*, XXVII, March 2, 1912, 1846-1849.

—— "The Mentally Defective as Cases in the Courts of New York City." *Medical Record*, LXXXVII, February 27, 1915, 337-341.

Sears, F. W.: "Crime—Its Cause and Prevention." *Vermont Medical Monthly*, XVIII, November 15, 1912, 261-267.

Sehon, George L.: "Report of Committee on Prevention and Probation." *Proceedings of the American Prison Association*, 1910, 131-153.

Sellers, R. B.: "The Etiology and Elimination of Crime." *Transactions of the Texas Medical Association*, XXXVI, 1904, 309-315.

Sharp, Harry C.: "The Indiana Idea of Human Sterilization." *Southern California Practitioner*, XXIV, November, 1909, 549-551.

—— "Rendering Sterile of Confirmed Criminals and Mental Defectives." *Proceedings of the National Prison Association*, 1907, 177-185.

—— "The Severing of the Vas Deferentia and Its Relation to the Neuropathic Constitution." *New York Medical Journal*, LXXV, March 8, 1902, 411-414.

—— "Vasectomy as a Means of Preventing Procreation in Defectives." *Journal of the American Medical Association*, LIII, December 4, 1909, 1897-1902.

Shivers, M. O.: "Vasectomy: The Surgeon's Part in the Treatment and Prevention of Criminals and Defectives." *Journal of the American Medical Association*, LIV, May 14, 1910, 1634.

Silliman, Benjamin: "A Plea in Behalf of Phrenology." *American Phrenological Journal and Miscellany*, III, December, 1840, 130-141.

Sims, F. L.: "Asexualization for the Prevention of Crime and the Propagation of Criminals." *Transactions of the Medical Society of Tennessee*, 1894, 100-114.

Singer, H. Douglas: "The Sterilization of the Insane, Criminal and Delinquent." *Illinois Medical Journal*, XXIII, May, 1913, 480-485.

—— and Ordahl, George W.: "A Study of Prisoners at the Joliet Penitentiary." *Institutional Quarterly*, VI, September 30, 1915, 19-24; also *The Delinquent*, V, September, 1915, 1-6.

Sleyster, Rock: "The Criminal Physique: A Preliminary Report on the Physical Examination of 1521 Prisoners at Wisconsin State Prison." *Journal of the American Medical Association*, LX, May 3, 1913, 1351-1353.

—— "Physical Basis of Crime as Observed by a Prison Physician." *Bulletin of the American Academy of Medicine*, XIV, December, 1913, 396-407.

Smith, Samuel G.: "Typical Criminals." *Popular Science Monthly*, LVI, March, 1900, 539-545.

Sneve, Haldor: "Influence of Parental Diseases, Habits and Heredity Upon Juvenile Crime." *Bulletin of the American Academy of Medicine*, XIV, October, 1913, 359-368.

Spaulding, Edith R.: "The Results of Mental and Physical Examinations of Four Hundred Women Offenders—With Particular Reference to their Treatment During Commitment." *Journal of the American Institute of Criminal Law and Criminology*, V, January, 1915, 704-717.

—— and Healy, William: "Inheritance as a Factor In Criminality: A Study of One Thousand Cases of Young Repeated Offenders." *Bulletin of the American Academy of Medicine*, XV, February, 1914, 4-27.

Speranza, G.: "Criminality in Children." *Green Bag*, XV, November, 1903, 516-520.

Spitzka, E. A.: "The Post Mortem Examination of Leon F. Czolgosz, the Assassin of President McKinley." *Journal of Mental Pathology*, I, December, 1901-January, 1902, 195-209; also *American Journal of Insanity*, LVIII, January, 1902, 386-404.

—— "The Guiteau Autopsy." *American Journal of Neurology and Psychiatry*, I, 1882, 381-392.

—— "The Execution and Post-Mortem Examination of the Van Wormer Brothers at Dannemora." *Daily Medical Journal*, I, February 8, 1904, 1-2.

Spitzka, Edward C.: "A Contribution to the Question of the Mental Status of Guiteau and the History of His Trial." *Alienist and Neurologist*, IV, April, 1883, 201-220.

—— "A Reply to J. J. Elwell in re Guiteau." *Alienist and Neurologist*, IV, July, 1883, 417-438.

Spoerl, Howard D.: "Faculties versus Traits: Gall's Solution." *Character and Personality*, IV, March, 1936, 216-231.

Spratling, E. J.: "The Legal and Social Standing of the Epileptic." *Medical News*, LXXXIII, July 18, 1903, 112-114.

Spratling, William P.: "Epilepsy in Its Relations to Crime." *Journal of Nervous and Mental Disease*, XXIX, August, 1902, 481-496.

—— "Moral Insanity." *Medico-Legal Journal*, VIII, 1890, 220-226.

Stedman, Henry R.: "A Case of Moral Insanity with Repeated Homicides and Incendiarism and Late Development of Delusions." *American Journal of Insanity*, LXI, October, 1904, 275-297.

"Sterilization of Criminals." *Law Notes*, XXII, July, 1918, 65-67.

"Sterilization of Feeble-Minded and Certain Types of Criminals." *Survey*, XXIX, December 21, 1912, 374-375.

Stern, Heinrich: "Alcoholism and Crime. How We Should Deal with the Criminal Alcoholic." *Quarterly Journal of Inebriety*, XXIV, April, 1902, 148-152.

Stevenson, William G.: "Criminality." *Medico-Legal Journal*, V, 1887-1888, 158-179; 257-282.

Storer, Mary: "The Defective Delinquent Girl." *Journal of Psycho-Asthenics*, XIX, September, 1914, 23-30.

Streeter, Lillian: "A Relation of Mental Defect to Neglected, Dependent and Delinquent Children of New Hampshire." *Proceedings of the National Conference of Charities and Correction*, 1915, 340-352.

Stuver, S.: "Asexualization for the Limitation of Disease, and the Prevention and Punishment of Crime." *Journal of Materia Medica*, XXXIII, November, 1895, 167-170.

"Surgery for Criminality." *Journal of the American Medical Association*, XLVI, May 12, 1906, 1447.

Sweeney, Arthur: "Crime and Insanity." *Northwestern Lancet*, XVII, May 15, 1897, 203-211.

Swift, Edgar James: "Juvenile Delinquency and Juvenile Control." *Psychological Bulletin*, VI, April 15, 1909, 127-129.

—— "Some Criminal Tendencies in Boyhood: A Study in Adolescence." *Pedagogical Seminary*, VIII, March, 1901, 65-91.

Talbot, Eugene S.: "A Study of the Stigmata of Degeneracy Among the American Criminal Youth." *Journal of the American Medical Association*, XXX, April 9, 1898, 849-856.

Taylor, J. Madison: "Asexualization of the Unfit." *Alienist and Neurologist*, XXXIII, February, 1912, 10-12.

Teed, J. L.: "On Mind, Insanity and Criminality." *Journal of Nervous and Mental Disease,* VII, January, 1880, 62-73.

Thacker, J. A.: "The Psychology of Vice and Crime." *Cincinnati Medical News,* II, March, 1873, 101-117.

Thayer, Walter N. jr.: "What May We Do with Our Criminals?" *Survey,* XXIV, July 9, 1910, 587-589.

Thomas, John Jenks: "Retardation and Constitutional Inferiority in Connection with Education and Crime." *Journal of Nervous and Mental Disease,* XL, January, 1913, 1-16.

Thomson, I. D.: "Dipsomania, as Distinguished from Ordinary Drunkenness." *Transactions of the Medical and Chirurgical Faculty of the State of Maryland,* LXXXI, 1879, 156-171.

Tichenor, E. B.: "Anthropometry and Psychology." *Philosophical Review,* II, March, 1893, 187-192.

Town, Clara Harrison: "Mental Types of Juvenile Delinquents Considered in Relation to Treatment." *Journal of the American Institute of Criminal Law and Criminology,* IV, May, 1913, 83-89.

Trials—As Reported in the *American Journal of Insanity:*

Baker, Abner, jr.: III, July, 1846, 26-35.

Brown, Captain Joseph J.: XIII, January, 1857, 249-259.

Clark, William: XII, January, 1856, 212-237.

Daley: XLV, October, 1888, 191-206.

Farrer, Nancy: XII, April, 1856, 316-334.

Freeman, Charles F.: XL, January, 1884, 353-363.

Freeman, William: V, October, 1848, 34-60.

Freeth: XV, January, 1859, 297-306.

Furbush: IX, January, 1852, 151-166.

Greenwood, Nathaniel: V, January, 1849, 237-245.

Haddock, John: XI, April, 1855, 365-382.

Hammond, George: XVI, October, 1859, 168-184.

Holm, Anton: XXXI, October, 1874, 254-263.

Kellogg, Ashbell: VI, January, 1850, 247-254.

Manley, William: XLVII, October, 1890, 152-165.

Matteson, Perrine D.: XXXI, January, 1875, 336-344.

Maude, Patrick: XVI, April, 1860, 484-486.

Otto, Peter Louis: XLV, October, 1888, 207-219.

Pierce: XXVIII, January, 1872, 399-409.

Rich, Samuel S.: XVI, April, 1860, 369-384.

Rogers, Abner, jr.: I, January, 1845, 258-278.

Sloo, Robert C.: XV, July, 1858, 32-68.

Speirs, William: XV, October, 1858, 200-225.

Sprague, Charles: VI, January, 1850, 254-263.

Windsor, Captain John: VIII, January, 1852, 227-267.

Van Meter, M. E.: "A Plea for Sterilization as a Prevention of Crime and Disease." *American Journal of Dermatology and Genito-Urinary Diseases,* XII, July, 1908, 288-295.

Vaughan, Victor C.: "Crime and Disease." *Proceedings of the American Prison Association,* 1914, 292-301.

Voigt, F. M.: "Crime and Criminals." *Proceedings of the National Prison Association,* 1888, 246-250.

Waite, Edward F.: "The Physical Bases of Crime: From the Standpoint of the Judge of a Juvenile Court." *Bulletin of the American Academy of Medicine,* XIV, December, 1913, 388-395.

Walsh, J. J.: "Insanity, Responsibility and Punishment for Crime." *American Journal of Medical Science,* CXXXVIII, August, 1909, 262-269.

Warren, John C.: "The Collection of the Boston Phrenological Society; A Retrospect." *Annals of Medical History,* III, 1921, 1-11.

Wayland, Francis: "The Incorrigible: Who Is He, and What Shall Be Done with Him?" *Proceedings of the National Prison Association,* 1886, 189-197.

—— "Incorrigible Misdemeanants." *Proceedings of the National Prison Association,* 1887, 225-241.

Weidensall, Jean: "Criminology and Delinquency—Annual Summary." *Psychological Bulletin,* X, June 15, 1913, 229-237. (Bibliography.)

Weir, James, jr.: "Criminal Anthropology." *Medical Record,* XLV, January 13, 1894, 42-45.

—— "Criminal Psychology." *Medical Record,* XLVI, September 8, 1894, 296-299.

—— "The Criminal Type as Exemplified by the Murderer of the Wratten Family." *Report of the Board of Health, Indiana, for the Year Ending October 31, 1893,* XII, 215-220.

—— "The Sexual Criminal." *Medical Record,* XLVII, May 11, 1895, 581-583.

Westcott, L. A.: "A Radical Treatment for the Prevention of Crime and Disease." *Medical Council,* X, September, 1905, 330-332.

Wey, Hamilton D.: "Criminal Anthropology." *Proceedings of the National Prison Association*, 1890, 274-291.

—— "Notes and Observations." *Twentieth Year Book of the New York State Reformatory at Elmira, for the Year 1895,* (1896) 63-102.

—— "Physical Training Department." *Seventeenth Year Book of the New York State Reformatory at Elmira, for the Year 1892,* (1893), P. 1–P. 45.

—— "A Plea for Physical Training of Youthful Criminals." *Proceedings of the National Prison Association*, 1888, 181-193.

—— "Short Notes in Anthropology." *Eighteenth Year Book of the New York State Reformatory at Elmira, for the Year 1893,* (1894), 152-181.

Wholey, C. C.: "Cases of Moral Insanity Arising from Inherent Moral Defectiveness." *Journal of the American Medical Association,* LXII, March 21, 1914, 926-928.

Widen, L.; "Young Criminals in the Nebraska State Penitentiary." *Survey,* XXVII, November 18, 1911, 1221-1225.

Wight, J. S.: "A Plea for the Treatment of Criminals." *American Journal of Neurology and Psychiatry,* II-III, 1884-1885, 128-140.

Wilcox, Reynold Webb: "Habit Producing Drugs and Crime." *Bulletin of the American Academy of Medicine,* XV, June, 1914, 149-155.

Williams, Tom A.: "The Sterilization of Degenerate Criminals." *Atlanta Journal-Record of Medicine,* LVIII, October, 1911, 371-373.

Wilmarth, A. W.: "Pathological Conditions Accompanying Mental Defects in Children." *International Congress of Charities, Correction and Philanthropy,* Eighth Section, 1893, 14-16.

Wilson, J. C.: "Peculiarities of Conformation in the Skulls of Criminals." *Philadelphia Medical Times,* XV, October 18, 1884, 50-51.

Wilson, Thomas: "Criminal Anthropology." *Report of the Smithsonian Institution,* 1889-1890, 617-686.

—— "Criminology." *Proceedings of the American Association for the Advancement of Science,* 1900, 294-300.

Wines, E. C.: "Cause and Cure of Crime." *Princeton Review,* I, May, 1878, 784-814.

Wingate, U. O. B.: "Suggestion, Not Hypnotism and Crime."
Medico-Legal Journal, XI, 1893-1894, 220-223.

Winter, Henry Lyle: "Hereditary Neurotic Condition and Acquired
Instability and Disease Associated with Crime." *New York
Medical Journal*, LXVI, November 6, 1897, 621-624.

—— "Notes on Criminal Anthropology and Bio-Sociology. Being
a Study of Seventy-three Irish and Irish-American Criminals
Made at the King's County Penitentiary, Brooklyn, New York."
State Hospitals Bulletin, II, 1897, 462-498.

Wise, P. M.: "The Barber Case—The Legal Responsibility of Epileptics." *American Journal of Insanity*, XLV, January, 1889,
360-373.

Witmer, Lightner: "Criminals in the Making." *Psychological Clinic*,
IV, January 15, 1911, 221-238.

Witter, John H.: "The Physical Basis of Crime from the Standpoint
of the Probation Officer." *Bulletin of the American Academy of
Medicine*, XV, April, 1914, 102-104.

Wood, Horatio C.: "Neuropathic Insanity in Relation to Crime."
*Transactions of the Medical Society of the State of Pennsyl-
vania*, XXIII, 1892, 92-104.

Woodbury, Frank: "The Relation Between Crime and Insanity."
*Journal of the American Institute of Criminal Law and Crim-
inology*, IV, July, 1913, 282-284.

Woodruff, C. E.: "Some Thoughts Relative to the Etiology of Degeneration." *American Journal of Insanity*, XLVII, October,
1900, 203-214.

—— "Who Are the Unfit?" *Medical Record*, LXXVI, August 7,
1909, 213-216.

Woodward, Samuel B.: "Homicidal Impulse." *American Journal of
Insanity*, I, April, 1845, 323-326.

—— "Moral Insanity." *Report of the Massachusetts State Lunatic
Hospital*, 1837, Appendix, 171-182.

—— "Medical Jurisprudence of Insanity. Report of the Trial of
Abner Rogers, jr., Indicted for the Murder of Charles Lincoln,
jr., late Warden of the Massachusetts State Prison." *American
Journal of Insanity*, I, January, 1845, 258-278.

Wright, H. W.: "A Consideration of Constitutional Inferiority."
New York Medical Journal, LXXXVIII, December 26, 1908,
1217-1222.

—— "The Problem of the Criminal in the Light of Some Modern Conceptions." *Journal of the American Medical Association,* LXI, December 13, 1913, 2119-2122.

Wright, Thomas Lee: "The Disabilities of Inebriety—An Inquiry Respecting the Nature of Drunkenness and of Its Responsibilities." *Journal of the American Medical Association,* XIV, March 8, 1890, 332-336.

—— "Drunkenness and Its Criminal Responsibilities." *Quarterly Journal of Inebriety,* XII, October, 1890, 345-351.

—— "The Equitable Responsibility of Inebriety." *Journal of Nervous and Mental Disease,* XVII, December, 1892, 867-879.

—— "The Inability to Discriminate Between Right and Wrong Disguised by Automatism." *Medical Record,* XXIV, July 14, 1883, 31-34.

—— "Inebriety; A Study upon Alcohol in Its Relations to Mind and Conduct." *Alienist and Neurologist,* III, 1882, 217-239.

—— "The Invariable Tendency of Drunkenness to Crime—Whence Comes It?" *Quarterly Journal of Inebriety,* IX, April, 1887, 65-72.

—— "Observations on the Criminal Status of Inebriety." *Alienist and Neurologist,* XII, January, 1891, 1-18.

INDEX